The Return of
Civil Society

The Return of Civil Society

THE
EMERGENCE OF
DEMOCRATIC SPAIN

Víctor M. Pérez-Díaz

Harvard University Press
Cambridge, Massachusetts
London, England

First Harvard University Press paperback edition, 1998

First published in Spanish in 1987 by Instituto de Estudios Económicos, Castelló 128–6, 28006 Madrid, Spain.

Publication of this book has been supported by a grant from The Program for Cultural Cooperation between Spain's Ministry of Culture and United States Universities.

Library of Congress Cataloging-in-Publication Data

Pérez-Díaz, Víctor.
  [Retorno de la sociedad civil. English]
  The return of civil society: the emergence of democratic Spain / Víctor M. Pérez-Díaz.
    p. cm.
  Includes bibliographical references and index.
  ISBN 0-674-76688-1 (cloth)
  ISBN 0-674-76689-X (pbk.)
  1. Representative government and representation—Spain. 2. Spain—Politics and government—1975– 3. Regionalism—Spain. 4. Trade unions—Spain. 5. Catholic Church—Spain—Political activity.
  I. Title.
JN8210.P4713   1993
946.083—dc20   92-29941

Contents

Contents

Acknowledgments

A first version of this book was published by the Instituto de Estudios Económicos of Madrid in 1987. The present version builds on the previous one but departs from it in crucial respects. I have added the first chapter and thoroughly transformed the second one, where the core argument of the book is presented. I have kept, with some variations, the chapters on the church and socioeconomic and regional mesogovernments, have revised thoroughly and condensed my argument about the Spanish workers, and have introduced other alterations in my last chapter on unions and workers in general, while I have set aside those chapters of the Spanish book that deal with the business community, the educational and health professions, and the transformation of peasants into modern farmers. Also, portions of this book have appeared previously in English in P. A. Hall, ed., "European Labor in the 1980s," in *International Journal of Political Economy* 17:3 (Fall 1987).

When the Spanish edition was published, I expressed my gratitude to many friends, colleagues, students, and institutions that helped me in a variety of ways. My debt has increased considerably during these last years.

I have greatly benefited from my discussions with colleagues and students at the Center for European Studies at Harvard, the departments of political science at the University of California at San Diego and the Massachusetts Institute of Technology, the Committee on

Western Europe of the Social Science Research Council, and the Center for Advanced Studies in Social Sciences of the Juan March Institute of Madrid. The Juan March Institute gave me the opportunity to rewrite this book; and the Fondo de Investigación Económica y Social and the Foundation of the Instituto Nacional de Industria in Madrid provided me with the financial and institutional support to do most of the empirical research on which parts of this book are based.

I would also like to thank most heartily for their kind encouragement Daniel Bell, Suzanne Berger, and Juan Linz. Ana Buenaventura, Juan Carlos Rodríguez, and Jacqueline de la Fuente helped me, patiently and graciously, through the last states of putting the final version together, including bibliographical references, editing, and typing.

I want to take this opportunity to thank my wife, Marina, once more, for her love, trust, and fundamental determination. I also want to pay tribute to the memory of my father, Miguel Pérez Poyo, to his detached benevolence towards a world he loved without quite feeling fully committed to it, or in any need to take it too seriously; to the stubborn independence of his spirit, his resilience, sense of fairness, deep compassion, and ultimate benevolence; caring so much, expecting so little, and yet so full of hope, the lightness of his humor always ready to undo his disappointments; so easy to forget grievances, and so grateful for the unexpected, softer side of life.

The Return of
Civil Society

1

The Emergence of Democratic Spain

I begin with a personal observation which is related to my general argument: I belong to a generation of Spaniards who first assumed professional and political responsibilities in the late 1950s and early 1960s, in the belief that the institutional framework of Francoism was both inimical to us and an impediment to solving Spain's problems in a spirit of freedom, justice, and creativity. We believed then that, for all its limitations and internal tensions, and with all the reservations that our own youthful maximalism advised, western Europe and the western world as a whole provided us with keys to a better understanding of our situation and a better future for our country.

The idea that solutions to Spanish problems were to be found in Europe had been a traditional notion of the liberal intelligentsia in the country for more than two centuries, and in adopting this attitude we, the new generation, were doing nothing more than assimilating this tradition, at least in part. One of its eminent representatives was José Ortega y Gasset, who claimed: "Spain is the problem, Europe is the solution" (1963, p. 521), echoing similar sentiments expressed by Joaquin Costa and the "regenerationist" literature of the late nineteenth and early twentieth centuries.[1] Ortega was referring to the appropriateness of a program of profound "regeneration" or transformation of Spanish culture and institutions, taking as a model (or, at the very least, as a source of inspiration) central and northern European countries such as France, England, and Germany: their universities, their public opinion, their economies, and their political institutions. In sum, he was referring to a program which today many people call modernization.

Evidently, neither in Ortega's time nor in our own has it ever been thought that Europe could provide an unequivocal and definitive solution for the many and varied problems of Spain. Furthermore, it was clear not only that Europe in turn had many problems to solve but also that Europe was to some extent a problem in its own right; of this there was painful evidence in the form of two world wars. Nonetheless, Europe, and in particular the Europe which had emerged from the Second World War, was an example of how certain fundamental problems of economic growth, coexistence, and freedom, which seemed so intractable and in need of such a disproportionate expenditure of energy on the part of the Spaniards, could be tackled. Above all, Europe appeared to offer the appropriate institutional framework within which we in Spain could face up to new, different, and more stimulating problems which, though we might not be capable of solving them, would require us to give the best of ourselves in order to confront them. In short, those of us who were members of the generation belonging to the late 1950s and early 1960s considered ourselves to be, on the one hand, dissenting from the predominant culture and institutions of Francoist Spain and, on the other, hopeful of the possibility of anchoring our dissent in the European experience of that time.

Usually the dreams of one generation are fulfilled only in the lifetime of the next, if at all. Therefore, it has been our great privilege as a generation not only to have harbored visions of change but to have been witnesses to, and protagonists in, the changes we desired, to the extent that institutions which were a fundamental part of European life a few decades ago have today come to be an accepted part of Spanish life as well. We feel very grateful for this—although it would not be easy to identify the object of our gratitude—and also perhaps proud. However, it is a pride tempered by the knowledge that it was our good fortune to have experimented with the institutions of capitalism and liberal democracy in the context of western Europe in the 1970s rather than the 1930s, as our parents had had to do, with disastrous results. It is further tempered by the understanding that we have been participants in rather than the protagonists of a very complex historical process of accommodation and adjustment between Spain and Europe, which took place almost uninterrupted from the mid-fifties to the mid-eighties, half of this time under Francoism and the other half under a liberal democratic regime.

My main argument in this chapter deals with the emergence of a new democratic tradition in contemporary Spain. I contend that the gradual emergence of liberal democratic traditions of institutions and values in civil society preceded, and prepared the way for, the political transition of the 1970s, and that, in combination with the invention of a new "tradition" in our political culture, those societal traditions enhanced the chances for the consolidation (and institutionalization) of the new regime. The result has been a process of synchronization and homogenization of the culture and institutions of Spain with those of Europe.

Before going any further I should offer a brief clarification of my use of certain terms. To the expression *civil society* I give a rather specific meaning that I explain at some length in Chapter 2. In short, it denotes a *type* of society that combines, to one degree or another, markets, voluntary associations, and a public sphere. Yet in any change of regime (and this includes the change from an authoritarian or totalitarian regime to a democracy) a distinction can be made between the processes of *transition* to, *consolidation* of, and *institutionalization* of the new regime. This is an analytic distinction.[2]

Empirically the three processes are interrelated: they are not consecutive phases of a temporal order, but rather they overlap one another. In the process of *transition,* the basic rules of the game (and this is what a political regime is all about) are established, both within the political class and between the political class and society at large. These rules concern chiefly the limits of state power, the means of access of both politicians and society to that power, and the modalities for the exercise of such power. (In the case of Spain this process was concluded by the referendum on the Constitution at the end of 1978 for the country as a whole, and with the referendum on the Basque Statute of Autonomy in 1979 for the Basque region). This process should be distinguished from that of *consolidation* of the new regime, at the end of which there is a widespread expectation that the regime is going to stay, and its basic rules will be respected, since there is no credible threat to its existence, whether from a foreign invader, the army, guerrilla movements, a social revolution, or opposition parties. (In Spain this point was reached during the first socialist government, between 1982 and 1986.) The process should also be distinguished from *institutionalization* of the regime, at the end of which it is recognized as legitimate in the eyes of most of the population most of the time, and the basic rules of the political game not only prevail de facto but have been internalized by both politicians and society. (In Spain this process still has a long way to go.)

I first examine the emergence of societal traditions prior to the transition by demonstrating, in effect, how economic growth, social changes, and the demographic processes of the sixties (such as rural migration, the changes in agricultural structures, and the development of an industrial proletariat) were inseparable from institutional changes, which in turn were responding to cultural and political stimuli, for instance, in the areas of industrial relations, labor unions, and rural life as well as in the church and the mass media. These institutional changes were the result of a combination of endless conflicts and understandings within civil society, and between civil society and the public authorities. Businessmen, workers, priests, doctors, university professors and students, journalists, and many other social agents played a decisive role in these changes. But at the same time, the sometimes unforeseen and unintended consequences of certain political decisions by Francoist governments were also of crucial importance, for example, the rejection of a totalitarian model in the early 1940s, which allowed the church and Catholic organizations a decisive margin for maneuver, and the turnaround in economic policy at the end of the 1950s, which strengthened the links between the Spanish economy and world markets and unleashed the economic and demographic transformations of the 1960s. Finally, both the strategies of social agents and the policies of state agents were substantially affected by the fact that all of them had to establish these strategies and policies within the context of post–Second World War western Europe.

The final result was the emergence of liberal democratic traditions in society with the development of a reserved institutional domain relatively free from government intervention; institutions of self-coordination within society such as markets and networks of voluntary associations as well as social movements engaged in a complex game of conflicts and alliances; and a sphere of public debate. I call these traditions liberal democratic in the sense that they incorporate beliefs, imply commitments, and shape habits which are consistent with the principles of a liberal democratic polity. These principles include the proposal that a fairly wide arena be reserved for the exercise of the fundamental liberties of individuals and their organizations, thus defining the area of legitimate intervention by the state; the requirement that the state be responsive to the pressures which individuals and organizations bring to bear in defense not only of their particular interests but also of their own versions of the public interest; and demands for a public sphere, that is, an area of debate regarding the definition of the public interest. Also in the long run the result has been a process of synchronization or homogenization of the culture and institutions of Spain with those of Europe.

I then move on to the invention of a democratic tradition in our political culture which is "new," or different from that of previous ones (such as those of the nineteenth century or the first decades of the twentieth century), as a result of the trauma of civil war and the experience of Francoism.[3] I show how such a tradition has required the elaboration of a new cultural idiom, including an array of new political symbols, such as sacred texts (the Constitution), exemplary institutions (the monarchy), and rituals (democratic elections and the signing of social pacts); and a new understanding of Spanish history (in particular a reconstruction of Spanish collective memory) and the articulation of ennobling myths (such as a reinterpretation of the civil war as an unavoidable tragedy).

In general the development of a cultural political idiom that allows politicians and society to articulate and give meaning to their new institutional experiences may be helped by two factors: first, by the establishment of a plausible link between the present and the past (in Spain this involved a reassessment of the civil war); and second, by the forging of a plausible link between the present and a future state of affairs that seems both desirable and achievable. It was generally believed that Spain could arguably aspire to a type of society such as that embodied in present-day western Europe, and that Spain was in fact already becoming more and more like a western European country. In fact this European reference, and the construction of a European identity for Spain, has been one of the most crucial mechanisms at work throughout the entire process of transition to and consolidation of democracy.

In turn, for these links to be forged, some prior ideological "house cleaning" or forgetting may be needed. At least in the case of Spain two sets of ideologies had to fade gradually away: those of national Catholicism on the right (see Chapter 3) and of social radicalism on the left. Both had provided in the 1930s the cultural preconditions for the kind of intense and divisive politics one may refer to by the name of *absolute politics*.

In short, my argument involves certain general ideas about the important role societal traditions and political symbolisms *(sensu lato)* play in the process of transition, consolidation, and institutionalization of a democracy. It is in fact the main point of this chapter that, in terms of the Spanish experience, the success of democratic transition and consolidation (and, later, of democratic institutionalization) depends to a great extent on the previous emergence of liberal democratic traditions in society, and on the invention of a cultural political idiom, including political symbols, and the cognitive maps and moral orientations embodied in such symbols, by means of which both the elites and the population at large give meaning and mobilize commitment to those regime-building processes.

I next assess the potential as well as the limits of my argument for explaining the democratic transition and consolidation in Spain. I start by discussing other structural and actor-oriented arguments that give causal preeminence to factors such as international conditions, modernization, political culture (in a narrow sense), and the succession crisis of the authoritarian regime, finally focusing on an argument that emphasizes bargaining among elites. By contrast, I suggest that the crucial choices made by the elites and by the population at large are interstitial choices, and are to be understood as largely shaped by and dependent on already existing social traditions or rules of the game as well as the corresponding cultural understandings, and on the constraints imposed by the army. Although this last is an important qualification, it should be pointed out that the army itself is in turn influenced by its own traditions and its own understandings. The Spanish army responded to transitional events not so much as a strategic actor (since it may be shown that specific groups within the army had their own agendas regarding the transition, though the army as a corporate actor did not) but rather as a bearer of its own local tradition.

The general point underlying my argument is that transitions to as well as processes of consolidation and institutionalization of political regimes are often understood as sequences that follow from critical choices made by elites, social groups, and the population at large. But the fact is that only very rarely do these people face problem situations as rational choice makers, weighing the costs, benefits, risks, and probabilities of success of several alternatives, in the short, medium, and long run. More often they simply react to the situation at hand and to others' responses to it in the framework of previously existing traditions that shape their preferences and their definitions of the situation. As I mentioned, choices, while being at times critical, tend to be interstitial and heavily dependent on, and embedded in, already existing or emergent traditions.

By *traditions* I mean sets of institutions (that is, rules and expectations) and cultural practices (that is, beliefs and evaluative statements embodied in rituals, myths, or ideologies) which have come to form a regular and expected part of everyday experience (Gray, 1986, p. 34; Shils, 1975, p. 182). Culture and institutions belong together, since institutions are both carriers (or expressive vessels) and reinforcing mechanisms of culture. Therefore, institutions give values and beliefs a structure of plausibility (Douglas, 1988; Berger and Luckmann, 1967, p. 93) or viability (Thompson, Ellis, and Wildavsky, 1990). This extended concept of tradition comes close to the classical notions of ethos or mores, which denote both an actual way of living and a set of normative statements or beliefs about life, about what constitutes a "good life." Awareness of the fit between one's actual behavior and those rules and any underlying cognitions may vary considerably. Different authors such as Hayek (1960), Shils (1975), and Bourdieu (1972) have all suggested the critical importance and the pervasiveness of rule-following activities in which the actors have a very limited awareness regarding these norms, which they take mostly for granted, and the consequences of their acting according to them. This is not to say that those rule-following activities can be considered irrational, or as being on the borderline between meaningful and meaningless behavior.[4] Tradition-bound or rule-following behavior is implicitly rational insofar as people know these traditions, understand their consequences, and are therefore in the position of having tested them in different situations over time.

Thus, political transitions can be reconstructed ex post facto as critical choices by the elites, but most often those choices are not so much deliberate calculations as belated reactions to ongoing processes the elites hardly understand, much less control. They may well start out with very limited knowledge and understanding of even their local circumstances, not to mention the international situation, and full of dubious preconceptions about them. Moreover, it is not easy for them to learn from their mistakes under the pressure of the many confusing and unexpected events of the transition. If they are allowed to fall back on their own experience, they may try to cope with uncertainty by adhering to their ideological tenets and reverting to a pattern of behavior that served them well in adjusting to, even surviving, the previous authoritarian regime (in the case of people engaged in bureaucratic maneuvering within the state or in opposition politics). By contrast, external pressures require them to learn quickly the potential for and the limits of society's support and of the army's attitude. Such learning is conditional on the politicians' gradual understanding of the societal traditions and the culture in which those traditions are expressed.

In the last two sections of this chapter I explore other themes which complement and extend the central argument. As a critical counterpoint to the theme of the relative success of the transition to and consolidation of democracy and the process of Europeanization in Spain, I analyze some problems relative to the institutionalization of Spain's democracy and its specific characteristics. This leads to a discussion of some of the tensions between the process of western Europeanization and the persistence or re-creation of traditions moving in quite the opposite direction, with special reference to the phenomenon of clientelism, and the emergence of traditions in the sphere of public debate which are quite worrisome from the normative viewpoint of the desirability of that institutionalization.

SOCIETAL TRADITIONS

In the course of one generation Spain has become a modern capitalist economy, a liberal democratic state, and a tolerant, pluralist society which is largely secular with regard to the majority of its economic and political concerns, and based in principle on respect for values common to other western societies, including individual freedom and human rights. This has been the result of a profound institutional and cultural transformation of which the most outstanding aspect has been the democratic transition. As a result, although Spain may still lag behind many other countries in western Europe with regard to living standards, levels of productivity, and the quality of its political institutions as well as institutions of research and higher education, these standards now seem accessible; if they are not already within our grasp, at least they are now within our reach.

It should be remembered that in the aftermath of the civil war things looked, and in reality were, very different. At that time Spain was also trying to catch up with Europe, but with a very different Europe. Spain's models were Nazi Germany and Fascist Italy (which were not, it must be said, so very different from the models that many other fascist or authoritarian regimes and movements all over continental Europe were trying to emulate at the time). We know that the victory of the Allied forces in the Second World War decided the fate of those models. The peoples of continental Europe were liberated from or overthrew those regimes, mainly as a result of the invasion of foreign armies, which contributed decisively to the transition to and consolidation of the liberal democracies of western Europe (Herz, 1982) and to the so-called people's democracies or communist dictatorships of eastern Europe. Within a few years the countries of western Europe had begun to rebuild their economies, expand their markets, set up their welfare states, consolidate their party political systems and democratic institutions, and grow and prosper in all directions.

In contrast with these European democracies of the 1940s and 1950s, Franco's Spain looked anachronistic and backward. The Spanish state was organized along strictly authoritarian lines. A military dictator held supreme power, "by the Grace of God," according to the official line, but in reality by relying heavily on his comrades in arms, the Catholic church, the business community, large numbers of peasant smallholders, and the urban and semiurban middle classes, some of whom belonged to the Fascist party, which at its peak had almost a million members. Labor unions were suppressed, and the attempts of anarchists and socialists to organize them clandestinely were harshly punished; but professional and to some extent business associations were permitted, though always subordinate to "the regime"—an expression which, in the parlance of the time, referred to a variety of institutions, organizations, and individuals implicated in the possession and exercise of state power.

The Francoist state appeared to dominate civil society. This was of course in keeping with the manifest ideology of Francisco Franco and his supporters, who defined the "new state" as opposed to what they called the "liberal state." In general, the tasks of the liberal state tend to be limited to those which provide an institutional framework for individuals, families, and private organizations to carry out goal-oriented activities, whether they be for selfish or altruistic motives. The liberal state has few common objectives or general interests of a substantive and nonprocedural nature; and the few it does have tend to be articulated through continuous debate among social actors who pursue objectives in which general considerations combine with private interests, and which, moreover, are, or may be considered, "legitimate." By contrast, totalitarian and (frequently, but not necessarily) authoritarian states claim to have national objectives, linked to historical projects and missions, which justify their appeals to "the nation" (or a plurality of nations) to support them in their task. What is more, these states maintain that such objectives express the profound desires and feelings of the nation, and thus they pretend to a sort of mystical or quasi-mystical identification between the nation and the state.

The nation-state that emerged after the civil war in Spain had ambitions and pretensions of precisely the latter nature. Many of its leaders dreamed of constructing a homogeneous Catholic society, organizing the economic and social life of the country along corporate lines, and yet being capable of converting Spain into an industrial and even a colonial power of some importance. Borrowing from the experience of a variety of historical periods, the Francoist state tried to combine what it considered an up-to-date version of a medieval parliament with some features of sixteenth-century imperial Spain, including the characteristic concessions to the preeminence of the counter-reformist Catholic church, and the trappings of nineteenth-century European colonial powers and contemporary fascist regimes.

The fulfillment of these grandiose designs of the state and its associated elites, principally the church, required either a favorable or a relatively neutral external environment. Only in such a context could the state and the Spanish ruling classes concentrate on the task of imposing their will on a society made up of an appreciable number of enthusiastic followers, but an even larger number of demobilized and disorganized people reduced to passivity and fear. As it was, the relative isolation of the country after the defeat of the Axis powers was a condition favorable for ensuring the domination of the Francoist state and its associated elites and fostering their illusion of a society constructed according to their ideals.

For many years the link between Spain's external isolation and the probability of success in the task of internal domination was very strong. It was expressed in a complex symbolism of separation from the outside world and of victory over internal enemies, such as the myth of Numancia[5] and the ritual of "victory parades." But if the success of the Francoist experiment depended on the stability of external factors, it was also particularly vulnerable to any changes in the external context. When the fascist powers began losing the war in 1942, Franco had to opt for coming to terms with the western democracies on the common ground of anticommunism. After some years in purgatory, the Francoist state was accepted by the democracies as a rather shamefaced member of the second order. But western support, as demonstrated in 1953 by the pacts between Spain and the United States and the concordat with the Holy See, proved to be conditional, first, on Spain's opening up to the international capitalist economy and, second, on the reinforcement of semipluralism (or limited pluralism) in its society, and in particular, respect for the autonomy of the church and Catholic organizations. These conditions proved to be the decisive catalysts for the far-reaching transformations in Spanish life which were to occur in the decades that followed.

During the 1940s Spain was still an agrarian society, with approximately half of its labor force employed in the agricultural sector. Small and medium-sized peasant holdings dominated the rural landscape of the northern *meseta*, while the latifundios, with their corresponding masses of an underemployed rural proletariat, were the typical feature of a large part of the southern *meseta*. Traditional production techniques and deficient forms of organization, combined with harsh climatic conditions and semiarid soils, prevailed in large parts of the country. Yields were low, and agricultural production rose only slowly as the increase in the amount of land under cultivation affected increasingly marginal lands with decreasing yields. At the same time, industrial development was uneven and, on the whole, slow. The protectionist laws of national industries and the privileged circuits of credit and public investment gave an initial boost to industry, which, however, soon ran out of steam, given the scarcity of capital movement, the shortages of and difficulty of obtaining imported machinery, the indecision of leadership, and the organizational deficiencies of businessmen and the managerial class as a whole, combined with the weakness of domestic demand. By the mid-1950s it was clear not only that the Spanish economy was facing a crisis in its external sector but that in general it had lost its bearings.

The second half of the 1950s and the early 1960s were a time of crucial changes in the economic policy of Francoism and, as a result, in the relation between the state and society. In the final analysis, these changes were caused by Spain's involvement in the network of geopolitical alliances and economic (and, as we shall see later, cultural) interdependencies among the western democracies. Placed in a critical situation in which it was necessary to make a choice, as the immediate consequence of the failure of its economic policies and the crisis in the external sector, the Spanish government decided to put an end to the import-substitution policies with which it had tried to stimulate industrial development and fulfill its dreams of autarky, which derived both from its initially fascist ideology and from its partially self-imposed international isolation (see Anderson, 1970). This move may well have been influenced by the failure of the economic policies of General Juan Perón and his subsequent loss of power in Argentina at the end of the 1950s (Waisman, 1987).

As soon as it became clear that Spain was heading decisively in the direction of an open economy which would be integrated into international markets (a move endorsed very quickly by the reports of the World Bank and other organizations), massive quantities of capital, commodities, and people began to flow across the Spanish borders, bringing with them all sorts of institutional and cultural transformations. The ability of the state to stand guard over the country and thus control the fate of its population came to an end. The grandiose designs to which I referred earlier came to be seen as delusions of grandeur, reduced to the rhetorical exhortations, vestiges of another era, still to be heard in the speeches of the head of state, then finally silenced and forgotten altogether.

Peasants and agricultural laborers became industrial or construction workers and urban residents. Millions migrated to the towns, leaving the countryside depopulated. By the mid-1970s the portion of the working population actively engaged in agriculture had fallen from 50 percent to about 15 percent. Agrarian technology, professional agricultural training, and rural schooling underwent profound changes; and the traditional institutions for the social control of rural life (authoritarian families, interference from schoolteachers, priests, and local authorities in moral matters and habits, and patterns of deference toward traditional elites) were gradually eroded until they finally disappeared (Pérez-Díaz, 1973, 1992a). Millions of tourists invaded the coasts of Mediterranean Spain, while millions of Spaniards emigrated northward, often to spend years living and working in Germany, France, Holland, or Switzerland; thousands of students and young professionals went abroad to study; entrepreneurs imported machines; foreign investors poured capital into the Spanish economy; and consumers became accustomed to buying foreign-made goods.

As these interchanges increased in frequency, their significance soon became clear for all to see. It could be summarized as a massive, all-pervasive learning experience. Spaniards were exposed to institutions and cultures, ways of accomplishing things in all spheres of life, which were simply far more efficient than their own in achieving some of their traditional objectives as well as other objectives which they were rapidly learning to appreciate: a better, more comfortable standard of living, offering more money and resources but also increased freedom of movement, more opportunities to prosper and get ahead, less subjection to authority, more knowledge, and more varied ways of relating freely among themselves. In this way Spaniards learned from, imitated, and wound up identifying with the people of western Europe, their institutions, and their way of life.

I should point out that this external influence was not operating in a vacuum nor simply by contagion. Therefore it is useful to examine in more detail the mechanisms by which external influences combined with endogenous processes to produce these changes. The central mechanism was the activation of latent conflicts which already existed in the heart of Spanish life and society. Thus, as soon as the state lost it capacity to keep the gates of Spanish society closed, and as soon as foreign goods, messages, and people came flooding through those gates, the otherwise latent economic, social, cultural, and political conflicts were activated, putting pressure on the existing institutional framework and forcing Spaniards to experiment with new institutions, inspired to some extent by European models.

Thus, for example, economic change was accompanied by three institutional changes of enormous importance for the system of industrial relations. These had to do with collective bargaining, strikes, and workers' associations. Some of the changes were not fully legalized but were more or less tolerated from the late fifties to the mid-sixties. Driven by the economic development of the 1960s and based on the Ley de Convenios Colectivos of 1958, collective bargaining spread throughout industry and generated the need for some recognition of workers' representatives with whom to negotiate, and some tolerance of strikes as a pressure mechanism in negotiations. The Ley de Jurados de Empresa then granted some measure of freedom for the election of workers' representatives within companies. This law was used intelligently, first by local leaders of various origins and later by clandestine unions such as the Comisiones Obreras and the Unión Sindical Obrera, which managed in this way to ensure a margin of some tolerance on the part of the authorities, or rather alternating periods of tolerance and persecution, which never reached the extremes of repression which had crushed the socialist and anarchist organizations in the first phase of Francoism. In time a modification was introduced into the legal regulations that classified a strike as an offense, establishing a distinction, of doubtful application, between a "political" strike and a "professional" strike. As a result, days lost to strikes rose from about 250,000 per year in 1964–1969 to about 850,000 per year in 1970–1972 and 1.5 million per year in 1973–1975 (Pérez-Díaz, 1979, p. 19).

The result was that at the time of the democratic transition, the working class had accumulated ten or more years' experience of massive strikes, collective bargaining, and representative unions. All these institutions were semispontaneous re-creations or inventions of the workers, who were quick to take advantage of both the decisions and the de facto tolerance of the Francoist state as well as the opportunities for wage increases offered by economic growth. When it came to shaping these institutions, the workers drew on models from their own European experiences. All of these institutions replicated the models of collective bargaining, industrial conflict, and labor union representation that had existed in Europe for a long time, and to which Spanish workers were exposed, directly or indirectly, as a result of their emigration to Europe.

But it was not only economic and social institutions that were affected by the changes. So were the basic institutions for the creation of culture and the socialization of new generations. The decisive turn taken by the country between the mid-fifties and the early sixties is not reducible to a change in economic policy which opened up the country to the outside world, with consequent effects on economic and social life. The new economic policy (introduced in 1959 with the Stabilization Plan and consolidated in the years following) was both a symptom and a preview of the broader changes to come in the mentality—that is, in the implicit paradigm—of the elites and the country as a whole. The nucleus of this change with regard to the mentality of the Francoist establishment (Catholic priests and leaders, professionals, businessmen, and some of the politicians themselves) was their realization of the failure of the corporate, authoritarian, counter-reformist, and autarkic aims incorporated in the ideal of a "well-ordered society" such as they had conceived of in the 1940s. From that moment on it became increasingly evident that such an ideal did not constitute a credible scenario for the future of Spain.

At the same time, the Catholic church and religious experience in general were also subject to a process of profound transformation (see Chapter 3). The church was challenged inexorably from all directions. After the death of Pius XII the Spanish church had become increasingly at variance with the dominant tendencies of the majority of other western churches, including the Vatican itself. Its teachings, and above all its attitudes, its very spirit, were out of step with the others'. Although this was known and discreetly discussed, the split was so marked at the Second Vatican Council that it came as a traumatic shock for the Spanish church, whose bishops had attended, most of them in the belief that they represented the soul of orthodoxy. Instead, in some confusion, they were forced to resign themselves to superfluity and irrelevance.

Taking advantage of the moment, priests and laymen more in tune with the spirit of the times, or as they put it with the "breath of the Holy Spirit," pressed the older generation of bishops and leaders of the religious orders to introduce intellectual, moral, and organizational changes under threat of open rebellion. Whether Basque nationalists, democrats, or leftists of whatever ilk, in one way or another they challenged the church to modify the authority structure of its ecclesiastical institutions, its definition of its role in society, and ultimately its alliance with the Francoist state.

By the time of the democratic transition the Spanish church had come so far in its transformation as a consequence of the combined pressure of the universal church and the rising generation that, instead of upholding what had come to be its sign of identity during the first stage of Francoism—that is, its identification with the winning side in the civil war—not only was the church no longer proud of its leading role in defining the war as a "crusade," but it began to ask the Spanish people's forgiveness for having failed to avert the war.

To this should be added the fact, no less revealing, that such a gesture, overwhelming in its symbolic importance, went almost unnoticed by the general public. During that time the conflict between priests and Catholic leaders of various ages and persuasions had been acted out against the backdrop of a country that had begun to turn away from the practice of a religion requiring such high drama, and to lose interest, if not in religion itself, at least in ecclesiastical affairs. This attitude was probably the natural extension of a traditional posture of reticence or hostility toward clericalism in a country which in other respects considers itself Catholic. In other words, the Spanish people went through a process of detachment from the church, even, one might say, a moderate secularization in the broadest sense, while maintaining a minimal allegiance to it in the sense that while they still received the sacraments, their interest in the dogmatic and moral teachings of the Catholic church declined dramatically, and their interpretation of morality relative to their practical decisions in almost all areas, and especially in matters of private morality, became an increasingly personal affair.[6]

At the same time, institutions for the creation and dissemination of secular culture also underwent extraordinary changes. By the early 1950s the milieu of artists and intellectuals was already far removed from the influence of both the state and the church. The attempts made by Catholic "integrists" (aligned with the Opus Dei movement) to gain control of the university system failed precisely because of the fierce resistance offered by the liberal Catholic intelligentsia, represented by figures such as Joaquín Ruíz Giménez, Pedro Laín, and José Luis Aranguren, during the first half of that decade.

It is clear that by the mid-fifties, influenced partly by this intellectual elite and partly by the existence of an earlier liberal tradition of Ortega, Unamuno, and the "'98 generation," many of the "best and the brightest" among the university students felt alienated not only from the Francoist state but from the entire dominant social and religious culture. In reality their intellectual orientation was increasingly focused in an altogether different direction, beyond the borders of Spain; and if they upheld the Spanish liberal tradition, it was above all because it encouraged them to look toward Europe. The books they were reading with greatest interest were existential, Marxist, and analytical works, the majority of which were non-Catholic or anti-Catholic, inspired by Heidegger, Sartre, Camus, Nietzsche, Hegel, Marx, and Popper. When they decided to act, they reinvented a tradition of student movements with social and political undertones which was inspired by European models, such as French university unionism. This new generation found its signs of identity in opposition to Francoism, and large numbers of young people became committed to a university movement which managed to dismantle the Falangist organization in the late fifties and to consolidate the democratic student organizations throughout the sixties.

By the time of Franco's death in 1975, Spanish universities had developed a political culture hostile to the regime of the day. The initiation rites for new students called for their participation in acts of protest and unrest against the political and academic authorities. The consequences were not limited to the universities: in years to come, as these students graduated, a generation of young lawyers, journalists, doctors, engineers, and economists brought new values, ideas, and demands to their spheres of professional activity. They challenged established patterns and the predominant culture of the organizations in which they had begun to work, whether in professional associations, newspapers, hospitals, or businesses. This pressure led to slow alterations in the authority structures and a continuous renegotiation of situational definitions within these organizations.

As a result of these processes, by the mid-seventies the economic, social, and cultural institutions of Spain were already quite close to those of western Europe, and the cultural beliefs, normative orientations, and attitudes of the people that accompanied the workings of these institutions had become fairly similar to those of other Europeans. This was one of the main reasons why the political change to democracy took place so swiftly and, apparently, so thoroughly, in spite of the enormous problems to be overcome, much to the astonishment of those foreign observers who persisted in looking at Spain through the prism of the 1930s, the civil war, or the first decade of Francoism.

If we now examine the *end* of the process which I have outlined, before the moment of transition in the mid-seventies, the first thing to acknowledge is that Spain's economy was a modern one, already ranking tenth among capitalist economies worldwide. It included a booming service sector and a broad industrial sector, and agriculture was undergoing a rapid transformation, as were the institutions governing industrial relations. Economic development had created a working class recently uprooted from its rural origins but eager to reap the benefits of continuous increases in real wages, and an incipient welfare state which had begun to develop in the sixties. Toward the end of the seventies the standard of living of the average Spanish worker was about two thirds that of the average French worker and quite close to that of an Italian. In the last years of Francoism, when workers were mobilized for collective action, their main objectives were economic and organizational, as they attempted to achieve better wages and fully legalized labor unions, free from the restraints imposed by the semitolerance of the sixties and the violent reprisals of the early seventies. Both their behavior and their attitudes during those years, and even more so during the transition itself, displayed a restrained, limited, yet significant acceptance of the authority structure of capitalist enterprises and the fundamental facts of a market economy, an attitude not very different, in fact, from that prevailing among other workers in western Europe. And although from that time on there would be intense conflicts of interest, frequent strikes, clear support for the so-called class unions (those of socialist and communist inspiration), and a growing preoccupation over the economic crisis and high unemployment levels, the workers nonetheless continued to maintain this attitude; indeed, the degree of legitimacy and trust invested by workers in the economic system was sufficient to preclude any real support for radical alternatives, and the record of past economic prosperity encouraged hopes of a sustained recovery (which was to come later, in the mid-eighties). When it became clear that workers supported the system, the class unions were forced to follow their lead (see Chapters 5 and 6).

A second point that should be emphasized is that by the mid-seventies the intense ideological conflicts of contemporary Spanish history had abated considerably. The ideological origins of both the right and the left were in crisis, and those tending toward one persuasion or the other seemed willing to accept a peaceful compromise with their opponents as the result of a long and complex process. Many Falangists on the one hand, and many anarchists, communists, socialists, and anticlerical intellectuals, on the other, had mellowed and come to adopt more moderate attitudes as a result of ideological evolution, reflection on the reasons for the civil war, and observation of both international changes and events within Spain, including the evolution of public opinion.[7] As for the Catholic church, it was no longer inclined to preach a holy crusade, or to support Francoism as in the past; on the contrary, many Catholics were looking for some accommodation with secular forces and the new democratic regime.

Most important is that for at least fifteen years (between the early sixties and the mid-seventies), the great majority of Spaniards, better educated than in the past and out of touch with ideological politics, had been taking part in the functioning of the economic, social, and educational institutions of civil society, which had offered them experience in negotiating, encouraged a growing confidence in their own judgment and ability, and systematically rewarded pragmatic strategies and compromises. At the end of this period the majority had little inclination to participate in any new ideological battles, and their vision of the world had become rooted or embodied in countless social rituals of negotiation and dialogue, generally based on values such as reason, freedom of choice, tolerance, prosperity, individual happiness, and citizenship. As a result, by the mid-seventies it had become apparent that the differences between Spain and western Europe with regard to both economics and culture had become merely a question of degree.

This homogeneity also applied in the political sphere, and uninterrupted democratic rule since the mid-seventies has only increased it. Spain now has a political class composed of people of different origins and persuasions, some originating in the "families" of Francoism and others in different sectors of the opposition, including communists, socialists, liberals, and Catalan and Basque nationalists. In spite of their differences they coexist in a civil way; they compete in elections; and they learn their trade in the exercise of state, regional, and local power. Politicians and bureaucrats handle official business year after year. They attend to the rituals of public life, solve problems, keep the usual confusion of politics within reasonable limits, and frequently endure insoluble difficulties with a degree of dignity. They have even been able to develop a reasonable consensus on the basics of foreign, regional, and economic policies which very few appear to question. Democracy has become the norm, an expected and accepted part of

the everyday life of the Spanish people (with only some reservations, which I examine later in this chapter).

I must emphasize, however, that while the societal traditions that developed during the last twenty years of Francoism played a crucial role in preparing the way for democracy, the success of democratic consolidation hinged on the combining of these traditions with a new tradition of *political culture* before and during the transition process.

THE INVENTION OF DEMOCRATIC SPAIN

The culture of a society is made up not of a set of stable and consistent beliefs, normative orientations, and their corresponding institutions, but of a repertoire of many such cultures or cultural traditions which have accumulated throughout history as responses to various problems. It is a complex repertoire in which these traditions may coexist peacefully, interrelate, or stand in open conflict with one another. They may be linked by some common ground which they all share, or by points of orientation over which they all disagree (Laitin, 1988). At each stage in the evolution of society a new generation, faced with new problems, turns to this repertoire of cultural traditions to use as instruments with which to interpret and solve those problems (Swidler, 1986). This may oblige it to choose among several possible interpretations of its history, ancient and modern, although in reality this will be not a single choice but numerous choices, for different segments of the population will choose different interpretations and transitions, and thus engage in cultural debates from different viewpoints. These substantive choices lead to other choices relative to the manner and intensity of adherence to one tradition or another. In some cases commitment to a tradition may be only superficial; in others people may anchor their lives and personal trajectories to it. They may adopt a critical attitude toward a cultural system, or accept some of its elements while rejecting others, or take some elements out of context and introduce them into a new context, or combine elements; they may even "invent" new traditions (Shils, 1975; Hobsbawm and Ranger, 1983).

In contemporary Spain we see the emergence and, to some extent, the invention of a new tradition and a new identity: that of a democratic Spain in contrast to a Francoist Spain, connected in a problematic way with pre-Francoist history, from which it is cut off by the trauma of the civil war. Tied to this denotative nucleus of a democratic Spain we find connotations of modernity ("modern Spain" as opposed to "traditional Spain," or perhaps "backward Spain") and of belonging to Europe (a "European Spain" as opposed to a "different Spain" or the "isolated Spain" of the past). This new tradition is, up to a point, a deliberate institutional and cultural construct, the result of an effort by Spaniards to combine the imitation of western models with the application of learning, in a harsh school, from within their own experience.

Spaniards have constructed a set of quasi-sacred texts, discourses, myths, rituals, and icons that pervade everyday politics. In doing so, they have taken some elements from the past—from the liberal monarchy of the restoration, from the republican tradition, from the two sides of the civil war and the Francoist period—as referents, both positive and negative, for this new tradition. Thus, they have built their system of political institutions on the cornerstone of the 1978 Constitution, which was designed to avoid the pitfalls associated with the earlier Constitution of 1931. But the contrast between the two constitutions is softened by the obvious fact that both are liberal democratic experiments resting on similar political principles. Although the most visible symbols of the republican tradition have been avoided, most of the substance of that tradition has been incorporated through the unquestioned acceptance of the principle of popular sovereignty. And even if the monarchic flag has been retained, the Hapsburg emblem, associated with both traditional Spain and Francoism, at its center has been replaced by the Bourbon emblem, loosely associated with the Enlightenment of the eighteenth century and the constitutional monarchy of the nineteenth century. Controversial monuments such as the Cross of the Valley of the Fallen, near Madrid have receded into the background and been given no public attention. Matters of contention have been deflected by other means. Thus, Spaniards have put together symbols that used to stand against one another and have made them coexist peacefully side by side. Streets may be found which are named either after Francoist generals of the civil war or after republican or leftist figures. And, in a most telling display of the symbolic politics of peaceful coexistence, a statue of Franco on horseback in front of a complex of official buildings in downtown Madrid stands less than a hundred meters from the statues of two leading socialists of the

Second Republic, Prieto and Largo Caballero, both dead in political exile.

Throughout these years the integrative role of politics has been emphasized over and over again, as much in the design and functioning of Spanish institutions as in political discourse. The Constitution of 1978 symbolizes national reconciliation and accommodation between right and left, between the church and anticlericalism, between capitalism and social reform movements, and between the center and peripheral nationalisms. The monarchy has gradually emerged as a unifying symbol of the nation, apparently of ever-increasing importance. National elections (and, to a lesser extent, regional and local elections) have been used routinely as forums in which to pronounce ritual speeches about the virtues of a democratic system that abhors political violence; and political campaigns based on images of moderation have repeatedly demonstrated their success at the polls.

Moreover, for many years both during and after the transition, a crucial part of political life has consisted of a series of pacts and understandings among the different political and social forces. The Constitution was the result of such a pact between the left and the right; and other more or less formalized understandings were reached between the political class, the armed forces, and the church. The regional pacts between centrists, socialists, and local political elites have absorbed many of the conflicts arising from the institutionalization of a system of regional mesogovernments, or autonomous communities (see Chapter 4). The social pacts among politicians, bureaucrats, unions leaders, and the business community have probably been instrumental in legitimizing the economic system and upholding the anti-inflationary economic policies of both centrist and socialist governments, thus reducing the level of industrial conflict and helping to consolidate the professional associations (see Chapters 4 and 5).

This institutional effort has been paralleled by a collective cultural effort, partly conscious and partly unconscious, to forget some fragments of Spain's history while keeping alive or reinterpreting others. The Francoist past has been not so much denounced as silenced. References to personal involvement in the civil war are avoided; the symbols of both victors and vanquished have been passed over or have lost their salience; the church has forgotten its crusades, and the communists and anarchists have forgotten their revolutionary goals; the death penalty has been abolished; and the country has been busy portraying itself as peace loving and eager for dialogue, reconciliation, and mutual tolerance. It could even be said that one of the reasons why the Spanish people took so long to react, and in such a hesitant manner, to the violence in the Basque region has been the difficulty of reconciling their pacific image of themselves and their institutions with the grim reality of political violence. They have reacted to this difficulty by taking refuge in the ritual denunciation of such violence as irrational, absurd, or useless, overlooking the fact that from the viewpoint of the Basque terrorists and other nationalist groups, political violence has been a very "rational" instrument in the fulfillment of their objectives for quite some time.

As I have said, in constructing this new tradition of democratic institutions and culture, Spaniards have combined the imitation of successful western models with lessons from their own experience. Looming large in the collective memory of that experience is the image of the crucial experiment that failed: the Second Republic, followed by the civil war of 1936–1939. The success of the present experiment in democracy has depended, and still depends, on the *adjustment* between European models, actual circumstances, and that particular piece of collective memory which is the civil war. It might be added that one of the reasons for so much misunderstanding between Basques and other Spaniards during the political transition has been their very different experience of that war.

For a large part of its modern history Spain had lived through a debate between two great complexes of cultural traditions so intense that many referred to it as the debate between "two Spains," modern versus traditional, secular versus Catholic, but also liberal versus authoritarian. The conflict affected all spheres of life—religion, social relations, the economy, and political institutions, as well as Spain's sense of history and collective identity—and it culminated in the civil war, a twentieth-century conflict which was in essence the last of a series of wars and uprisings left over from the nineteenth. But the war marked a decisive turning point in the course of that secular debate and has served as a reference point for the invention of the new tradition of a democratic Spain.

The civil war remains open to conflicting interpretations. Opposing yet simple Manichaean readings have traditionally been favored by both the right and the left, the winners and the losers, as if the war had been a struggle between the forces of good and evil. Yet there is room for a more ambiguous and subtle argument. It could be said, for example, that, although the fascist and military forces who rebelled in Spain in the 1930s acted "wrongly," they did so because they counted on the support of peasants, Catholics, and the middle classes, whom they believed to be "justifiably" alarmed by radical threats from the extreme left and by the indecision and incompetence of the moderate left. It could also be added that the whole process of confrontation in Spain was compounded by the imminent clash between German and Italian fascism, Soviet communism, and the western democracies, all of which, like Olympian gods, or demons, presided over and interfered in the death throes of Spanish domestic politics. This complex argument, with some variants, was the object of increasing commentary and debate during the fifteen or twenty years preceding the democratic transition.

It is interesting to note that this was the argument which finally prevailed, probably assisted by the process of transition itself. Many members of the generation that grew up during the final stage of Francoism came to interpret that part of their collective memory in the light of this reasoning, distancing themselves from the traditional posture of the combatants of the war, and refusing to take sides. As a result, the war came to be seen as the unfolding of a Greek tragedy, and therefore took on an aura of tragic inevitability. This characterization may have dubious validity from the viewpoint of a detached observer (and it will probably be revised by future generations), but it had momentous consequences for the participants in later events.

The crucial point now is to comprehend that if the civil war was a tragedy, this has vital moral implications for political discourse. The share of guilt and responsibility must be more or less evenly distributed among the combatants, since both sides were to blame, and the total amount of guilt and responsibility must also be reduced, since neither side was entirely guilty so much as each was responding to threats from the other. Moreover, both sides became pawns in the larger game of world politics which overwhelmed them. Finally, if a tragic reading of the war is extended to include postwar developments, surely the guilt the parties had to bear has been further expiated through suffering: the losers under the repression they endured for well over a generation, and the winners, to a lesser extent, by seeing their heirs renounce their monopoly on political power and lose control of the state a generation later.

The civil war has been the decisive moral and emotional reference point for the contemporary Spanish transition to democracy in much the same way that the English civil war of the seventeenth century was the moral and emotional reference point for the sociopolitical arrangements which were to open the way for modern liberalism. The Spanish civil war has been the national drama ever present in the public consciousness, while democratic politics has provided countless opportunities for the symbolic ceremonies which have nullified this experience. Democratic institutions themselves can be understood as ceremonies of national reconciliation. The political class, and the economic, social, and cultural leaders who have supported the new regime, have been the principal actors and officiators in the majority of these ceremonies, while the country has generally been cast as spectator, chorus, or accompaniment, with the political arena providing a scenario par excellence.

Conventional sociology and political science consider the state only in terms of its practical or instrumental dimension: as an agency for ruling over society, with a monopoly on legitimate violence, and for the solution of (some, supposedly crucial) collective problems. From this point of view political sociology may explain many phenomena but finds it difficult to explain the intensity of the feelings of attraction or repulsion which politics arouses in many people; neither can it explain the affective bonds which link them to the state and to the personal, institutional, and material symbols of patriotism and partisan loyalties, their confidence in leaders, and the passions which mobilize the energies necessary for participation in public life. As a matter of fact, reduced to a mere game of interests, political life itself lacks interest and meaning, both for the usual practitioners and for the general public.

In reality the state has two dimensions: it is to some extent an agent of domination over and negotiation with society, sometimes with the aim of solving collective problems; but it is also to some extent a supposedly exemplary focus of society. Systematic attention to this dramatic, symbolic, and affective dimension of the state is crucial for understanding not only the transition to but also the workings of Spanish democracy, all the more so inasmuch as in the Spain of transition the ceremony of restoring peace to the community has been almost continually interrupted by violence. This has accentuated the necessity and urgency of the state rituals aimed at exorcising the destructive or demonic forces that threaten civil life.

EXPLAINING A SUCCESSFUL DEMOCRATIC TRANSITION

Two kinds of explanations are usually advanced for successful transitions to or consolidations of liberal democracies: structural explanations and actor-oriented ones.[8] Structural explanations emphasize economic or cultural conditions, both domestic and international, while actor-oriented explanations focus on the critical choices made by strategic actors, who may be constrained by those conditions but are also able to shape and transform them. These are sometimes considered opposing approaches, though it is easy to see them rather as complementary (Lipset, Seong, and Torres, 1991). Once the two extreme positions of determinism and unrestrained free-choice arguments—economic, cultural, and so on—are set aside, we are left with the traditional view (rephrased so often and in so many different languages) that the two elements of constraining factors and bounded choices (or choices with some degree of freedom) on the part of the actors are interrelated elements which require each other as parts of the same argument. The question, then, is to move beyond those rather unexciting dilemmas of structuralist versus actor-oriented arguments, and to explore ways in which those structural factors operate and the actors' moves can be better understood. The answer may lie in a view that holds traditions, rules, or institutions to be the core of those structural factors, and in the corresponding view that sees the actors less as choice makers than as rule followers (or as rule deviants or rule breakers).

Thus, modernization theories can be viewed as exponents of structure-oriented explanations of the emergence of democratic regimes. Prevalent in the 1950s (Lerner, 1958; Lipset, 1959), these theories suffered from the lapse into authoritarianism of one after another modernizing country during the 1960s and early 1970s. Yet the more recent wave of democratization felt throughout the world seems to have partly vindicated that theory, or some new version of it. Its proponents claim that a positive correlation (or rather, an N-curve relationship) has been established between economic growth and democracy (see Lipset, Seong, and Torres, 1991, pp. 14ff.). Nonetheless, in order to move from this observation to a persuasive causal explanation, and to do so while avoiding economic determinism, the authors are required to look into the intermediate mechanisms between the two variables. The argument they emerge with holds that economic growth is somehow responsible for the increasing social expectations and demands of the masses, and for the increasing capacities of the elites to satisfy these demands. Still, the question of why these demands should include demands for political freedom and democratic institutions, and why, therefore, the game pitting demands for greater material well-being (along with more educational and employment opportunities) and the elites' capacity and willingness to satisfy them should be played within the framework of a democratic regime rather than any other type of regime remains unanswered—unless other historical or cultural factors are allowed to enter the picture (Lipset, Seong, and Torres, 1991, pp. 26ff.). But when they do enter, the end result is a downgrading of the explanatory status of the independent variable (that is, of economic growth), which becomes neither a sufficient nor even a necessary condition but only a facilitating condition, an "important aspect" of democracy (see Lipset, Seong, and Torres, 1991, p. 31).

But if one problem with some of the structural explanations is the weakness of their discussion of the intermediate variables, the problem with many actor-oriented explanations is their tendency to lose sight of the constraining factors and to overemphasize the uncertainty of the situation and the contingent nature of the actors' choices. These choices seem to be only (or mainly) constrained by the interplay between different strategies and by the actors' previous choices (and the paths constructed by the breakdown of authoritarian regimes and the first steps of the transition; see Karl, 1990). If this approach is pushed to extremes, as happens in Guillermo O'Donnell and Philippe Schmitter's account (1986) of democratic transitions, events are "explained", or rather described, as unlikely combinations of *fortuna* and *virtù* (though this *virtù* is itself little more than an empty label, since it is made to refer to actors, characters, and goals which are so ill defined as to be largely the result of the events themselves). Thus, the authors are not interested in explanations (as they dismiss what they call normal scientific approaches for understanding social processes of some complexity); they are content to provide an ideal description, constructed on the basis of (and given some plausibility by its apparent fit with) isolated bits and pieces of a few instances of democratic transitions.

Implicit in the tentative conclusions offered by O'Donnell and Schmitter is a set of theoretical assumptions that may serve as a contrasting starting point for the position for which I argue in this section of the chapter. The authors assert, first, that democratic transitions are to be understood as resulting mainly from critical choices made by strategic political actors (both hard-liners and soft-liners of the authoritarian regime, as well as opposition forces), with some input from social elites and elite-led social movements. Second, these choices are made in a climate characterized by a considerable degree of uncertainty regarding the rules of the game, whether applied during the transition or at the end of it. Third, these rules, and the Constitution in which they are enshrined, are invented and bargained over by these political elites. Finally, the implication is that the political actors are the protagonists of the process since they either have at the outset or develop policy programs and institutional designs which they try to implement through critical choices that shape the entire process.

By contrast, I would assume, first, that most people, political actors included, only rarely confront situations as choice makers. Usually they face them as rule followers, in the context of traditions and institutions that shape their preferences and their sense of what can be done. Choices do exist and may have momentous consequences, but they are interstitial and heavily dependent on those traditions even when they diverge from them. At the same time, actors may be precluded from seeing this, since their self-understanding, their everyday life, is embedded in a cultural idiom of "finalism." This applies particularly to political actors and their ordinary political life: the only way they can articulate their own experience is through a language of goals, projects, programs, objectives, and the like. Second, when the time comes for a regime transition, for a change of rules in the political game, actors find themselves in a situation of only relative uncertainty, since they still get most of their definitions and preferences from background assumptions and meta-rules of the game which already exist, not in the political realm but in other areas of social activity, that is, in the realm of civil society. Third, the new political rules are not so much invented *de novo* as translated, so to speak, from these meta-rules of social, economic, and cultural life. The new regime's viability, its chances for success, hinges precisely on the appropriateness of this translation: it will be viable only if, and only to the extent that, there is a good fit between the rules of politics and the meta-rules of society. Fourth, civil society thus plays a central role prior to and throughout the processes of transition and consolidation. It is from this civil realm that the meta-rules of the political game emerge, together with the background assumptions, social predispositions, and standards of appropriate behavior—standards governing our definition of what is "normal," how things are expected to work. The implication is that civil society is already *there:* it does not have to be resurrected as the result of sociopolitical mobilizations taking place at the time of the transition.[9]

Starting from this point I mean to attempt an interpretation of events in Spain which combines the role played by civil society with the development of a cultural political idiom; the army's willingness to limit the degree of violence and to give politics a breathing space, room to develop; and finally, the critical choices of the political class. But first I examine some alternative explanations and look into some factors which have usually been given credit for the success of the Spanish political transition: a favorable international context (Spain being a semiperipheral country in the western world, its political institutions had to adjust to those of the core nations); a set of socioeconomic and cultural changes (some authors group these together under the label of "modernization") and the structural strains those changes put on the authoritarian regime; the spread of new attitudes and opinions among the population concerning political institutions and political participation (which would indicate the existence of a democratic political culture prior to the transition); a crisis of succession within the authoritarian regime (owing to Franco's dying without having appointed a leader to replace him); and, above all, the ability of the political elites to settle their differences and agree among themselves on a new democratic regime and to lead the country down the path of a brokered transition: a *reforma pactada/ruptura pactada.*

I deal briefly with the first four factors (the international context, the modernization thesis, the predemocratic culture, and the succession crisis) and then focus on the idea of elite bargaining. I argue that taking this last factor as the main one overestimates the capacities of the political elites and their ability to influence events. Finally, I advance my own explanation, according to which Spain's political leaders showed a remarkable ability not just to lead but to learn from the course of the events; to adjust to two fundamental sources of pressure (from social traditions and from the army); and, in the process, to contribute toward the development of a new cultural political idiom. Those pressures both constrained and provided an opportunity for the elites' decisions. They converged in pushing these elites through a course of bargaining and compromise among themselves, which found its expression in the political culture.

To begin with, the international context, although largely in favor of democratic change (certainly more so than in the 1930s), exercised a limited influence and could exert pressure only through domestic factors. Many examples of peaceful coexistence between authoritarian regimes and western democratic polities over long periods of time demonstrate the limits of this explanation. It is obvious that a democratic capitalist environment may be unfriendly to but also quite understanding of and compatible with an authoritarian regime. And so it was with the Francoist state for more than twenty years.

Insofar as the influence of changes associated with modernization (economic growth, improved rates of literacy and formal education, rise of mass communications and urbanization, and so on) is concerned, it is worth remembering that these changes do not translate themselves into political change in any predetermined way; also, they are fully compatible with totalitarian as well as authoritarian regimes. In fact, many fascist as well as communist states were built in the belief that they were the epitome of modernity, certainly more so than the "decadent" liberal democracies of their time. More to the point, the Francoist state combined a traditional outlook on politics and culture with a modern economy, and it attempted to gain legitimacy in the eyes of the Spaniards by pointing at the economic growth of the 1960s. In fact, many Francoists interpreted the results of the referendum of 1966 and the mass demonstrations of December 1970 as a corroboration of the theory that modernization was helping, not hurting, the authoritarian regime (Preston, 1986, p. 34). The point is that for these changes to have some specific effect on politics, they have to be connected with other institutional, organizational, and cultural changes, and must be incorporated into social traditions.

The evidence concerning the democratic political culture of Spain prior to the transition is soft, but it tends to show that democratic culture was very weak.[10] This is not to imply that the basic cultural orientations of the Spaniards regarding their society, collective problems, recent history, and near future had not changed. Change ran very deep indeed, as I have shown. But these cultural changes were to a great extent implicit, and were embedded in the social traditions to which I have alluded. By contrast, public opinion surveys in the 1970s showed that the Spaniards' explicit attitudes and opinions toward political institutions and personnel reflected a general lack of interest in politics, and that most people were rather acquiescent toward the Francoist regime. They may have wished for more say in the election of political leaders, but they showed little sympathy for political parties; in addition, they wanted a strong leader to solve most of their collective problems, they expressed indifference to the would-be king, and they harbored feelings of respect for Franco himself.

With regard to the crisis of succession in the authoritarian regime, it is true that Franco's death was in itself a crucial event, compounded by the fact that he had no successor willing and able to carry out his legacy. In Franco's final years, as he was gradually moving down the path to senility (and in the midst of feverish public expectations of his imminent death, but with no action taken to hasten it), he was able to anoint only two second-rate political figures (Luis Carrero Blanco and Carlos Arias), possibly capable of presiding over caretaker governments but with no leadership qualities of their own, and a would-be king whose loyalty to Francoism had always seemed suspect. But the critical point is that there was no political milieu from which a hypothetical willing and able successor could draw support. In the background there stood a Francoist political class, ready to abandon politics for the pursuit of private interests,[11] and an army with a limited veto power, which was accustomed to obeying and standing on the sidelines of politics.

Many scholars have focused on bargaining among the elite as a chief explanatory factor for the success of the transition. Undoubtedly there is much to recommend this claim. Whatever the structural conditions may be, transitions are unique sequences of events, the direction of which is, at critical points, highly contingent on the vision, will, and capacity to act of small numbers of strategically placed individuals (Linz, 1987). Certainly the history of the Spanish transition cannot be written without giving proper recognition to the way in which King Juan Carlos and, above all, Adolfo Suárez guided their plans for political reform through the murky waters of the Francoist establishment, and to the way they persuaded public opinion and the political opposition to play by their rules, as well as to the way in which that opposition (along with the church and other socioeconomic elites) responded to, helped shape, and supported those plans. This they did in record time. In less than one year, between July 1976, when the king appointed Suárez prime minister, and June 1977, when the first free elections took place, Suárez was able to persuade the Francoist parliament and the army in the fall of 1976 to accept a national referendum on the law for political reform; to hold the referendum in December 1976 which gave him a clear mandate for scheduling free elections; to legalize the parties, including the Communist party, in the spring of 1977; and to hold elections in June 1977. Then the new Cortes convened, and a new Constitution was drafted and approved by a referendum in December 1978; in the meantime, a broad consensus was being reached among the parties concerning a set of socioeconomic policies, including the Moncloa Pacts in the fall of 1977 and the Statutes for Regional Autonomies between 1977 and 1979.

In light of this series of crucial decisions, it seems that the Spanish transition should indeed be understood mainly as the result of bargaining among political elites—of the *reforma pactada/ruptura pactada* between government and opposition (Maravall and Santamaría, 1986). This characterization, however, overstates the role of these elites and assumes that they had resources of wisdom, will, and capacity for mobilizing support which in fact they lacked.

To begin with, initial public expectations regarding the new king were mixed. He was an ambiguous symbol for political change, as he could be seen both as a guarantor of continuity and as a promise of reform. Juan Carlos owed his position to Franco. As one among several candidates, he was chosen because he seemed able to combine and embody two sources of legitimacy: that of a traditional monarchy and that of the Francoist regime. Juan Carlos was educated under Franco's close supervision, and in 1969 he became Franco's officially recognized heir in a solemn televised ceremony in which he had to pledge before the Cortes, on his knees with his hand upon the Bible, to support Franco's political principles. At the same time, Juan Carlos was supposedly an obedient son to his father, Don Juan, who seemed by contrast a man of liberal predilections, who thought that the only chance for a restoration of the monarchy lay not so much in a compromise with Francoism as in the new king's being seen as a king for all Spaniards, an idea possibly implying a policy of national reconciliation between the two sides in the civil war, as well as hopes for a liberal political regime.

Now, if the king could initially be seen as the repository of contradictory loyalties, the same might be said of the class of politicians and civil servants who made up the semireformist wing of Francoism, and who came to power along with the Suárez government. They had made their career under Franco, and they had a long record of acquiescence and opportunism, some experience in the ways of public administration, propaganda, and political repression, and a rather erratic and unimpressive record regarding political reform within the Francoist institutions. Some of them thought that Franco's death offered an opportunity for a break with the past, while others accepted the new situation in the belief that years of economic growth and law and order, the rise of the middle classes, and the spread of consumer culture made possible a continuation of the past.

Meanwhile, most of the lawyers, journalists, functionaries, academics, and professionals who held posts in the opposition parties at the time of transition were not in a much better position to understand and act on the situation. The liberal parties had little organization and few members, and their leaders were not well known (the most widely respected one, Dionisio Ridruejo, had died in 1974, a year before Franco). They were rather apprehensive about what sort of political preferences the public might show after forty years of Francoism.

Socialists and communists, the leftists in general, were also ill prepared to deal with the new situation. They had trained themselves in a rhetoric of radical confrontation that reflected a superficial understanding of the circumstances of Spanish society. The communists, for instance, refused for a long time to accept as a fact the economic growth and social transformation of the country since the 1960s, and they expelled from their ranks those leaders who recommended taking these facts into consideration in order to revise their strategy.[12] It took time for the left to acknowledge that the envisioned agrarian reforms of the 1930s no longer applied to the conditions of the 1960s. The socialists, with fewer ideological hang-ups, waited, however, until the mid-1970s, and then adopted a radical stance, enshrining Marxism in the structures of the party.[13] In general, while the experience of opposition politics provided useful training in intraparty political maneuvering (Gillespie, 1988, pp. 212ff., 267ff.), drafting manifestos, and handling the media, it was a mixed blessing for helping the politicians understand the problems of the country. My general point is that, given this record, it was to be expected that the new political class would enter the period of transition with a rather distorted local knowledge of the Spanish scene, and would be unable to foresee and plan in advance what ought to be done. Rather, their best opportunity lay in their instinct for survival, and in their ability to learn from and adjust to events and the public's reaction to them.

As a matter of fact, at critical turning points in the spring and winter of 1976 and the summer of 1977, it was the public response that proved to be the key factor. First, during the period between November 1975 and June 1976, the Francoist political class as a whole procrastinated and was deeply divided and hesitant. The critical test that demonstrated the Francoists' failure and prepared the way for the king's decision to appoint Suárez as prime minister was the popular agitation and general restlessness that spring, which revolved mostly around the collective bargaining arrangements taking shape at that time in an atmosphere of increasing alarm over the impending economic crisis, unleashed by the oil shortage of 1973. Second, by contrast, when Suárez took the initiative for political reform in the fall and winter of 1976, it was the opposition parties' turn to hesitate, and to advise against participation in the December referendum on political reform. The people made clear by voting in the referendum that they trusted Suárez's intentions and his political judgment. Finally, the elections of June 1977 were the public's third critical intervention. By demonstrating the general inclination toward political moderation at the expense of the extreme left and extreme right, these elections pushed aside many of the politicians' expectations, fears, and hopes about the potential either for radical politics or for continuity with the past. The results set the tone for the tasks of writing the Constitution and working out other compromises on socioeconomic policies, relations with the church, and the regional question. Thus, the political elites were successful not because they were able to lead the public but rather because they were able to learn from and follow the public mood.

This learning reached the elite mainly from two quarters: from society and from the army. Social traditions gave support to moderate policies, and the army threatened sanctions on immoderate ones.

These positive and negative reinforcements were the carrot and stick that drove home lessons the politicians either would never have learned or would have been tempted to forget. The politicians' main merits consisted in their being able to translate these opportunities and constraints into institutional designs and policies.

As I have indicated, the traditions that prepared the way for the political transition had been developing, almost without interruption, for about fifteen to twenty years before Franco's death. These were initiated by social groups which had certain incentives and opportunities for change. As migration, technical innovations, and economic growth altered the framework of urban as well as rural life, these groups faced new situations which required them to establish new ways of living. At the same time, these people had access to novel cultural artifacts which allowed them to redefine their situation and give new meaning and direction to their actions: for instance, the models of present-day European unionism, the dissenting traditions of the European intelligentsia, the *aggiornamento* of the church, and new consumer patterns. As the groups initiated these traditions, they gradually moved onto center stage of the social system, and the impact of these traditions on the rest of the population became ever greater. That impact was reinforced by the mass media (by television since the 1960s, and by the press, taking advantage of the Press Law enacted in 1966). The result was that by the mid-1970s the way of life in civil society had become to a large extent liberal democratic. Mutual tolerance and bargaining according to agreed-upon rules of the game became the norm. Checks on the use of power by people in positions of social, cultural, and economic authority were routinely enforced. Demands for increasing levels of freedom were repeatedly made in the expectation of being honored. The articulation of all sorts of interests and ideas in the public arena became commonplace. In time this discourse came to be considered normal, and was granted an aura of naturalness.

By contrast, what looked increasingly abnormal, exotic, and different was the Francoist state and the Francoist regime. The reversal of normality and abnormality between the first and last stages of Francoist rule was almost complete. In the 1940s and 1950s the state had almost succeeded in shaping (through a variety of instruments, including intimidation and a timely alliance with the church) large segments of Spaniards' daily life. The street being a symbol of everyday social interaction, the state's ability to rule over the street was an obvious indication of the government's ability to fit in with the ordinary life of its subjects. But by the early 1970s the emerging social traditions of change, bargain, and dissent were setting the tone of the street, while the diehard Francoists, known as "the bunker," were seen as people taking refuge in an enclosed space, entrenched against the reality surrounding them. Hence the success of the rhetorical appeal of Suárez's public speeches in the fall of 1976, in which he urged the people to approve the law for political reform. These speeches were couched in the terms of an opposition between the normality of social life, or the life of the street, and the abnormality of political life. Suárez issued his political call on the grounds that the new law would bridge the gap between the two and would translate the rules of ordinary life into politics; that is what the change to political democracy was all about.[14]

Social traditions rooted in the experiences of nearly two decades explain the public disposition at the time of the transition. Still, although these traditions existed and translated themselves into interventions by the public at critical junctures, and although specific leaders were quick to grasp the implications for initiating policies, it does not follow that the majority of the politicians were capable of learning. Their ability to learn could be diminished by their own preconceptions, which were anchored in their previous experience and the peculiarities of their position. They could stand by these preconceptions for quite a while, even in the face of the evidence. They could be unrealistic as long as they were not confronted with "recalcitrant experiences" (Quine, 1953; see also White, 1981) whose consequences they could not escape. One of these recalcitrant experiences was the presence of the army.[15]

As a matter of fact, we know that many politicians on the Francoist side half believed their own official propaganda, which appeared to be corroborated by some measure of success—for instance, by economic growth, law and order, and diplomatic recognition. Franco himself was seen as a shrewd and realistic appraiser of situations and of men. He had been able to steer through the complicated (and initially hostile) international scene of the 1940s and 1950s, moving from Nazi sympathizer to (marginal) member of the western alliance. But his ability to learn from the developments of the 1960s and early 1970s was much more limited. He was led to believe, by his own propa-

ganda, that economic growth and the rising middle classes would provide additional legitimacy to his regime. Instead, he had to live with
an array of complications which resulted from those developments,
and which he did not understand. To begin with, he understood very
little about the economy. In addition, he did not realize the importance of the students' discontent or the workers' mobilization; and he
could not make sense of the regional and nationalistic revival. He
reacted to these developments by holding to the simplistic view that
the unity of Spain was being threatened by social and territorial conflicts. Thus, he returned to the beliefs which had helped him justify his
own rebellion in the 1930s. Losing the church's support, even seeing
its gradual detachment from the state, disconcerted him. In the face of
all this he procrastinated, and allowed for only limited and minor institutional reforms, indulging in wishful thinking which convinced him
that everything was under control ("atado y bien atado," tied up and
well tied up). But Franco's misconceptions were mirrored by those of
many of the politicians who succeeded him. As we have seen, not a
few of the politicians of the right harbored unrealistic hopes about the
willingness of the population to support the continuation of the
Francoist institutions; and many opposition politicians entertained
their own brand of unrealistic hopes about the radicalism of the
masses. Those biases were checked, as I have mentioned, by societal
traditions and by the presence of the army, a topic to which I now
turn.

The Spanish army did not stand at the beginning of the democratic
transition as a force divided and defeated in war, as the Portuguese,
Greek, and Argentine armies did at the beginning of their own
national transitions. On the contrary, the Spanish army was perceived,
and perceived itself, as victorious and united. It had won the civil war,
and that memory was the key to its self-conception and to the image it
projected to the outside world. A solemn ceremony was held every
year on the anniversary of that victory, in which the army marched
along the main streets of the capital and every provincial town. At the
same time, Franco avoided testing the military in foreign wars and
adventures. He did not enter the Second World War, despite Nazi
pressures to the contrary, nor did he get entangled in military confrontations in North Africa, so that once the French conceded independence to Morocco, he followed suit; he did not engage in colonial
wars in Guinea and the western Sahara, instead losing both territories

without a fight when the time came. In this way the army's strength and unity were preserved. That unity was a goal of paramount importance. The army was haunted by memories of past divisions: the Moroccan war, the organization of the Juntas de Defensa, the dictatorship of Primo de Rivera and the Second Republic, right up to the civil war, when the army split and a significant part of the officer corps, as well as many generals, remained loyal to the Republic (Payne, 1967). Thus, Franco and the military took care to monitor dissent among the ranks. This became an increasingly pressing need by the early 1970s, in view of the Portuguese revolution. Hence the swift and decisive manner in which the threat posed by the organization of a group of democratic officers was dealt with in 1974.

But, however united and even ready to act the army was at the time of transition, it was unclear what specific moves could be expected from it. Here we have to take into consideration the army's traditions, which grew out of the long period of Francoism. First, there was a tradition of its self-understanding and self-justification as guarantor of the unity and continuity of the country against threats posed either by domestic forces such as regionalism, political factionalism, or social conflicts which might end in a general breakdown of law and order, or by foreign invasion. This was the rationale behind the army's rebellion in 1936. Second, there was a tradition of remaining in the background of political life, of playing a marginal role in the control of political institutions and the establishment of public policies. Only rarely were military men part of Franco's inner circle, where most crucial political decisions were made; and, even more important, the army did not take upon itself the role of modernizing agent, in contrast to the way the Brazilian and Peruvian armies of the 1960s and the dissenting Portuguese officers of the 1970s understood their historical task. That task was left in the hands of Franco, or rather of a segment of the civilian political class. Third, in the absence of the excitement and opportunities provided by wars and engagement in politics, the military's everyday experience had evolved within the narrow horizons of garrison life, focusing only on the anxieties surrounding the waiting list for semiautomatic promotions up the military career ladder. The army became risk averse, legalistic, tied to the status quo, while allowing a moderate, semiprofessional, and apolitical trend to develop in its midst. Thus, we understand why the army, once Franco disappeared, found little incentive to intervene, provided the politicians understood that the transition should be compatible with most of the army's traditions, and above all that it should not appear to threaten the fundamental unity and continuity of the country. This was ensured by the fact that the legal framework was kept in place and that the king, who had carefully cultivated his links with the army, remained a symbol of the continuity underlying the institutional changes.

Let me summarize by saying that, in explaining successful transitions to democracy, four main causal factors should be considered: traditions within civil society that have accustomed the population to polycentric forms of order such as markets, social pluralism, and public debate; a cultural idiom that emphasizes the integrative role of politics and moves people away from absolute politics; the military's acquiescence in accepting a limited role for itself; and the politicians' ability to learn from and adjust to the foregoing factors as a precondition for playing a constructive role in the transition—in designing the institutions, initiating policies, and properly performing their symbolic role.

More particularly, civil society prepares the way for the democratic transition through a variety of mechanisms. Society intervenes at critical junctures and shapes *crucial events*. In this way people create recalcitrant experiences that refute politicians' expectations (for instance, about the masses' radicalism) and perhaps also the politicians' dreams about the feasibility of absolute politics. Societal traditions influence the *institutional design* of the new political regime by establishing meta-rules of the game that set limits and provide orientation for the Constitution and other political institutions. They also shape *policies* by indicating the contours of popular acceptance of political experiments in areas such as those of economic, regional, and educational policies. They therefore *educate the political class* by requiring it to go through a short yet intense period of training in pragmatic politics. More particularly, social traditions teach politicians not to take their claim to political representation literally and to understand that the people's long-term consent to the politicians' rule is conditional on performance. These traditions also *educate the army,* in that they shape the army's perceptions of the degree to which the new institutions are compatible with its understanding of its own mission for maintaining the basic social fabric and the unity of the nation and defending it from foreign aggression. They help in the creation, enrichment, and spread of *political symbols* that provide the new politics with a way to express itself. They shape the *basic, often tacit understandings and dispositions of democratic politics*. In effect, they develop expectations about a polycentric order and limited government; they create habits of bargaining, mutual toleration, and compromise; they mark the dividing line between what is normal and abnormal, realistic and unrealistic; and they lay the foundation for a self-concept of the collective subject which engages in democratic politics (namely, the nation or some "plurinational" collective entity) as a moral community engaged in an ongoing conversation with itself regarding its problems, its goals, and even its own identity.

By focusing on civil society I do not mean to imply that unless a fully developed civil society exists, the chances for a transition are minimal or nonexistent. My point is that a *successful* transition will come about only if, and only to the extent that, a civil society or something like it either predates the transition or becomes established in the course of it. This raises extremely interesting questions concerning those situations when transitions start while civil society is still fairly underdeveloped. It may be that in these cases charismatic leaders, wise institutional designs, and exogeneous factors can play a role—not in making up or substituting for the civil society which is not there, but in helping the process by which such a society comes about. This role would require elites to pay close attention not only to the design of political institutions but also, and mainly, to the design of social institutions such as markets, social pluralism, and the public sphere.

THE UNCERTAIN INSTITUTIONALIZATION
OF LIBERAL DEMOCRACY

The successful transition to and consolidation of Spanish democracy was achieved by the promulgation of the Constitution and the creation of a generalized and stable expectation in the country that liberal democracy was no longer threatened by the use of violence or the victory at the polls of antisystem parties. But the full institutionalization of the regime implies that the rules of the game have been internalized, that is, accepted as legitimate and reasonable, practiced by the majority of the population, and therefore transformed into predictable patterns of behavior as part of normal, everyday customs. In Spain this process is still going on. So far the record is a mixed one, with considerable accomplishments but also with significant limitations.

On the accomplishment side the list is quite impressive, and to some extent this book will bear witness to those successes. To begin with, the political institutions of a liberal democracy have been established and tested, as of this writing, through a period of about a decade and a half. The old and deep conflicts between the Catholic church and a secular society have been largely superseded as the result of a rather baroque historical development involving the state, the church, and the whole of civil society, which I analyze at some length in Chapter 3. The experience of that decade and a half, despite occasional disturbances, has sealed the reconciliation. The cleavage between the center and the periphery, and the tensions between the civil authority and the military which arose at least in part in connection with it, has been to some degree resolved, most notably through the institution of regional mesogovernments, without gravely endangering the political system, social pluralism, the market economy, and the basis for a common collective identity most Spaniards could relate to (see Chapter 4).

Most important, two key sets of institutions typical of civil society—markets and voluntary associations—have been reinforced and have undergone a dramatic (though still inconclusive) process of development. As we will see in Chapter 4, the Spanish economy underwent a very difficult period of internal adjustment up to the mid-1980s, when unemployment rose to 20 percent of the active population. But, as a result of a combination of intense foreign investment, cautious economic policies, and the adaptive strategies of business and unions (see Chapter 5), the basic macroeconomic equilibria were maintained, and inflation gradually went down (from an annual rate of increase of 24 percent to about 6 percent between 1977 and 1990), while foreign capital kept coming in, and employment appeared to be on the way to partial recovery by the late 1980s. At the same time, there was a nearly complete transformation of the agrarian sector (Pérez-Díaz, 1987, pp. 353–389), a protracted industrial restructuring still in the making by the early 1990s, and an overhaul of the way in which the financial markets operate in the country. But for all the problems of the Spanish economy, its dynamism was quite remarkable, some indication of which is provided by the increase in the number of new enterprises which registered with the Official Registrar of Commerce: up from 10,294 in 1979 to 70,164 in 1988.[16]

At the same time, there was, as I have mentioned, a development of the organizational capabilities of both business and labor. Business entered the political transition from a position of weakness. It enjoyed no close ties with the main political parties, faced what seemed at the time a wave of worker radicalism, and did not have an all-encompassing organization to represent its interests. In a matter of a few years, however, business found the principles of a market economy enshrined in the Constitution, organized itself around the CEOE (Confederación Española de Organizaciones Empresariales) and other groups, and participated in "social pacts" with unions it learned to live and deal with (see Chapter 4). Businessmen also learned to deal with the new political class. They developed links, though not very strong ones, with centrist and rightist political parties, and succeeded in arranging for a mutually beneficial accommodation with a socialist government.[17]

In turn, the industrial workers, and to some extent the employees in the service sector, were somehow represented by two main (and rival) union federations, the communist-led Comisiones Obreras, or CCOO, and the socialist-controlled Union General de Trabajadores, or UGT. These unions faced the double challenge of the political transition and an acute economic crisis with mixed feelings and very limited knowledge as to the proper strategy to follow. Thus, though they may have maintained on occasion the rhetoric of social radicalism, they proved able to adjust to the perceived demands and expectations of their constituencies (see Chapter 5). As a result, although these unions did not succeed in attracting many affiliates, they managed to retain their capacity to represent, and apparently to maintain a sizable amount of influence over, the working population, even if the unions' uncertainties made it difficult for them to play a leading role in shaping current developments (see Chapter 6). The evolution of these professional and labor organizations may be seen as part of a wave of social activism and new initiatives in all areas of social, economic, and cultural life. Thus, the total number of associations required by law to register a copy of their statutes with the Ministry of the Interior rose from 9,629 in 1970 to 35,589 in 1980, and 74,884 in 1989.[18]

But, however impressive these accomplishments have been, they should be considered against a background of some ambiguity, where other contrary trends have also appeared. Thus, throughout the years of democratic rule, four traditions or tendencies have emerged that, if unchecked, may have the potential for steering the country in the direction of a clientelistic polity and society, and for a systematic distortion of the public sphere. These are the tendencies of the political parties to become increasingly oligarchic; to articulate a public discourse which does not accord with their actual behavior; to insulate themselves from public opinion while obscuring their dealings with certain powerful interest groups (and particularly with the economic establishment); and to engage in some policies regarding the lower classes that foster patterns of dualism, clientelism, and deferential politics. By blurring the boundaries between the state and civil society, these trends constitute a danger that the public accountability of state authorities may become diminished, and possibly that a pattern of collusion and understandings between strategically well-placed actors on both sides of the fence between the public and the private sector will be established at the expense of what can be defined as the general interest.

To begin with, the major political parties in Spain have relatively few members compared to their European counterparts.[19] They make little effort to attract new members and apparently even less effort to attract people of independent judgment. This is not because they value ideological purity, (for they are all pragmatic and try to appeal to the electorate at the center of the ideological spectrum), but rather because, lacking such purity, they are extremely careful to preserve the party as an apparatus under the control of its leaders. Thus, members are required to be loyal and obedient to the party oligarchy. (The party leaders call this a concern for the unity of the party.) It is not that the leaders do not have good reason for wishing to maintain unity: the socialists had a long tradition of divisiveness which proved disastrous for them on various occasions, particularly before and during the civil war; and a bitter history of intraparty disloyalty led to the collapse of the UCD (Unión de Centro Democrático), Suárez's original party, which was the government party during the transition. Yet, in their zeal to safeguard party unity the incumbent oligarchs and their followers seem to demonstrate defensiveness, pessimism, and a fear of freedom.

This oligarchic control has been favored by a number of institutions. I will mention only two of them, leaving aside others, such as the electoral system of proportional representation with "closed" lists of candidates. A high ceiling on electoral costs has combined with the unwritten rule that this ceiling must be highly elastic to raise the threshold of access to the electoral market for new parties. This puts incumbent party leaders in a most favorable position vis-à-vis challengers and dissidents, whose threat of splitting the party would scarcely be credible, since a new party would find it very difficult to enter the electoral market. Also, the procedural rules of the Cortes, and the way in which they have been applied by its presidents, have drastically reduced the opportunities for public speech available to members other than the party spokesmen and has reduced the position of the ordinary member of parliament to that of an automaton with finger poised to press the voting button when advised to do so by his party spokesman, a gesture which awaits its reward at the critical moment when party candidates are chosen for the next elections.

The confusion in the public discourse of the parties has several causes. To begin with, by overdramatizing their differences, some parties have tried to conceal the fact that there is much continuity and similarity in the foreign, economic, and welfare policies of the governments of the center right (1976–1982) and center left (since 1982). Nothing could be more logical, given that these policies are variants of Spain's long-term historical pattern of increased involvement in the western world (which, as we have seen, was given a decisive impetus in the late 1950s). But to admit to this similarity is apparently taboo. Therefore it must be disguised by rhetorical appeals to the symbols of identity of the different parties, particularly when the time approaches for an electoral campaign; then flags are waved, partisan enthusiasm is brought to a pitch, and attempts are made to arouse the tribal instincts of the electorate and spur them on to attack the other parties.

Another variation in this general pattern of rhetorical ambiguity consists in defending policies which the party leaders have no intention of putting into practice. Again, at times of uncertainty such as elections or political crisis, party politicians apparently decide that they are facing an impressionable general public, which demands only a few brave words with a touch of moral indignation (such as "We have come this far, we'll go no further," "Something drastic has to be done," "We need a change," and so on).[20]

It also seems that the temptation to employ this high-flown rhetoric becomes all the more irresistible when a party is in opposition. For instance, when in opposition the Spanish socialists created the impression that they had designed a new economic policy, stressing issues of redistribution and state intervention which they later proceeded to forget, just as they forgot their appeals for Basque self-determination once they came to power.[21] In the field of foreign policy the socialists wanted to have things both ways: they entered the 1982 electoral contest by coining the slogan "OTAN, de entrada no" (which meant approximately either "No entry into NATO" or "NATO, no entry yet"). This policy then began to unravel year after year until it was in tatters, and finally became "OTAN, de entrada si" (Yes to entering NATO) in the run-up to the referendum on this issue in March 1986. In turn, the Partido Popular, which has been in opposition ever since, has also adopted impeccably opportunistic positions at critical moments, as indicated by its recommendation of abstention in the NATO referendum, which was as inconsistent with its own principles as it was symptomatic. Let us observe, however, that if politicians have used these rhetorical tricks again and again, it is because they have been successful; the people have let them get away with it and have voted for them afterward.

To this emerging tradition of rhetorical ambiguity if not outright duplicity can be added another: that of the triviality and lack of precision which surround the debate about the most important problems facing the country. The decision on whether or not to join NATO was on the verge of becoming merely a vote of confidence in the government, and was rarely discussed on its own merits. Even Spain's entry into the European Community in January 1986 was not the object of much public debate, despite its extraordinary consequences. Discussions of economic and welfare policies are usually limited and sprinkled with stereotypes and subterfuges. It seems as though the political class has hardly any interest in stimulating debate on addressing the country's major problems, such as how to improve the competitiveness of the economy; how to boost experimentation in the design of business, health, and educational institutions and research and training centers; and how to protect the environment. The poverty of debate over the national budget (not a terribly exciting subject in most democratic countries) is just one more symptom of this lack of interest—all the more revealing given the well-established tradition of a huge disproportion between the approved budget and the actual amount of government spending, and of a lack of effective jurisdictional control over that spending after the fact.

Behind these traditions of rhetorical vagueness we may suspect there is a fear on the part of politicians that if they admitted they do not know how to solve these problems, and this admission emerged in their public rhetoric, then they would lose their legitimacy to govern. If that were the case, it would be an indication of the politicians' failure to understand that, in ordinary times and in complex societies, state governance serves little more than three purposes: to fulfill the ritual functions of integration in a society which, by means of its markets and its associations, already coordinates itself to a very large extent; to deal from time to time with the obstacles which accumulate in the path of economic growth and other areas by making some critical decisions to remove blockages; and to propose some topics for public debate which may prove useful in reinforcing the public's commitment to liberal democratic institutions. If this were so, then the politicians' self-image as being the force that solves the great problems of society or fulfills some grandiose historical mission would be little more than compensation for their own insecurity as they faced problems they barely understood and could not control. The truth of the matter is that, given the limits of human knowledge and the increasing complexity of events, no one knows or could know how to "solve" such problems; and this is precisely the reason why the solution to these problems must be left open to constant experimentation and debate.

The insulation of the political parties and the political class from public opinion manifests itself in several ways. One is the lack of transparency in the dealings between politicians (whether individuals or groups) and the private sector. The practice of "insider trading"—that is, the transfer of privileged information from the public to the private sector, or vice versa, by individuals for their own benefit—is an ancient institution in Spain which has flourished in the shadow of all kinds of regimes, from pre-Franco days up to the present, particularly in the years of economic bonanza after 1986. It is reinforced, moreover, by the practice of what the French call *pantouflage,* or the movement of people between the public and private sectors, doing business one day with the sector they were regulating the day before. Commissions, tribunals, and parliamentarians have rivaled one another in their discreet treatment of these matters (as was demonstrated during the debates which took place in parliament throughout 1988, and in the work and conclusions of the parliamentary investigating commission on trafficking in influence). In fact, insider trading and *pantouflage* are two institutions that have reinforced the consolidation of the Spanish establishment, anchored in key sectors of the business community, and its working arrangements with the party in power. Blurring of the boundaries between the private and the public sector has eased the way for a new metamorphosis in the Spanish establishment by means of networking, establishing channels for personal contacts, and avoiding open markets, meritocratic competition, and public scrutiny. The occasional outbreak of scandals and rumors has only reinforced what it was supposed to expose, because the reports have been so inconclusive that their very reiteration seems to suggest that the process has to some extent become inevitable.[22]

Likewise, the opacity of party finances may seem to endanger the long-term credibility of the political system, for the lack of reliable information, combined with the exposure of specific scandals, produces a generalized sense that the parties cannot pay their electoral expenses without resorting to illegal methods, including massive violations of the tax laws. This problem is further exacerbated when politicians, instead of acting clearly and promptly in this respect, take advantage of the occasion by flaunting their disdain, or reply to questions by casting aspersions on the intentions of those who denounced the practices (thus fueling expectations of impunity and tolerance, if not of complacency).[23]

Those practices of patron-client relationships within the parties and between the parties and the socioeconomic elites, together with the corresponding rhetorical ambiguity, find their mirror image in similar patterns (and a similar rhetoric) involving the relations between the political class and significant segments of the lower classes, particularly in connection with certain socioeconomic public policies which have attempted to deal with the consequences of the high rate of unemployment (between 15 and 20 percent during most of the 1980s and early 1990s). The fact is that a fairly well protected core of Spanish labor has grown up, surrounded by a periphery of unemployed people (mostly young men, as well as women and older workers discouraged from entering, or staying in, the labor market), only 30 to 40 percent of whom receive unemployment benefits. They are trying to survive within the "safety net" of their extended families' support, and of two peculiar institutions either tolerated or fostered by the government: the underground economy and what in rural areas is called *empleo comunitario* (community employment).

Although this underground economy is by definition hidden from the public eye, and so reliable estimates of its extent are lacking, it is generally admitted that entire industrial districts (such as the so-called shoe districts of the Levant) and large parts of sectors such as textiles, metallurgy, and professional services, as well as the building industry, count on it to prosper and even survive. (Martínez Estévez and García Menéndez, 1985; Casals and Vidal Villa, 1985; Benton, 1990).[24] Business in those sectors and regions apparently could not succeed if not free from the burden of paying taxes, social security, and the minimum wage; and apparently local authorities—quite often members of the Socialist or Communist parties—and local unions agree.

Thus, we find a curious experiment in the peaceful coexistence (or cohabitation, so to speak) of an illegal microcorporatism at the local level, which condones the underground economy, and the legal macrocorporatism of the national "social pacts," which pushes up the level of the taxes, social security compensation, and wages which apparently make it so difficult for local entrepreneurs to stay in business. Although formally contradictory, these two brands of corporatism are in fact complementary to each other. Both have an acceptable degree of legitimacy in the eyes of local authorities, police, and unions, as well as social and cultural elites at large, including the local priests; and they are not questioned by the regional or even, in any form that threatens to translate itself into action, by the national authorities. That legitimacy has been wrapped up in arguments of moral reasoning as well as convenience by appeals to the needs of the lower classes but also of the businessmen, private interests, and the common good. It has been formulated in terms of a reasonable and realistic compromise. This is most forcefully argued from the local viewpoint, since the ones who will suffer the consequences seem somehow far away and do not quite belong to the local moral community: distant businessmen affected by unfair competition; workers prevented from entering the labor market because of these practices; overburdened taxpayers or contributors to social security. This moral reasoning seems flexible enough to further accommodate itself to the fact that earnings in the underground economy may be simultaneously supplemented by unemployment benefits.

But state public policy provides us with another piece of evidence as to how moral political arguments are combined with systematic cheating under the law. In towns with a large rural proletariat, it is possible for anyone who can document working on a farm for sixty days to get community employment benefits for the whole year. Official certification is easy to come by if the local officials decide not to look too carefully into the facts. This seems to have been the practice in large parts of southern Spain. While this has helped a very vulnerable sector of the population to get through hard times, it has also had critical social and political consequences, since it has provided a massive following for the socialists throughout Andalusia and Extremadura, with a well-established clientelistic network, and has thus strengthened the hand of the southerners within the Socialist party.[25] Of course, the extension of benefits is expected to be reciprocated by a deferential vote.[26] Let us merely observe that the proliferation of this kind of clientelistic practice in the countryside cannot be explained by the characteristics of the peasantry. In Andalusia, prior to the Francoist period, there existed a powerful anarchist tradition opposed to caciquism, or clientelism, although there are also traces of an earlier socialist tradition of using the state to create a socialist network (Gillespie, 1988, p. 202). In northern Spain, at least in Castile, the general trend away from traditional forms of clientelism on the right was already visible by the 1920s (Pérez-Díaz, 1992a).

Shifting perspectives from the political parties to civil society, however, makes it clear that civil society also bears responsibility for these phenomena. The liberal democratic regime and the institutions of markets, social pluralism, and the public sphere offer a variety of opportunities for society to articulate its values and interests, thus shaping the content and the form of the public debate, as well as to resist the parties' eventual oligarchic tendencies and to check the development of a clientelistic network or system of relations between state and society, whether at the upper echelons of society, among the lower classes, or in between. To the extent that these trends and traditions have been allowed to develop, we must assume that so far both Spanish politicians and Spanish society have been reluctant to internalize some of the basic normative orientations of those "free" or "open" societies to which most liberal democracies belong. These basic normative orientations require some consideration.

PROMISES AND LIMITS

A cultural tradition includes both a culture proper (a set of beliefs, rules, and values) and an institutional setting. Culture and institutions are interlinked. Institutions are both culture carriers, or "expressive vessels," and reinforcing mechanisms of that culture by way of the distribution of rewards (or sanctions) for acceptable (or unacceptable) behavior. But institutions have to be properly designed, actually established, and then put to work over a period of time and tested against a variety of situations, wherein people have to demonstrate once and again their commitment to the basic rules of the game and their corresponding normative orientations. Thus, in the case of recent Spanish history, while it is true that Spaniards have incorporated the mainstream western cultural traditions of liberal democracy and civil society, it is also true that the record so far shows both the promise and the limits of their ability to translate these traditions into smoothly operating institutions.

We may assume that the fundamental institutions of western-style "free," "open," or "civilized" societies (Popper, 1966; Hayek, 1960) include the rule of law, open markets, social pluralism and a public sphere, a democratic polity, and a rational yet publicly accountable modern bureaucracy. But for these institutions to work properly, people within both society at large and the state must internalize a set of normative ideals and formal, universalistic rules underlying those institutions. They must acquire a sort of "tacit wisdom" (by analogy to the "tacit knowledge" to which Michael Polanyi refers; see Polanyi, 1967). And this in turn requires a period of sustained self-discipline and moral exertion during which the proper orientations and the emerging institutions may find an opportunity to reinforce one another.

Now, implicit in all those institutions are three basic sets of formal, universalistic rules whose internalization defines peoples and societies as "civilized" or "uncivilized," according to the normative standards of an open society. These rules require that work be carried out with professional honesty, eschewing fraud, sloppy standards, or cover-ups for technical incompetence; they require respect for truth, and, therefore, formal logic and rational argument in intellectual exchanges and moral debates; they require respect for the individual's dignity and free choice, as well as for the property and physical integrity of all members of the community, irrespective of their power, wealth, status, gender, religion, or ideology. These rules of work, rational knowledge, and sociability imply, therefore, respect for the individual's private space. This is the space in which we make choices for which we may then be held responsible in the areas of work, cognitive activities, and social interactions. Prominent among these choices are those concerning the groups and other individuals with whom we choose to develop a moral and affectionate commitment; in other words, these are choices relating to the moral communities to which an individual wishes to belong. These rules require people not only to be ready to submit to external sanctions if they break them but, above all, to have the inner conviction that such rules, and the corresponding inner space, are, so to speak, sacred, and that these rules, and their own attachment to them, constitute the signs of identity of their membership in civilized society. It thus follows that only if this inner conviction is sufficiently widespread can we speak of a civilized society; if this is not the case, we can only talk about a promise of civilization, still to be fulfilled.

To the extent that these formal, universalistic rules do not apply fully to the institutions of a given polity and society, we may observe that the rules of the game of democratic pluralism and the due process of law, open markets, and meritocratic competition may be systematically distorted. They are made to coexist with, and are subverted by, other, very different rules, such as those on the model of patron-client relationships. Those clientelistic arrangements insulate producers from the effects of their own poor professional performance and the deficient quality of the resulting products or services; they limit or otherwise modulate the access of members of society to the market, to the unbiased application of the law, to the bureaucracy, and to political power; and they qualify their membership in the social and political community. They favor those who belong to the clientele in question, and place in the hands of the patrons the power to shelter or to expose, to distribute such access among their clients, and to define the quality of their membership in society. Such distorted arrangements can be observed in all modern societies. But the point is whether they are contained within certain areas of life or are all-pervasive, whether such arrangements actually condition the greatest part (or a substantial part) of social life or are of only marginal importance. Within Europe it is generally admitted that such arrangements are more visible and deep-rooted in the Mediterranean countries, at least in comparison with those of central and northern Europe (Eisenstadt and Roniger, 1984).

Such arrangements have to be *disguised* in those societies which claim allegiance to the formal, universalistic rules and the institutions of free or open societies. Those disguises can take many forms, from the dogmatic assertions of political ideology, local or regional patriotism, national character, religious beliefs, or professional ethics to various kinds of ideological eclecticism and ambiguity.[27] But whatever the disguise, the crucial practical consequence of it is that individuals and organizations are thus able to shield themselves from the effects of the open competition of cultural traditions, politics, professional services, markets, products, and so on. They place themselves within networks under the protection of patrons, political leaders, bureaucrats, or influential friends, and they expect to benefit from the eventual coalition between these networks, or from the eventual outcome of their conflicts with one another.[28]

The existence of strong clientelistic arrangements has implications for the type of political discourse, the motivational orientations of individuals, and the reputational structure of society. Thus, a pattern of rhetorical ambiguity or even duplicity may develop as the least costly way to reduce the cognitive dissonance between the ideals of an open society and the realities of a clientelistic one. This ambiguity represents a middle ground where it seems possible to make emphatic and reiterated assertions of democratic principle or of attachment to the rules of open markets along with de facto toleration of, or eventual participation in, oligarchic politics (or avoidance of tax laws or of regulations concerning employment benefits, the funding of political parties, insider trading, and so on). Tolerance of this kind of ambiguity may be greater the more the public is habituated to confusing political statements, unfocused journalism, imprecision in the use of legal and administrative language, poor educational standards with regard to written and oral presentations, and other similar rhetorical traditions.

These arrangements imply the compatibility of an external respect for legal formalities, the officially declared rules of the game, with the conviction that in fact many of these formalities are impossible to implement or to comply with (for instance, those regarding the underground economy, insider trading, or the funding of political parties). This conviction would be embedded in, and reinforced by, all sorts of customs and practices, with the result that, were these circumstances to persist or to become more general, an inner respect for the law and the rules of the game would gradually wane, or disappear altogether. In this context it is to be expected that many individuals would develop a particularistic set of motivational orientations. Let us remember that individual motivational orientations are to a significant extent institutional and cultural constructs, and that institutions and moral traditions provide individuals with definitions of self-interest and social obligation which are considered acceptable or legitimate in a given community. In the absence of strong traditions of group loyalty (as in Spain), it seems likely that many individuals would use most organizations and patron-client networks in an instrumental fashion, and that they would give primacy to a narrow definition of individual (or family) self-interest. Thus, they may be led to play the game of exchange among themselves and with the public authorities, in the spirit of exacerbated hyperindividualism which characterizes those who are proud of outsmarting everybody else. And if they happen to be politicians or civil servants, they may use their specialized knowledge of the inner workings of politics and public administration for their own advancement by means of insider trading, *pantouflage,* and the like.

The resulting reputational structure may seem confusing, thus adding to the general climate of uncertainty and cloudiness of the public debate. On the one hand, it is to be expected that, under these conditions, a reputational structure may develop which would grant the greatest honor (and give social approval and a sense of achievement) to those who make it to the top, and thus acquire the power to share out their own privileges among their present or potential clients. On the other hand, remnants of various traditional moralities combined with the explicit standards of a free society would undermine this ethic of success in the pursuit of self-interest.

In sum, these more or less fragmentary clientelistic arrangements and patterns of rhetorical ambiguity point to the limits of the establishment of a liberal democracy in Spain, and possibly in other countries as well, and to some of the existing dangers for its eventual institutionalization. It is now time to return to the core of my argument, to try to locate developments in Spain in that context, and to understand these developments from the perspective of a more general historical process, one I will refer to as the return of civil society.

2

The
Return of
Civil Society

Although democratic transitions depend on prior social traditions and the emergence of a new political culture, the crucial test for the consolidation and institutionalization of democracy is how successful the new democratic state is in the task of handling the basic problems of the country. This task is a challenge for both the state and civil society, and the way it is met has important repercussions for the relations between them. This test was a particularly difficult one in Spain, for it took place at a time of profound transformation—economic, social, and cultural—within that group of western European countries Spain was so eager to be a part of.

This chapter deals with socioeconomic and political developments in western Europe, particularly in the period following the Second World War. I argue that a process of institutional experimentation took place as a response to those developments, with the result that civil society considerably extended the scope of its operations and its responsibilities. First I examine the general problem of the relations between the state and civil society in modern times, and I propose a definition of terms as well as a conceptual schema. Then, I advance some views on the general pattern of relations between the state and society and the reasons underlying the cycles of expansion and decline of state protagonism. This leads to the theme of the rise and fall of the state as the bearer of a moral project, and a brief excursus on the state-centered tradition of theories of civil society.

The second part of the chapter—the core—focuses on relations between the state and civil society in contemporary Europe. I analyze the relative stability of the 1950s and 1960s; the social and political turbulence of the late 1960s and the 1970s; the economic crisis of the mid-to-late 1970s and its consequences on economic growth, social integration, and politics; and the processes of adjustment and institutional experimentation following it, whether in a neocorporatist or in a neoliberal direction. I point out that cultural issues such as the definition of solidarities and moral communities have been central to the entire process, particularly during the period of uncertainty and experimentation.

The chapter ends with a reference to recent developments in eastern Europe, which indicate a reemergence of civil society and suggest a corroboration of some of the main points of the previous discussion.

THE CONCEPT OF CIVIL SOCIETY

Some of the problems we face in trying to apply the concept of civil society to the present situation in Spain lie in the ambiguity of that concept. This is to some extent the result of a complicated intellectual history.[1] The term *civil society* was first used in its broadest sense as a synonym for *political society.* Then its meaning shifted to being the opposite of the concept of the state. This is how the term tends to be used today. I will refer to some aspects of this history later. For now I want to start by making a clear distinction between two different meanings that may be attached to the term, and by applying other terms to each of these two meanings: civil society *sensu lato* (or "civil society one") and civil society in a more restricted sense ("civil society two").

Civil society *sensu lato,* or the first meaning of civil society, denotes a set of sociopolitical institutions including a limited government or state operating under the rule of law; a set of social institutions such as markets (or spontaneous extended orders)[2] and associations based on voluntary agreements among autonomous agents; and a public sphere in which these agents debate among themselves and with the state about matters of public interest and engage in public activities. This is the kind of civil society to which the Scottish philosophers of the eighteenth century such as Adam Ferguson referred (see Ferguson, 1980). This concept corresponds to the actual sociopolitical systems or historical configurations of Great Britain and the United States through most of the nineteenth century as well as, for some authors, the essentials of the blend of liberal democracy and market economy typical of contemporary western societies (Okun, 1979). The idea of civil society as a set of sociopolitical institutions has proved compatible from the very beginning with a range of intellectual traditions, including those loosely labeled "classical" and "modern" liberalism, "civic" or "republican" traditions, and so on.[3]

This construct of civil society *sensu lato* has an internal consistency. It is "civil" inasmuch as its autonomous agents are "citizens" (as opposed to mere subjects of a despotic ruler or of a ruling caste) and therefore members of a "civilized" society (as opposed to a barbaric or backward one). But the point is that they may be citizens *only* because they are autonomous agents, and they may be autonomous vis-à-vis the state *only* because the state has a limited power to enter these agents' reserved domain.

It also follows that there is an important dividing line within civil society *sensu lato* between the state and the citizenry. This division provides us with a starting point for the development of the second concept of civil society, or civil society in a more restricted sense, which refers to social institutions such as markets and associations and the public sphere, and excludes state institutions proper. The former are areas of social life that may generally be considered outside the direct control of the state (Held, 1989, p. 6).

But this autonomy may exist either in a full or in a more mitigated way. It exists in full only when the state is part of a civil society in the first sense, that is, when it is a limited state operating under the rule of law. Otherwise, the institutions of civil society in the second sense (markets, associations, and a sphere of public debate) would exist in a more mitigated and less developed way within the framework of other historical configurations, such as those presided over by authoritarian and totalitarian regimes (for instance, Franco's Spain and the eastern European socialist societies).

Thus it may be argued that the development or emergence of civil society in the second sense within an authoritarian or a totalitarian regime prepares the way for its transition to a liberal democracy and a full-fledged market economy, and thereby to the full establishment of civil society in the first sense. (This is a point I made with regard to Spain in Chapter 1.) In turn, it may also be argued that, once the first form of civil society is established, it reinforces the institutions of the second form and makes possible further developments of markets, voluntary associations, and the public sphere. The connection between the two concepts is a close one, but it is not one of mutually necessary implication. Civil society in the first sense cannot exist without civil society in the second sense as a part of it, but the reverse does not hold true: the latter may exist within or without the former.

For the sake of clarity, throughout the remainder of the book, I will use the expression *civil society* to mean the second form: social institutions such as markets and voluntary associations and a public sphere which are outside the direct control, in a full or in a mitigated sense, of the state.[4] I have decided on such a use of the term because I think that choosing one's terms is not merely a matter of stipulative definitions. At least in some cases, and unless current usage has confused the concepts beyond repair, we may be well advised to take into account the fact that words are "carriers of historical experience."[5] My understanding of the term corresponds broadly to what has become accepted usage in sociopolitical discourse today. It seems to me that, by the late 1980s, in countries as different from one another as those of southern Europe and central Europe, more and more people understand civil society as something apart from the state, and use the term in the context of arguments that focus on the problem of how to define the proper boundaries and the proper relations between them.[6] Indeed, it has been the urgent need for a better understanding of these relations that has pushed so many sociopolitical actors to reinvent or to apply anew the concept of civil society. Thus, the distinction between the state and civil society appears to be a logical, historical precondition for analyzing the relations between them, while blurring that distinction seems to lead to analytical and normative confusion.[7]

From the start, and once again for the sake of clarity, I want to differentiate my use of the term from that of others and to offer my reasons. First, I include the sphere of public debate within the area of civil society. My rationale is that I understand civil society as being composed of agents involved both in private dealings and in debating and acting out different versions of the public interest; this includes collective agents such as interest groups and social movements. I want to stress the link, and the compatibility, between these two dimensions of the agents' behavior, and I disagree with those who believe that civil society concerns itself only with private or particular interests. By contrast, other authors feel that a different term, *political society*, should be used for those societal actors engaged in public debate and public-oriented activities.[8]

Second, in my account the social institutions of civil society include both markets and voluntary associations. This explains civil society's internal complexity (Keane, 1988b, p. 64) and its peculiar blend of cooperation and competition among its constituent units. By contrast, other authors maintain that civil society is composed solely either of markets [9] or of voluntary associations (interest groups, social movements, or intermediary bodies).[10] Jürgen Habermas, for instance, considers the core of civil society to be constituted by voluntary associations which he sees as standing outside the state *and* the economy, understood as being systematically integrated actor fields having a logic of their own.[11]

Third, from my viewpoint markets and voluntary associations and the public sphere constitute a system of cooperation and competition involving a very large number of autonomous agents. This system encompasses a variety of areas of life (economic, social, political, and cultural) and exhibits a relatively high degree of self-coordination. These assumptions run counter to two basic tenets of the theories of civil society in the Marxist tradition. First, Marxists use the term to denote a particular location in society. Marx reduces civil society to the market economy,[12] Gramsci to sociocultural institutions. Second, they consider this location to have a privileged strategic importance, and they link their theory of civil society with a theory of class struggle (in Gramsci, a struggle for hegemony; see Bobbio, 1988) which furthermore points to a radical transformation, and eventually the disappearance, of civil society.

The State and Civil Society

The state and civil society face each other as two differentiated sets of actors and institutions engaged in a number of reciprocal exchanges. But in order to understand these exchanges we have to take into account the fact that the state confronts civil society in a plural capacity. First, the state has the "real" status of being both a coercive apparatus and a service provider.[13] But the state also has the "symbolic" capacity of being a prominent actor in the public sphere.

As a coercive apparatus the state claims a monopoly on the use of force as a precondition for maintaining external and internal peace, while as a provider of a variety of services it helps society attain economic prosperity, social integration, and a sense of collective identity. As a result, the state is expected to enhance the capacity of society for survival (Mann, 1986b, p. 119) in an environment of geopolitical confrontations, international economic exchanges, and cultural pluralism. In exchange, the state asks for society's consent to its rule, that is, consent to the state's claims to preside over domestic exchanges and to oversee exchanges with the rest of the world, and to maintain boundaries and gateways.

Given the fact that the state is both a coercive apparatus and a service provider, an expression such as *state rule* has a built-in ambiguity. It refers both to the state's ruling over society and to the state's contributing to the task of regulating or coordinating society. It suggests both a system of unequal exchanges, in which the state stands above society, and a system of equal exchanges, in which the state and society stand on the same footing and bargain with each other.

The long-term stability of all these exchanges may well hinge, as Max Weber suggested, on the civil society's perception of the legitimacy of state rule, since neither fear of coercion, custom, nor expediency is enough to ensure such stability (Weber, 1978, pp. 31ff.). Nonetheless, since the state is not only a coercive apparatus but also a service provider, the actors' attribution of legitimacy to state rule depends not only on the formal character of that rule but also on its content. Hence, we should distinguish between a formal and a substantive legitimacy. The social agents ascribe *formal* legitimacy to the state's orders by virtue of tradition, affective or value-rational faith, or by considering the state's positive enactments to be legal.[14] At the same time, these agents ascribe *substantive* legitimacy to the state's orders by virtue of the link they establish between these orders and the state's ability to provide for society's survival and prosperity, in other words, the state's ability to solve fundamental problems or deliver public goods such as defense against external enemies and provision of internal security, economic welfare, social integration, and collective identity.

The state—or rather the rulers who occupy state positions—tries to persuade the social agents to attribute substantive legitimacy to its orders by instrumental and by expressive means, that is, by way of effective actions and by way of symbolic performances (Pérez-

Díaz, 1992b). In other words, the state rulers may either actually solve the problems of society or express the hope that the problems will eventually be solved someday, thus persuading people to live with these problems without turning to other rulers to solve them. Given the limited ability of any rulers to solve the basic problems facing any given community for more than a brief period of time, symbolic performances play a crucial role in obtaining the society's consent.

It thus follows that, both in their actual performance of providing services and in their symbolic performance of persuasion, the state's rulers have to engage in bargains of all kinds with civil society. Therefore the rulers of liberal capitalist societies need the cooperation of socioeconomic elites such as businessmen and union leaders if they are to deliver the measure of prosperity (that is, economic growth and social integration) on which their substantive legitimacy depends; they need the cooperation of territorial elites to articulate a sense of collective identity for the entire nation; and they also need the cooperation of cultural elites to persuade people of the legitimacy, both formal and substantive, of their rule.

It is a matter of empirical inquiry to determine the form and the intensity of the mutual dependence on which political rulers and socioeconomic, territorial, and cultural elites stand with regard to one another in each particular situation. But in general, three sets of circumstances act to constitute their relationships. First, the state's rulers make up a heterogeneous body composed of several groups and organizations: government officials, legislators, judges, civil servants from different departments and agencies, and the military. They all have a vested interest in being seen from the outside as part of a unitary state, and they may sometimes work together as a unitary actor;[15] but often the state's actions are the result of bargaining process within the state between coalitions made up of different state agents (Allison, 1971).

Second, the state's rulers are only one part, even if the most important one, of a more extended and even more heterogeneous group we may call the political class, which is composed of state rulers and the party in power, but also of opposition political parties and a periphery of professionals involved in the workings of government and politics (and, more particularly, in shaping the agenda for the public debate, such as lobbyists and political journalists).

Third, the socioeconomic, territorial, and cultural elites of civil society stand at the top of organizations, social movements, interest groups, and currents of opinion over which they usually have only limited control. Thus, it cannot be taken for granted that they will deliver their constituencies' consent to whatever bargains they may strike with the state's rulers.

The result is that the relations between the state and civil society at any given moment are made up of constellations of sociopolitical coalitions constantly crossing the boundaries between them.[16] Over time these constellations achieve some limited degree of stability as the result of institutional and cultural factors so they may be understood as following one another in a sort of meaningfully patterned sequence. Before we turn to a consideration of the general outlines of that sequential pattern for western Europe in modern times, I want to make three final points.

First, there have been long historical cycles in western history marked by alternating phases of state protagonism and societal protagonism, with the state playing the more or less dominant role. This process is what I refer to when I use the metaphor of the ebb and flow of the state tide. Second, some sociopolitical coalitions push for state powers and activities to grow, and others restrain them. There are critical junctures (see Lehmbruch, 1991, pp. 131ff.) at which choices are made by these coalitions, leading either to paths of state aggrandizement or to paths of state containment. At some of these junctures opportunities are heavily stacked in favor of one path or another. Thus, wars and revolutions are usually followed by periods of state growth. By contrast, the emergence of institutions of representative government and market economies are more likely to lead to a containment of the state, although this is not necessarily so. Third, underlying those choices and the processes that proceed from them are profound cultural changes in the definition of the state's role in modern society. It is my belief that the general tendency toward state growth over the last two hundred years or so has been supported by a vision of the state as the bearer of a moral project, which has been called by different names—nationalism, modernization, and social reform, among others. Today we are witnessing a generalized crisis of such a vision (and among its corresponding institutions) in both western and eastern Europe. The theme of the return of civil society is an expression of that crisis.

The Ebb and Flow of the State Tide

Taking a long view of the relation between state and society throughout European history, we see that it has followed a pattern similar to the ebb and flow of the tides, the alternation of advances and withdrawals of land and sea. Hegel suggested that the sea is a metaphor, a symbol, for "infinity and inquietude."[17] Even when it looks calm, the sea is in a permanent state of agitation and anxiety. People who live on the coast traditionally engage in discovery and exploration and dedicate themselves to commerce and to piracy, to cultural exchanges, questioning, and experimentation. The sea is therefore a fitting symbol for a civil society fired by the interests and the passions of myriad individuals, constantly changing, bargaining among themselves, coordinating their activities through a spontaneous extended order. By contrast, the inland territories are the setting where we expect different kinds of institutions and individuals to control things—state rulers and state institutions—and we expect them to impose a different kind of order. Instead of bold ships there are imposing buildings which sit firmly on the ground. Rulers of such empires act out their dreams of order by imposing their rule over quiescent subjects, with the cooperation of armed forces and civil servants. The boundaries of the territory are clearly established and well guarded, and large monuments are constructed as a symbol of the rulers' wishes for stability and permanence.

The metaphor suggests some of the structural differences between states and civil societies, their belonging together in a common scenario, and an alternation of phases, with the implicit assumption that there will always be a "next phase" when civil society or the state will take charge. More to the point, the metaphor suggests that something is wrong with the fairly generalized assumption that the modern state is a rational development, and that it should be expected to grow in the future.[18]

Throughout western history the relative importance of the state vis-à-vis civil society has undergone enormous changes. The Greek polis blended the state and civil society to such a degree as to create the illusion of the absence of a private sphere. This, of course, applied only to the Spartan-style Greek polis, not to Athens, where, according to Pericles' funeral oration,[19] an equilibrium of sorts was achieved between the public sphere and private interests. In any case, the Greek polis, for all its considerable powers over its own society, had a very limited territorial scope. Greek cities belonged to Hellas, a system of intercity relations, itself a part of an even larger system of states. At critical moments most of Hellas would come together against a foreign invader. The effort succeeded against the Persians but failed against the Macedonians and, even more decisively, against the Romans.

The Roman republic, and the Roman Empire, saw the gradual development of a relatively strong state able to hold together an extended land mass and a coastal territory, and to defend it successfully for a considerable period of time. In the meantime, Roman law allowed for the consolidation of the basic institutions of civil society, such as private property, rules of contract, corporate entities, and so on. Eventually, however, the state proved unable to keep the society together and to defend it. It was replaced, at least in the West, by a myriad of decentralized sources of political power. After a protracted period of confusion, which lasted until the beginning of the second millennium A.D., a new sociopolitical order gradually emerged (Mann, 1986a, pp. 373–415). It was characterized by a loose fit between three sets of cultural, socioeconomic, and political networks: an extended network of church institutions, later to coexist with the universities and other learned circles; a fragmented economic space, where local agrarian systems (usually organized around cities, rural communities, and seigneurial domains) coexisted with regional markets and international commercial routes; and a multipolar political order within which kings, the feudal nobility, the cities, and the church battled for preeminence.

Still, it took another five or six hundred years to build the modern European states, those of the sixteenth and seventeenth centuries, which were organized around the political supremacy, if not the full-fledged sovereignty, of kings. Now, if we understand the situation as one of a "market" of political institutions, the development of the institutions of the European states was the result of a combination of factors, some belonging to the supply side and others to the demand side of that market. On the supply side, it was obvious that kings, and their own patrimonial functionaries, were willing to increase their coercive and administrative powers. But their drive was successful only because it proved to be consistent with two developments on the demand side of the equation.

First, domestic demands within society encouraged state growth.

The church, the peasants, the urban nobility, the emerging bourgeoisie, and the rural nobility became supportive of the king's claims at various critical points in the process because they perceived the king as willing and able to guarantee a solution for their own problems, either by upholding customary rights, by enacting new privileges, by guaranteeing the application of the common law, or through extraordinary provisions. Second, systemic pressures pushing in the same direction resulted from the fact that each state was enmeshed in a network of states and entangled in a competition for wealth (land, population, markets) as well as prestige and political influence. This led them to emulate one another and engage in war. This in turn generated domestic demands within society for state protection against foreign attack. Thus, the states were able to initiate and profit from the vicious cycle[20] of establishing new taxes for the purpose of building up standing armies, and building up standing armies for the purpose of extracting more taxes. In this way, the military-taxation machines of the absolute monarchies of the ancien régime were created (Tilly, 1975, p. 23).

Then, as a Januslike institution[21] placed between a set of domestic agents and a set of foreign states, the state tried to take advantage of any favorable combination of domestic and international pressures to increase its economic and demographic base and the loyalty of its population, since both were needed for enlarging its tax base as well as its army. Hence the state's need to pay increasing attention to its role as a service provider, and to the cultural and symbolic aspects of its rule.

At the same time, the (relatively) strong European states of the ancien régime witnessed a parallel development on the part of their civil societies. The states tried to coordinate this development and use it for their own purposes, with mixed results. In the long run some civil societies outgrew the control capacities of the states, and this opened the way for states of a different kind. In cases where this did not occur, civil societies remained underdeveloped, but in the long run the states declined.

Thus, socioeconomic and cultural transformations prepared the way for a situation in Great Britain between 1640 and 1690[22] when critical choices were made that checked the development of an absolute monarchy. As a result, an early combination of a representative government and a market economy was tried out. This institutional experiment presided over a spectacular development of civil society. This, in turn, helped stimulate new experiments in North America and France in the late eighteenth century. By contrast, when states succeeded in keeping their civil societies under strict control, these societies remained underdeveloped, and those states declined. The Spanish state built up a relatively efficient military-taxation-administrative machine and obtained some impressive results with it in the sixteenth and seventeenth centuries. But it did so at the cost of impeding the development of rural and industrial Castile (Pérez-Díaz, 1992a) and neglecting that of the rest of Spain. For this it had to pay the price of prolonged decline, with a slow recovery late in the eighteenth century, which provided a limited basis for the institutional transformations of the nineteenth century. Prussia did something roughly equivalent, but on a smaller scale and in a more systematic manner; and the price it paid was to become a bellicose but backward country with a hypertrophied military-taxation machine, a garrison state with a dwarfed civil society (Carsten, 1954), which was thoroughly defeated by Napoleon. This led, in turn, to the reforms that opened the way for a different equilibrium between state and society in the nineteenth century.

During the nineteenth and twentieth centuries western countries experimented with different varieties of liberal states, authoritarian regimes, and totalitarian systems. These different political regimes provided different institutional frameworks for the continuous negotiations between states and civil societies regarding the boundaries between them, as well as the distribution of resources and the rules of the game. And the game was a very complex one, with alternating phases of state and societal protagonism. In a sense it was not a zero-sum game, since both states and societies increased the range and the volume of their activities: the states expanded their coercive apparatus, budget, administrative structure, intellectual resources, and personnel; and civil societies increased in all their dimensions—economic, social, political, and cultural—as seen in the development of organizations of all kinds (firms, unions, churches, media, universities, sports associations, and so on). But with regard to the *relative* importance of the state and civil society, we may observe three different phases: first, a liberal phase; next, a state-centered one; and finally, our present phase of uncertainty and search for a new equilibrium.

We may broadly consider the nineteenth century to be a "liberal century," at least with regard to most of western Europe (and the

United States), with civil society playing the protagonist and the state playing an important but limited role in social, economic, and cultural matters. By midcentury, however, this state of affairs was under attack by Catholics and conservatives on one side and socialists on the other, and by the intensification of nationalistic sentiments. By the time of the outbreak of the First World War, it was under very severe strain (Dangerfield, 1961).

The war had dramatic consequences for the way politics would be conducted throughout the rest of the century, for the states' capacities and willingness to intervene, and for the expectations people developed about the proper role of the state. After the war, the liberal tradition seemed increasingly out of place.

The very experience of total war in 1914–1918, the socioeconomic and cultural uncertainties of the succeeding decade and a half, and the emergence of two totalitarian systems and other authoritarian regimes that spread all over continental Europe, as well as, once again, the experience of a second total war in 1939–1945, combined to produce three trends: politics was understood by many as "absolute politics," setting the ultimate goals of entire societies;[23] the states' capacities and will to intervene grew; and people became used to that trend and took for granted that it would continue in the future. As I will discuss later in this chapter, the postwar period did not radically alter the course of these historical trends, and so the general belief in the state as the key institution of the social order has been part of the zeitgeist for most of the twentieth century. It is only since the early 1980s that a new change of phase has been initiated which implies a critical reassessment of the state's role.

The Rise and Fall of the State as Bearer of a Moral Project

Underlying the process of formation of the national states in western countries and the different phases of state and societal protagonism over the last two centuries,[24] there was a cultural process at work. States appeared and then grew, and not merely because those institutions filled an empty space between an international order and a domestic arena, or because a series of fortunate, daring, and ruthless rulers were able to take advantage of the competition between states to play off against one another the demands of different groups within their own population. They appeared and grew also because (and to the extent that) all the institutional inertia and group strategies were embedded in a political culture, at the heart of which we find an argument that portrayed the state as the bearer of an extraordinary moral project. By contrast, the gradual loss of plausibility of this argument lies at the heart of the present-day change of phase in the relative prominence of state and society, and at the heart of society's increasing resistance to further state growth.

The rise of this notion of a moral project required the cooperation of political elites and cultural elites. While the monarchs and their allies did the actual work of defeating rival contenders, rounding up territories, and developing armies and tax-levying systems and other institutions, an intellectual tradition developed which took a relatively consistent view of the modern state and instilled meaning and moral justification in those practical endeavors. In order to do that, these state intellectuals had to construct a metaphysical fiction, a theory of state sovereignty, and a moral argument.

As a result of the metaphysical fiction, the state acquired an autonomous existence. Although the term *state* was first used with a denotation close to the modern one in the sixteenth century, not until the eighteenth century did it come to refer to a corporate actor, transcending the human beings of which it was composed, including the state's rulers (who began to identify themselves as "the first servants of the state") and their families or dynasties (Skinner, 1978, pp. 349–358). This corporate actor was said to have a will, a vision, and a capacity to act on its own.

At the same time, the term took on a sort of aura, inspiring awe and respect. After much indoctrination by secular and religious elites, this aura was gradually accepted, and finally taken for granted, by the population. The invention of the concept of sovereignty played a crucial role in this process, for it allowed the ruler to be more than a suzerain, or bearer of supreme power, in which case he would still have to reckon with others who had an autonomous power source of their own, either a religious or a secular one. Now, by being the bearer of sovereign power, the state could pretend to be the source of all the other powers. Thus, the state would permit these other powers to exist, but only as subordinate to state power and contingent on state recognition, since, at least on principle, the state's powers could not be limited or checked by any other institution.

But since these were extraordinary claims—indeed, they ran against the institutional complexity and political fragmentation of much of the European experience—they had to be grounded in an elaborate moral argument, which was driven home through a prolonged period of indoctrination, institutional work, and the "shock therapy" of catastrophic wars.

The dramatic religious wars of the sixteenth and seventeenth centuries provided the decisive stimulus, and the initial structure of plausibility, for that moral argument to take hold (Berger, 1971). Kings grounded their claims to absolute or sovereign power on the need to guarantee domestic peace and to avert civil wars, which they did either by insisting on the religious conformity of their subjects or by allowing only a limited degree of religious toleration. Thinkers of different persuasions, such as Pascal and Hobbes, agreed that civil war, whether because of religious or constitutional considerations, should be considered the worst of all possible evils; that justice or the public good should be defined first and foremost as the kind of social order that would make civil war impossible; and that the public authority should uphold that order, and should count on their subjects' submission to it.

Successive generations of intellectuals expanded this moral argument in different directions. They ended up with three theories which fleshed out the moral tasks of the modern state: those of nationalism, citizenship, and modernization. First, they made the state responsible for the defense of a new principle of collective identity in a world of competing nation-states. Second, they made the state responsible for the creation of a community of citizens and of a public sphere where these citizens would meet their rulers on a nearly equal footing. Third, they made the state responsible for the economic prosperity and the social integration of society—or, to use a term which would come into play in the twentieth century, they made the state responsible for modernizing the country.

Once this work was done, the next step was to convince people not only that the world should be understood as divided into a number of such sovereign states, each one, on principle, second to none, but also that all of world history should be read as a sort of epic drama portraying the process of formation of those states and the challenges by which they test their sovereign claims against one another. An additional dramatic effect was obtained by pointing at the different historical configurations (or combinations of types of economic growth, social integration, and political regimes) of the various nation-states;

by asserting that a higher morality was embedded in one configuration as against another; and finally by persuading people of the absolute value they should grant these assertions so as to be ready to fight and die for national interests and national values.

Thus, an all-encompassing "master fiction" (Geertz, 1983) developed, combining a cognitive map (which appealed to the need people had for orienting themselves in a perplexing world) and a dramatic script[25] (which appealed to the people's emotional needs for expressing their altruistic, aggressive, and self-destructive drives).[26] This master fiction became persuasive enough to be taken for granted by several generations of Europeans in the course of the nineteenth and twentieth centuries. As a result of it, people developed feelings of moral obligation, and even of a sacred duty, vis-à-vis the state, and went as far as to justify the sacrifice of their property, their liberty, and their lives for their country. This moral disposition was put to a bitter test in a succession of wars.

Now, in stating that today we are witnessing the decline of the state as the bearer of a moral project, I mean that this master fiction has lost its plausibility. It has become increasingly doubtful that in today's world the state is or should be the bearer of a national identity, the state is or should be the focus of public life, the state is or should be the main actor in a process of modernization and therefore the key to economic growth and social integration. This argument underlies my discussion later in this chapter of the western European scenario during the post–Second World War period.

Intellectual Traditions of Civil Society

For a long time civitas and polis, civil society and political society, were used as interchangeable terms; in this sense we may say that civil society was coterminous with the state (Keane, 1988b, pp. 35ff.). But by the seventeenth and eighteenth centuries the term *civil society* was being used in the context of a particular intellectual and historical debate which lay at a crossroads in the history of western society, one path leading to the consolidation of constitutional governments and the other to the consolidation of absolute monarchies.[27]

And so by this time civil society was coterminous not with the state as such but rather with a specific type of state or political association characterized by the rule of law, limited government, and an active citizenry. This was the kind of state being built in England throughout the eighteenth century, in contrast to the kind of state that prevailed over most of continental Europe. Thus, at the heart of the theories of civil society stretching from John Locke (Locke, 1970, pp. 154ff.) to Adam Ferguson, we find a combination of ideas, institutions, and social groupings that support one another: those of limited government, a tradition of containment of the king's powers, and a core of citizens able to combine their involvement in the market with their involvement in the public sphere. Adam Smith, Edward Gibson, David Hume, and Adam Ferguson were aware of the need to put together all these elements if civil society (in our first sense) were to emerge and to persist—and to avoid corruption and decline. This was a society-centered tradition insofar as the emphasis was on the limits of the state and the potential of society to govern itself. During the nineteenth century, Tom Paine, Benjamin Constant, and Alexis de Tocqueville developed this tradition, made a sharp and fast distinction between the state and society (civil society in our second sense), and looked for ways to confront the new forms of state despotism of the nineteenth century, including the despotism of a democratic state (Keane, 1988b, pp. 39ff., 55ff.).

The state-centered intellectual tradition of civil society was based in very different analytical and normative assumptions, with the result that mixing the two traditions has created considerable confusion. Hegel is at the heart of this confusion because of the ambiguity of his thinking, but ultimately he belongs to the state-centered tradition. A similar ambiguity underlies Marx's thinking, but he too belongs to that tradition. According to them, civil society (in our second sense) lacks the ability to organize itself and to grow. Hence, it must be shaped by conscious, deliberate design, the main designer being the state (for Hegel), or a revolutionary group in control of the state (for Marx). Despite obvious differences between the two, both theorists shared a deep distrust of civil society, and they argued for the primacy of a strong state, albeit different versions, which was to be the bearer of an exalted moral project.

Hegel's thinking on civil society was ambiguous, first, because of a terminological ambiguity, and second, because of his ambivalence regarding civil society. To begin with, Hegel used the same term with two meanings. In the first instance he referred to a stage in a succession of ethical communities, from the family to the state (that is, civil society in our first sense), including the administration of justice by means of a system of laws, courts of justice, and public authority, as well as society proper, all roughly corresponding to the sociopolitical configuration of England by the early nineteenth century. In the second he referred to an element within the most modern of those ethical communities (that is, to civil society in our second sense). This civil society in a more restricted sense would be a part of the "modern state," corresponding roughly to the sociopolitical configuration of Prussia in Hegel's time.[28]

But even within the limits of this latter, more restricted sense of the term, Hegel's understanding of civil society was unclear. Apparently the term would refer to markets (or "systems of needs") and corporations or professional associations. But since corporations in Hegel's system were strongly dependent on public authorities, there was a tendency in Hegel, and even more in his interpreters, to locate corporations in between civil society and the state, and to reduce civil society to the market.[29]

But then, even Hegel's view of civil society qua market was an ambivalent one. On the one hand, he had a very critical view of civil society and a very benign view of the state. Hegel thought civil society was unable to guarantee sustained economic growth and social integration. It was prone to economic crisis, generated extreme inequalities and extreme poverty, with the result of producing a class of have-nots who were left out of the system of property, and therefore had become the battlefield for a war of all against all.[30] Hence, the need for the state's corrective action, which would compensate for the failures of the market and would produce social integration.

Furthermore, civil society could not create a sense of collective identity; only the state could do this, by reconciling a variety of particular interests through a public or common interest. And it was finally up to the state to educate people in the moral sentiments, or ethos, of patriotism and civic virtue. Therefore, Hegel had a very positive understanding of the state, and more particularly of state officials. He entrusted them with the main responsibility for accomplishing all the state's tasks, and therefore for providing economic prosperity, social integration, a sense of community, and a moral education—not to mention the assertion of the nation's interests and values in the world arena. He believed that state officials had the correct views and understanding of the public interest, and also the moral commitment to (or the ethical will of) the collective good as well as the capacity to implement this commitment. This is the reason why Hegel referred to them as a universal class.

Yet Hegel was fascinated by Adam Smith's understanding of the market as a self-coordinated system, and by Smith's metaphor of the invisible hand. He translated this metaphor in his own terms as "the cunning of reason," as the implicit universality of particular interests, in other words, as the unintended result of a collective good being produced by people whose only (or main) concern was the pursuit of their particular goals as they coordinated their activities through the market.[31] But a translation and a change of label did not make for a better understanding of the market. The fact is that Hegel's argument about the market (or the system of needs) as a system of implicit universality was an inconsistent one. It was in the logic of Hegel's argument that what is implicit would eventually become explicit or "self-conscious."[32] Time and learning from actual experience should make this possible. Therefore, people should be expected to increase their awareness of the universality of the system of needs. They should be expected to learn that the market system as such was a collective good which should be protected, and should be made to work properly, for the sake of the general interest. But if this were the case, then the educational role of state officials should be expected to be greatly reduced, or even to disappear in the long run. People would learn, and as they learned, their teachers' roles would fade away.

Still, these bureaucrats would have a transitional, if crucial, educational role to play for a period of time. The trouble was that even the attribution of this transitional role to the bureaucrats was inconsistent with Hegel's own reasoning. That is, if the market was a collective good, and the bureaucrats' raison d'être lay in their superior awareness of the collective good, it follows that one of the most important educational tasks of the bureaucrats would be to educate the public in the virtues of the market. But here a difficulty arose, for there was nothing in the day-to-day experience of bureaucrats that would enable them to do this job.

Let us not forget that it was also in the logic of Hegel's arguments that ideas and institutions go together. According to Hegel, ethics were a matter not of good intentions and isolated decisions but of the individual's actual sustained course of behavior in the framework of a body of social mores (Hegel, 1967 paras. 141–152). And if Hegel thought so highly of the bureaucrats, it was because the bureaucratic institutions shaped a bureaucratic ethos that predisposed these individuals to behave properly in the pursuit of the public interest.[33]

But the point is that precisely because they were embedded in those institutions and shared in that ethos the bureaucrats were not in a position that fostered an understanding of and concern for the proper functioning of the market. In other words, given their actual experience, it would be unrealistic, and therefore irrational, to expect them to have the vision, the will, and the capacity to implement the kind of collective good that was the market system. Whatever experience the bureaucrats might have of the markets, it was alien, or at best marginal, to their everyday experience. The ordinary fulfillment of their duties did not predispose them to understand the market. The type of order created by the market was the opposite of the hierarchical organizations to which they belonged. Their training made it hard for them not to try to interfere with the markets wherever they found them. That training led them to be suspicious of whatever they did not control, and by definition markets tended to escape their control.

In conclusion, far from making a substantial contribution to the theory of civil society, Hegel made a doubtful and inconsistent contribution to it.[34] He fueled a terminological and conceptual confusion and pushed forward a state-centered view of civil society, with the implication of a fundamentally overcritical view of modern society and an extravagantly benign view of the modern state. Still, he maintained a modicum of appreciation for the self-regulatory mechanisms of society, such as markets and—to a very limited extent, and always under the vigilant eye of the public authorities—corporations, just enough to lend some plausibility to a tradition of liberal interpretation of Hegel's political philosophy.[35]

Marx pushed Hegel's ambivalence toward civil society even further, and ended up by taking an even more negative view of it. To begin with, Marx all but ignored civil society in our first sense and focused his attention almost entirely on the second.[36] He then proceeded to reduce civil society to the market and to a battlefield for class struggle. Marx rejected any claim of implicit universality for the market system, which he characterized as torn apart by its internal contradictions, unable to provide for self-sustaining economic growth, and on the way to a (presumably imminent) terminal crisis. Moreover, the market was unable to generate social integration and to provide the basis for any kind of moral community. On the contrary, the capitalist firms as the basic productive units of the market, and the market itself as the anatomy of civil society, were institutions inimical to any sort of moral community. The social classes were aggregations of individuals playing different roles in the firms and in the market, and these classes were engaged in a struggle to the death against one another.

Thus, once again civil society seemed unable to provide for economic growth, social integration, and a sense of community. This time neither the Hegelian state, with officials as its protagonists, nor any kind of bourgeois state could make up for these deficiencies. But even though Marx rejected Hegel's plea in favor of the bureaucracy, he did not reject Hegel's assumption that there should be a universal class; and he continued to search for it. The assumption was rooted in the misunderstanding, which Marx shared with Hegel, that the stability of the social order was impossible without a collective agent, or subject, in a position to gather all the relevant information, design that order, and maintain it in a deliberate way. The universal class was supposed to be that kind of agent. But then, Marx believed he had discovered within civil society a particular social class potentially endowed with the attributes of a universal class—with the vision, the will, and the capacity to implement the collective goods of economic growth, social integration, a collective identity, and membership in a community. All this would be attained by means of a class struggle, a social revolution, and a thorough transformation of the social, political, and economic system. That universal class was the industrial working class.[37]

The problem, however, was that Marx's hostility toward civil society as a whole translated itself into a deep ambivalence even toward that part of civil society for which he had such great expectations. (Pérez-Díaz, 1984). In the final analysis, neither Marx nor most thinkers in the Marxist tradition could find arguments and empirical evidence persuasive enough to justify his portrait of the working class as universal. The actual working class appeared to be a frail foundation for the new order. It looked as if this working class alone could not be entrusted with full responsibility for the task. The job that had to be done could be done by that class only within the framework of organizations whose leadership and cadres might or might not belong to the working class themselves—first the revolutionary party, then the socialist state—and it could be done only in combination with other classes, while the responsibility for deciding on and handling these interclass coalitions would lie with the party and the state. Moreover, since the tasks of class struggle, social revolution, and the construction of socialism were to be conducted despite the opposition of powerful enemies, the revolutionary party and the socialist state were to be seen as armies fighting a war. Therefore, the authority of their leaders had to be strengthened. Hence, the subordinate position of the working class would be reinforced de facto; at the same time, in compensation, rhetorical praise for the symbolic value of the working class would be pushed beyond all limits.

EUROPE AFTER THE SECOND WORLD WAR

In the decades following the Second World War, the role of the state as a service provider grew considerably, encompassing more and more services and occupying an ever more prominent position in the economic and social life of most western countries. This was so in Europe more than in the United States, despite the fact that social security and family subsidies had increased spectacularly in the United States since the 1930s (Feldstein, 1985; Skocpol, 1985b), together with the development of public utilities and regulatory agencies. In Europe, northern and central states tended to grow more than the southern ones (OECD, 1981; Flora and Heidenheimer, 1981).

The state facing increased socioeconomic responsibilities demanded a new name: the "interventionist" (or "developmental," or "Keynesian") state, on account of the high level of active government intervention in the economy (fixing aggregate demand, regulating economic activities, redistributing income, assigning resources to production, and so on). But the name did not do justice to the institutional complexity. The state was also called a social democratic state, or at least a state based on a social democratic compromise, because of the combination of a mixed economy (with markets and state intervention), massive social transfers, and the unions' strong role, in the framework of liberal democratic political institutions. But the label did not quite fit the fact that the state was designed and managed by conservatives, Christian-democrats, and liberals, as well as by social democratic parties. Finally, it was called a welfare state because it seemed that, by engaging in all these activities, the liberal democratic state was widely increasing the scope of its service operations and accepting primary responsibility for the welfare of the country, including full responsibility for self-sustained economic growth and social integration.

The construct of the welfare state had historical and ideological roots in the state traditions of the old regime. During the nineteenth century many liberal as well as conservative politicians believed that the state had a mission to keep the country together and integrate the lower classes within the social fabric and a moral obligation to maintain the welfare of these classes. In England the Tories reacted against the danger of a country divided into two nations as a consequence of the industrial revolution, commercial spirit, and mechanization (Smith, 1967). In Germany liberal nationalists such as Friedrich Neumann (Mommsen, 1981), social democrats such as Ferdinand Lasalle, and conservatives such as Bismarck (Taylor, 1955) believed in the possibility of reaching an understanding with the working classes on the principles of nationalism and state responsibility for social welfare. These considerations were reinforced by Christian traditions as different as Wesleyan Methodism and corporate Catholicism, and influenced by electoral politics. Conservative politicians often took the lead: it was a conservative, Bismarck, who first established the basic institutions of the European welfare state, just as it was another conservative, Disraeli, who first extended electoral rights to a sizable sector of the European working class.

But to this initial spur must be added other causes: social demands and pressures coming from within the state apparatus and the political class. The social demands for state intervention came from diverse quarters: from the socialist branch of organized labor (both socialist parties and socialist unions), though not so much from the anarcho-syndicalist unions; from the entrepreneurial class hoping for state contracts and state protection against foreign competition; from the professional sectors of the middle classes interested in state-guaranteed employment in social services such as schools and hospitals; and from the peasants eager for state subsidies and protectionist tariffs. We must also take into account the pressures from within the state and the political class: from party politicians, army officers, and civil servants wishing to expand their area of influence and patronage and to justify their roles by adding new tasks requiring more resources and more personnel. Thus, sociopolitical public spending and regulatory coalitions developed, the work of which was in turn greatly facilitated by an array of cultural factors, constitutional mechanisms, and systemic pressures.

Within the liberal tradition a normative consensus grew up around the idea that all modern governments should make provision for the indigent and disabled and should concern themselves with issues of health and the dissemination of information, and that there was no reason why the bulk of these service activities should not increase with the general growth of wealth. Meanwhile, within the socialist and social conservative traditions there developed the normative consideration that the state should intervene in the economy to make the distribution of income conform to a given conception of social justice (Hayek, 1978, pp. 256–257). In turn, nationalism, which had fully developed during the nineteenth century, provided a basic ideological structure for articulating the pressures of these coalitions and to some extent, with the help of Keynesianism, for mixing up these traditions (Hall, 1989). At the same time, a variety of institutional mechanisms (budget regulations, parliamentary proceedings, networks of intermediation, and others) fleshed out those beliefs and normative considerations, and favored the success of public spending coalitions.[38] Finally, since nation-states could exist only in an environment of competition with other nation-states, systemic pressures forced the states to increase their warfare capabilities and, as a complement and a counterpoint, their welfare capabilities as well.

All these conditions were in place by the beginning of the twentieth century. Then, between 1914 and 1945 Europe underwent a series of dramatic and demoralizing experiences. Two wars of total destruction decimated the population, and totalitarian politics and authoritarian regimes spread over continental Europe. These crises deepened people's dependence on the state, reinforced their acquiescence to drastic increases in state power, and shaped their expectations that such a level of state power was permanent and could only increase.[39]

In the western societies, where liberal democratic institutions were restored, the effects of these expectations, of the memories of solidarity against a foreign invader, and of the need for reconstructing the economy all combined to reinforce acceptance of a level of state power and intervention that was much higher than what had existed prior to 1914, though of course much lower than in the defeated Nazi and fascist states.

Nevertheless, whatever the causes (that is, the sociopolitical coalitions as well as cultural and institutional factors) for the emergence of the European welfare states, the main reason for their survival in the decades following the Second World War lay in the apparent success of the experiment. People became convinced that the expansion of the state's activities was helping to resolve the problems of economic growth, and in fact during the 1950s and 1960s the economies of OECD (Organization for Economic Cooperation and Development) countries grew steadily. At the same time, social conflicts seemed increasingly manageable.

The higher degree of social integration in all these countries was the result of four sets of combined factors. First, economic growth combined with a deliberate social policy to ameliorate the material well-being and life opportunities of the working population. Growth allowed for substantial increases in real wages and nearly full employment; at the same time, rates of occupational activity rose, with increasing numbers of women, peasants, and immigrants joining the ranks of the urban working population. Economic prosperity meant higher and, above all, more stable incomes for workers, thus smoothing out conflicts of interest with the managerial class. These workers had an opportunity to buy houses, durable consumer goods such as cars and appliances, and insurance policies. But in addition, social policies were implemented so that the workers received state protection in two key areas: social transfers (such as unemployment subsidies, public schooling, health insurance, social security, and housing subsidies) and state regulation of the labor market (intended to protect job stability).

Second, socioeconomic and demographic factors combined with cultural ones to reduce the cultural division between the working population and the middle classes. Geographic mobility and occupational changes accompanying the development of a service economy lessened status differences between social classes (Goldthorpe, 1978) and eroded the closely knit working-class communities where a culture of class struggle had earlier taken root, but which now became increasingly marginal. At the same time, the development of public education and the diffusion of a culture of mass consumption homogenized the speech and the life-styles of workers and the middle class. Although this did not wipe out class differences entirely in the short run, it took a significant amount of heat out of the remaining conflicts of interests and led to a gradual weakening of the plausibility of radical politics.

Third, a set of cultural dispositions and institutions developed, which in turn facilitated class compromise. A democratic culture and democratic institutions in the political field contributed to the general understanding that, whatever the nature and intensity of social conflicts, the subordinated classes should have ways to make their voices heard and to defend their interests. The welfare state should protect the individual's freedom to join a union, and should allow for workers' representation within firms. Two kinds of bargaining mechanisms were institutionalised at a macro level in the postwar period which helped to create a climate of social and political compromise and which reinforced a consensus on some key socioeconomic policies: consociational interclass agreements between populations defined along ideological-religious, linguistic, or ethnic lines in some countries, such as the Netherlands, Belgium, and Switzerland (Lijphart, 1975, 1977); and neocorporatist agreements between business and organized labor, with the government often joining in (Schmitter and Lehmbruch, 1979).

In turn, these neocorporatist agreements were helped by three sets of cultural and institutional conditions regarding the unions' behavior: first, the unions became more and more sensitive to the benefits of a market economy, and more willing to defend the relative position of the nation's economy in the world market, as in the case of Sweden, or willing to accept most of the consequences of anti-inflationary policies, as in the case of Germany; second, the unions developed an understanding of the long-term effects of their own behavior on the economy (possibly the system of centralized collective bargaining was an incentive for the unions to develop this understanding); and third, the unions were strong enough to force their rank-and-file members to comply with their directives. Wherever these three conditions applied, and the unions were strategically moderate and organizationally strong, neocorporatist agreements followed, as was the case in several northern and central European countries. Wherever the unions were radical—that is, uninterested in the long-term consequences of their actions on the market economy, or hostile to it—and weak, no similar agreements could be put in place, as was the case in southern Europe.

But even in countries where a significant segment of organized labor adopted a radical, transformative view of politics and the economy, the rank and file did not follow suit. Thus, a functional equivalent to neocorporatist institutions was the implicit social pact established between rank-and-file workers and the sociopolitical and economic elites who were the main engineers of the welfare state. As a result of this pact, the workers expected economic growth, social services, and political freedoms, and in exchange they acquiesced in, and even supported, the existing political and economic institutions. This implicit social contract underlay the compromises that labor organizations made (what we may call the social democratic compromise with capitalism), and limited the margin for effective dissent.

Finally, the alternation of right and left in governing these countries, both sides committed to the basic tenets of the welfare state, blurred even further the traditional ideological division within European politics and reduced the likelihood that social, political, and ideological conflicts would coalesce, whereas, by contrast, just such a combination of conflicts set the stage for the high drama of the 1930s. Short of being used as symbolic vessels for highly charged political emotions, "left" and "right" lost most of the aura and the appeal they had had in the past. Although the labels still maintained some remnants of their old meaning, particularly for the militants of the political parties, they gradually became used as shorthand images and heuristic devices that simplified complexity and sometimes facilitated electoral choices by cutting through the vagueness of half-understood issues and evasive political leaders.

Turbulence in the Late 1960s and the 1970s

The relative equilibrium of the 1950s and 1960s was followed by an unsettled period characterized by intense industrial conflicts, the emergence of new social movements, a severe economic crisis, and policy uncertainties. At the time some radical critics of the social democratic compromise argued that this turbulence made for a fundamental crisis within the existing political and economic system. According to them, capitalism was suffering a crisis of legitimacy in the late 1960s and early 1970s, later compounded by a crisis of accumulation throughout the 1970s.[40]

The fact is, however, that in the end the turbulence of these decades left the fundamentals of western societies still standing. There was no radical crisis of the liberal democratic state either in the United States or in western Europe, where Italy's "difficult democracy" remained difficult but resilient (La Palombara, 1987; Spotts and Wieser, 1986), while Spain, Portugal, and Greece joined the ranks of the democracies, and other countries followed suit in South America, Southeast

Asia, and central and eastern Europe. Nor was there a radical crisis of the typically western blend of welfare state and market economy. The welfare state survived and even prospered during the seventies, as shown by the steady increase of state expenditures in many countries despite some partisan rhetoric about dismantling the welfare system (Wilensky, 1981). It was only later, in the 1980s, that a process of experimentation took place which included a cultural change in the way the role of the welfare state was perceived and a half-sustained effort at containing its growth.

As a matter of fact, a real radical crisis did take place later, in the second half of the 1980s, not in the liberal societies but in the socialist ones. This was a combination of a crisis of legitimacy and a crisis of accumulation; and it was a terminal one, which destroyed the socialist order, much to the embarrassment of the western critical intelligentsia and most western academics, who had been unable to foresee it. All things considered, the turbulence of the time had a dramatic flair that captured people's imagination in the west and produced lasting cultural effects.

Let us start by considering the socioeconomic conflicts of the late sixties and early seventies. These conflicts increased as the result of a contracting labor market and an expansionary economy, coming after a period when increases in real wages lagged behind gains in productivity (Adam and Reynaud, 1978). They acquired greater virulence in countries where collective bargaining was decentralized and poorly institutionalized, and unions were either relatively weak and radical because of their links with strong communist parties, as in Italy and France, or so focused on distributional policies that they were indifferent to the long-term consequences of their behavior on the economic performance of their country, as in the United Kingdom.

Although the workers' core demands were semitraditional in character (pay raises and reduction of wage differentials in favor of semiskilled labor), qualitative demands were also made regarding working conditions, worker representation on the shop floor, and a voice in decision making. Some of these demands had already been met in countries such as Germany, where workers' councils and codetermination were already well-established practices in large firms. But in other countries such as France and Italy, where these demands sounded extreme, the increased level of economic conflict was interpreted as a symptom of a general malaise within the industrial system.

This interpretation was seemingly reinforced when these conflicts coincided with others of a different nature initiated by social movements or loose organizations of ecologists, feminists, ethnic minorities, regionalists, and university students. These movements were both instrumental and expressive. People wanted to advance their interests while at the same time making a statement about their values and their collective identity.

The ecologists defended local environments, but they also protested against a commercial or productivist orientation present in both the public and the private sphere which threatened the general quality of life. The feminists were interested in enhancing women's opportunities for better jobs and more responsibility in the economy and in politics; but they also put in question what they considered to be a male-dominated world, and they hinted at a rearrangement of gender relations in all areas of life. The ethnic minorities and the regionalist movements aspired to a redistribution of real and symbolic resources among ethnic and regional groups, but they also challenged the traditional preeminence of core ethnic, regional, and national groups and the underlying principles, myths, and rituals which in the past had pulled different groups together within the larger society. The university students, for instance in France and Italy, fought for lower tuition, better conditions for intellectual work, and larger state budgets for education, and for state protection against external competition (for example, by defending the state monopoly, or quasi-monopoly, on higher education); but at the same time they made passionate statements regarding the desirability of a more humane, more cooperative, less competitive society.

All these movements pointed at important elements of malaise throughout the social body, revealed problems, and had considerable influence in setting the agenda for public debate. At the same time, they all tended to shape this public debate in such a way that a remedy to those problems was to be sought, first and foremost, through state action. The state was the focus toward which these movements directed their demands. In this respect there was no break in continuity between these social movements and the elites which invented and managed the sociopolitical compromise on which the equilibrium of the welfare state of the 1950s and 1960s had rested. The cultural affinity between them was a profound one. This helps to explain two critical features of the drama of the late sixties and seventies. First, it explains the ambivalence of the elites when they faced the attacks of the leaders of those movements, since they came from the same cultural environment and shared a common language. Second, it explains the relative ease with which many movement leaders, after a training period in confrontational politics, joined the ranks of civil servants, party politicians, and professionals employed in or dependent on the public sector.[41]

The ambiguity built into these economic conflicts and social movements could be perceived from the outset, in the events of May 1968 in France, which were heralded as the expression par excellence of the crisis of the liberal capitalist societies. Swaying with the endless tide of their own words, intoxicated by a sense of the power of their ideas, and all of this mixed in with a strong dose of moral indignation and at least a few drops of complacency, the Parisian students and the supportive intelligentsia proclaimed the beginning of a new era. The movement claimed to be reminiscent of 1789, but in fact it was more like 1848.[42] After a few weeks the industrial working class made a settlement with the government for significant but not extraordinary gains in real wages;[43] the majority of Parisians got ready for their summer holidays; and the majority of Frenchmen gave a vote of confidence to De Gaulle.

What defeated the student revolution was not state violence but rather fatigue, and worse still boredom, with a festival which had gone on too long. A modicum of transformative symbolism had been a welcome relief in the routines of everyday life. But afterward, people realized that, all things considered, most of these routines were fairly acceptable, and the basic institutions of liberal capitalism were good enough for them. All they really wanted was to introduce a few reforms, add some improvements, make the institutions more open and more flexible, and try new ways of living with them. They were far from willing to make a radical break with the socioeconomic and political order. This tacit and sobering discovery was a telling finale—indeed an anticlimax—for a drama which had been played out with such a display of rhetorical exuberance.

In turn, the economic crisis of the mid-seventies seemed a much more serious challenge to the established order. Instead of a crisis of capitalist legitimacy, this was a crisis of accumulation, for the capitalist system seemed overwhelmed by circumstances and unable to deliver economic growth. Yet once more there was irony in the fact that, in time, a gradual consensus emerged in the public, across the entire political and social spectrum, to put its trust in the market economy, even, if necessary, at the expense of the welfare system.

The crisis arose from a combination of factors. The way was prepared by a financial crisis fueled by the manner in which the United States had financed the Vietnam war. It was precipitated by steep increases in the price of raw materials (chiefly oil in 1973 and 1979, after the war in the Middle East and the Iranian revolution), and aggravated by increased competition in world markets, owing to the ascent of the Japanese economy and of that of the new industrializing countries, within the framework of increasing economic internationalization.

The OECD countries reacted with policies which, though diverse, did have some factors in common (Schmidt, 1983). First, they focused on the oil crisis of 1973 in the expectation that this would be a temporary incident, and tried to cushion its effects. The governments provided companies with subsidies to compensate for the increase in energy costs, kept their long-standing policy of extensive labor market regulations, stepped up the volume of social transfers in order to cope with the rise in unemployment, and went along with the escalation of workers' demands for wage increases to compensate for inflation. This was the prevailing pattern followed by governments of the right and of the left (for instance, social democrats and bourgeois parties in Sweden, Labour and Conservatives in Great Britain). The result was "stagflation": a decrease in the growth rate and employment and an increase in the rate of inflation.

By the time of the oil crisis of 1979, the governments had adopted a different attitude, having learned from previous experience. Now they expected the situation to last, and so they aimed at making structural or positive adjustments in their economies (OECD, 1981). Most of the governments, the central banks, the economic profession, and even the political class and the public gradually reached the same diagnosis. The internationalization of the economy (in capital flow, energy, industrial products, or services) was held both irreversible and desirable. Countries should keep their economies as open as possible and try to improve their competitiveness in the world markets. Changes in demand, in the structure of relative prices of the inputs, and in the rate and nature of technological innovations would be increasingly difficult to predict and the behavior of the markets more and more uncertain. Governments and central banks could do little more than try to create conditions which would help firms adjust to a continuously changing and largely unpredictable environment.

At a minimum it was felt that a strict monetary policy should control domestic inflation, and coordination among monetary policies should make this task easier. The mix of other policies was left to some experimentation. There was an expectation that the state would have to cushion some of the social effects of its anti-inflationary policies. It was expected, too, that the state would try to invest in infrastructure of various kinds. Given a tradition of state intervention, it was to be expected that, at least in some countries, the state would engage in industrial policies which would favor sectors and firms that looked promising—and would bet on the taxpayers' disposition to pay for the wrong choices and on the electorate's forgetfulness come the next election. A margin of inconsistency in fiscal policies was also to be expected. But at least in principle there was consensus that the general aim of states' policies should be to reduce the external disequilibria of their economies and to improve their competitiveness in the world markets. These were the accepted standards against which the performance of the domestic economies and economic policies would be judged.

Now, the implementation of policies consistent with this diagnosis created considerable strains in the social democratic compromise of the 1950s and 1960s, particularly in three policy areas: those of wage policies, social transfers, and labor market policies.

First, from the priority given to anti-inflationary policies and from the emphasis put on firms' competitiveness in world markets, it followed that labor costs should be contained, particularly as energy costs increased. Labor was to be persuaded to accept limits on raises. This was accomplished almost overnight in Japan. It took longer in western Europe, though the adjustment was easier where unions were strong and moderate (characteristics usually found together with neocorporatist institutions; see Scharpf, 1984).[44]

Second, anti-inflationary policies, together with the need to encourage productive investment, were supposed to require the reduction of public deficits, and even the containment of public spending. However, this ran counter to a historical trend which was the result of sustained deliberate policies by spending coalitions, and of the combined inertia of well-established institutions and social expectations, which in some countries were enshrined in legal entitlements. Moreover, massive social transfers were needed to compensate for unemployment and for a policy of wage containment. Therefore, resistance to public spending reductions was widespread, and on the whole relatively successful, including in the United States and the United Kingdom.

Third, there was disagreement on the need to make the labor market more flexible. In fact, the expression "flexibility of the labor markets" covered two quite different phenomena, as it referred to both the external and the internal labor markets. Regarding external labor markets, most European economies became less and less flexible during the 1950s and 1960s, for it was generally understood that, as part of the social democratic compromise, employment should become more stable and compensation for dismissal more costly in terms of time, legal proceedings, and expense for the employers. For some observers there was a distinct trend for the "status component" of the employee's position in the firm to prevail over its "contract component" (Dore, 1973; Streeck 1985, 1986). In the face of the economic crisis, however, many companies felt compelled to reduce their work force in order to survive and to compete. Moreover, provision had to be made for continuous adjustment of the work force to a changing economic scenario. Thus, two questions arose: first, how to redistribute the socioeconomic costs of massive dismissals among the firms, the laid-off workers and their families, employed workers, the rest of society, and the state, not to mention the foreign countries from which many of those laid-off workers had come; and second, which kinds of jobs should be expected to provide stability in the future and which should not.

In most countries the way to address both questions was to apply de facto a dualistic formula, usually half hidden under a cloud of social rhetoric. According to this formula a protected core of workers kept the guarantee of job stability (together with the corresponding social security benefits), while a periphery of underprotected and unprotected workers did not. Underprotected workers included new entrants in the labor market, usually young men, who had to settle for temporary contracts, as well as those unskilled and semiskilled workers (largely young people, women, older workers, and migrants) who were the first to go in case of dismissals, and for whom getting back into the market would be difficult. Unprotected workers included the unemployed whose benefits had run out, and those who were working in the underground economy.

This formula was quite compatible with neocorporatist institutions,[45] since the unions used those institutions as an instrument for maintaining the job stability of the protected core and for obtaining minor advantages for (and as a forum for making rhetorical statements with regard to) the periphery of underprotected and unprotected workers. And they knew that, as a result of this dualism, foreign workers would be sent home by the thousands, that older workers and women would have few incentives to search for jobs, and that many laid-off workers and new entrants in the labor market would find no jobs, or only jobs in the underground economy offering low wages, poor working conditions, and no social security protection.

By contrast, flexibility of the internal labor market referred to the rules of intrafirm mobility and the ways in which tasks were defined and social and professional interactions were organized. The corporate culture and the institutional design of the firm were extremely important in this regard, and they appeared to be connected to each other. Wherever an organizational culture of "high trust" between employer and employees existed, as was the case in many Japanese and German enterprises, a substantial degree of flexibility in the rules of the organization and the definition of employees' tasks occurred. This was not the case in organizations with a culture of "low trust," as was traditional in Anglo-Saxon and Latin European countries. In turn, the institutional precondition for this culture of high trust, and the organizational flexibility that went with it, seemed to be a substantial measure of job stability, or lack of flexibility in the external labor market.

It may be that this combination of flexibility in the internal labor market and inflexibility in the external one enhanced the survival capacity of Japanese and German firms, particularly as the effects of such a combination were reinforced, and apparently required, by changes in technology and in the composition of demand. At least this was the argument put forward by some analysts of the rise of what is variably called neoindustrialism, flexible specialization, or new productive systems.[46] But it may also be that events had been moving toward the application of a dualistic formula to areas within the firm, with a core of permanent workers (to whom the corporate culture of high trust and the rules of organizational flexibility would apply) and a periphery of more transient and less integrated workers; and to a network of organizations, with a core of firms which guaranteed permanent employment and a periphery of subcontractors or client firms which did not.

In any case, it is worth considering that this combination of internal flexibility and external inflexibility pointed in a direction that was disquieting from the viewpoint of labor traditions as they had been shaped by the social democratic compromise of the 1950s and 1960s. Because a culture of high trust, in which employees share the employer's goal of enhancing the competitiveness of the company in the world markets, might result in a sort of microcorporatism (Streeck, 1986), it would fit poorly with the basic institutions, long-term strategy, and ideological traditions of the class-centered European brand of unionism, since microcorporatism would ask for more and more decentralized forms of collective bargaining (thus reducing the institutional role of the national unions), and would pay lip service to an ideology of class solidarity which some unions were trying to keep alive, at least as a sign of collective identity, and as a justification for their own leadership role. I discuss this matter further in Chapters 5 and 6.

Redesigning the Welfare State: Institutional Experiments

As a result of pressures for change in state policies and institutions in all areas, the equilibrium of the welfare state of the 1950s and 1960s was put into question. In turn, the responses to these pressures depended on a variety of economic, political, and cultural circumstances—and allowed, therefore, for a good deal of variation.

Two sets of experiments with the institutional design of the welfare state took place during the 1970s and the 1980s: the development of already existing neocorporatism, which seemed to fit better with a social democratic tradition as well as with a conservative one; and deregulation, privatization, and the expansion of open markets, associated with a neoliberal political philosophy.[47] For all their differences, these experiments shared a common trait in that they widened the scope of civil society's intervention in the organization of socioeconomic activities.

This shared trait should be emphasized all the more in view of the fact that, for all the declared incompatibility on matters of principle between neocorporatists (that is, social democrats or welfare statists) and neoliberals, in real life their rhetoric, institutions, and policies were often mixed up. During this period in many cases political rhetoric, institutions, and policies fit rather poorly with one another. Liberal governments kept the welfare states growing, and socialist governments privatized and deregulated the economy, while the electorate kept sending mixed signals about their preferences. Therefore, my discussion is meant to refer to general trends or orientations, not to clear-cut critical choices unambiguously made or fully implemented in most countries. As a matter of fact, under a rhetoric of "choices," most governments and electorates tried to avoid making them as they muddled through the problems of the 1970s and 1980s.

The core of neocorporatism consisted of an institutional pattern of consultation between business and labor, with government's explicit or tacit intervention, in order to prepare for, to formulate, and to implement certain key socioeconomic policies, such as wage, social, and labor market policies. Since businessmen and workers were represented by their professional associations, including business organizations and unions, these associations were expected either to be strong enough to guarantee their members' compliance with those policies which had been agreed on[48] or to be close enough to their members' sentiments so that a rejection of the agreements by these members was out of the question. As a matter of fact, it was also expected that a tradition of social pacts (or concerted policies) would strengthen those associations' hand vis-à-vis their members so that in time a more predictable rank-and-file business and working community would develop. And it was further assumed that state officials and the leaders and cadres of those interest associations would get used to one another, come to trust one another, develop a common language, outlook, and set of interests, and foresee the consequences their games would have on the economy, politics, and society as a whole.

In the troubled 1970s the state found new reasons for reinforcing (or, if necessary, inventing, as in Spain; see Chapter 4) this tradition of social pacts and the scope of neocorporatism. The state was interested in sharing the risks and the costs of difficult policy decisions, thus shifting part of the responsibility, the credit, and the blame to unions and business (Berger, 1985a). Also, debating and signing the pacts was, irrespective of their real effects, an educational experience and a symbolic performance that might enhance the moral authority of the state officials, at least for a while. At the same time, the state's offer involved a challenge and an opportunity for business and union leaders to influence events and to take part of the credit for a more cooperative social climate, and even for an economic recovery if one happened to come along. It was also an opportunity for the leaders of the professional associations to strengthen their personal positions in their own organizations, learn about one another's strategies, and discover how to handle the public debate.

Being on the defensive, the union leaders tried to work out different compromises, for instance, trading off their acquiescence in containing wage increases and introducing some job flexibility for increases in social transfers (subsidies to sectors or companies in crisis, pensions, or unemployment benefits) and selective benefits for the unions (monopoly on legal representation, subsidies or positions for union leaders in state agencies). The range of possible trade-offs could be extended to include helping political leaders close to the unions succeed to positions of state power. In effect, even if the unions did not obtain significant concessions from the government, they might argue that by softening their demands, they had increased the chances for a leftist party to stay in or to come into power. As a matter of fact, it could be pointed out that by hardening their positions, the British unions facilitated Margaret Thatcher's electoral success in the late 1970s.[49] In contrast, by half accepting the austerity policies enacted by a leftist government, the unions added to the credibility of the Spanish socialist government in the eyes of the middle classes, a critical factor in explaining the latter's electoral support for socialist candidates throughout most of the 1980s.

Of course, employers could identify more easily than unionists with the kind of policies that followed from the diagnosis and the pressures I have discussed. Since, by the 1980s, the main lines of economic policy had been agreed on by both the left and the right, the employers' dilemma was to decide which kind of government was best suited for implementing those policies. There was no compelling reason for business to restrict its choice to the right, or even the center right. Any leftist party eager to stay in power could be equally eager to do the job, and to apply for business support. The comparative advantage of the left was precisely its relationship with the unions, which made it better able to persuade them to go along with those policies. Certainly British labor had to wait until the early 1990s to be ready to be persuaded. But the German socialists under Helmut Schmidt's leadership, the Spanish under Felipe González, and the French (after

1983) under Laurent Fabius and Michel Rocard proved they could be relied on much earlier.

The problem was that agreement on the basics of an economic policy did not make for agreement on the actual implementation of that policy and its translation into specific and timely government action. This difference is of considerable importance. Not only were the states' capacities limited, but also the governments had to make their own trade-offs between economic soundness and short-term electoral considerations. Such a situation has the potential to produce mutually inconsistent policies and/or a pattern of procrastination (see Chapter 4). The neocorporatist institutions, which had been designed, and were expected to work, to facilitate the public's acceptance of socioeconomic policies, could therefore act as an impeding mechanism if the union leaders decided to use them to block or defuse the effect of those policies.

The neoliberal experiment in redesigning the welfare state tried to learn from all these experiences; but it also started from a philosophical position according to which the historical trend of state aggrandizement, with or without the agreement of organized interests, was to be contained, and possibly reversed.[50] This trend, it was argued, served neither the public interest nor the private one. Public spending coalitions were to be checked. Thus, unions were targeted as one of the main obstacles to the kind of adjustment required by the new economic environment, together with business's propensity to ask for state protection, and the state's proclivity to grant it in exchange for increased regulatory powers and an ever-greater share of the national wealth.

From a neoliberal perspective, the state's task was not that of sharing responsibility with the interest groups in organizing economic and social life (as was implied in the neocorporatist experiment), but that of moving out of that sphere as much as possible, and reducing its (and their) responsibility. The state's responsibility was to be reduced in favor of markets, that is, the self-regulatory capacities of individual firms, individual families, and individuals *tout court,* which would interact as freely as possible with one another under the rule of law. Certainly collective goods were needed, and the state could play a significant role in providing them, but it had no right to claim a monopoly for that provision; it was to be just one agent among many in an open market of social services.

A neoliberal philosophy shaped the agenda of the U.S. and British governments of the 1980s, which resulted in the implementation of an array of policies. Some referred to "institution building," and tried to create a framework of laws and institutions which would enable free and open markets to work properly (including laws on property rights and the rights of voluntary associations; see Starr, 1990). Others were liberalization policies (sometimes called deregulation policies, though in fact they imply either reforming existing regulatory agencies or setting up new ones) aimed at reducing the state's policy of closely supervising various kinds of activities. And "privatization" policies were aimed at shifting the balance between the private and the public sectors in favor of the former by selling off parts of the state sector. To this list may be added the policy of contracting out public services to private firms, which would then provide collective goods using public funds and operating under some public guidelines (Starr, 1990, pp. 41–45). There was a general hope that these sets of policies would help increase the degree of competition in the economy.[51]

The policies of the Thatcher and Reagan administrations aimed at, and in fact resulted in, an expansion of free markets in a variety of areas: labor markets, capital flow, trade, financial services, and manufacturing. By contrast, the administrations were rather cautious in trying out policies of privatization and deregulation in social sectors such as health and education which lay at the heart of the welfare state. Here the traditional role of the state in providing these services (and, by implication, in being the main institution for expressing social or national solidarity) was somehow reluctantly maintained, at least in fact if not in theory. However, in the field of education at least a plausible argument, if not a systematic policy, was put forward to advance the cause of the voucher principle, according to which the responsibility of the state would be limited to providing families with the money to pay for their children's education. It would be up to the parents to search out and choose the school that best suited their own preferences, among a variety of competing private and public schools, none of which would receive additional state subsidies. This method was proposed, from different ideological perspectives,[52] in the hope that it might result in a process of social learning and, ultimately, in better education. The principle behind the experiment was the implicit expectation that people would learn from their mistakes: parents would learn how to choose wisely, and school administrators, public or private, would learn how to provide a good education and how to market it to discriminating consumers. The hope was that an entire society of discriminating consumers would eventually emerge.

A similar principle, and a similar expectation, underlay other experiments in the field of public health. Here the (presumably discriminating) consumers would be entitled to shop around and choose the doctors and the hospitals they preferred. These would therefore be required to compete for patients, thus ending up in a hierarchy of reputations that supposedly, in the long run, would reflect the quality of their performance.[53]

The plausibility of these schemas was reinforced by the fact that, in liberal capitalist societies, they were similar to the ones that were already in place both in the economy and in politics. Fostering the competitiveness of firms and increasing the reliance on markets were the fundamental normative tenets which could be deduced from the prevailing diagnosis of the economic situation. At the same time, democratic politics was based on the assumption that voters make reasonable choices between competing parties (and, eventually, between competing policies and institutions), learn from their mistakes, and try to correct them by voting for different parties or policies next time. Without this assumption democratic politics would have to be considered undistinguishable from demagoguery and political manipulation, which was precisely the position traditionally taken by the totalitarian critics of democracy, both fascists and communists.

Whether because of the apparent success of some of the economic policies put forward in the United States and the United Kingdom during the 1980s, or because of the relative cognitive and moral consistency of neoliberalism with the prevailing economic diagnosis and the tenets of democratic politics, the fact is that there was a limited diffusion of neoliberal arguments, policies, and institutions throughout Europe, including the countries ruled by socialist governments. Deregulation and privatization as well as the introduction of market principles in the public sector were policies gradually adopted in socialist France, socialist Spain, and even, up to a point, in social democratic Sweden (Immergut, 1990).

It is worth noting, however, that in these cases the adoption of fragments of neoliberal policies and institutions was the result less of emulation and ideological conversion than of these governments' pragmatic disposition to adjust to the consequences of systemic pressures they were not in a position to resist, much less to control. In effect, the internationalization of the economy created the conditions for a competition among regulatory regimes, in which some neoliberal sets of policies and institutions finally prevailed. More particularly, the process of European economic integration, which was already a factor in François Mitterrand's change of heart in 1983, pushed the national governments even further in the neoliberal direction through the second half of the 1980s and beyond.[54] At the same time, this external push converged with other pressures from within the domestic economies. The growth of an underground labor market eroded much of the rationale for the existing regulations of the official labor market, in the same way that a thriving black market in illegal money eroded much of the rationale for the existing regulation of the financial markets. Although these two types of markets might coexist peacefully in the short run, and even complement each other, by contrast this coexistence eroded the moral basis which in the long run was absolutely indispensable for a properly functioning economy, including a modicum of trust in the legal system and in the honorability or civic ethos of the public authorities.

Redefining Solidarities

These experiments in institutional design of a neocorporatist or a neoliberal sort shared the common trait of giving more and more power to civil society. Moreover, as the foregoing discussion suggests, in so doing these experiments permitted more and more responsibility to lie in the ultimate units of society, namely, individuals. These individuals might belong to organizations. My contention is, however, that in today's world of organizations the links between individuals and their organizations are increasingly loose.

To begin with, the very process of institutional experimentation at a time of increasing turbulence fostered a mentality of trial and error, which tended to exclude dogmatic assertions of ideologies and programs and asked for explicit and deliberate individual choices. The public had to be convinced time and again of the desirability of both the goals and the ways to attain them. The time when political and social leaders could decide these questions and count on the public's tacit consent was over. The public was more assertive, but also the turbulence of the 1970s and 1980s diminished the self-confidence of politicians, civil servants, professional experts, unionists, and business leaders. The world looked much less predictable than in the past. Those political and social elites were not so sure they understood what the situation was or even what their own goals were.

Over the last twenty to thirty years or so, the churches, for instance, have had to adjust to the changing and contradictory demands of the faithful or else resign themselves to growing indifference and disaffection (see Chapter 3). Political parties saw the electoral vote becoming more and more volatile after repeated attempts to deceive themselves about the presumed stability of the electoral blocs (Nie, Verba, and Petrocik, 1979). Both unions and companies had to deal with the fact that the loyalty of "their" workers could not be taken for granted, that it was divided between company and union, and that in any event it existed in limited amounts, since most workers refused to identify themselves fully with either side, partly because their commitment to their own families often came first (Goldthorpe et al., 1968a).

Now, it may be said that, in general, the degree of freedom individuals have with respect to the conditions that frame their experience varies considerably and depends on many factors. But it seems to be greater both in times of crisis or acute turbulence, as in the 1960s and 1970s, and in times when some order is expected to come about as the result of the quasi-spontaneous coordination among large numbers of autonomous agents, each pursuing his or her own goals, and this is precisely the type of social order western societies of the 1980s seemed to be approaching.

In these circumstances social integration would be the consequence not of people living together under similar conditions, or working within the same organizations, or sharing the same goals, but of critical choices made by those individuals to adhere to the rules that make possible this extended order of many-sided and multiple interactions and to abide by the moral traditions and moral communities that go with these rules. Hence the crucial importance of explaining the emergence and development of the individual's moral sentiment of solidarity. As a moral sentiment, solidarity implies a commitment on the part of a morally responsible agent. States, societies, nations, classes, even organizations are not morally responsible agents. Only individuals are. Therefore it is only in individuals and in their choices that we can find the key to the problems of social integration, particularly in times of crisis or acute turbulence, or times that approach the condition of extended spontaneous order.

The problem is that, as the accumulated result of living in times first of trouble and then of spontaneous order, the moral choices individuals made became largely problematic. The links between these individuals and the organizations to which they belonged (and the institutions in which they were embedded) became loose. They belonged to them, but with reservations, with a certain ambiguity; or they belonged to several of them which they might play off on occasion against one another. Their collective identities became soft.

Let us consider the case of the workers' moral attitudes vis-à-vis the market economy, the companies, and the unions (on this more later; see Chapter 6). During the 1950s and 1960s the workers' consent to the functioning of a market economy was tacit and instrumental. It coexisted with a ritual denunciation of capitalism by union leaders and leftist politicians—the same ones who were making a compromise with business and governments to keep the economy running. The turbulence of the late 1960s and 1970s exposed to light this mild form of schizophrenia. At the moment of truth, people made their choice in favor of liberal capitalism and stood by it through the economic crisis.

It seems safe to assume that if most people believe that their country's economic system is grossly unfair and therefore unacceptable from a moral viewpoint (either because it allows a minority to exploit a majority of have-nots or because income disparities, with or without exploitation proper, are allowed to grow in ways that may seem utterly unjustifiable), they will have great difficulty in persuading themselves that a public discourse of civic duty, due respect for the law, and patriotism is meaningful, and indeed that they belong to the same nation as that minority of exploiters, of people exceedingly rich and powerful and possibly above the law. The Marxist tradition articulated an extreme version of this negative view, portraying capitalism as a system of class exploitation and the nation as a battleground for the class struggle. According to this doctrine there was no moral community between the classes, and any moral community that might exist stopped at the boundaries between them. The fact is, however, that the European workers of the postwar period rejected this extreme negative version, as demonstrated by their behavior.

At the same time, their explicit statements were often hesitant, confused, or ambivalent as they declared capitalism to be "unjust." In light of workers' actual behavior in support of capitalism at critical junctures, statements such as this require interpretation. It might be that the workers judged capitalism against the yardstick of a good or even perfect society, patterned on the ideal of the family, an arcadian peasant community, or any other gemeinschaft type of community—a society free from internal conflict, where people cooperate with one another, decisions are made by near-unanimous consent, and resources are distributed according to merit or to need, ranked on a uniform scale of preference. In this utopia we might find echoes of hundreds of years of Christian moral teaching and village and guild traditions, or the traditions of "tribalism" or "closed societies" to which Popper and Hayek refer (Popper, 1966; Hayek, 1988). In fact, all these moral traditions were reactivated by contemporary unionism (see Chapter 6).

Nonetheless, these moral sentiments toward capitalism became intertwined over time with other sentiments arising from a different perspective: from seeing capitalism not against the yardstick of a beautiful dream but in comparison with its available historical alternatives, in a complex world where a consensus about the scale of preferences among so many basic units of society cannot be expected. Thus, when workers made moral judgments which were preferential judgments among the available alternatives (Klein, 1981), then the value or desirability of capitalism increased dramatically. The market economy was justified because it provided access to things which were valuable in themselves, such as material prosperity, individual freedom, or moral sociability in small or large moral communities, possibly including the communities of firms and unions (see Chapter 6), and it did so better than those alternatives.[55] This is how workers ended up believing that the market economy might be morally acceptable, or morally tolerable, or fair enough.

Now, when the mass of European workers came around to this idea and acted on it in making critical choices in the 1960s and 1970s, the leaders, the cadres, and the militants in the unions and the parties of the left who had strong ideological commitments and intense feelings of moral indignation found themselves at the end of their tether. If they stood by their ideal of socialism as the dream which could not be given up, they conceded defeat in real historical terms, which were the very terms their Marxist training made them think were the only relevant ones. But if they faced facts squarely, they could no longer blind themselves to the realization that, for the vast majority of their constituencies (and possibly for themselves), socialism was no longer a plausible alternative to capitalism. Thus, the two phenomena—the moral acceptability of capitalism and the crisis of plausibility of socialism—came together and influenced each other and reached a climax in the 1980s.

At a micro level the workers' moral, if unenthusiastic, acceptance of the capitalist firm paralleled their moral, and equally unenthusiastic, acceptance of the market economy. But in this case the unions were able to make a more credible argument than socialism was able to advance at the macro level. Thus, workers were solicited by conflicting claims on their loyalty from unions and companies.

Most often firms dealt with their employees on purely instrumental terms. Yet at times they also issued a call for some form of solidarity, particularly if, whatever the reason, management became interested in creating a culture of high trust. At the basis of this culture there must be the perception of a rough equilibrium between workers' contributions to and rewards from the firm (in terms of wages, conditions, voice, and so on), and of a common interest or goal. From this it follows that the management's authority would be considered legitimate (so that consent to its directives would not be merely instrumental), and the firm would be a meaningful focus for feelings of solidarity, pride, and loyalty, and for a moral community of some sort.

In turn, the unions challenged the firms' claims to the loyalty of their workers. This they did from three different standpoints. First, from a *radical* perspective (corresponding to a theory of class struggle), the unions demanded their workers' full emotional and moral commitment to their cause. The union claimed to be the only moral community workers could properly belong to, and management and ownership were by definition excluded from it. Thus, the characteristics of intense intraunion solidarity—a clear-cut split within the company between "them" and "us" and outright hostility toward "them"—went together. Second, from a traditionally *reformist* perspective the unions kept their distance from management, rejected the proposal that the company was a moral community, calling it a deception, and tried to adopt a long-term strategy of radical reform, thus, questioning the basis of the market economy. But still, it was a characteristic of this traditional reformism that the unions were also willing to live with their companies as they were, to make tactical compromises, to wait for better times, to engage in businesslike instrumental exchanges with management, and to encourage the workers to do the same. Third, from a *microcorporatist* perspective, the unions took on the task of cooperating with the firm on matters of common interest while pressing for specific reforms. In this case the unions took for granted that the workers would have a double loyalty to the firm and to the union, and would try to live with this ambiguity. This implied the union's acceptance of the company's claim to be a moral community itself, and of management's claim that its authority was legitimate.

But under existing conditions it was left more and more to the workers themselves to define their solidarities and to decide the identity and the shape of the moral communities they would adhere to (see Chapter 6). To a significant extent western workers took a detached view of both the company's and the union's claims to their loyalty, and they combined an instrumental and a moral attitude toward both, in part because they were interested in the welfare of their own families (Goldthorpe et al., 1968a) and in part because, for reasons which had to do with the general climate of the times, individuals tend to be careful investors of their limited moral and emotional capacity for commitment and thus reduce the risk of a bad choice by diversifying their moral investments and by keeping in reserve a part of their emotional resources, refusing to invest them in any organization whatsoever.

In sum, the relations between civil society and the state in western Europe from 1945 to 1990 underwent three distinct phases. First, there was the relative equilibrium of the welfare state from 1945 to the late 1960s. This was a period of economic growth and apparent social integration, the latter resulting from various developments. Economic prosperity under conditions of a relatively stable international economic environment made possible socioeconomic policies conducive to continuous increases in real wages, social public spending, and job security, thus satisfying a variety of social and economic needs of a majority of the population. At the same time, status differences lessened; bargaining mechanisms were institutionalized at a micro and at a macro level, favoring a pattern of mutual accommodation between conflicting interest groups; and the traditional ideological division between left and right was considerably reduced and made less dramatic. The implicit cultural assumption underlying all these developments was that the state should take more responsibility for the general welfare of society.

Second, by the late 1960s and early 1970s the system appeared to be in deep crisis and heading, in a sort of *fuite en avant,* toward a new institutional design with even more state intervention, since the main thrust of most of the socioeconomic conflicts and social movements (and perhaps also the prevailing tone of the diagnosis of the intelligentsia) was to put more demands on the state. Curiously enough, this *élan* of transformative politics proved to be a historical mirage. The events of the late 1960s were the swan song of radical politics, soon to be all but forgotten in the unexpected turn of events in the late 1970s and the 1980s.

Finally, by the late seventies, the tide had turned. It took time for people to realize the depth and the scope of the change, but the fact is that the state found itself in the position of taking less and less responsibility for events it could not control. This gave way to two institutional experiments. Refurbishing the neocorporatist tradition was the logical defensive and conservative reaction of people committed to maintaining most of the social democratic compromise of the past; but even so, the content of the socioeconomic policies decided on and enacted within the frame of these neocorporatist institutions resembled more and more their neoliberal alternative. Neoliberalism was a risky attempt at checking, and even reversing, the historical trend of state growth. In point of fact, both experiments were mixed up in government policies and in the actual functioning of both existing and new established institutions, and compromises were made between them. Underlying both experiments was a general sense of a return of civil society, in the form of new arrangements being worked out between public authorities, markets, and voluntary associations.

In connection with these developments, there was also a sense of relative cultural indeterminacy that pervaded the public sphere. Beliefs and moral traditions had been connected in the past, in a relatively firm and clear way, to smoothly functioning organizations and institutions such as churches and Christian-democratic or conservative organizations, leftist parties and unions, firms and markets, even national states. Under the conditions of turbulence and institutional experimentation from the late 1960s to the 1980s, people had to take a new look at, and to decide on their commitments to, the core institutions of a liberal democracy and a market economy. At the same time they had to face up to the task of redefining these commitments, as well as the solidarities and collective identities that might be connected to them. And they had to find new ways in which their moral sentiments could be anchored in a set of institutions at a time when these very institutions were in the process of being redesigned.

As a final caveat I would like to point out that my argument so far has not been and is certainly not meant to be one of positing society against the state. Far from it; a theory of civil society incorporates both institutional settings and focuses on their continuous interaction. The state, of course, may or may not play extremely useful roles as service provider, as coercive apparatus, or as symbolic performer. It is obvious, for instance, that the state may cooperate in establishing, and may even initiate, the kind of institutional experiments I have referred to, and that the defense of the country is a precondition for whatever experiments may eventually take place. Even if the state's traditional claim to be the bearer of an exalted moral project is questioned, it still has at least a minimal moral mission of helping to keep society together, and allowing people to define and pursue their own moral projects. The point, however, is to be aware of the limits of such a role, and to look as carefully as possible at the boundaries between the state and society.

These boundaries can be, and are expected to be, continuously crossed in both directions. This is an argument not for blurring the distinction but, on the contrary, for making it sharper and clearer, as this is a precondition for establishing the accountability of the public authorities and the quality of the public debate. It is also a precondition for fully recognizing the capacity of society to solve, or to take the initiative in solving, most of its collective problems, including those of self-coordination and material and spiritual growth.

The implication, therefore, of pointing out the limits of the state is that of assessing the potential of civil society. This, it has been argued, is not a matter of mere ideological "rediscovery" (as if the state of the art of academic debate would require us to bring civil society back in) but rather a matter of historical record. The evidence seems to show that the wave of new liberal democracies currently being established all over the world, the institutional experimentation with open markets and voluntary associations, even the new terms in which the logic of state regulations and the welfare state tend to be discussed all point in the direction of a return to or reemergence of civil society—a civil society which is certainly a far cry from the caricature of a market society of self-seeking, narrow-minded individuals unconcerned with the general interest.

The Problematic Return of Civil Society in Central and Eastern Europe

A further corroboration of my argument can be discerned in the collapse of the totalitarian regimes of central and eastern Europe,[56] which has resulted from the combination of a profound crisis of the Marxist states and the communist parties on the one hand, and of a new assertiveness of civil society on the other.

First, let us consider the crisis of political ideas and political institutions. Contrary to what most Marxist western intellectuals have argued (particularly when they tried to put some distance between themselves and the communist parties of their own countries), Marxist ideas and Marxist institutions (particularly in the socialist states and communist parties of central and eastern Europe) went hand in hand in a long-standing, unbroken tradition of a century and a half in the case of the parties and between forty and seventy years in the case of the states.

The claims of those institutions to be the bearers of an exalted moral project were therefore given ample opportunity to prove themselves. Some western scholars might still imagine that the efficacy of the sociopolitical model of the Soviet Union had been recognized the world over,[57] but to the subject populations in both the Soviet Union and other European socialist countries it was increasingly obvious that these states had failed on almost all counts in the domestic arena and were unable to deliver a dynamic economy, an integrated society, a meaningful public sphere, and even a strong collective identity. By the 1980s it was also obvious that, on the international scene, the Soviet Union was lagging far behind in its military and economic competition with the West. At last the Soviet leadership, and the Soviet state, felt obliged to give up the pretense of presiding over a superpower and to face up to their inability both to deliver the essentials of economic growth and a sense of national identity and to stand up to western competition.

Mikhail Gorbachev's performance in dismantling the Soviet Union's totalitarian institutions from within (initially a baroque strategy for restoring the economy and catching up with the West) was astonishing. At the same time, his wavering, procrastinating, and merely symbolic performance regarding substantive issues over too long a period suggested that totalitarian states and parties were unable to understand a complex and changing situation such as the one the Soviet Union was going through.[58] State and party functionaries remained fixated on a conceptual schema that made it extremely difficult for them simply to understand the rules of a market economy, and this cognitive difficulty was compounded by their repugnance at losing control of the situation.

More generally, the course of Gorbachev's protracted process of reform made clear the irrelevance of Marxist theories for helping to define and to solve the problems at hand, and of Marxist morality for motivating people to perform their duties as citizens, workers, or members of a national community. This was extended to Marxist symbols, which were drastically devalued. Images that embodied and gave sensuous expression to the Marxist traditions (icons such as the red flag; statues of Lenin; the hammer and sickle; slogans referring to class struggles, vanguard parties, and the construction of socialism; mythical tales of the October Revolution; shrines such as Lenin's tomb, and so on) no longer evoked feelings of respect or fear. They became embarrassments, waiting to be desecrated or soon forgotten.

Thus, the situation in the Soviet Union was such that, after seventy years of communist rule—which could at least claim to have promoted a process of industrialization and defended the country against Hitler's armies—Marxist institutions, ideas, and symbols were no longer credible. In most of central Europe there seemed to be no room for debate about the massive loss of legitimacy of the socialist states and the communist parties, since this loss had already been proved, and repeatedly so, since the 1950s by armed revolts, popular resistance, and other manifestations of general discontent, which had been duly put down by the national communist parties with the help of the Soviet Union.

In contrast with this collapse of established political institutions and their corresponding political culture, there was everywhere in both central and eastern Europe a reemergence of societal institutions and organizations, as well as a public sphere, which prepared the way for the political and economic transitions of the 1980s. It came about as a result of a combination of four developments: the emergence of social traditions connected with a variety of socioeconomic, demographic, and cultural changes; the use people made of cultural traditions, some endogenous and others external to those countries; the presence of organizations or networks able to initiate the development of a new public sphere; and, last but not least, the crystallization of some of these developments around a search for a new identity, which in some cases adopted the form of an explicit appeal to a rebirth or return of civil society.

To begin with, economic and social changes associated with industrialization and urbanization, including a technological revolution in communications and the upgrading of public education, increased the people's ability to make individual choices and to engage in horizontal communications and all sorts of extended orders such as markets and networking (F. Starr, 1988, 1990). This combined to create pressures in favor of reserved domains for individuals, to be protected by the law and courts of justice.

At the same time, the new opportunities for choice, and the renewed pressures for a larger reserved domain, were perceived as such and fought for by people whose cultural framework was gradually changing; and in turn this framework shaped these people's expectations and aspirations. Since Marxist ideology was waning, fewer and fewer people articulated their experiences within the framework of a revisionist Marxism. Most people turned to other cultural idioms for understanding their problems of economic growth, social life, and nationality, and for grounding their personal choices. They resorted both to endogenous local traditions that had managed to survive the Marxist regimes and to available information about western traditions.

Nationalism, religion, memories of a bourgeois secular culture or a liberal tradition[59] before the socialist revolution of 1917 or the Red Army's invasion after the Second World War provided some reference points. To these were added the more recent memories of resistance or dissidence (Budapest in 1956, Prague in 1968, Poland's church and workers' tradition of defiance, the Russian dissidents). In turn, the West provided ready-made institutional models of liberal democracies and markets, which were easy to detect underneath the more obvious behavioral patterns of mass consumption and a variety of lifestyles.[60] Finally, in the course of developing those social traditions, and of taking stock of these cultural influences, there was a corresponding growth of organizations and social movements (Starr, 1988).

All of this coalesced around a new identity which was searched for and then forged. The way was prepared by the debate over the theme of civil society. At some point the subject population of most of these countries defined itself as different from, and opposed to, the established political class: the *nomenklatura*. This act of defiance was a critical step in the process of emancipation from totalitarian rule. Such defiance was symbolized by a name: the name of civil society. This civil society was said to have been reborn (Rupnik, 1988). The term was used as part of a specific argument within the public debate of which the expression *rebirth* or *return* of civil society was understood as a metaphor.

The argument ran like this. Civil society as a set of institutions and actors differentiated itself sharply from the state and the political class. Social actors and institutions claimed to have an existence of their own, which was not a result of the state's activities, and they proved this existence through their ability to resist the state. They rejected the state's claim to monopolize the public sphere and challenged the state's definition of the public good, whether in terms of economic growth or in terms of social consensus. They also rejected the state's claim to have the chief responsibility for providing these goods, while they asserted their own capacity and responsibility and claimed they were better placed than the state to solve the problems of growth, social integration, and even national identity. Hence, they asked for institutional changes in the political system that would shift the balance between the state and society in favor of the latter, and this implied asking for a liberal democracy, a market economy, a pluralist system of interest representation, and cultural pluralism. (To return to the terms defined at the beginning of this chapter, they made a claim that a civil society in our second sense already existed to some significant degree under communist rule and should be given a chance to push forward the establishment of a civil society in our first sense.)

These claims were advanced and fought for in different ways and on different terrains according to local circumstances. In Poland they were advanced mainly by the church and the unions; in Hungary they came about initially through the development of the so-called second economy; in Czechoslovakia they were fought over mainly in the field of the public sphere and by cultural dissidents.

In Poland both the Catholic church and Solidarity challenged the state and the party. For many decades the church was an independent source of social integration, cultural traditions, and a national identity. Partly as a result of this, the Polish students were never fully indoctrinated in Marxism-Leninism.[61] The Polish peasantry for its part was able to survive, having avoided the fate of its Russian counterpart in the 1930s, when anywhere from 6 to 11 million people died in the course of the collectivization of the farms, and about 30 million peasants were forced to migrate to the cities. On the basis of these experiences, and taking advantage of the internal splits within the party and the Marxist intelligentsia, Solidarity emerged. It was to begin with an autonomous interest group for the workers, and then for the peasants, the students, and a variety of professional interests. It was also a social movement, that is, a type of voluntary association with both a loose following and the ability to enter and to shape the public debate and to make a statement regarding general social issues (Arato, 1981–82). This in turn created a training ground for a new political leadership to emerge. Solidarity went so far in claiming to address itself to solving the general problems of society that it established a network of organizations for the coordination of thousands of units engaged in the production and distribution of economic goods and services. This was done in open defiance of the official channels of the state-controlled economy in an attempt to prove the near irrelevance of the state institutions.

In Hungary, János Kádár's policies allowed for the development of a second economy during the 1960s. This was his attempt to come to terms with the memories of the revolt of 1956 and the repression that followed. He tried to legitimize the communist regime by showing it to be compatible with a modicum of economic prosperity and individual freedom in private life, provided that people managed to hold two jobs (one in the official economy and another in the second economy; see Stark, 1990; Rona-Tás, 1990) and renounced political freedom. *Pari passu,* segments of the intelligentsia took advantage of Kádár's relaxation of cultural controls to distance themselves from Marxism and approach western academic circles. This created a society that some witnesses characterized as hybrid and confused (Hankiss, 1990, p. 190). However, the fact is that people apparently lost some of their basic confusion and became passably lucid regarding three fundamental points: that economic growth would eventually take place only by pushing reforms in the direction of a market economy and not by coming back to a command economy; that the prospects for a better future, in both economic and cultural terms, lay in rein-forcing links with the West and not with the East; and that Kádár's attempt to increase the legitimacy of the communist state had failed.

In turn, the Prague Spring of 1968 was the symbol of a devolution of power from the state to society that, once made, was felt to be just and long overdue. Alexander Dubček's rather bland and amiable lead-ership was mainly symbolic, and seemed a fitting part of the entire symbolic process of the devolution of power. Most of the sociopolit-ical, economic, and cultural initiatives of that brief period moved hesi-tantly in the direction of a liberal democracy, a marketlike economy, and cultural pluralism. Gustav Husák's policies in the wake of the Soviet armed intervention, by contrast, attempted to reverse this incipient trend on all fronts. However, resistance was organized, this time around a nucleus of cultural dissidents. They succeeded in cre-ating a forum or reserved space for a public debate where moral and intellectual principles opposed to those of the Marxist state would prevail. The principles of truthfulness, open inquiry, rational criticism, and mutual toleration stood against the principles of ideological dog-matism, party or state interest, propaganda, and mere opportunism (Havel, 1988). Then, and again through a process of networking, the influence of this cultural regime (in the sense of a set of rules for cul-tural exchanges) spread across the boundaries of that reserved domain, and the forum finally became a public one.

All these experiences in different countries demonstrated the via-bility of alternative institutions (collective bargaining and strikes, mar-kets, rules of public debate, and so on), alternative organizations, networks, and social movements (churches, unions, networks of dissi-dents, and the like), and alternative cultural idioms (market philos-ophy, religion, nationalism, remnants of bourgeois liberalism, village traditions) to Marxist institutions, organizations, and ideas when the time came to handle problems of economic growth, social integration, cultural creativity, or national identity. These practical demonstrations took place over a prolonged period in the 1970s and 1980s. They prepared the ground for the final collapse of the communist states, which occurred at the very end of the 1980s, when a breathing space or window of opportunity was created as a result of the increasing inability and/or unwillingness of the personnel heading those Marxist states and parties to employ violence against their own populations to the extent that they or their predecessors had done in the past.

3

The Church and Religion in Contemporary Spain: An Institutional Metamorphosis

In the 1930s the Catholic church was persecuted in one half of Spain and exalted in the other, with men killing and being killed for reasons which were to a significant extent religious. A decade later a new alliance seemed solidly established between church and state. And yet the next twenty years, from the mid-1950s to the mid-1970s, were to witness a new avatar or transformation of the Spanish church as it distanced itself from its historical allies and drew closer to a liberal democratic regime which it would have condemned in earlier times, while accepting a situation of religious pluralism. This drama of the church's persecution, exaltation, estrangement, and accommodation with a changing temporal order can be understood only by looking into the relationships between the church and that temporal order, namely, the state and society, within the larger institutional and cultural framework that shaped those relations. In this chapter I explore the emergence and erosion of the alliance between the Catholic church and the Francoist state, and the religious forms and experiences associated with that alliance.

This is not a tale of decay or collapse of the Catholic church or Catholic religious experience in confrontation with the modern world.[1] In fact, our drama ends with an accommodation that implies intense soul-searching, risk taking, and innovation, all of which attests to the adaptive capacity and resilience of the church and the depth of people's religious commitments. The key to that accommodation lies in the symbolic and institutional negotiations that took place during the fifties and sixties between the church, the state, and civil society. The issue underlying those negotiations was the new religious demands arising from strategically situated social groups. These demands arose in connection with new problems and a search for solutions to those problems. The people who made the demands challenged the structure of plausibility of the church's doctrines, and therefore pressed for their reformulation and for corresponding institutional and organizational changes. My account tries to show the links between the emerging religious culture and its institutional framework by looking into the mechanisms that made those negotiations (and, in the end, that accommodation) possible.

At no time, however, can the religious offers of the church and the various religious demands of state and society, even under the best of circumstances, have more than a limited fit. Religion may have the effect of "consecrating" the existing political and economic arrangements, as Pierre Bourdieu suggests (1971b, p. 310), but it may also have the contrary effect of a "prophetic denunciation" of those arrangements; most often it may have *both* effects, for different audiences and at different times.

Regarding this limited fit, three comments are in order. First, this limited fit is *not* bound to be a handicap for the survival of church institutions and religious experiences; on the contrary, it may provide an opportunity for experimenting with new institutions and with moral and cognitive innovations that may prove successful (and compatible with the original tradition), thereby enhancing the adaptive capacities for survival of church and religion. Second, this limited fit demands accommodations in both directions. Church and religion may submit to the pressures arising from modernity no more than modernity itself (for instance, a liberal democratic regime or a full-fledged market economy) may be shaped by the influence of the church and people's religious experiences. Finally, the difficulties of such a fit between the church and a national temporal order are compounded by the fact that the relationship is played out in a larger international context that has some influence on the opportunities and constraints national states and national societies experience in defining their religious demands.

For the purpose of my discussion I will define religion as a set of cultural orientations—that is, beliefs and morals more or less codified in creedal form—linked to actual behavior embedded in institutions and rituals that are basically consistent with those orientations, characterized by the fact that they rest on a careful consideration (hence the term *religio,* from *relegere;* see Jung, 1967) of supernatural or sacred entities held to be autonomous or independent of the believer's will. At least in the western tradition (Berger, 1971) such supernatural or sacred entities are held to be autonomous, and they have evolved into gods or other spiritual agents with which believers engage in various forms of interaction. Within such a tradition an experience is usually considered to be religious only if and when such interactions, (or the expectation of such interactions) take place, and not simply when individuals experience a sense of awe before an unknown, indeterminate force (an "oceanic feeling"; see Freud, 1962) and/or face up to basic existential questions (Bell, 1980).

These interactions may be mediated by specific sets of actors and institutions, such as churches, that would share in the sacred character of those supernatural entities. Instead of following Durkheim in defining the church as the whole of the moral community for both the mediating actors and institutions and the mass of religious believers, I use Weber's distinction between the church as a producer (or coproducer) of religious offers and the mass of believers as the bearers of religious demands (Weber, 1978; Bourdieu, 1971a). Within the Catholic church, therefore, I distinguish between two sectors: the church proper, comprising its leadership and administrative apparatus (papacy, episcopate, secular clergy, and religious orders, which may be referred to as the hierarchy, ecclesiastical class, priesthood, and so on); and the laity, or the church's social basis ("God's people," the mass or community of believers, the faithful). The community of both sectors makes up the Catholic church in its widest sense, and perhaps from the church's viewpoint the most theologically correct one; but in my judgment there can be no satisfactory explanation of the transformations affecting the *whole* without analyzing each individual part, and without distinguishing between the strategies of the ecclesiastical body (which produces the "religious offer") and the attitudes, mindsets, or behavior of the faithful (who make the religious demands). Such being the case, I shall use the term *church* to refer only to the ecclesiastical body.

Typically a church offers a religious message to its followers and potential followers which combines three elements: a message of *meaning,* a message of *salvation,* and a message of *moral community,* all of which (at least in the western tradition of monotheistic or polytheistic religions) take as their reference point a god or other supernatural figures,[2] which the church represents, from which it receives its spiritual resources, and with which it mediates. Thus, within these three messages is included the implicit message of the church about itself as the source of meaning, salvation, and community.

The message of *meaning* refers to the point that religion offers (or claims to offer) a schema, a mental order, an explanation of causes and purposes in marked contrast to the apparent chaos of reality, the incoherent fragmentation of daily life, natural and historical cataclysms, the mysteries of death and the future, and ignorance of the past (Geertz, 1973; Berger, 1971). The creation of the world, original sin, redemption through the incarnation and sacrifice of God, the spiritual community among generations alive or dead, hope of an afterlife, the task of rebuilding the Kingdom of God on earth: all these are elements of a vision which seeks to encompass the totality of human experience in a coherent way. The message of *salvation* is to be understood in its widest sense. It is not only a question of setting the mind at ease by creating order but also, and more especially, a case of satisfying human affections and emotions. This message refers to salvation from diverse forms of danger and suffering, whether famine, illness, or drought, or feelings of guilt and impurity, loneliness, the anguish of death, tedium, daily routine, or uncertainty about the transience of time. Finally, the message of a spiritual or religious *moral community* is implicit in and forms part of the message of salvation. The communication of the religious message already implies such a community, and the supernatural referent, the mediator, and the receiver of the message all form part of it. It may be a community including gods, virgins, saints, angels, and the dead, and of course bishops, clerics, and the faithful, as in the case of the Catholic church—a community both visible and invisible, in this life and in the life hereafter, a community which is already part of the message of salvation because it advises, consoles, and resolves frustrations and grief.

In the case of the Catholic church the messenger is also a *prominent* part of the message itself. This emphasis is one of its defining characteristics with respect to other Christian churches, in particular most Protestant ones. What this means, first of all, is that the religious message of meaning is accompanied by a heavy emphasis on the *teachings* of the church when the time comes to determine that meaning. It is not for each individual to question the divine Word in the sincerity of his heart and the light of his reason; it is for him to accept fundamentally the interpretation proposed by the church (that is, the spiritual leadership at the head of the organization, together with professional theologians and other clerics): a church which is infallible in matters of faith and morality. It is not for the people to decide on their course of action; it is for them to adjust such a course to the prescriptions, the advice, and the spiritual direction of "wise and saintly" priests. Naturally, there is leeway for choice in making personal decisions, but the criteria are already laid down.

Second, the religious message of salvation is accompanied by a similar emphasis on the *sacramental intervention* of the church. Salvation is, in the final analysis, participation in the state of grace—that state which makes us safe and saintly, both in this life and in the next. Grace is not the outward sign but the reality of communion with God. Therefore, since the Catholic church dispenses the sacraments, it must hold, in the strictest sense, the key to the communication of supernatural grace or divine life which flows between God and mankind. In this way the church not only consoles and uplifts morally, or intercedes with rogations and other similar acts before supernatural figures, but administers the greatest of all religious and supernatural gifts as well.

Finally, from this we see the *centrality* of the Catholic church in the moral or spiritual communion of Catholics with God and supernatural figures. In fact, in everyday preaching the co-protagonism of Christ and his church is emphasized and reinforced by images of loving identity between the two. This centrality appears as much in ordinary teaching as in the sacraments, and it is summed up in that mixture of sermon and ritual which is the Mass. An example of Catholic ceremony par excellence, the Mass "deconstructs" the temporal community and reconstructs it again on its own terms, in a sacred place, at a sacred time, centered on the priest and his acts, both rational and magical.

This is the religious offer (creedal as well as ritual and institutional) made by the Catholic church to meet the demands for meaning, salvation, and spiritual community by the masses of its actual or potential followers. These demands are, as they have always been, most diverse in content as well as in intellectual articulation, emotional depth, and scope.

Depending on people's location in the economic, social, political, or cultural system, they may formulate religious demands for the justification or legitimation of their privileged position, or for compensating their underprivileged situation (Weber, 1978). These demands may be more or less explicit and fully articulated, even systematized (for instance, by traditional peasants and by urban intellectuals). They may diverge as to their intensity or their extent (Groethuysen, 1927). They may be backed by deeper or more superficial emotional and moral commitments to act them out; and they may be applied to a more or less extended area of beliefs, morals, and actual behavior.

The church may try different strategies for meeting these demands. Ultimately it is faced with a strategic dilemma between, on the one hand, adapting its offer to the demands of different groups and, on the other, articulating and shaping these very demands; thus it is the demands which, for better or worse, adapt to the offer. And, as it happens with so many organizations facing a market for their products, the church may very well opt for a situation of monopoly, thereby increasing its chances of shaping the population's religious demands. Hence the crucial problem of the church's relation to the state which alone can guarantee that monopoly position, putting at the church's disposal the state's own monopoly over the legitimate use of force.

From the start, the contrast between a monopolistic religious market and a competitive one (or a situation of religious pluralism; see Berger, 1971) could not be greater. In the case of a monopoly over the religious offer, the Spanish Catholic church has no rivals. There are no other cultural elites—Protestant clerics, Jewish rabbis, Muslim mullahs or ulemas, freethinking intellectuals, perhaps even atheists—with whom to compete for souls. These souls are reduced to being consumers of religious products (creeds, rites, institutions) the production of which is none of their concern. Strictly speaking, the church is not "offering" but imposing upon them beliefs and religious practices; its religious power implies in fact the use of temporal power to place sanctions on heterodox beliefs and practices, either directly or through an intermediary (usually the state). It offers these believers submission or humility as a value in itself, appealing to the servile or submissive instinct in people, as part of its messages of meaning, salvation, and community which are encoded in its teaching, its sacramental potency, and its central location within the community of saints. The margin for individual freedom is reduced to the acceptance of the religious product with a greater or lesser degree of fervor: the choice is whether to be an enthusiastic or a lukewarm Catholic. But it is not open to believers to reject the product or to substitute another, unless they are prepared to receive the corresponding sanctions, including temporal ones. This drastic reduction of individual freedom is justified because there can be no room for error or for sin, and because, mankind being weak and sinful, the roots of freedom are already corrupt.

This has been the ideal situation enjoyed, or sought, by the Catholic church throughout significant periods of history, almost all of which time it has relied on (or tried to rely on) an available or kindred temporal power. This ideal is clearly illustrated in the famous speech by the Grand Inquisitor in the parable by Dostoyevski, with a singular justification: if Jesus Christ had come to give or restore freedom among men, giving them the opportunity to choose his person and his message, the church, more realistically, would have understood that freedom was an excessive burden which many men do not want, and it would have offered them a pact whereby, in return for their submission, they would be secure and well governed and would have their needs satisfied (Dostoyevski, 1964, pt. 2 bk. 5, 5:204ff.). The Christian community is now a flock, led by its shepherds, through our earthly valley, toward the kingdom of heaven, protected from false shepherds and evil beasts.

However, this model has two drawbacks. It leaves the church open to pressure from both the temporal ruler and the political opposition to that ruler. In the first place, even if the church remains immune, to a certain extent, from the demands of many of its followers, it cannot claim the same immunity to pressure from the temporal power, on whose good will it depends, once the supreme ideal of a theocracy is demonstrated, for one reason or another, to be impractical. If it is not possible to consider the state as an instrument subordinate to the church, and if the relative autonomy of the two spheres is consolidated, it is essential to come to an agreement, negotiating and renegotiating with the temporal power, *do ut des,* for the purpose of receiving state support in exchange for services rendered: a contribution to the legitimacy of the state and its rulers and the habituation of its subjects to obedience; administrative services, policing, and control of social customs; exhortations for the defense of the nation or for the conquest of other nations; tolerance toward the morals of the court; resignation toward temporal interference in religious affairs and (increasingly) the exercise of exemplary moral functions by the state in accordance with the interests and motives of its rulers. All of these necessarily convert the church's monopoly on spiritual power into an imperfect one.

A second drawback is that the situation creates a bond between religious and temporal power which, in the long run, may be counterproductive, since the groups which oppose the incumbents of temporal power, given the support which the latter receive from the church, come to be defined (and define themselves) as enemies of the church as well. Thus the ground which is gained today may be lost tomorrow, and the greater the instability of a political regime or its political base, the greater the risk to the church.

This situation of religious monopoly supported by temporal power contrasts with that in which the church cannot, or has no wish to, shun the presence of other cultural elites in a more or less open competitive market of offers of meaning, salvation, and moral community, with or without religious referents in the strict sense. At times when the church could not rely on a well-disposed temporal power, and even sometimes when it could, strategies leading to the installment of a neutral temporal power, whether nondenominational or even of a different denomination, have been undertaken in order to keep the religious market open—at least open enough for the Catholic church to continue competing (proselytizing, educating, and so on) with other denominations. This situation differs drastically from the earlier one insofar as, in this case, the religious product cannot be offered independent of demand. As a limiting case we could posit a situation of "consumer supremacy" in which consumers were free to choose between alternative religions and other cultural offers and thus to condition, by means of their preferences, the form and content of religious messages in the short or long term.

At the same time, in any situation either of monopoly or of religious pluralism the church must decide how to design its institutional structure to allow for more or less lay participation in the government of the church and in the formation of the religious offer (in theological and moral argument, participation in rituals, co-direction of denominational associations, and so on). Obviously, the greater this participation is, the fainter the line becomes between ecclesiastics and laymen; and since this line seems to be a distinctive feature of the Catholic church, it is therefore to be expected that the participation of the faithful will not rise above a certain limit. Ideally, in the aforementioned model of the shepherd and his flock, the only participation required of the flock would be to bleat their acquiescence to the decisions of the shepherd and frolic in the meadows. But this relative passivity can lead to inattention in times of danger, for example, when the wolves attack. Then it would be preferable for some of the sheep to know how to defend themselves and, incidentally, their shepherd. In other words, there are circumstances which demand a response from believers, moving them to action against adverse temporal powers or competitive cultural elites. Their passivity, their inertia, or their lack of willpower then become a risk and could even be interpreted as acts of resistance to clerical influence, a kind of deliberate indifference, a rejection of the religious commitment, or a silent challenge to the moral authority of the church. It may then seem less dangerous to admit the right to a voice in ecclesiastical organization (although rebels may come forward who, in time, must be brought to heel or coopted) than to suppress all such mechanisms and then be faced by an obstinate wall of silent dissent, of followers who have lost their religious sensibility and turn a deaf ear to the anguished cries of their shepherds in danger.

Whether the situation is one of monopoly or one of religious pluralism, and whether more or less participation by laymen is allowed by the church's institutional structure, the church must nonetheless opt for either extending or reducing the area of beliefs, morals, and behavior affected by its religious messages and submitted to the church authority. This may range from a maximalist position in which all of human life is subjected to religion (combining a maximum of intensity with a maximum of extension of religious experience) to a minimalist position in which religion is reduced to regulating specific acts of external piety. As a matter of fact, for a very long time the Catholic church opted for a dual strategy according to which a minority of ecclesiastics and selected laymen received the vocation of a full religious life, while the majority of the faithful carried out the duties of their temporal state, with the addition of pious and ceremonial activities, under the supervision of that ecclesiastical minority, although in times of religious fervor the church tended to extend its area of influence over the laity, wrestling with the resistance of artisans, farmers, intellectuals, and others.

In summary, the great strategic dilemmas of the Catholic church which I have discussed apply to a situation of either religious monopoly or religious pluralism for any religious offer, thus leading to religious power sustained either by religious and temporal sanctions or by religious sanctions alone; the internal structure of the process of producing the religious offer, and the greater or lesser degree of participation by believers in the decision-making processes of the church; and the delimitation of the area, be it large or small, of the beliefs and behavior to which the offer applies, and thus the area of religious influence.

If we were operating in a vacuum, an ideal space, and we imagined a strategy to maximize returns of the resources and powers of the church while minimizing the risks, we could make three assumptions. First, that the church would tend toward achieving a monopoly situation, and thus recourse to temporal sanctions, claiming to have at least indirect *potestas* on the state, without forgetting that this carries the disadvantages of the cost of interference by the temporal powers in religious affairs and the risk of a hostile reaction toward the church on the part of those in the opposition who may one day take over. Second, that the church would tend to reduce to a minimum its followers' participation in its decision-making processes, although this might result in a lack of interest or even apathy among these followers, who may not rally to the defense of their shepherds and their faith at critical moments. And third, that the church would tend to extend to the maximum the area of beliefs and behavior to be affected by religion, although this would be limited by the interest of the church both in preserving the duality between church and followers, a differentiation partly justified by the differential extension of the area of religious life to be influenced by religious considerations, and in not exacerbating the resistance of the laity to the expansion of the church's influence.

Given the caveats which I have introduced into the strategy of maximization of returns and minimization of risks, it may be imagined that the church's decisions concerning these strategic dilemmas depend on the specific historical context in which the maximization strategy is to be carried out, and the likelihood and strength of resistance rooted in the religious demands of various social groups.

THE SPANISH CHURCH'S OPPOSITION TO MODERNITY

Given the premises just discussed, the initial feelings of intense opposition of the Catholic church toward the modern world are easily explained, together with the ambivalence which it has continued to feel right up to the present day, for the modern world signifies an end to the position of almost total cultural monopoly held by the church and the introduction of considerable competition in the field of religion.

The Catholic church of medieval times was a long way from being a monolith. It was differentiated by a multitude of schools, interests, and currents of opinion. But all these differences implied a fundamental creedal unity, and over all of them hovered the shadow of ecclesiastical authority (and, in principle, the ultimate threat of inquisitorial proceedings or their equivalent against consistent and recalcitrant believers in heterodoxy). Where earlier this church had been unique, modern times saw the introduction of a multitude of Protestant denominations and humanistic, scientific, philosophical, and literary circles, thereby eroding de jure or de facto ecclesiastical authority and the power of its threats, particularly since now the church was under the protection of temporal powers persuaded of the new ideas and either hostile to the power of the church or avid for its wealth. Under these conditions, after a running battle lasting for two centuries, often between opposing fanatics, tolerant regimes were established throughout almost all of Europe, and this meant a relatively open market for beliefs.

At the same time, the message of those new and very different ideologies generally coincided in proposing a radical devaluation of the importance of the church. The Protestant denominations tended to displace the church from the center of the arena of religious life to its outer edge. The importance of its teaching was weakened in favor of the value accorded a personal interpretation of God's Word, which, moreover, could be read by the believer himself in his own home. The power of the church to tie or untie, to administer divine grace, was denied or substantially curtailed. The center of the spiritual community shifted to the personal drama of a direct relation with Jesus Christ.

Similarly, the message of scientists and humanists or men of letters, and of secular humanism in general, consisted of a relative devaluation of the religious message, since they reconstructed the messages of meaning, salvation, and moral community with at best a weak connection to religious referents. Natural science could account for a world with a God who was either absent or reduced to his minimum expression. The emerging social sciences of economics and politics could account for their spheres of knowledge with only marginal reference to revelation or even morality; neither Adam Smith nor Machiavelli needed a church or divine message of any kind in order to explain their respective worlds. Furthermore, the hope of salvation or liberation from much human frustration and suffering became increasingly bound to the expectation of material and moral progress resulting from the growth of knowledge of nature and society and from individual or collective human action. This progress meant the certain though problematic advance toward achieving a community which would be prosperous, free, integrated, and just, of which the historical models, to the extent that they existed, were not the Christian societies of the past, with their traditional monarchies and economies that were either agrarian or dominated to some extent by the guilds, but, at least for some people and in some crucial aspects, resembled rather the pre-Christian classical societies, with their idealized models of the Greek city-state and the Roman republic.

This does not mean that in the construction of economics and politics as autonomous spheres of human life we cannot trace religious foundations. Weber pointed out the Calvinistic religious impulse underlying certain economic experiences (Weber, 1958); and an argument can be made about the importance of the congregations of saints for an understanding of the rise of modern representative institutions (Walzer, 1970), or of the religious leagues for an understanding of the emergence of political parties (Koenigsberger, 1955). But the issue is that once these institutions were established, the logic of their development came to minimize systematically the initial religious referent. In other words, the experience of how these institutions functioned and the nature of their place within a wider context led people to substitute them for their initial motivations and the meaning which these had given to their actions. This is what has been called the process of "secularization" in the largest sense, implying both institutional and cultural changes that take people and organizations away from the institutional authority of the church and weaken their religious referents.

Religious truth, interpreted by the church, was no longer the governing principle which gave meaning to the totality of experience; on the contrary, modernity meant a fragmentation of this experience into autonomous spheres, each with its own principles. In political life these were "reasons of state" or, later, the "general will"; in economic life the logic of the market and business profit; in intellectual life the search for truth based on natural reason and observation. This vindication of autonomy did not long remain in the terrain of principles but was institutionalized so that, little by little, the church began to lose its political power, its properties, and its control over education and the diffusion of ideas.

The final implication of this market situation in which the church had to compete with Protestant denominations and secularized currents of thought and practices was the recognition of the individual conscience as the final judge of one belief over another. Thus, what may be called the recognition of consumer supremacy arose in relation to the products on the market, whether symbolic, intellectual, or religious. That this recognition was not formal and explicit from the start of the process does not mean that it was not implicit, nor that it was not visible enough to the church, which possessed the lucidity born of a state of perpetual alertness common to institutions which are hypersensitive to their enemies.

We may come to the conclusion that, given the strategic orientation of the Catholic church, and given the characteristics of modernity just outlined, it is understandable that the church could not but be profoundly opposed to that kind of modernity. Modernity threatened its strategy: it substantially reduced the resources of the church and increased those of its opponents, in this way minimizing the probability of success of its strategy and multiplying its costs and risks. The market situation of religious pluralism, with the competition of so many powerful rivals, the tendency to reduce religion to a limited area of life, the dwindling importance of the ecclesiastical body, and the principle of freedom of conscience all forced the church to revise its historical trajectory. It could either revert to a model of evangelical simplicity, universal love, and ill-defined institutions, adopting what some considered to be its original message; or it could remain consistent with its structure and history and accept the challenge of modernity by opposing it in an attempt to mark out territory in which to maintain the ideal of a Christian society under the moral authority of the church, while at the same time learning from modernity about the best ways for implementing its defensive strategy and achieving its goals. This second option was the one that was put into practice, constituting that immense historical operation known as the Counter-Reformation.

The Counter-Reformation was an extraordinary dogmatic and moral rationalization of what was in fact an almost instinctive reaction on the part of the church to safeguard some territories over which an agreement with the temporal powers could be reached in order to ensure the monopoly of its religious and cultural offer, to maximize its sphere of influence, and to reinforce the subordination of believers. It achieved this to a considerable extent in its own pontifical states, in the kingdom of Castile and other territories belonging to the king of Spain, in the territories of the House of Hapsburg in general, including large segments of Italy, and with great difficulty in France, where it had to brave the consequences of a civil war and accede to the demands of royal power for almost three centuries.

Even so, this was not merely the perpetuation of times gone by. The Counter-Reformation meant an expansion of the religious sphere and an increase in its intensity. This trend toward expansion and intensification meant a growing presence of religion in the public and private areas of human life. The eucharistic play, the auto-da-fé, church imagery, baroque sculpture and painting, the missions, and popular preaching launched religion into the public arena. But at the same time, the new religious orders, with the Jesuits in the forefront, transmitted a kind of intimate, ordered, methodical religiosity which required discipline and the animation of the spirit, a reorientation of energies, and a rationalization of religious experience, above all among the noble estates and the middle class. To this was added the founding of seminaries, the insistence on teaching and control over social customs by the clerics, and the reorganization of the ecclesiastical structure, with increased emphasis on the parish as the basic organizational unit, on the presence of resident parish priests, and on the work of these priests in controlling their parishioners.

That extraordinary effort to articulate traditional religious values, beliefs, and institutions in a new environment came together with an attempt to differentiate the religious offer to meet the demands of diverse audiences. On the one hand, the church had to deal with a nobility and a middle class which had developed an interest in the economic, political, artistic, and intellectual innovations associated with modernity. Some degree of accommodation with these innovations had to be achieved if religion was to retain its plausibility for that new breed of *gentilhommes* and bourgeois. The new Jesuit order was set to explore to the limit that strategy of accommodation all over Europe, as it did following the same logic with regard to nonwestern cultures. The church, however, did try to keep the customs and beliefs of most ordinary people under tight control.

A study of certain regions of Castile, the Tierras de Curiel y de Peñafiel, between the sixteenth and eighteenth centuries gives an illustration of what this systematic effort by the ecclesiastical institution came to mean in the daily lives of peasants and rural dwellers (García Sanz, 1989; see also Domínguez Ortiz, 1973; and Pérez-Díaz, 1992a). It shows how the church absorbed a substantial portion of the agricultural production of the zone through tithes and other incomes; it was present in local politics; it filled the changing seasons with significance; it sanctified the rites of birth, marriage, and death and exorcised evil spirits; it dominated public life. It had the means to place sanctions on blasphemy, work on Sundays and holidays, extramarital sexual relations, the consumption of meat during Lent, the retention of tithes (nearly one third of the heavy fiscal burden peasants had to bear), singing and dancing by young people, and the failure to observe the precepts of annual confession and communion (to be marked in the appropriate registry books).

Nevertheless, this strategy of control met with some resistance. Nobles and councilors resisted any loss of control over local affairs. Peasants acquiesced but kept many of their own customs. Moreover, the ecclesiastical institution itself did not function properly. The bishops were continually admonishing priests not to carry arms, gamble, sing, dance, or attend bullfights; not to dress up or have commercial dealings; not to enter taverns or brothels nor to live in public concubinage—admonitions whose emphasis and reiteration suggest a priesthood whose flesh was weak and whose moral authority was only modest. However, the program of reform (or counter-reform) was in no way invalidated as a result. Quite the opposite. Everything, the church thought, would resolve itself in time with improvements in the ecclesiastical organization, more visits by bishops and archdeacons, better seminaries, more theological and moral formation, more popular missions, greater vigilance over social customs, and more catechism.

Naturally the Catholic church could not easily renounce this state of affairs and its program for the betterment of the world. And thus, in those countries which remained Catholic after the religious wars of the sixteenth and seventeenth centuries, the struggle of the Catholic church against modernity continued—against capitalism, the modern state, and later against liberal democracy and secular culture—for all these institutions implied a curtailment of the church's power, a reduction of its influence, and competition for its souls.

This long struggle between church and modernity has meant a slow though dramatic process of apprenticeship and adaptation on the part of the church: slow because it has been only in the last fifty years or so that the church has made its peace with that world, and only in the Second Vatican Council has it officially recognized this; and dramatic because it has caused extraordinary tensions resulting in periodic explosions of antireligiosity, anti-Catholicism, and anticlericalism, even if these explosions have become less violent over time with the reduction of the church's hostility to the modern world (and vice versa, but that is another story), in such a way that to some extent it is now possible to talk about not just an adaptation of the church to the modern world but a reciprocal adaptation.

From the point of view of analyzing the adaptive mechanisms of Catholicism and the modern world, the case of Spain since the civil war constitutes a piece of historical evidence of singular interest. This is because the Nationalist victory led to a systematic attempt to realize the ideals of the Counter-Reformation at the height of the twentieth century, including the establishment of a state religion and the total conversion of society to Catholicism. In only two generations we have witnessed the failure of this historic project, the conversion of Spain into a "modern" nation, and a reconciliation of the church to its new circumstances. During this time the mutation of the Spanish Catholic church has been extraordinary. It is as if we had been watching a play in several acts, complete with changes of scenery, of plot, and of the personality of the characters, and even of the emotional tone—furious in the thirties, exalted in the forties and fifties, troubled and inquiring in the sixties, moderately euphoric throughout the seventies, and discreet, showing a sense of both satisfaction and disillusion since the eighties.

In the 1930s the church was an actor in the civil war. It saw itself as martyr and militant, as the protagonist of the crusade pitting one half of Spain against the other, in which the middle classes were divided, the peasants were divided, and the workers were apparently "de-Christianized" (although perhaps the belligerence of the leaders and officials of political and labor union organizations should be understood in the context of the indifference to, or respect for, religion, if not the church, felt by a large part of their rank and file).

In the 1940s and 1950s the church was the "church triumphant." Its alliance with the temporal powers appeared stable. By delegation it wielded state authority in matters of education and the regulation and supervision of morals through the adaptation of legislation to ecclesiastical doctrines, preferential treatment for educational institutions belonging to the church, institutionalized mechanisms for the exercise of power and influence on the part of the church in public affairs, and ecclesiastical censorship of entertainment. In other words, a species of moral and cultural mesogovernment (see Chapter 4) had been created whereby the church was empowered with state authority in educational and other matters. To this was added its extraordinary influence and control over the public and private spheres of society.

From the mid-1950s and throughout the 1960s we witness an erosion of the earlier equilibrium and of the confidence of the church in itself. It could not withstand the problems it had with intellectuals, workers, capitalism, regionalism, political power, and mass morality. During these years a countercurrent emerged within the Spanish church which questioned the solutions of the church triumphant and which received a decisive impetus from the Second Vatican Council. These were critical years, full of doubts, internal divisions, and conflicting hopes.

Throughout the 1970s the internal conflict drew to a close and the consequent change of alliances took place; the distance from authoritarian power increased; and an understanding with a new political class, a liberal democratic regime, and a nondenominational state grew. These were years of moderate euphoria because this extremely delicate operation was successful and because the church was reliving an experience of co-protagonism in the events of the transition to democracy.

Since the 1980s the church has been taking stock of its situation. It has been reduced to just another pressure group, obliged to come to terms with laws of which it only partly approves or of which it completely disapproves, with limited influence over the political classes, and, what is even more surprising, with a variable influence, tending toward the precarious, over civil society. The church has become aware of a phenomenon which had been gathering momentum for over twenty years: the daily life of the masses has slowly been slipping out of its sphere of influence.

THE CIVIL WAR: ITS RELIGIOUS DIMENSION
AND ITS HISTORICAL BACKGROUND

The one hundred years which stretch from the end of the Napoleonic wars to the 1930s can be understood as a long drawn-out struggle between the Catholic church and the liberal regime in search of a modus vivendi. The point of departure was one of profound reciprocal ambivalence. The Spanish ecclesiastical body did not openly oppose the fall of the ancien régime; in this they were indecisive and prudent, as was common among the enlightened European clergy of the eighteenth century. But the experience of the French Revolution and the Napoleonic era convinced the church of the convenience of an alliance between the throne and the altar which would hold in check the tide of liberalism which seemed bent on creating a nondenominational state with religious freedom and a considerable reduction in the wealth and power of the church (Artola, 1959). Later it became clear that the legitimists, or Carlists, had no historical future. Their influence would reach no further than precarious control over marginal areas of European society, such as the Basque region between 1833 and 1840 and between 1872 and 1876. Thus, the church was obliged to come to an understanding with "lesser evils": doctrinaire liberalism, "moderantism," and the Cánovas restoration.

The objective of these tactical understandings from the point of view of the church always centered on limiting the freedom of other beliefs and obtaining from the state a commitment of support or preferential treatment for the church (subsidies, tax exemptions, support of church education, laws compatible with ecclesiastical doctrine on questions of morals and social customs, and so on). In exchange, the church renounced any active or consistent support for enemies of the regime, lent it an air of legitimacy, and concurred in habituating the masses to acquiescence under the established order. This understanding was achieved only after numerous confrontations, including the expropriation of ecclesiastical lands and possessions, the expulsion of religious orders, disputes between science and religion, school wars, and so on, accompanied in Spain and elsewhere by the burning of churches and convents, the murder of priests, and other atrocities and sacrilegious acts.

Tactical understandings and a gradual approach toward a modus vivendi continued to take place between bourgeois society and the Catholic church, in spite of anticlerical offensives and hard-line Catholicism. They were fostered by the positions taken by popes such as Leo XIII on political *ralliement* and social affairs, which led to the two currents of liberal Catholicism and social Catholicism, which were influential in various parts of Europe, though not in Spain until much later (Laboa, 1985; Payne, 1984).

The cataclysms in Europe resulting from the Great War and the period of revolution and counterrevolution in the 1920s and early 1930s were additional cause for a profound disturbance in the already unstable relations between the church and the modern world. The rivalry of the church with the liberal order seemed to pale before the onslaught of the socialist and extreme nationalist movements which surfaced as the leading figures of the new situation. The church in the thirties and forties found itself in the middle of a triangle of adversaries, caught between liberals, fascists, and anarchists, socialists, and communists (to the extent that we can consider those three branches of the original tree of the Socialist International as one), and it had to choose one on which to depend, trusting that its adversaries detested one another more than they detested the church. The situation, of course, was not uniform throughout Europe; it was very different in France and Italy, on the one hand, and in Spain, on the other.

In France and Italy to a large extent the church had overseen with a spirit of sympathy and understanding the emergence of an authoritarian corporative regime and the marginalization of liberals and socialists or anarchists. But the outcome of the Second World War, the ultimate national defeats, and the German occupation which both countries had experienced, in very different ways, meant, at a given moment, the crucial experience of the involvement of a substantial part of the church and many Catholics in movements of resistance. These experiences legitimized their ultimate intervention as co-protagonists in the liberal democracies which were set up in these countries at the end of the war. The shared experience of risks and sacrifices in the name of national independence and the creation of a liberal democracy (with the addition, or otherwise, of social and economic reforms of a populist nature) was to cement together the moral community of socialists, liberals, and Catholics in these countries, the results of which were to underlie and limit partisan tensions in the postwar period. This, in turn, would make possible the strategic alliance of social democrats and Christian democrats on the subject of national reconstruction, the welfare state, and the construction of a united Europe.

However, if the experience of resisting German invasion or German occupation was crucial to the churches of Italy and France in the thirties, the crucial experience of the Spanish church was very different. The latter found itself in the middle of a civil war, confronted by a republican-socialist coalition in parliament and socialist and anarchist masses in the streets, and so made common cause with the military, conservatives, and fascists united in the political project of an authoritarian corporative regime.

The religious problem in Spain in the thirties was highly charged owing to two circumstances: first, the extreme attitude taken by the people of that period toward the problem, in part the inheritance of a tradition of highly dramatic conflicts; and second, the combination of this with other serious political, social, and economic problems which occurred at the same time, and in such a way that the church and religion were to be found at the center of an intense argument over the consolidation of the political regime and social reform. Both factors turned a difficult religious problem into an insoluble one.

It is not credible that in the thirties Spanish civil society had ceased to be Catholic (in spite of the much-quoted and rather confused statements of Manuel Azaña on the matter).[3] Few Spaniards were not baptized, and, during the Republic, there were few civil marriages, few divorces, and few burials of a civil nature. Probably the majority of Spaniards felt vaguely Catholic sentiments, although their attitude toward the church and the priesthood was, in many cases, indifferent or ambivalent. But although the majority may have been Catholic within these limitations, the fact is that the Republic placed a liberal political sector and some intensely anticlerical socialist and anarchist organizations at the center of the political stage (Ramírez, 1969). This anticlericalism was the legacy of several factors: the anticlericalism of the liberals and progressives of the previous century, who resented the "moderate compromise" between church and state; the reactions by many intellectuals and some segments of the middle class against the agreements between the church and the Cánovas regime, and against the Catholic revival at the end of the century (which was a consequence of the flow of French religious orders to Spain following French anticlerical legislation, and of the dynamism of organizations such as the Jesuits); and the annoyance and distrust aroused among many politicians by the collaboration of Catholic institutions with the dictatorship of Primo de Rivera. Furthermore, the anticlericalism of the 1930s was heir to a tradition of popular anticlericalism with a bloody history dating from 1834–35 and from the *semana trágica,* the "tragic week" of 1909 (Payne, 1984; Ullmann, 1968).

The anticlerical offensive of the Republic left the church and Catholic believers disconcerted, as they had adopted a reticent, wait-and-see attitude toward the new regime. They soon felt obliged to defend their institutions and their beliefs. Constitutional compromise was not possible (Gunther and Blough, 1981). The expulsion of the Jesuits and the limits imposed on other religious orders and on public manifestations of the cult and Catholic teaching displayed an unequivocally hostile attitude; these and the burning of churches and convents almost within a month of the Republic's being declared were an indication of the intention of some not merely to limit the church but to destroy it, relying on the deliberate passivity of the government (as was demonstrated by the negative attitude of Azaña and the Socialist ministers to the demands of Miguel Maura to use the forces of law and order; see Maura, 1966, pp. 249ff.).

The church reacted to all this by mobilizing the masses of peasants and the middle classes and channeling them into professional and political right-wing organizations, prepared for by decades of careful organizational work (Castillo, 1979; Montero, 1986). The extreme right soon took upon itself the task of conspiring to overthrow the regime. The moderate right refused to state its unambiguous loyalty to the new institutions and openly flirted with authoritarianism. Meanwhile, faced with the relative success of the moderate right in the elections and their eventual accession to power, part of the left wing reacted with a social revolution in 1934, which, although it failed in only a few weeks, was not without its share of bloodletting, accompanied by the burning of churches and other rituals of desecration of religious symbols.

This history of quarrels, radicalism, and violence erupted, as we know, into a three-year civil war which involved all sectors of the population. At the rural level the peasants from the northern *meseta* with smallholdings or medium-sized farms confronted the anarchist and socialist masses of peasant smallholders and landless laborers of southern Spain. The middle classes of liberal or anticlerical sentiment were opposed by other sectors of the same classes with moderate or conservative leanings, who, with varying degrees of enthusiasm, made the cause of the defense of religion their own. As for the leaders and officials of the workers' organizations, the majority were antireligious and anticlerical, although it is doubtful that those feelings were shared by the mass of workers. Once the war had begun, a leader such as Andrés Nin could boast of having resolved the problem of the church "by getting to the roots": "We have suppressed its priests, the churches, and the Cult"; and *Solidaridad Obrera* (an anarchist paper) could also call for "the church to be torn out by the roots . . . we must seize all their possessions . . . the religious orders must be dissolved . . . the bishops and cardinals must be shot" (Ruiz Rico, 1977, pp. 22–23). *El Socialista* had already declared that progressive man, "more than anticlerical, has to be antireligious . . . [and that] socialism is incompatible with Catholicism or any other religion" (Gunther and Blough, 1981).

Unequivocal testimony of the extent and intensity of anticlerical and antireligious feeling in a large part of the country was offered by the murder of almost seven thousand priests and members of religious orders during the first months of the war in the Republican zone: 4,185 members of the diocesan clergy (almost one priest out of every seven) and 2,648 in orders. In some areas the majority of the diocesan clergy were executed, as in Barbastro (88 percent), Lérida (66 percent), and the city of Tortosa (62 percent), or nearly so, as in the provinces of Ciudad Real (40 percent) and Toledo (48 percent) (Payne, 1984, p. 214). All of this violence occurred with no other justification or excuse than that of a collective act of cowardice and barbarity, just as, in their time, the murders of the clergy in the uprisings of the nineteenth century had been precipitated by rumors of the poisoning of public wells. This also corresponded on the Francoist side to the bloody reprisals and systematic repression carried out by groups behind the lines, invoking motives of spiritual reconquest and identifying Spain, Catholicism, military revolt, and authoritarianism as one and the same.

This crucial experience of being part and victim of a massive blood-bath was decisive in shaping the mentality of those who lived through those years, especially that of adolescents and young adults who were later to attain positions of authority within the church and the state in the decades that followed. For the church in the Republican zone, the experience had been one of unremitting persecution: brutal from the first moment, endless, and then, when tempers had cooled, toned down by the Republican government's need to improve its image in the eyes of world opinion (Payne, 1984, p. 215; Ruiz Rico, 1977, pp. 59–62). The experience on the Nationalist side was completely different. It was the apotheosis of the crusading spirit, to some extent deliberately encouraged by the leaders of the insurrection, but also an expression of genuine feeling among broad sectors of the population. Many young people from the peasant or middle classes were infected with a patriotic religious fervor which, according to the individual, either concealed or gave meaning to the dangers of battle. With the odd exception, the position of the bishops was unequivocal. Although their famous collective letter of 1937 made no actual mention of the word *crusade*, there can be no doubt about what they felt their position to be. The church gave its wholehearted support to the military revolt, both morally and, except for some initial caution, diplomatically. Time and again it referred to the revolt in terms of a religious war and to a defense of the Catholic religion (Ruiz Rico, 1977, pp. 45–59). And what the high clergy stated, at times permitting themselves the luxury of some mental reservation for the benefit of future historians, the lower orders shouted loud and clear. As a result, both factions activated powerful memories of the intervention of the clergy in feats of arms throughout Spanish history: the Reconquest; the religious wars in Europe; the fight against the infidel and the violent repression of internal heterodoxy; and, more recently, the familiar figure of the guerrilla priests struggling against Napoleon, and the priests of the apostolic factions of the 1820s and of the Carlist factions of the 1830s and 1870s.

THE CATHOLIC CHURCH TRIUMPHANT

The designation "church triumphant" can be applied to the Catholic church during the period of its alliance with the government of General Franco, when the ideals of a state religion and the total conversion of society to Catholicism were flourishing. The church was not to renounce these ideals until it had assimilated the lessons of the Second Vatican Council during the late nineteen sixties. This period originates with the beginning of the war in the Nationalist zone, thus spanning, in the broadest sense, almost thirty years. However, two phases must be distinguished: in the first, continuing until the mid-fifties, there was almost complete unanimity within the church as to the strategy of alliance with the powers that were (a phase I discuss in this section); and in the second discrepancies occurred with the appearance of countercurrents of thought that prepared the way for a profound alteration in the relations between the church and temporal power (a phase I shall cover later in this chapter).

I must insist that only by understanding the tragedy of the civil war and the contrast between the experiences of the church in the Republican and in the Nationalist zones is it possible to understand the decades that followed. The church, martyr and militant, persecuted to the death and fighting to the death, was now the church triumphant. The feelings, shameful but genuine, of fear, hate, terror, and indignation which had metamorphosed into the fighting spirit of crusade during the war could afterward convert themselves into expressions of pride and remain associated with the definitive triumph of the Cross. In order for this metamorphosis of feeling to be possible, it was necessary for the memories of martyrdom and crusade to be perpetuated, protected, and exalted in collective memory. With this object in mind, thousands of monuments evocative of a cult of "the dead for God and for Spain" were built all over the country, anywhere near, or forming part of, church buildings, thus associating suffering and torment with triumph and religion with nation (in much the same way that, after the First World War, monuments to the dead soldiers in the squares of French and German villages became reminders of that war and of nationalistic sentiment; see Mosse, 1975). Together with the monuments came the rituals and then the succession of myths and legends. Parades, processions, panoplied entrances, dedications to the Sacred Heart and to the Virgin, protestations of Catholic faith and obedience to the pope were the occasions for thousands of ceremonies associating the church with the state, united, directly or indirectly, by the bloody experiences of the war.

The church at that time was deeply united (with the noteworthy exception of a segment of the Basque clergy) in the saintly spirit of what might be called Christian vengeance, a vengeance which consisted of piously converting those condemned to death on the way to their execution, comforting those in prison, and dedicating its energies to eradicating the seeds of the diabolical enemy from both the state and society (Laboa, 1985, pp. 142–143).[4] It was united not only in its feelings but also in its plan of action, which Cardinal Gomá summarized in these words: "Leaders! Unfurl the sails of Catholicism . . . ! Let there be no law, no chair, no institution, no newspaper beyond or against God and His Church in Spain!" (Laboa, 1985, p. 144).

From the civil war and the historical events leading up to it, the Spanish church had learned a number of lessons, some relating to the state and others relating to civil society. With respect to the state, the lesson seemed clear. In the long term, tactical understanding with the liberal state had brought catastrophic consequences. The intransigent distrust and reticence of the Spanish Catholic church toward liberalism had been confirmed and aggravated by the Republican experience. A "lesser evil" was not good enough. The church's political goal had to be full realization of the ideal: a denominational state fully consistent with the church in its structure, its legislation, and its civil servants, subordinate to it in at least some areas, and providing the resources for the church to carry out its objectives.

The new Spanish state was denominational almost from the first moment (after some initial indecision), and it remained so, it could be said, ad nauseam. Its basic laws and ordinary legislation were overflowing with declarations to this effect. The speeches and the signs of identity of its leaders, the public rituals, the affirmations of ecclesiastics and their presence in state offices emphasized it: from modest chaplains in the Fascist unions or the Frente de Juventudes (Youth Front) to members of the Councils of the Realm, of the regency, of the state, of the Falange, and of parliament. The state repressed, harassed, ostracized, excluded from teaching posts, or censored, depending on individual cases or situations, Protestants, Freemasons, freethinkers, non-Catholics, Marxists, anarchists, and so on, which is to say practically all the imaginable rivals of the clergy. The new state promised that its legislation would correspond to Catholic norms; not only did it keep its promise, but it also ceded jurisdiction over the matrimonial separation of Catholics to the ecclesiastical tribunals. Furthermore, it decided that the church could exercise control of and surveillance over moral and religious teaching in all types of educational establishments, state or otherwise, as well as appoint the teachers of these subjects in state schools and run their own teaching establishments (almost half of all the centers of secondary education in the country). Likewise, the state permitted the church to censor artistic and literary works and to maintain its own newspaper network, amounting to almost one fifth of all newspaper circulation in 1956, and other publications, amounting to nearly 70 percent of all publications in the country around 1957 (Hermet, 1985, pp. 195ff.). What this meant was the creation of a moral and cultural mesogovernment in the hands of the church, which could share in the decision making and execution of policies on moral education and the control of social customs, backed up by an explicit legal framework, and relying on its endorsement by state authority.

Finally, the state also contributed all sorts of material resources to the church, and with great generosity. This was a subject of vital importance, since the brief experience of the Republic had taught the ecclesiastical dignitaries a lesson in the unpredictability of relying on civil society for taking care of the church's finances (Payne, 1984, pp. 201–202). The subsidies from the Francoist state were substantial: in the early 1970s they were calculated on the order of 5 billion pesetas a year, the equivalent of a medium-sized ministerial budget (Hermet, 1985, p. 26). But the state did not limit itself to subsidies (through endowments for the normal functioning and personal expenses of the diocesan clergy, wages and salaries of ecclesiastical personnel employed in the public administration, or subsidies to church-run education); it also added tax exemptions and direct investment or investment aid in the construction or reconstruction of religious buildings.

Naturally, although approaching the ideal, the Spanish state was not "perfect"; perfection would perhaps have required the state's total subordination to the church. The result was that causes for discontent remained, some far from negligible, and they were to flourish in the future. The church, for example, had to come to an understanding, at times difficult and inconvenient, with one of the key elements of the regime, the Falangist party, which had grown from 36,000 to 362,000 members between 1936 and 1938, stabilizing at a little less than 1 million affiliates around 1942 (Hermet, 1985, p. 273). The Falange played a very important political role in the first years of the regime and pressed for the creation of a strong and relatively secularized state. The church had to accept the absorption of the Catholic agricultural unions, the Catholic student federations, and other Catholic unions in general into the Falangist apparatus, just as it had previously had to accept the disappearance of its own Catholic political parties. At times it was necessary for the church to fight against state censorship; and it had to make a concerted effort, when the time came, to protect the specialized branches of Catholic Action. It was never satisfied with the regulation of university education and the de facto limitations on aid to and development of universities belonging to the church. In general, it always viewed with misgivings the totalitarian cries of Falangism, which rang in its ears like the weak but recognizable echo of German Nazism. The tensions between the church and the Falange, although contained within limits and balanced by numerous points of agreement, were never superficial. In fact, tensions between the Falangist and Catholic youth movements were endemic throughout the Francoist period. And it is worth our while to consider as variations of the same the tensions existing between Falangists and the Opus Dei movement in the 1960s and 1970s, which resulted in the split within the Francoist political class in its final stage. This tension even came to affect decisively the structuring capacity of parties of the center right during the transition to and the consolidation of democracy, for it is possible to find traces of the old enmities in the mutual distrust existing between the *azules* (the Falangist blueshirts) and Christian democrats of the defunct UCD (Union for a Democratic Center).

On the whole these tensions were at the time of only secondary importance. The fact is that for decades, owing to the Francoist state, the church enjoyed the full benefit of privileges which, in the context of the age, were exorbitant, although distinguished prelates overly eager to emphasize today their distance from a regime which has retrospectively been converted into *non sancto* have tried to minimize the contribution of the state to the fulfillment of the desires of the church.[5]

However, it was not enough for the church that the state should be denominational. This had to include the total conversion to Catholicism of the state's leaders as well as the historic project of a complete conversion of society in all its aspects: political, economic, and cultural. The church provided the state with a supply of political families. Between the mid-forties and mid-fifties the members of the Asociación Católica Nacional de Propagandistas (National Catholic Association of Propagandists) controlled key sectors of the government, and from the mid-fifties members of Opus Dei took over. Even so, this was only the most visible area of a wide network of associations for the formation of political leaders and of forums for debate. The church also tried to widen its influence in the economic sphere, although here it had to limit itself to little more than rhetorical declarations. In reality, economic space was dominated by the logic of the market and state intervention, both of which operated according to their own principles. This was recognized as compatible with the doctrine of the church, although its ideals would have been oriented toward some form of social corporatism, apparently not very feasible. The church had little to say about the economy other than some mental reservations and high-flown statements about the redistribution of wealth, the relief of poverty, and the vague advocacy of minor reforms. Nevertheless, this did not mean that Catholics as such could not set about the task of promoting economic growth and, incidentally, acquiring wealth for themselves. The fact is that the sanctification of these enrichment operations was to be a distinctive characteristic, at the beginning, of one of the most important Catholic associations of the day, the Opus Dei. Finally, occupying cultural or intellectual space meant excluding all the cultural rivals of earlier times. As we have seen, this was the purpose of the church's cultural mesogovernment, although it did have its limits. Beyond these limits were to be found technical and professional knowledge, and the sphere of university education, over which the control and surveillance of the church was usually reduced, intermittent, and, even then, relatively lax.

To all this was added the occupation of the people's interior or inner sphere, the zone of private conduct and conscience. In this respect what characterized the church at that time was its totalizing impulse; it wanted to embrace all aspects of life, body and soul, and for this, purposive coercion was not sufficient. It required persuasion as well; but this was applied in different ways in different parts of civil society. Simplifying that society, we can distinguish two worlds: that of the middle classes, source of the "select minorities," and that of the subordinate classes, or those normally destined to occupy subordinate positions in political, economic, or cultural organizations of all kinds. Initially the church preferred to address itself to the middle classes.

The efforts of the church to Catholicize the Spanish middle classes had begun much earlier. Throughout the nineteenth century the church had let large segments of them slip through its grasp. Curiously enough, even if Spanish liberal Catholicism had lost its doctrinal battle to the hard-liners or traditionalists (Laboa, 1985), to a large extent it won the contest in daily life. Spanish Catholics could be Catholic in church and perhaps in the home, but they did not feel subordinate to the will of the church in the public sphere, that is, in most political, economic, social, or cultural matters. They applied the liberal principle of the relative autonomy of different spheres of life. They thought the reduction of the influence of the church to questions of faith, cult, and social customs to be for the best. The clergy responded with pain and indignation to this systematic strategy of Spanish Catholics, which it branded as inconsistent, unenthusiastic, and full of concessions to the modern world; and, in compensation, the church tried to recoup its losses through its influence on women and young people, whom it wished to turn into fervent Catholics.

From this arose the educational and organizational efforts, and the effort to control the media, of the Jesuits and other orders between 1880 and 1930. But they always thought that they had begun late, and that their adversaries, the Institución Libre de Enseñanza, the '98 generation, Ortega, Unamuno, other *maîtres à penser,* and other institutions, had achieved a cultural influence which outstripped their own.

After victory in the civil war, the ecclesiastics thought that the moment had come to intensify their attempts to control these middle classes, with the help of the new state, through control of secondary education and the creation of a network of parallel or complementary organizations for the guidance of adolescents and young people. Organizations such as the Jesuits or Opus Dei, each one with its own style, responded to this need for the total conversion of "select minorities" originating in the middle classes, in whom they saw the leaders of the next generation. They tried to reach young people, who combined intense religious experience with the aim of carrying out God's will on earth and rebuilding the world according to the criteria of the Catholic faith and morality. They did not want indifferent, lukewarm Catholics. They wanted those who would commit themselves and their lives totally to the ideal of Catholicism, whose morality would call for surrendering themselves to a vocation of combat, and whose attitude toward the world would be one of permanent struggle against it. But if the world was there to be conquered, they had to live in a state of constant vigilance because the war had to be won again and again. Their mold must be heroic, their rhetoric one of conquest, their style almost military. Self-control, discipline, heroism, and asceticism: such were to be the moral and emotional keys to their behavior.

From this we can see the importance which sexual morality was to have in the formation of such people. The ethos of self-control was inseparable from efforts toward the systematic rationalization of religious conduct. However, the motivational structure of the insistence of the clergy on sexual themes, with the consequent appearance of an obsessive sexual climate around the Sixth Commandment, was somewhat more complex. This is because to the systematic rationalization of conduct were added three other, rather different motives which were not wholly consistent with it. The first was to follow a code of decorum fitting for those who aspired (or should aspire) to leadership, each according to his ability, among professionals, bureaucrats, and businessmen, which is to say, according to each prevailing code of ethics. The second was to follow the generic norms of protecting monogamous, heterosexual family relations, which, however, had always been compatible with wide margins of permissiveness for men in Catholic societies. Above all, the third called for building a psychological structure which would combine the hostility against the world felt by these young people with their subordination to men of the church, for if the young people repressed their sexual impulses, they did so by nourishing a certain aggression against the flesh, temptation, permissiveness, worldly ways, and the world itself. Thus, if they overcame temptation, they became soldiers of the faith; but if, being weak, they succumbed, they were therefore guilty and in a position of psychological dependence, needing the absolution which only an ecclesiastic could give them. The repressive treatment of sexuality therefore caused a substantial number of these apparently privileged and high-powered members of the middle classes to live psychologically and morally in alternating states of grace and sin, of ecstasy and depression, thus demanding the delicate intervention of the Catholic priest, who, with his experience of confession and spiritual direction, could soften the transitions between one state and another, admonish and console, reduce the feelings of incoherence, and set the bearings of each individual soul.

As for the subordinate classes, the church had to differentiate between the peasants, who had supported the Nationalist movement, and the urban working classes and farm laborers of the south, who had opposed it. The church could capitalize on its long dedication to the large numbers of peasant farmers and smallholders in the northern half of the country and use them as a breeding ground for religious vocations. The task of reconverting the working classes to Christianity, however, promised to be rather more difficult. The first goal, in any case, was to exclude any organizations which could claim the moral leadership of these classes: anarchists, socialists, communists. The only remaining competition came from the Falangist party. Incapable of preventing the formation of vertical unions controlled by the Falange and the absorption into them of its Catholic unions, the church tried to establish at least some safeguards and guarantees for Catholic labor organizations, particularly the specialized branches of Catholic Action. But, in the final analysis, it would be impossible to win over the souls of the people if the church's messages of an intellectual nature were not accompanied by moral and emotional messages of salvation and community attuned to the experiences of the people.

The Spain of that period was a country destroyed and impoverished by war, marked by scarcity and hunger, trying to find its bearings in the midst of autarky, arbitrary and not very competent state *dirigisme,* and the black market, with the bleakest of economic prospects. There was none of the economic development or mass consumption that would come later. It was a country of "limited goods" (Foster, 1967), which is to say, of reduced aspirations and expectations. In a world of backward villages and provincial capitals—including, of course, Madrid, where the struggle to survive imposed an oppressive, some-what coarse life-style of limited scope—it could be expected that many people would try to make sense of their lives by upholding values of self-sacrifice, renunciation, austerity, and respect for hierarchies and patron-client networks such as those proposed by the ecclesiastics.

In addition to that, the church also offered some messages of com-munity which were quite appropriate to the situation. Spain in the forties and fifties still felt the recent memory of a civil war which had caused almost half a million deaths and at least as many exiles. It had been an immense moral and emotional trauma for the country. Spain, a nation of survivors surrounded by memories of the dead, was at the time, and to a certain extent, also a nation of fratricides. Consciously or not, the country was having to live with feelings of horror and guilt—which helps explain the peace of the ensuing years, including during the transition to democracy forty years later.

The church could offer some consolation for this experience and these feelings of guilt, in part because suffering was inevitable, since the earth was, after all, a vale of tears, but also in part because it could compensate to some extent for the memory of the community that was destroyed with the hope of creating a new moral community here on earth. As the counterpart to the broken society of the thirties, the church proposed a community reconciled. On the one hand, it offered the defeated a way out of their humiliation and resentment; and on the other, it offered the victors, stained with blood, the opportunity of redeeming themselves by adopting the historic project of a new national moral community: a hierarchical community in which the select minorities and wholly Catholic middle classes would exercise a leadership of responsibility and concern for the moral and material well-being of the subordinate classes.

In fact, as we shall see, the efforts of the church, through its institutions, its practices, and its messages, were well, if not totally, rewarded by success. The presence of the church and religion in the public and private spheres was overwhelming. It was a presence to be found in buildings, the professions, large public meetings, flowers, music, and banners; all that was missing were the autos-da-fé and an ethnic expulsion to repeat, with all the resources of the twentieth century, the spectacle of the baroque Catholicism of the sixteenth and seventeenth centuries. The performance of the seasonal sacraments became universal, and attendance at Sunday Mass increased enormously, showing a decline only once more, toward the beginning of the 1960s (Hermet, 1985, pp. 68ff.). The conversion to Catholicism of the masses, and equally of all the social classes in the country, was carried out during those years, and not only in its external aspects. The fact is, since the spread of opinion surveys in the late seventies, it seems that all the social strata of the country, including urban workers, have declared themselves to be Catholics by an immense majority, the differences in percentages across the classes being relatively small and the declarations of orthodoxy being equally large (until more recent times) and fairly uniform (Fundación Foessa, 1981, p. 435). This means that if it was no longer possible to talk about a Catholic middle class and the de-Christianized masses (as could be done with some accuracy in the thirties), this was due to a process of conversion to

Catholicism during the intervening years, a process in keeping not only with the pressure from temporal powers and the social climate but also with the massive efforts to catechize which took place at that time in a context free from competition with other religious creeds and ideologies.

THE RETREAT FROM "NATIONAL CATHOLICISM"

The problem now consists of explaining how and why such a state of affairs could become transformed during these years and especially how and why one sector of the church played a decisive part in this transformation. The explanation must contain, in essence, an understanding of the motives and mechanisms by which members of the church themselves drew away from the ideal of a denominational state and the project of a Catholic conversion of the whole of Spain, which they were later to refer to disparagingly as "national Catholicism," in an oblique attempt to degrade and taint the phenomenon by association with "national syndicalism" and "national socialism" (Alvarez Bolado, 1981, p. 231).[6]

In order to understand the process of transformation of the 1950s and 1960s it is first necessary to understand the conditions permitting the perpetuation of this state of religious-ecclesiastical affairs in the 1940s and early 1950s, in other words, to understand the structure of plausibility (Berger, 1971) of that national Catholicism, and thus the conditions underlying its relative success.

The gravity of the attack suffered by the church in the 1930s allows us to understand the general thrust of its response and the intensity of the feelings associated with it. Even so, neither the thrust nor the intensity can explain its specific content. For this we have to look into the cultural premises that shaped that response. These refer us to an earlier historic or societal project which was an expression of the ideals to which a majority of the Spanish church had aspired for at least half a century prior to the civil war. These consisted of the creation of a denominational state and the dream of a total conversion of Spanish society to Catholicism. These ideals were stated again and again in the seminaries, in Catholic circles, and in Catholic publications by the bishops, preachers, and the most influential religious orders, with the Jesuits at their head—conservative, traditionalist, and absolutist ideals which were stimulated by the difficulties and frustrations of achieving any tactical understanding between the church and the liberal regime, and by the recurring waves of anticlerical propaganda. This mentality dominated the Spanish ecclesiastical milieu to the extent that, as I mentioned earlier, the modernist wave which swept Europe at the turn of the century passed unnoticed in Spain (Laboa, 1985, pp. 95ff.; Payne, 1984, p. 160; González de Cardedal, 1985, p. 243).

In spite of this, neither the thrust and intensity nor the content of the response can explain how this project was actually carried out and how the church was able to maintain such a course over a long period of time. For this to be possible it was necessary for an environment to exist in which external pressures were extremely weak, almost a historical vacuum, so as to allow the church to give free rein to its plans for spiritual conquest. This, in turn, required the simultaneous occurrence of three factors: a relative isolation of the Spanish church with respect to the universal church (which, because of its global responsibilities, could exercise a restraining influence on the Spanish ecclesiastics); a state which needed the church at least as much as if not more than the church needed the state; and a civil society without the strength to resist the combined efforts of church and state.

The presence of the universal church in the domestic arena was weak at that time because it was trying to survive a world war, searching for a balance between the sides and waiting to see what would happen next; and each one of its national churches had very serious problems of its own to solve. Under these circumstances Spain could be considered by the Vatican as isolated from what was happening in the rest of Europe. With the outbreak of civil war, the Vatican never concealed its preferences and its support. However, almost immediately afterward, taking Europe as a whole and considering the panorama resulting from that world war, the church began a positive reconsideration of the liberal democracies, which had to bring it, sooner or later, to a critical reconsideration of the Spanish regime itself. At that moment, though, such a conflict was still a long way off, and likely to remain so while the historical process of the cold war reinforced the preoccupations of the church with regard to the containment of the Soviet bloc. This seemed to counsel some bridge building between the liberal democracies and the Franco regime, all the more so when, in their vehement and anachronistic way, the

Spanish seemed to be reviving the almost forgotten desire of the universal church to become the moral center of the world, with the state included within it.[7]

As for the state, it lacked the means and the motivation to confront the church. The state needed the church for two reasons. First, it needed an apparatus of legitimation and daily, routinized civic socialization of both the elites and the masses which was relatively coherent and distinct from, though complementary to, the Falange; such was the apparatus of the church. Also, this need was tied to Franco's crucial decision to opt for being the head of a personal and authoritarian government but not, in the strictest sense, the leader of a totalitarian regime and a totalitarian party—a decision which he made, almost from the start, with the support of the army, the business sector, monarchic circles, professional bodies, and the church itself. The second reason was that once the Axis powers had lost the war, the survival of the regime in the new international context depended to a large extent on the good offices of the Catholic church. Thus, it could not oppose itself to the church; but even had it been able to, it would not have wished to do so because the leaders and officials of the new regime were infused with a genuine respect for the symbols and institutions of religion, and this applied even to a large part of the Falange itself.

Spanish civil society emerged from the civil war with a very low level of internal structure and few powerful voluntary associations. Spain had been characterized by the weakness of its voluntary associations (Linz, 1981). The new regime had banned the organizations of the losing side (parties, unions, cultural associations) and enforced the integration into state or semiofficial hierarchical schemes of many of the associations of the winning side as well. The church had little to fear in the way of resistance from a society which was deliberately kept at a minimum level of self-organization; with a few exceptions in the areas of business enterprise and cultural life, the church was virtually alone in being able to develop its own associations. Also, civil society had no means of resisting the church, neither was it morally or psychologically inclined to attempt it. The losers of the civil war entered the new era subjugated and faced by the prospect of continuous repression and systematic exclusion, which they hoped the church could relieve, while the winners were, at the very least, predisposed to respect the church. And so together they all formed a society suspicious of itself and in a state of tension and exhaustion which made it receptive to the ecclesiastical message.

As a result, the Spanish church was able to devote itself to the task of Catholicizing the state and society because (and to the extent that) it found itself in a historical moment which allowed it an extraordinary margin of freedom. That is to say, the Spanish church benefited from a universal church, and the Vatican in particular, sympathetic to its aims, but also occupied in recovering from the trauma of a world war and trying to survive the instability of the postwar period; a state of like mind, which was furthermore incapable of exerting real pressure upon it; and a prostrate civil society with neither the will nor the capacity to resist it. While these conditions remained in effect, the Spanish church could, with the collaboration of the state, devote itself to a wonderful game of historical anachronism, recreating the Spain of the ancien régime in the middle of the twentieth century.

Unfortunately for the historical project of national Catholicism, of all these factors only that of the state's relative weakness was to remain comparatively stable. It was obvious that under the conditions of postwar Europe the Francoist state could increase neither its will-power nor its capacity to oppose the church. It could not dispense with its support, except at the risk of a seemingly suicidal *fuite en avant,* a fleeing toward a kind of populist, secular fascism which would play on anticlerical sentiment, the dream of autarkic industrial growth, and social demagogy, as Perón tried to do in the Argentina of the forties, with unfortunate consequences. In fact, the Francoist state did just the opposite, the result of which was that the regime, in order to survive, and the church, partly to help the regime, committed themselves to a long-term strategy aimed at placing Spain within the network of western diplomatic and defensive alliances, which meant, in consequence, leaving Spain in an irremediably anomalous position with regard to the liberal democracies, and directing the Spanish economy toward integration with the world capitalist economy. These decisions, both crucial, were made in the fifties, and both were prepared, argued over, and carried out by Francoist ministers belonging to Catholic groups, the Propagandistas in one case and the Opus Dei in the other.

The result was to increase substantially the vulnerability of the system to outside pressure and to open a Pandora's box of hopes and ambitions within the country. First, what sprang from this box were the resources and motivations, the institutions and cultural orientations, which civil society needed if resistance to the church was to spread. Second, there appeared the resources and motivations, the institutions and cultural orientations, to strengthen the bonds between the Spanish and European churches, which meant, over time, a growing receptivity on the part of the national church to the winds of change blowing in from the universal church. And third, there appeared the resources and motivations, the institutions and cultural orientations, whereby, as a final consequence, the internal unity of the Spanish church was to be split. In this way the scene was set for the second act of this drama.

THE EDIFICE CRUMBLES:
CHANGES IN SOCIETY, POLITICS, AND THE CHURCH

The fifties marked the peak and the turning point of the alliance between the Francoist state and the Spanish church. Catholic ministers played the leading role in crucial decisions on foreign and economic policy, and diplomatic isolation came to an end, placing the country clearly within the western orbit. Meanwhile, the church was flourishing in all its manifestations. The Concordat with the Holy See was signed in 1953, confirming the public status of the church, and a combination of associations, religious practices, and manifestations of the cult occupied the public and private arenas of the nation. The public sphere was full of eucharistic congresses, catechismal gatherings, meetings of secular associations, processions, and popular missions. The private sphere was full of spiritual exercises *(ejercicios espirituales)*, exercises for improving the world *(ejercitaciones para un mundo mejor)*, short courses on Christianity *(cursillos de Cristiandad)*, retreats, days of meditation, and devout evenings. As a result, the number of those taking holy orders rose, and the size of the ecclesiastical body increased (Hermet, 1985, pp. 28ff.). However, these same years were to see the beginning of a countercurrent of thought concerning a separation of the church from its alliance with the temporal powers. Just as the last bricks were being cemented into place, the foundations of the edifice were beginning to crumble. Let us now analyze the causes and mechanisms of this collapse.

My central argument follows from the propositions just stated: that the less resistance the church encountered from civil society, the state, and other international agents, the more freely it could carry out its historic project of national Catholicism. As resistance increased, it would place constraints on the activities of the church and raise the cost and risks of its strategy. Beyond a certain limit the rising costs and risks would result in the need for the church to revise its strategy by means of altering its hierarchy of values and turning to a reinterpretation of its doctrinal repertoire in order to do so.

As we shall see, this is what happened throughout the 1950s and 1960s: the resistance of civil society began to increase, challenging the church and religion with new demands and new problems; the structure of the political arena began to change, with the slow emergence of a new political class which was no longer descended, strictly speaking, from either the winners or the losers of the civil war, and which was to offer the ecclesiastics an understanding on very different terms from those of the past; the international context was changing in the sense that the pressure of the universal church on the Spanish church increased substantially; this external pressure implied a reinterpretation of the doctrines of the church, a new religious offer, and a new strategy with respect to temporal power; and all these pressures were internalized by some parts of the ecclesiastical body, producing conflict within the Spanish church between so-called conservative and progressive elements.

Naturally, this interpretation constitutes a simplified analytical reconstruction of events the real development of which was considerably more complex. The various factors emerged with differing degrees of intensity at different times in the chronological sequence, and the interdependence between these factors also varied over time.

New Problems and Challenges for the Church

The Spanish church of the 1940s and 1950s wanted to conquer the world, but this also meant conquering souls. Force was not sufficient; it was also necessary to persuade. This required "negotiating" with the various social groups, adapting the religious offer to their demands for meaning, salvation, and community. The body of ecclesiastics which occupies the center of the church organization can, perhaps, formulate its religious offer independent of demand (as suggested by Bourdieu and Saint-Martin, 1982), but this is not possible for those on the periphery of the organization and in direct contact with their followers, and even less so if they are working in a territory which they themselves define as "missionary" and thus to be "saved," or "problematic," that is, one whose problems are to be "solved" in a religious manner.

From the church's viewpoint, its central task was to overcome societal resistance to religious and ecclesiastical persuasion concerning the best way to formulate and solve people's most salient problems. During the fifties the church had to face up to several critical difficulties that became more acute as time went on. I shall now identify and discuss three kinds of problems, intellectual, social, and moral, to which another kind, regional problems, could be added as a result of the reemergence of strong assertions of regional identities to which local churches tended to be highly receptive, particularly in Catalonia and in the Basque region.[8]

First, there was the *intellectual problem,* that is, the challenge that many intellectuals and others in the university milieu raised to the church's (and the state's) attempt at hegemonic control over cultural life. The majority of the better-known intellectuals of the thirties had scant sympathy for the victorious political regime and the church triumphant (not that this implies any great enthusiasm for the losing side either). They belonged to a cultural world alien to that of the church, and the latter had not exactly opposed or mourned their exile or proscription after the war. Nevertheless, one sector of Catholic intellectuals soon came to adopt a rather different attitude. For various reasons they identified themselves primarily as truth seekers, not as defenders of orthodoxy. Therefore these intellectuals were sensitive to both the values intrinsic to their sphere of action, such as truth and intellectual creativity, and to the necessary condition of their realization, which is freedom of thought. For this reason they respected the frequently non-Catholic or heterodox liberal intellectuals of earlier generations who had been intellectually honest (that is, honest with themselves in their search for the truth) and creative; and for the same reason they believed that they themselves formed part of an intellectual community wider than that of Catholic intellectuals. This made them intermediaries with the exiles of that time and with the principal figures of contemporary thought.

This being the case, the foundations for a conflict with the church triumphant were laid from the very beginning. Furthermore, this group of Catholic intellectuals of a liberal persuasion looked sympathetically on the work, and at times the person, of writers such as

Unamuno, Baroja, and Ortega, who had been and often still were denigrated by the majority of ecclesiastics of the period (Sopeña, 1970). In reply to such attacks these liberal Catholics (men such as Aranguren, Laín, and Marías) vindicated their respect for their predecessors as masters of their forms of thought and of moral and aesthetic sensibility. And if such masters had accepted the influence of Dilthey, Kierkegaard, or Nietzsche, this new generation, a hybrid of Catholicism and liberalism, was prepared to incorporate Heidegger, Barth, Jaspers, or Sartre, as it would later incorporate fragments of Hegel, Marx, and the analytical philosophers. As a result, these intellectuals made two fundamental decisions: to affirm the principle of the autonomy of intellectual activity, without subordination to ecclesiastical authority, and to consider in a positive way the main trends of non-Catholic contemporary thought.

In the fifties the liberal Catholic intellectuals were a force of the first order on the Spanish cultural horizon, already starting to build an institutional and organizational niche for themselves. They had a network of personal relations, more or less formalized intellectual collaboration and periodic meetings or gatherings (like those at Gredos), a collection of works published or in the process of being published, and influence in university circles (lectureships or academic posts, as in the case of Laín and Tovar, who were the presidents of two public universities at the time of the Ruiz Giménez ministry); and around them formed a concentric circle of young clerics and secular university students. All this was in opposition to a similar community, with an even more important institutional network, which had formed around the hard-line conservative intellectuals, one of whose sectors, the Opus Dei, had developed the strategy of occupying posts in the state universities, the creation of a private university (in Navarre), and the formation of wide old-boy networks of increasing influence in the business community and the state administration.

In this way the intellectual problem, which had initially been posed as a conquest of the intellectuals by Catholicism, became a conflict between opposing strands of Catholic intellectual thought, in which liberal Catholics criticized what they judged to be the intolerant Catholicism of the church triumphant and its *non sancta* alliance with authority. The outbreak of the conflict took place within the walls of the university with the student disturbances of February 1956 at the Complutense University of Madrid. They were a milestone in the cultural and political history of Francoism, and from then on a process began in which, even if the intellectual Catholics lost their academic posts (as did Laín and Tovar in 1956) or their lectureships (as did Aranguren in 1965), their opponents lost their influence, and the Opus offensive to occupy more territory came to a halt.

The attempts of the academic powers to control university life could not impede the diffusion of liberal and radical ideas among young lecturers and students. This diffusion took place as the result of travel abroad, books brought in from outside, a network of bookshops, publishers, university magazines, informal gatherings, experimental theater, film societies, student unions, and political organizations. Thus, in spite of a political regime and official culture very different from those of the rest of Europe, from the sixties on, the content of debates among a large minority in Spanish university circles became increasingly homogeneous with that of European universities, and its evolution continued on a par with it. Thus, from the end of the fifties and the early sixties, it was obvious to many of the priests close to the intellectual and university milieux that the only way in which to exert any moral or religious influence over them was to respect, and to some degree follow, the course of events.

Something similar occurred with the *social problem* (or, as some would call it at the time, the *problema obrero,* or worker problem). Among the social problems of the nation in the early fifties, the agricultural problem was just as serious as the worker problem, but it soon became clear that the latter was becoming more pressing year by year, even if this was only as a result of rural migration and the conversion of peasants into urban laborers. Moreover, this problem caused a syndrome of violently contradictory feelings among the clerical estate. The working classes seemed to be returning once again to the center of the stage, like a great red belt of poverty and resentment encircling Madrid and other large cities, there, yet again, to be reconverted to Christianity. Around this time, too, the church was feeling the need to make its peace with the working classes and with its own conscience, after the terrible memories of the civil war and the aftermath of repression. These workers were the image not only of the church's persecutors but of the poor in the Gospels, who, if they had persecuted the church, had perhaps done so partly through the fault of the church itself in not knowing how to approach them, and had done so with good reason because the church had become a party to injustice.

What we find during the fifties is a growing number of priests undergoing a spectacular change in their attitudes toward what they increasingly called the "working class" (instead of "the poor classes"). The feeling began to spread among them that it was necessary to change the terms of the debate on the social question and thus the resulting norms of behavior. There had to be less talk of charity and more of justice, implying that justice was on the side of the workers and that it was time for a reinterpretation of Catholic social doctrine, time to direct the action of the church less toward exhortation and more toward support of social claims.

A number of Jesuits played a crucial part in this change, some of them from the Catholic workers' organizations. The HOAC (Hermandades Obreras de Acción Católica), the JOC (Juventudes Obreras Católicas), and Vanguardia Obrera had been forming and consolidating themselves throughout the forties and fifties, and after a number of years they began to take the "workers' front" line, drawing away from the moderate tradition of Catholic trade unionism (Hermet, 1985, pp. 232ff.). At their height (the early and mid-sixties) they were of decisive importance for the reactivation of the worker movement and the formation of trade unions such as the USO (Unión Sindical Obrera) and Comisiones Obreras; for example, of the seven leaders to be accused in the first trial against the Comisiones Obreras in Vizcaya, six belonged to the HOAC (Hermet, 1985, p. 235). In the mid-fifties another Jesuit, Padre Llanos, previously renowned for his support of the Falangist movement, began his version of an experiment by French worker priests, going to live in a slum suburb of rural immigrants in Madrid, and arranging meetings between workers and university students. At the same time other Jesuits, such as Díez Alegría, undertook the task of reinterpreting the social doctrine of the church, accepting some of the basic Marxist characterizations of capitalism, with the help of the concepts of alienation, exploitation, profit, and the class struggle. Such practical and theoretical impetus had a profound influence on young Jesuits, priests, and university students, and enjoyed the sympathy of the liberal Catholic intellectuals as well. This current of advanced or progressive social Catholicism felt justified by the economic and social events of the sixties, when, as a consequence of the combination of economic growth and a more permissive legal framework (which made collective bargaining, trade union representation, and union elections all possible to some extent), a workers' movement emerged and developed of which the leaders originated in part from the rank and file of the Catholic organizations themselves.

But this trend had to coexist with others. On the one hand there was the main trend of social corporatism of the papal encyclicals, from Leo XIII to Pius XII, with which the church was attempting to establish an equilibrium between the two evils of socialism and capitalism and at the same time to live discreetly with the latter. On the other there was the secondary trend of frank acceptance of the market system and capitalist enterprise with all its consequences, compatible with a degree of public intervention and the redistribution of wealth, in a way that was acceptable to, for example, the Catholics of Opus Dei. For them, making capitalism function was also a way of making the country prosper and carrying out the will of God. They also felt that their vision of Catholicism and history was corroborated by the spectacle of Spain's economic growth in the sixties and the success of their own strategy for coming close to the central locations of political power. In short, the development of these social and intellectual problems ended in a rupture of the unanimity of the church's message and in the gradual emergence of two opposing subcommunities, with a fairly broad and indecisive segment in the middle.

To this situation was added *the moral problem*. In effect, the Spanish Catholic church, in its determination to Catholicize the nation, had decided to control the private sphere. This meant the suppression of divorce, jurisdictional control over separation proceedings between Catholic spouses, censorship of public entertainment and literary works including the press, suppression of brothels, and control over moral conduct at dances, in the streets, and on the beaches, which is to say, control over all public space. This the church tried to do by battling tirelessly against immodesty of dress, indecency of gesture, obscenity of speech, and various other manifestations of what, for the church, represented lewdness or shamelessness. In positive contrast, the church actively promoted the values of chastity and sexual abstinence, reinforcing it with a powerful cult of the Virgin, insistence on the sacraments which demanded or conferred ritual purity, such as communion and confession, and the exaltation of the family, organized on the basis of an indissoluble marriage and subject to the authority of the parents, especially the father.

The realization of this project to organize the private lives of the

Spanish people had never been an easy task. Not even in the most promising areas (as, for example, in the villages of Old Castile, a region with a high density of priests, firm religious beliefs, and frequent religious practice) was the real control of the private lives of the peasants very strong, at least during the preceding century and a half. In any case, the probability of success of such a project was steadily reduced throughout the 1950s and 1960s as a result of the combination of economic growth, demographic changes, and the spread of a mass consumer culture.

Economic growth provided the means to satisfy rising aspirations of material well-being, while rural depopulation reduced the weight of local opinion, and in particular that of rural priests in village life. The spread of mass consumer culture changed life-styles and frames of reference. This spread, however, was not the automatic result of economic growth, urban attraction, the tourist invasion, emigration to Europe, and the development of the mass media. The new mass consumer culture already had some roots in traditional culture (more in actual moral experiences than in any articulated moral theory),[9] first, because a component of hedonism was part of the moral tradition of the peasant class as much as of the urban lower or middle classes, and second, because attached to it there was a tradition of the social obligation of family heads to provide a better life and material comfort for their families, as a token of moral concern for their welfare and as a symbol of family status within the larger community.[10]

This consumerism was condemned by the ecclesiastical hierarchy and Catholic intellectuals of all shades, whether hard-line, liberal, or social, who understood little of those local moral traditions. Nothing could be more logical, of course, than this misunderstanding, since nothing seems more typical of cultural elites than their lack of appreciation or even their contempt for popular culture. This meant that mass consumer culture was accused of vulgar materialism by some and of alienation by others; and it was condemned by both conservative and progressive ecclesiastics. What is certain is that, in its way, this hedonistic or consumer culture, which the masses developed more or less spontaneously the moment they had the opportunity to do so (together with some models of reference which facilitated the specification of objectives, the search for means, and the distribution of information), was a moral act, and a revolutionary act of rejection of the moral culture of asceticism and limited aspirations proposed by the church in the previous decade, much as eastern European consumers would later reject the culture of limited aspirations for personal well-being proposed by their communist ideologues. Over time, this rejection came to contain two basic components: the creation of a permissive culture with regard to sex and a culture of moderation in relations of authority, beginning with those of the family.

The regions of the country where economic prosperity was greatest, the tourist invasion most widespread, and the hedonistic culture most deeply rooted, which is to say, the Mediterranean coasts of the Levant, were those in which change was fastest and most visible, especially among young people, although sooner or later the spread of this mass consumer culture and hedonism became generalized throughout the country.

This silent revolution of social customs, which neither priests nor intellectuals understood at the time, began at the end of the 1950s and continued to grow during the 1960s and 1970s. The rules of love and sexual courtship were changing, in the streets and discotheques, on the beaches, and in the women's magazines. In addition, the rules governing the exercise of paternal or maternal authority within the family, the control over timetables, comings and goings, advice and admonition were also changing. Little by little the situation went from one in which parents made the law and the children submitted to it; next to one in which parents made speeches and their children assented gravely, in relative silence, with the mental reservation of planning to get even behind their backs afterward; then to one in which parents ended up witnessing, first in amazement and later with resignation, the sight of their offspring doing whatever they wanted, whenever they wanted to do it, sons and daughters in whom, for lack of better advice to give, parents tried to instill a minimum sense of self-preservation, alerting them to the dangers of premature pregnancy and, in the years to come, drug addiction.

As a result, the priests themselves began to abandon their role as jealous guardians of popular sexual morality, relaxing or minimizing the importance of personal confession and even beginning to question the grounds for their own celibacy. In the long run all this ferment caused a generalized devaluation of authority, not only in the bosom of the family and ecclesiastical institutions but everywhere, in schools and university classrooms, in factories and the workplace.

Changes in the Political Sphere

From about the mid-fifties the political scene was modified, gradually at first and then more quickly and more profoundly. What had seemed to be a strong state in the 1940s and 1950s, with a resolute political class, a generalized acquiescence of the population to this class, external support, and the absence of viable alternatives, and which therefore seemed to be an authoritarian political regime with a future, began to look less and less strong as time went on. The decisiveness of the regime's leadership slowly began to falter, although this did not become visible until the 1970s, in Franco's old age. But the internal divisions of the Francoist political class had been worsening since the mid-sixties, the signs of social agitation and restlessness had been increasing, and the distance from the outside world and the reticence of the Vatican and the European Community had remained constant or increased.

This was happening in spite of the fact (and indeed partly because of it) that the Francoist state sometimes seemed to have committed itself to a halfhearted semireformist strategy on the road toward moderation. In the long term this strategy was demonstrated to be erratic and unsuccessful. What emerged, in contrast, was an alternative political class which gained strength in such a way that, given the turn of events, it seemed increasingly likely to have a chance of success, and which (unlike in the 1930s) did not seem hostile to the church. In that sense the continuity with the political classes that had won or lost the civil war was broken.

That the Francoist state, which in the 1940s and 1950s had looked ahead to a brilliant future, should become by the 1960s and 1970s a state with a doubtful one was an extraordinarily important change for an institution such as the Catholic church, which, for reasons of organizational structure, past recollections, almost its very nature, tended the near-continuous reformulation of its long-term strategies. However, all this took place over a relatively long period of time and across conflicting perceptions and evaluations of the situation occurring within the church. The majority of the ecclesiastical body and the hierarchy were not convinced that the regime had no future until the beginning of the seventies. Until then, this moderate or conservative nucleus within the church maintained as their main strategy the basic idea of an alliance with the state which was fitting for the church triumphant. The demonstrations of support for the political regime on the part of the hierarchy therefore continued; and as a result, the teachings of the Second Vatican Council on religious freedom were received with great care being taken to avoid their negative implications for the understanding between the Spanish church and the Francoist state. The hierarchy was sympathetic to that semireformist strategy, and prominent Catholic groups, both within the church and in public life, took an active part in the formulation and execution of that strategy.

The last fifteen or twenty years of Francoism are sometimes portrayed as years of contradiction between a socioeconomic structure which was changing and a political structure which was resisting change, of which the final result was the political transition which reestablished an equilibrium between society and the economy on the one hand and the political system on the other. This approach minimizes the effect of cultural factors and simplifies the interplay between politics and socioeconomic factors. One of its weak points consists precisely in its not taking sufficiently into account the changes in political strategy of the Francoist state during its last two decades: what I have called its halfhearted semireformist strategy or its tentative move toward moderation.

Evidence of this strategy is, however, abundant. The state's repressive policy was modified throughout the sixties. Repression there certainly was, but to a much lesser degree, and thus of a different quality, than in the forties and early fifties. Repression continued to weigh heavily on the communists and later on the Basque separatists but only lightly on the liberal, social democratic, and socialist opposition. Not only was there a reduction in the degree of political repression, but throughout the fifties and sixties the Franco regime formulated, with relative clarity, a political project for a new version of an authoritarian regime with four main characteristics. First, economic development was to be based on a mixed economy, with growing influence of the markets, increasing internationalization of the Spanish economy, and state intervention in planning similar to that of France. All this was implemented by economic policy in a systematic and continuous way from 1959, with the stabilization plan for that year, and successive development plans—an economic policy, incidentally, which had considerable success. Second, a welfare state developed, with an expanding system of social security and the resulting network of hospitals and general medical care, as well as the generalization of primary and secondary education. All of this took place during the sixties and seventies. Third, there was an extension of freedom of expression and the right to associate typical of civil society, which was, to some extent, the result of the Press Law of 1966 and the acceptance, whether de jure or de facto, of an area in which social pressure could be brought to bear on labor issues by means of the institution of collective agreements and labor tribunals, trade union elections, and the legalization of strikes connected to labor issues. Finally, there was a hesitant and eventually aborted attempt to create a limited field of political representation.

This project of reforms from within Francoism was welcomed by the church and carried out by Catholics connected with, above all, Opus Dei (whose political weight was becoming increasingly decisive), but also by the ACNDP (Asociación Católica Nacional de Propagandistas) and traditionalist circles. This naturally gave rise to the corresponding internal struggles to change the balance of forces within the different political families of the regime, with the accompanying build-up of ambitions, alliances, and enmities which were to form the substratum of political experience of that section of the Francoist political class which was to lead the transition to democracy fifteen or twenty years later. This could be characterized as a Bismarck-like project (as is suggested in Hermet, 1985, pp. 114ff.), were it not for the fact that it fails the crucial test, which in its own way the Second Reich was able to meet for a period of time: that of limited political representation. After the crisis of the antisocialist laws, the regime of Bismarck and Wilhelm II accepted a broad range of political parties, free elections, and free trade unions. Francoism never came this far, which is why its strategy can only be described as semireformist.

Thus the regime, having been capable of bridging the gap in its second phase—from, so to speak, the sixteenth to the nineteenth centuries—ran out of steam at about the point where it came close to the stage of political development that had previously existed in Spain by the 1870s, reducing its degree of historical backwardness to only one century. This may have been praiseworthy, and may even have raised the hopes of those Francoists with greater reformist impulses and a broader sense of history who, like Manuel Fraga, saw themselves in the mold of a Cánovas del Castillo (a self-perception which was to have interesting repercussions in the seventies). But it was an experiment which, taken as a whole, was not successful, first, because the crucial limitation on political parties and trade unions denied the raison d'être of the new, emerging political class; and second, because, at the same time, a cultural mutation was taking place in the country, as a consequence of which the combination of socioeconomic changes and semireformist policies only managed to nourish a Tocquevillean process of growing expectations of and aspirations toward freedom.

A sector of the church played a decisive role in the creation of this new political class and this change of mentality, for, in reality, during these years the church was playing not one game but two. The hierarchy and the majority of ecclesiastics continued playing the game of an alliance with the regime, while the other game, that of the dissidents, was being played by young priests and Catholic activists. This was to a great extent a generational distinction.

We should remember that in the early fifties a breach was to open into which a new generation would irrupt, a generation which had not fought the war and which refused to continue the work of its predecessors, setting itself up in opposition to them. This generation (and its major decisions) cannot be understood as a product of the historical situation or the effect of a combination of economic development and political tensions. Structural and institutional factors explain only the framework of objective opportunities which were available to that generation in pursuing its goals and standing up for its values. Therefore, its strategy is to be seen in the light of the dominant role played by cultural symbols and guidance in its process of moral and intellectual education. This process was influenced to a large extent by a crucial segment of young priests and Catholic activists. This religious and ecclesiastical intervention was decisive in breaking the continuity of political opposition to the regime, thereby substantially increasing its chances of success. The history of the political classes in the transition to democracy, although incorporating family and ideological traditions, is, nevertheless and above all, a history of discontinuity, the key to which lies in the intervention of this Catholic segment.

The dissent of the generation that followed that which had fought the civil war raises two questions. First, why, instead of pursuing its private interests, did a significant segment of this generation feel responsible for and concerned about the collective problems of its time, taking for granted that it had a mission to fulfill and should be determined to take action? And second, why in the process of so doing, instead of continuing the efforts of its parents, did it work in opposition to them? Its dissent was an oedipal revolution aimed at the symbolic death of the parents: the destruction of their work and their expulsion from positions of power. In that it had a remarkable success, since the new generation managed to change the political regime, and to a large extent it also managed to exclude its parents from political power, as much on the left wing as on the right.

But let us consider within this generation the group of young Catholics. It is obvious that part of the political generation of the seventies originated from the activism of Acción Católica, the Congregaciones Marianas, the Círculos Católicos, the Hogares del Empleado y del Obrero, the Vanguardia Obrera, the Hermandades Obreras, and the Juventud Obrera Católica of the fifties and sixties. This activism went well beyond its initial objectives and soon took up the fight against the SEU (Sindicato Español Universitario), setting up new organizations such as the local chapters of the SEU itself (since the mid 1950s), the SUT (Servicio Universitario del Trabajo), the activities related to the Pozo del Tío Raimundo (the neighborhood where Padre Llanos lived), the semiclandestine trade unions of the USO (Union Sindical Obrera) and CCOO (Comisiones Obreras), the publishing activities of Cuadernos para el Diálogo or the ZYZ publishers, and the political organizations of the FLP (Frente de Liberación Popular) or the ORT (Organización Revolucionaria de Trabajadores). These organizations and activities were sources of apprenticeship and training for political action, for the formation of militants, the accumulation of organizational resources, the drawing up of programs, and the making of alliances. With all this, the church began to implement, on the left, the parapolitical function it had traditionally implemented on the right (with the ACNDP or the Opus Dei), but through different ecclesiastics and with a different religious offer. The religious offer which the priests made to the generation of dissent was one that combined religious authenticity with a commitment to the struggle for justice and freedom.

If one analyzes the messages of priests and Catholic intellectuals in the early fifties such as Llanos, Díez Alegría, Alberdi, Sopeña, González Ruiz, Aranguren, Laín, and many others directed toward young Catholics, militants or activists of secular organizations, or simply those with religious problems, what most attracts attention is the emphasis on religiosity or a morality of "authenticity." In opposition to an emphasis on the positive, external religiosity of solemn ceremonies, attendance at Mass, the reception of the seasonal sacraments, and external professions of faith, and in opposition to the supposedly superficial religiosity of both bourgeois and popular culture, a call was made to the authenticity of these young people's convictions and religious feelings, to the intensity of their faith. It was an appeal to the inner workings of self-discipline and the systematization of everyday conduct according to religious ideals. In a sense such appeals extended Jesuit education as it was taught in the colleges at that time.

But here the call to a rationalization of religious life was carried to its ultimate consequences, probably in part because of the influence of moral and theological reflections of a Christian-existentialist nature (this was a time when intellectuals such as Aranguren were analyzing the Protestant faith and offering a sympathetic and intimate reading of the religious beliefs of Unamuno, and writings such as those of Karl Rahner were being widely read). In consequence, the religious believer was carried one step beyond the stage of rationalizing the religious life of secular people in the Jesuit way, that is, beyond subordination to a spiritual director. The religiousness of authenticity displaced the locus of the decision as to whether or not to accept a doctrine to the sphere of the believer's internal convictions, and converted teaching into an exercise of persuasion between equals instead of an act of imposition by a moral authority. This quasi-Protestant reform thus created an atmosphere of inner freedom and the ability to face up to new tasks. But for this ability to be translated in actual behavior, the formal religiosity of authenticity had to be combined with a religious commitment to temporal action, and the content of such commitment had to be defined as the struggle against the established order.

The religious commitment to temporal activities did not contradict existing religiosity but rather extended it. It was one more example of the worldly orientation typical of Spanish Catholicism, of its propensity to intervene in worldly affairs, including political and socioeconomic structures, in pursuit of the realization of the Kingdom of God on earth. From such a viewpoint the world of the thirties had been dominated by anti-Catholicism, and had to be changed; that of the fifties and sixties seemed to be dominated by pseudo-Catholics and also had to be changed. The categoric moral imperative was the same;

the only difference was the content of this world. The continuity of this fundamental impulse facilitates an understanding of how and why priests, such as Llanos, who participated with enthusiasm in the project for the total conversion of society to Catholicism in the forties, could then turn away, disillusioned, toward the prophetic denunciation of what they had helped create.

The doctrine of the need to fight for justice and freedom meant a radical devaluation of the world created by the church triumphant and Francoism. Having widened their horizons of reference to the universal church and the European nations, both priests and laymen engaged in this operation agreed that the church and the Francoist regime were isolated and anachronistic redoubts of those societies. The civil war was morally and religiously devalued to the rank of a class struggle, the Francoist state to a personal or fascist dictatorship, the religion of the church triumphant, national Catholicism, at best to a religion insensitive to the suffering and needs of a large part of the population, and at worst to a religion which was indeed the opiate of the people.

But it was not sufficient to detract from the adversary. It was also necessary to articulate a religious offer with a historic project for the future. Priests and Catholic intellectuals understood that they had been presented a unique opportunity. History was moving Spain in the direction of modern Europe, and also, or so it seemed to many, in the direction of an era of great social change, all of which placed the working classes at center stage. At the same time, the political situation of Francoist Spain made any action on the part of (non-Catholic) organizations linked to prewar parties or trade unions exceedingly difficult. These conditions provided dissenting priests and Catholic activists with a unique opportunity to become the leaders of the masses, to develop a representational function on behalf of labor unions and working-class parties by a sort of implicit or tacit delegation of trust. That seemed all the more plausible as the ranks of Catholic workers' organizations were growing to reach a membership of some 100,000 by the early 1970s (HOAC had about 30,000 members and JOC about 60,000; see Hermet, 1985, p. 237).

This religious offer, and the historic project implicit in it, was accepted by many young Catholics, probably because it responded to a diffuse and little articulated demand or disposition on the part of these young people. Recognition of the inner freedom of the laity seemed in keeping with the attitudes of a generation with a desire to succeed in circumstances of tension and difficulty. They had been educated in the idea that they had a mission or task to fulfill, and at the same time they felt freer and more capable than the previous generation; they had greater cultural resources, a more solid education, a wider horizon, and even a richer religious experience than their parents.

Furthermore, this generation, in spite of its ascetic education, was less willing to suffer for its sins and had fewer feelings of guilt. They had not hated or killed their fellow countrymen in a civil war; they had not stripped them of their possessions; they had not become rich on the black market or by manipulation of the state apparatus; neither had they degraded themselves by pretending to believe in extravagant doctrines, nor by accepting the judgment of people lacking in culture, of rigid and simplistic ideas. This is to say that they had an awareness of having killed less, robbed less, and lied and humiliated less than the previous generation. Therefore, it was logical not only that they should feel less guilt but also that they should be predisposed to feel indignation toward a generation which, being inferior in moral and cultural terms, was superior in the control of political, economic, and social resources.

In this way the doctrine of the struggle for social justice and a free political regime (with at least the freedom necessary to fight for that justice) provided justification for these young people's indignation and gave meaning to their activities. This does not mean that it is necessary to reduce these justifications to mere rationalizations. But it should be pointed out that, independent of the fact that these justifications may have an objective foundation, we can understand their appropriation as subjective truths only if we take into account the emotional element attached to them, and if we consider these young people's calculations of the costs and probability of success associated with their carrying out a course of conduct consistent with such justifications. Without such considerations, these justifications would have remained abstract recognitions of a truth but not commitments to effective action. In my opinion that emotional element and those calculations referred to a generational impulse, a subjective experience of moral superiority, and a relatively plausible historic project in the articulation of which the church and the clergy played a decisive role.

In this way the dissident critical or left-wing subculture developed and provoked division within the church, bewilderment among the hierarchy, and the irritation of the state, gaining momentum as the consequences of the Second Vatican Council started to unfold in the mid-sixties.

The Church in the 1960s

In the 1950s and early 1960s various segments of the church started to modify their strategies in relation to intellectual, social, and moral as well as political problems, taking into account the corresponding social groups. In part, that change reflected its adaptation to the demands of these groups (and in that sense we may label its conduct *mimetic*), but it also reflected a change, prior to these demands, in the mentality of the clergy, as a result of which the latter were able to influence the articulation and the content of those demands (and in that sense we may label its conduct *prophetic*).

This change in mentality was the consequence of a number of factors, among them, in particular, the exposure of young priests to the influence of the European churches from the beginning of the 1950s. During those years priests or would-be priests began to leave Spain to study in the theological centers of Innsbruck, Munich, Paris, and other major cities (González de Cardedal, 1985, p. 163). They found themselves in a situation in which they were forced to compare the intellectual poverty and isolation of Spanish neoscholasticism and the forms of traditional piety with the dynamism of the new theological trends and a process of liturgical renovation. They were forced to compare the stagnation of the Spanish church with the spirit of theological and liturgical renewal which was inspiring the European churches.

Behind that religious experience there was also an experience of organization, life-style, tolerance, and compromise, and a mentality which had incorporated modernity, which was compatible with religion and a vigorous church, as was, for example, the case with the German Catholic church, which discreetly made use of a nondenominational state (embedded in a renovated tradition of cooperation with the churches) and coexisted peacefully with Protestantism and a secular humanist culture. The historical background to this was a process of national reconciliation helped by the fight against Nazism and fascism, or by memories of horror and historical failure associated with the Nazi and fascist experiences, to which can be added the experience of European reconstruction, growth, and political stability based on an understanding between Christian democrats and social democrats, or even the experience of class conflicts within this European order which suggested compromises between, and joint ventures of, leftist Catholics and communists.

These differences were experienced by these young priests in places beyond the control of their superiors, and in an attitude of intellectual inquiry, personal freedom, and moral and emotional sympathy. In due course many of them managed to establish special relations with their superiors back home; or else they realized that these superiors lacked the theological foundation for controlling their meditations or sheltered behind the conflicts of jurisdiction between the bishops and the religious orders they belonged to. In these ways, on their return to Spain, at least initially, these young priests managed to construct niches of tolerance for their activities. Their example bore fruit among their colleagues, all the more so as translations of foreign works of a religious nature increased substantially in number during those years (by 1965 such translations made up 83 percent of dogmatic literature published in Spain; see Payne, 1984, p. 246).

It was only natural that these priests, and the people within their sphere of influence, were drawn into the very same milieu of liberal and dissident Catholics who were encouraging the aforementioned processes of intellectual, social, and political change. There was an obvious elective affinity between the two groups, and in time they came to form a religious subcommunity within the Spanish church. In this regard, what the Vatican Council of 1962–65 did was to lend its support to these processes of change which were already under way, accelerating them, precipitating the crisis, reinforcing the position of dissident priests and Catholics, and ensuring an outcome in their favor.

If, at the beginning of the 1960s, there had been a nucleus of the church made up of the hierarchy and the majority of the ecclesiastical body, with a periphery of critical priests and militants, what the Vatican Council did was to displace the center of gravity of Spanish Catholicism away from the nucleus to the periphery. From that moment on, independent of the position of power which they occupied within the structure of the Spanish church, the bishops found themselves on the defensive, with their influence slowly decreasing, while the marginal clergy and militants found themselves moving along with events. Although it could have prepared itself for these events, in view of the style and orientation of the pontificate of Pope John XXIII, the Spanish hierarchy did not expect the shock of the council. It had convinced itself that its alliance with temporal power and its historic project of a denominational state and an orthodox Catholic society approached the "Catholic ideal" more closely than the compromises, concessions, and tolerance of the European churches toward the modern world. To be rudely awakened from that dream and have to renounce that image of itself was very hard. The hierarchy could not recover from the shock of seeing itself as a marginal and anachronistic element within the universal church. Its delusions of grandeur collapsed before the document on religious freedom accepted by the council. From then on, change within the Spanish church became inevitable, for isolation was no longer possible and a schism was inconceivable; all that remained was to determine the tempo, the form, and the costs of the transformation.

Recovering to a large extent the spirit of that modernism which had been condemned at the turn of the century, the Vatican Council proposed a new way of relating the church to the modern world. In the political sphere the church no longer aspired to the support of temporal power, and it accepted that it must operate in a "market" of religious beliefs, that is, in a situation of religious pluralism. Without defining the ideal political regime, the church excluded totalitarianism, disparaged authoritarianism, and implicitly legitimized liberal democracy. In the economic sphere, its messages maintained the traditional ambiguity of those who accept capitalism and the reform of capitalism, seeming to settle for the kinds of mixed economies (with state intervention and free trade unions) which were prevalent in western societies. In the cultural sphere, the church accepted much of the criticism of the Enlightenment, recognizing the centrality of the values of freedom and reason, and taking to itself the heritage of humanism, modern science, and much of contemporary philosophy. As a result it implicitly reduced the significance of ecclesiastical teaching, proclaimed its respect for freedom and natural reason, and, explicitly or implicitly, declared its intention to renounce the use of sanctions against heterodox beliefs or practices, whatever the temporal situation in which they were to be found.

In this way its message of meaning left a wide margin for explanations and justifications of a natural character; its message of salvation

163

duly recognized the intrinsic value of programs and policies for reducing hunger and ignorance, for encouraging economic growth and the redistribution of wealth, and so on; and its message of community directed Catholics not toward the creation of Catholic cultures, isolated with respect to the surrounding community (as had been established, or attempts had been made to establish, since the middle of the nineteenth century), as the defensive answer to secular society, but toward the creation of nondenominational communities, made up of people with diverse beliefs but united by a common morality, for the realization of a project which offered the hope of salvation from moral and material misery and ensured areas of solidarity and mutual affection on earth. All this meant a reevaluation of spiritual tasks and an emphasis on themes of social morality, and, *sensu contrario*, it implied relegating the problem of the final stages of human life and sexual morality, those topics which had dominated the imagination and sensibility of Catholics for decades, to secondary status.

All of these changes, many of them important ones for the church as a whole, amounted to a Copernican revolution for the Spanish church. There arose resistance on the one hand and enthusiasm on the other, and thus the division of the Spanish church into two blocs, with a bewildered majority initially caught in between. In opposition to the dissident clergy was the traditional clergy grouped around the Hermandades Sacerdotales and other conservative circles, and the tension between them only increased with time. Along with this tension was a growing sense of uncertainty and mixed feelings on the part of the majority. In a survey carried out among the Spanish clergy in 1970, a clear division of opinion was observed on the political problems of the nation. The division was most marked between the generations, older people in favor of the status quo and the younger ones against it (Martín Patino, 1984, pp. 160ff.; Payne, 1984, p. 254). This division took on even more importance owing to the age grouping of the Spanish clergy as a result of the civil war: it was divided into two large groups, one of men under forty years of age, the other of men over sixty, with relatively few in between (Hermet, 1985, pp. 31ff.).

As well as highlighting this division, the survey reflected an extraordinary doctrinal insecurity among the majority of ecclesiastics. Already in the 1950s some priests had been disturbed by the apparent vacuum of official Catholicism and the evidence that the project of converting

Spain to state Catholicism was not succeeding. But what had been the unease of the clergy in the fifties faced with the failure of their project became by the end of the sixties the sense that there was no project at all. The clergy felt uncertain of their theological knowledge (39 percent) and their moral understanding (51 percent) and believed themselves to be without either the preparation or the capacity to direct the faithful on social (73 percent) or political (75 percent) matters. Consequently, they turned their eyes toward the process of education and training and expressed their profound discontent (51 percent) with the education they had received in the seminaries (Martín Patino, 1984, p. 161).

The bewilderment was deep and permanent. As a result, it is not surprising that, combined with a spectacular increase in all kinds of opportunities in civilian life—for economic improvement, intellectual development, political action, and emotional relationships—there was a crisis of religious vocation, although the process was not exclusive to the Spanish church, and was also to be observed in other European countries such as France (Bourdieu and Saint-Martin, 1984). There was a generalized move toward secularization throughout the clergy (some four hundred left the priesthood each year between 1966 and 1971); the number of seminarists dropped from about 8,000 in the 1950s to about 1,800 in 1972–73; and approximately one third of Spanish Jesuits abandoned the order between 1966 and 1975 (Payne, 1984, pp. 225ff.).

The bishops, only half understanding this state of affairs, adopted a defensive, tentative strategy. On hearing the results of the Vatican Council, Archbishop Cantero did not hesitate to speak of the need for "maintaining and strengthening the Catholic unity of Spain . . . whose civil expression . . . [should be] the confessionality of the state . . . in accordance with the Council" (Ruiz Rico, 1977, p. 197). In fact the hierarchy was not prepared willingly to alter its understanding with the Spanish state. Its application of the principle of putting some distance between the church and political power consisted of trying to prevent Catholic associations from aiming criticisms at the Francoist regime. By insisting on this they brought the final consequences upon themselves. When in 1966–67 the leaders of Acción Católica tried to lead the way by criticizing the authoritarian regime, Archbishop Morcillo reminded them unequivocally that "no branch [of Acción Católica], no organization could make declarations [of that kind] without authority; and that authority had never been given [by the church], or if it had, it had been revoked" (*Ecclesia*, 1 [1966], 935–939). Subsequently, after additional skirmishes, Acción Católica was deprived of its leaders, followed by the immediate collapse of the organization; it went from being a dynamic organization of 1.5 million members in the early sixties to a stagnating one of 100,000 by 1972 (Payne, 1984, p. 250).

However, this same incident proved that an attitude of intransigence could bring with it catastrophic consequences by activating dissenting voices within and causing massive exit from the church apparatus (Hirschman, 1970); thus, division in the church could be exacerbated and organizations dissolved. Neither did it seem very sensible to gamble unreservedly on a regime with a doubtful future. So, finally, the bishops began to persuade themselves that the times required adaptation and reform.

To this process of self-persuasion was added continuous and energetic external pressure from the Vatican, which was exercised by means of various institutional mechanisms. The Holy See decided to accelerate the extremely slow process of episcopal reflection and reduce the resistance of the bishops, modifying their organizational structure and composition. At that time the episcopate was led by a small Conferencia de Metropolitanos with preeminence given to the Conferencia Episcopal of all the bishops. It was found that, on the whole, the Conferencia Episcopal was composed of bishops who were relatively old and had been named jointly by the church and the state (which exercised a traditional privilege of presentation), and so it was decided to alter this composition drastically. Thus, bishops were to retire after a certain age, remaining as members with the right to speak but with no vote in the Conferencia Episcopal. Younger auxiliary bishops were named with the right to speak and vote in the conference, but in whose appointment the state could not intervene. Pressure was put on the Spanish government to name the Vatican's candidates as bishops by the simple ploy of reducing to one the trio of candidates which the Vatican usually put forward (Payne, 1984, p. 261). Finally, the government was publicly exhorted, time after time, to renounce the privilege of presentation. Through its apostolic nuncios the Vatican worked with prudence, care, and decision, and its strategy was successful within a very few years. In 1966, 65 percent of the Spanish bishops were over sixty years old, and the number of auxiliary bishops (those named only by the church) was just five out of a total of seventy-seven. By 1973, bishops over age sixty were only 40 percent of the total, and the number of auxiliaries had risen to seventeen (Ruiz Rico, 1977, pp. 189, 213). By 1971, the relative strengths in the Conferencia Episcopal were already such that an archbishop loyal to the Vatican line, Enrique y Tarancón, was elected president of the conference. This nomination marked the end of one phase and the beginning of another in relations between the church and the state, and in relations within the church itself. What had until then been a church confused and divided became, in the 1970s, a church determined to carry out a new historic and social project, and with it a strategy of detachment and even estrangement from the Francoist regime.

The Conversion to Liberal Democracy

At the beginning of this discussion I pointed out that the strategy of the Catholic church, in its attempt to achieve a monopoly over the religious offer, with the consequent alliance with temporal power, ran the risk that the political opposition of that moment would become a hostile force in the future. This risk increased considerably in Spain throughout the period under consideration, owing to the resistance of society, the changes in the public sphere, and pressures from the universal church. As a result, in due time the Spanish church opted for revising its strategy and accepting a situation of religious pluralism.

This occurred gradually over a period of time, but one key year can be singled out. In 1971 the balance of power within the episcopacy swung decisively in favor of those who supported a revision of the church's strategy with the nomination of Archbishop Enrique y Tarancón as president of the Conferencia Episcopal (Martín Patino, 1984, pp. 163ff.). Tarancón belonged to the moderate sector of the Spanish episcopate and had been elected by the Holy See as primate of Toledo in 1968 (in an operation similar in nature to that which was to take place some years later with the nomination of Suárez as prime minister in June 1977 in order to engineer the political transition). In the same year a joint assembly of bishops and priests was held which had an enormous impact on Catholic public opinion and whose conclusions were oriented in the same direction.

Once decided upon, the strategy of estrangement from the Francoist regime was carried out in a deliberate and systematic way, in spite of a rear-guard action by conservative sectors of the church which was to continue right up to the last moments of Francoism (one good example of which was the criticism offered by conservative priests of the conclusions of the joint assembly; see González de Cardedal, 1985, p. 167). The declarations of that assembly, the collective documents of the episcopacy from then on (particularly that of February 1973 regarding the relationship between the church and the political community), and the declarations of Tarancón himself, which culminated in the homily to the king in November 1975 on the occasion of his coronation, left no room for doubt about the reorientation of the temporal commitment of the church. Allusions, through careful use of language, to the desirability of a democratic regime were frequent. The key words were *harmony, dialogue,* and *public liberties,* including the freedom to elect political representatives. The church reiterated a positive evaluation of demands for freedom and justice, which was a thinly veiled reference to the demands of opposition parties and trade unions. It alluded again and again to the need for national reconciliation and a monarchy of all the Spanish people, as Tarancón conscientiously pointed out in his coronation homily (echoing a similar line of thought on the part of key members of the royal family). This moral-political discourse rested on a dramatic reconsideration of the most crucial event for the church in fifty years: the civil war. The ecclesiastics gathered together in the joint assembly of 1971 went so far as to recognize that "we have sinned . . . and we ask for pardon . . . since at that time we did not know how to be true ministers of reconciliation in the bosom of our nation, divided by a war between brothers." This statement was passed by a vote of 137 to 78 (Ruiz Rico, 1977, p. 236).

For the Francoist state, which had based a substantial part of its legitimacy on its Catholic qualities and on the support of the church, all this was a catastrophe, an aberration, and, to some extent, a betrayal. After all the state had done for the church, the latter, at the critical moment, was washing its hands of the future. Reminders about services rendered, the warnings and complaints of ministers such as those of justice and foreign affairs, fell on deaf ears (Payne, 1984, p. 265). The church hierarchy responded with a new demand by appealing to the Catholic convictions of its rulers to renounce the privilege of the presentation of bishops, which was one of the few mechanisms left to the state for exerting pressure on the church.

Many clerics responded by intensifying their support for the political and trade union opposition, with recourse to canon law (although this was in fact no more than taking advantage of a political privilege which had been granted by Francoism itself). In consequence, the ecclesiastical prison in Zamora began to fill up with priests, who reached the point of rioting in 1973 (Payne, 1984, p. 228), and the bishops themselves began to feel the effects of irritating the state. On the occasion of the funeral of Admiral Carrero Blanco in 1973, the notorious cries of "Tarancón, al paredón!" ("Tarancón, to the execution wall!" or "to the firing squad!") were heard; and in 1974 the government was on the point of expelling a Basque bishop from the country (the Añoveros affair). However, by these outbursts the state was merely betraying its weakness; it only managed to reinforce the determination of the church, even offering it the opportunity of figuring in the list of honor of those persecuted under Francoism.

Nevertheless, the estrangement of the church from the Francoist state was not just a simple inversion of alliances; it was part of a new understanding, and a more complex one, which the church reached in trying to place itself in a position equidistant from the democratic opposition and the reformist sectors of Francoism. Among the latter was the sector organized around the Tácito group, a group of Catholic civil servants and professionals, the majority of whom came from the Francoist political class, finally becoming a source of leaders and a laboratory for political formulas for the democratic transition (Rodríguez Buznego, 1986).

At the same time, the church increased its exchanges with the democratic opposition, a relationship made easier by three factors. First, the traditional leaders of the opposition parties had abandoned their antireligious and anticlerical attitudes dating from the civil war. Second, the new political class had to some extent been formed by the church, not only because the church had directly provided some leaders, outlines for programs, significant organizational resources, and ideological as well as institutional cover and protection from repression, but also, and above all, because the church had contributed toward shaping the overall experiences of many young people who had begun their political education in opposition to Francoism in the 1950s and 1960s. During those crucial years quite a number of these young people maintained their religious motivation and their ties with the priesthood and, as a result, the feeling of being part of a family, as reflected by a certain language, certain ways of thinking, and certain values. Perhaps they began in organizations such as the FLP, Cuadernos para el Diálogo, or the JOC, ending up in the PSOE, the Communist party, Izquierda Democrática, Convergencia i Unió, or UCD. These first experiences were very intense, with frequent interaction between these young Catholics and other non-Catholic young people, with the shared sensations of risk and a common adversary and feelings of belonging to the same generational community. Out of such experiences came patterns of dialogue and communication within the political opposition (as well as within civil society) which were later to become generalized during the years of transition, thus anticipating the characteristics of a community in which the winners and losers of the civil war were reconciled. From these experiences were born memories of recognition and respect, and even of gratitude and feelings of debt toward some sectors of the ecclesiastical establishment, which were to ensure crucial moral and political credit for the church at the time of transition.

Third, the fact that (in what was a very deliberate act on the part of the hierarchy) no Christian-democratic party was created contributed to the good relations between the new political class and the church, since the former ceased to fear any competition from the latter on its own territory. This fact was the result of a decision the church made mainly for two reasons. For one thing, the church lacked the capacity to form a party. It had practically destroyed its own organizations in the second half of the 1960s (recall the crisis of Catholic Action), and its militants had been committing themselves to other organizations. And for another, it lacked the overriding motive for the creation of a Christian-democratic party: the sense of a sufficiently serious threat to its core values and even bare existence. Communism and fascism, or their equivalents, were the historical reasons for which Catholics had overcome their internal differences and created a relatively homogeneous party in places such as Italy, for example, after the war. But Spanish fascism in the 1970s lacked force (as was to be proved with the first elections); and the moderate attitude of the Communist party and the continual experience of dialogue between Christians and Marxists in opposition to Francoism made the flag of anticommunism equally unviable.

As a consequence the church found itself playing a very important part in the years of the political transition, between 1975 and 1978, even without a party over which it could claim control or influence. On the one hand, it was capable of understanding and giving support to both the reformist sector of Francoism and the democratic opposition. On the other, it made a decisive contribution toward easing the hostility of the conservative right to the new democratic regime. It impeded a revival of the crusade spirit; it minimized the dangers originating from extremism; and, in general, it eroded or weakened the ideological foundations of any strategy of harassment of the democracy by the hard-liners of the state apparatus, particularly the army. Its direct and explicit support of the political transition was demonstrated by the positions it took, resulting in the acceptance of the Law of Political Reform in 1976 and the Constitution in 1978, which was accepted by the overwhelming majority of Spanish bishops, in spite of not inconsiderable reservations on some matters.

With the Constitution, the church accepted the principles of a non-denominational state and religious freedom (article 16), being satisfied with a recognition of what has been called the sociological fact of the Catholic church (in other words, a recognition that the Catholic church is a fact of life in Spanish society that the state is bound to respect), together with a declaration of the desirability of cooperation between the Catholic church (and other denominations) and the state. Recognition of the church in the Constitution was important also because it implied substantial freedom of movement for the church, whose structure and whose acts the state was committed to respecting. This was all the more important for the church inasmuch as Catholic doctrine, including that of the Second Vatican Council (Portier, 1986), has always set as the limit to the legitimacy of prevailing legislation (including the legality of a liberal democracy) that of "natural order" or "natural morality," whose content was to be interpreted chiefly by the church; and the church foresaw problems to come in the field of education, as well as legislation on divorce and abortion.

From that moment on, the church had to face up to a pluralistic situation not only with regard to religious beliefs and institutions but also in the political sphere. The church had not been able to control any of the new parties, nor did it seem to have much influence over the Catholic vote. In fact, the Catholic electorate, following a tendency observable in other countries (for France, see Berger, 1985b), dispersed its political preferences. This worked particularly in favor of the Socialist party, which has received a substantial portion of the Catholic vote, including the vote of practicing Catholics, who made up about 25 percent of the Socialist electorate between 1979 and 1982 (Montero, 1986, p. 157).[11]

In this situation of religious and political pluralism the Spanish church has apparently been reduced to just one more pressure group, which, in order to achieve its aims, must depend on the good will of its allies and the support of its rank-and-file members, which is to say, on laymen. Alliances and support of this nature can be problematical because the attitude of laymen toward the typical pretensions of the church (to amplifying its influence in their lives and reducing them to mere subordinates of the ecclesiastical organization) can be one of resistance. As I suggested earlier, if the church loses or renounces its monopoly over the religious offer, it may find that this is only the beginning of a series of compromises and concessions to the laity still to come.

In Spain the church, which no longer has an almost total monopoly over the religious or even the cultural offer which it has had in the past, has also had to confront laymen who were increasingly accustomed to exercising their freedom and had greater confidence in their own judgment—judgment which has increasingly diverged from ecclesiastical teaching, as was evident in the matter of divorce and abortion. For, while the church had used up all its energies in the 1960s and 1970s absorbing internal conflicts, putting its house in order, and ensuring for itself a dignified way out of Francoism and a role in the political transition, coming to an agreement with the corresponding political class, the evolution of civil society, its beliefs, feelings, and everyday practices had been taking its course. The consequence of this dual evolution, of the church and of society, has been a remoteness and a growing lack of relevance of the church's messages of meaning, salvation, and community in the eyes of a considerable part of civil society.

Ecclesiastical teaching has been relatively devalued on questions of public and private morality, on the former because the spectacular change of heart of the church with regard to Francoism can be interpreted as an attempt to draw closer to the dominant trends in secular thinking and to an accommodation with modern secular institutions. However praiseworthy this change may have been, it has shown not moral authority but rather the capacity to adapt.

The general perception of the increasing irrelevance of the church's teachings even in matters of private morality is the result of several factors. It may be partly attributed to the processes of the establishment and extension of worldly values, of searching for success or happiness on earth by achieving power, wealth, status, knowledge, affection, or sensual gratification according to one's preferences, but with only marginal reference to religious life, which have continued through recent years. In addition there is the fact that the church itself, in both its conservative and its progressive wings, has gradually devalued the laity's expectations and aspirations for achieving their salvation through sacramental practices, placing more emphasis on their participation in temporal activities. Finally, it must be taken into account that religious motivations in the search for a moral community are no longer played out against the background of a divided community of Spaniards, burdened by recent memories of a civil war. In opposition to the theater of self-destruction of the civil war, the years of transition and democratic consolidation have witnessed a theater of self-reconciliation, displayed in repeated ceremonies of consensus and rituals of understanding and the signing of agreements of all kinds—political and social pacts, regional statutes, understandings with the army and the church. As a result, the call of the church for social peace, however proper it may be, constitutes only one more voice in the polyphony of concord.

It is probable that as a consequence of all this, civil society has been reducing the intensity of its religious beliefs and the frequency of its practices; and that in this way, to some extent, it has been slipping away from the sphere of influence of the church. The vast majority of Spanish people today—86 percent according to the 1984 CIS (Centro de Investigaciones Sociológicas) survey—continue to consider themselves Catholic. But it seems that the proportion of "good" or practicing Catholics has dropped from about 56 percent to 31 percent according to some surveys carried out between 1976 and 1983 (Orizo, 1983, p. 177). Results of opinion polls cannot be taken as unequivocal indications of people's religious feelings and beliefs, not to mention their actual behavior, but are only rough approximations. At the same time, however, the internal consistency of these findings adds to their overall plausibility. These surveys suggest a marked reduction in the degree to which Spanish Catholics adopt the professions of faith and moral teachings of the church. Their orthodoxy thus seems limited. By 1969 the numbers of Spanish people who professed to believe in the infallibility of the pope (76 percent), the existence of hell (80 percent), the dogma of the Trinity (93 percent), and the real presence of Christ in the Eucharist (86 percent) were extremely high (Hermet, 1985, p. 72). But the CIS survey of 1984 found that those percentages had dropped considerably. The vast majority continued to believe in the existence of God (87 percent), but those who believed *without doubt* in a God who created the universe (59 percent), the divine nature of Jesus Christ (56 percent), and the existence of heaven (50 percent) were now scarcely a majority. Similarly, those who believed in the existence of the immortal soul (46 percent), the resurrection of the dead (41 percent), and the existence of hell (40 percent) were now a minority. It is true that the percentages are higher in the subgroup of practicing Catholics; but even then it should be emphasized that only two thirds of them accept without doubt the infallibility of the pope (61 percent), the resurrection of the dead (76 percent), the existence of hell (63 percent), and the existence of the immortal soul (68 percent). The proportion is reduced to between a fifth and a third in the subgroup of nonpracticing Catholics, 21 percent of whom believed without doubt in the infallibility of the pope, 26 percent in the resurrection of the dead, 25 percent in the existence of hell, and 33 percent in the existence of the immortal soul (CIS, 1984; Laboa, 1986, p. 90; see also Orizo, 1983, p. 173).

We also find that there are substantial numbers of Spaniards who consider themselves Catholics but nonetheless reject the teaching of the church on questions of sexual morality. This is not, of course, exclusive to Spaniards. It has been observed how, in the United States, a majority of Catholics reject the teaching of the church on the question of contraceptives (88 percent), the ordination of women (52 percent), the marriage of priests (63 percent), remarriage of divorcees (73 percent), and even abortion in the case of rape or incest (55 percent) (*International Herald Tribune,* November, 25, 1985). Similar findings can be observed in Spain: a sizable number of Spaniards accept the use of contraceptives (65 percent), the marriage of priests (54 percent), the dissolution of Catholic marriages (47 percent), and premarital sexual relations (45 percent) (CIS, 1984).

Furthermore, we have seen how the influence of the church in political life has been limited: for example, religious affiliation only moderately reduces the probability that a practicing Catholic will vote

Socialist. We also know that, in general terms, Spaniards think that the church should not have any influence in government (43 percent) (CIS, 1984).

It is even riskier to take the results of opinion polls as indicating the real weight and evolution of the influence of the church on the morality of the Spanish people, on their attitudes toward the basic values of social coexistence, and on their respect for other people and their property. The proportion of Spaniards who, taken at their word, accept the Ten Commandments would lie between 56 percent for the Eighth Commandment ("Thou shalt not lie") and 81 percent for the Fifth Commandment ("Thou shall not kill"), with figures ranging in between for the Fourth, the Seventh, and the Tenth Commandments (referring to honoring one's parents and respecting the property rights of others), the percentages being between seven and twelve points higher in the case of practicing Catholics (Orizo, 1983, p. 190; for comparisons with other European countries, see Stoetzel, 1982, pp. 339, 340). This suggests a relatively high degree of influence of the moral teaching of the church, at least regarding general declarations of principle. However, 61 percent of these same people manifested their belief that "there could never be absolutely clear-cut lines drawn between good and evil . . . What is good or evil depends on the circumstances at the time" (Orizo, 1983, p. 64). This poses questions about what the influence might be when the time came to make a real decision, particularly since a relative majority believe that the church does *not* have adequate solutions to the moral problems and needs of individuals (43 percent, as opposed to 39 percent who think it has), or the problems of family life (49 percent as opposed to 34 percent) (Orizo, 1983, p. 190), or else think that the church pretends to a moral authority which is not based on awareness of reality (41 percent as opposed to 27 percent) (CIS, 1984).

Finally, I must refer to what, for some sociologists of religion, has traditionally been the fundamental indicator of religiosity: the rate of attendance at Sunday Mass. The figure varies, according to different estimates, between 34 percent and 42 percent of the nation (Laboa, 1986), a relatively high figure, lower than that for Ireland but similar to that for Italy and much higher than that for France (see also Martín Patino, 1984, p. 196). It seems probable that there has been a decrease in this practice, particularly since the mid-seventies (Montero, 1986, p. 137). In the case of young people, we know that the frequency of attendance at Sunday Mass has gone down substantially from 62 percent to 35 percent between 1975 and 1982 (Toharia, 1985).

What is suggested by these data is certainly not the panorama of a thoroughly Catholic society, nor one in the process of becoming so. However, this diagnosis must be tempered by four considerations. First, it must be remembered that, in relative terms, the importance of the Catholic church in Spain remains considerable. Between 30 percent and 40 percent of Spaniards can be considered practicing Catholics. This may seem small in relation to the ideal of the church triumphant, which was a total conversion to Catholicism of the whole country, but the percentage is very high if it is compared to that of any other ideological group in society, as defined by other beliefs and moral attitudes. For example, the total of practicing left-wingers in the country (those who consider themselves to be socialists, communists, or of the extreme left, and who are active in trade union parties) probably does not reach even 5 percent of the population. Second, a distinction must be made between the ecclesiastical dimension of the process of slipping away from submission to the institutional authority of the church and its religious dimension (that of a weakening of personal religious beliefs and morals). And it must be pointed out that the latter is a very complex phenomenon indeed, about which we have only scarce and unreliable information, including the rather enigmatic responses to survey questions.

Third, the recent signs of dynamism in the Catholic church must not be overlooked. The decrease in religious vocations has reversed, and the slight increase in the numbers of seminarians seemed to be gaining momentum through the second half of the 1980s. New forms of organization have emerged such as Christian communities (neoecumenical, but also popular and charismatic), which seem to be prospering (Martín Patino, 1984, p. 192). Religion no longer polarizes the Spanish people, either politically or socially. At the end of the 1970s it was estimated that about 45 percent of people who considered themselves to be middle or upper-middle class were practicing Catholics, as were 38 percent of the lower-middle classes and 34 percent of the working classes (Martín Patino, 1984, pp. 202ff.). Yet, on the visit of Pope John Paul II to Spain in 1982, immediately after the Socialist victory in the elections of that year, a time when Catholic organizations were protesting against the Socialist legislation on education, mass demonstrations of an extraordinary extent were witnessed, showing the notable capacity and disposition of the Catholic masses for mobilization.

Finally, a positive sign of the dynamism and potential of Catholic culture in Spain may be seen in the fact that, even if practicing Catholics are less numerous among the younger generations than the older ones, certain details relative to the mood and nature of these younger Catholics suggest that they are more at ease in their environment and happier and more optimistic than young non-Catholics (or less conscientiously practicing Catholics). They feel more united with their families (58 percent as opposed to 47 percent of non-Catholics) and more in tune with their parents in their attitudes toward religion (68 percent as opposed to 25 percent), morality (66 percent as opposed to 36 percent), and politics (41 percent as opposed to 23 percent); they feel happier (only 9 percent of these Catholics felt unhappy or not very happy as opposed to 22 percent of the rest) and more optimistic about life (58 percent as opposed to 47 percent) (Toharia, 1985). So it seems that, once again, in the midst of a rather troubled situation for the church and Spanish Catholicism, it is possible to detect new if ambiguous signs of hope.

This study belongs to a genre of interpretive works of a general nature in which an analytical discussion is tied to a series of empirical observations about religion and the church in Spain since the civil war. Religion and religious experiences are central to this study inasmuch as it is about the content of the church's offer and the demands of its followers, and insofar as the phenomenon is a complex one, with dimensions relating to culture, beliefs, experience, morality, and organization (Glock, 1971). The focus of my argument, however, has been on explaining the causes and mechanisms behind the transformations in the church in response to its own conflicts and the pressures of the environment in which it moved, chiefly the state and civil society, during the crucial step from the Francoism of the 1940s to the liberal democracy of the 1970s and 1980s, and on doing so in the general terms necessary to cover such a wide and dramatic period while clearly retaining the outlines of an inevitably complex argument.

I have preferred to speak not so much of a process of secularization of Spanish life during this period as about a process of transformations, metamorphoses, or perhaps avatars. I use this term by way of analogy with its original meaning in Hinduism, as the incarnation of the deity (usually Vishnu) in human or nonhuman forms in times of crisis or tribulation, when the dharma, or universal order or law, is in danger, for the purpose of counteracting evil and reestablishing the balance. The doctrine assumes that these incarnations are various and (in late Hinduism) thus explain the existence of holy men. Obviously Christianity, with its doctrine of the unique incarnation of the deity in Jesus Christ, is incompatible with Hinduism; but this theological incompatibility is irrelevant for the purposes of using the term as an analogy (and one which is close, by the way, to theatrical experience) in the field of the sociology of religion. The changes in the historic project of the Spanish church (national Catholicism), in the religious offer or message of the church to its followers, in the structure of relations between the church and the state and society have been so profound that one may speak of the successive incarnations of different characters in a historical drama. In each new characterization or incarnation we see a response from the religious institution to a situation of disorder: a response directed toward a restoration of the balance which has been lost or the establishment of a new one.

As for the theory of secularization, it is now some time since it was shown to be ambiguous, at least in the most general terms (see, for example, Luckmann, 1969), so that it would have to be broken down into more specific propositions. The very term *secularization* lends itself to ambiguity, for it has a different connotation according to whether it refers to the reduction of the religious or of the ecclesiastical arena: religious or ecclesiastical secularization. In no way can these be considered identical. The religious area includes the explanations, justifications, and propositions of meaning which apply to the existence of divine or supernatural figures and to human interaction with these divine figures. The ecclesiastical area refers to certain more specific spaces within which a body of intermediaries plays an important role in interpreting meaning, administering the gifts of salvation (such as grace), and mediating in the interaction between human beings and the divine figures in such a way that those intermediary agents may exercise authority over these human beings.

So the three dimensions of meaning, salvation, and community apply to both the religious and the ecclesiastical spheres of human experience. This conceptual scheme implies the possibility of formulating hypotheses relative to the expansion or reduction of such spheres along all these dimensions, taking into account that the reductions in some areas and along some dimensions may or may not be compensated for by reductions in others. Finally, it is not sufficient to consider only the extension of the areas in question; it is also important to consider their intensity or depth, for a reduction in the extension of one area may be compensated for by an increase in its intensity, that is, in the importance or value assigned to the corresponding religious or ecclesiastical sphere.

Since the object of this study has not been the formal or systematic discussion of the secularization thesis, the reader will allow me to leave the application of the scheme just outlined to the case of Spain for another occasion. Suffice it to say that the evolution of the last one hundred years is a long way from demonstrating a general tendency which embraces all the areas I have been considering. The reduction of the ecclesiastical sphere, and perhaps of the religious one, seems evident at least between the beginning and the last third of the nineteenth century, but not since that time. The church seems to have recovered lost ground from the 1880s on, taking advantage of operations which had been set in motion decades earlier, in its understandings with the state as much as in its penetration of civil society. However, the events of the 1930s highlight the inadequacy of anything it had imagined. The outcome of the civil war, and even the experience of the war itself, meant an enormous expansion in both the religious and the ecclesiastical arenas, particularly in the latter. In any case, religion and church acquired extraordinary prominence in the 1940s, 1950s, and much of the 1960s in spite of various tensions. A denominational state and a total conversion of society to Catholicism appeared to go hand in hand for part of this period. What has happened since then may indicate a reduction in the ecclesiastical sphere but not necessarily a weakening, at least in relation to the church's public powers, especially if its situation in these years is compared to the political relationship of church and state and the new political class that emerged between 1965 and 1975. As for the signs of a reduction in the area of religiosity, these are inconclusive and at times ambiguous.

If, within the dramatic and eventful evolution over a century and more, we were to look for a pattern, I would propose the hypothesis of a spiral evolution, of chiaroscuro, or, if one prefers (and nothing could be more appropriate to the subject), a hypothesis of divine irony within the Spanish Catholic church. Irony is a play of contrasts in which reality is made to progress in such a way that in moments of triumph there appear the seeds of disaster, and in moments of crisis the seeds of hope, all in a strangely systematic way. In effect, each crucial development in Spanish life during these years has been for the church an ironic situation (Fussel, 1981), both better and worse than expected. When the Spanish church was on the verge of securing an understanding with the establishment of the restoration, crowning the efforts of forty years of alternate and combined tactical *ralliement* and hard-line Catholicism, and even succumbed to the temptation of acting with the support of the dictatorship of Primo de Rivera, it found itself besieged by the profoundly anticlerical offensive of the Second Republic and the anarchist masses, whose strength and enthusiasm for the task at hand the church had not been able to foresee. All of this brought the church to the verge of a terrible defeat. But from this crisis arose the possibility of a triumph such as the Catholic hierarchy had scarcely dared hope for even in its wildest dreams: the historic, almost miraculous possibility of repeating the sixteenth century four hundred years later—the triumph and exaltation of the church. Then, all of a sudden, from out of nowhere came the clerics themselves, some troubled or disillusioned, aware that the church had forgotten the workers, the peripheral nationalities, and the youth of the nation in its ambition for social and political leadership. The church discovered that a part of itself was questioning its own triumph and eroding the political-religious edifice of the Nationalist victory. Then, from the era of crisis, from a church disrupted and divided against itself, it reemerged with new vitality and a new capacity to carry out an extraordinary political reconversion. It had become the church of liberal democracy, so much so that even an important part of the success of the new political regime could be attributed to it, thus winning it the respect of the new political class and public opinion. But it also happened that, at the same moment, the church found itself caught up in a process of secularization (certainly ecclesiastical and possibly, to a large extent, religious) which had been taking place for almost thirty years: the slipping away, little by little, of civil society from within its sphere of influence. In each of these historical moments a triumph; in each triumph hubris (including forgetfulness of the period preceding the triumph) and in consequence the need to pay the price of that hubris in the form of a situation of crisis; and in each situation of crisis, finally, signs of hope for the institution: the irony of history or the irony of Providence.

With relation to the more specific evolution in the ecclesiastical arena since the crisis of the political-religious edifice of the church triumphant, it can be said that first, there has been a tendency toward the reduction of this sphere, and second, that within this sphere there has been an increase in the weight of the voice of the laity and the lower orders of ecclesiastics, a modest but visible democratization. The parallel with what has happened in the state over the same period seems obvious. Here there was also a retreat from authoritarianism in the last years of Franco, to the advantage of society, stimulated by social movements and organizations which wanted freedom of movement, even if afterward, once the new state was firmly established, the emerging political class proceeded to expand the volume of resources under its control, and, of course, the new state brought with it a democracy.

Even so, it cannot be concluded from a reduction in the area of influence of the church that there has been a process of religious secularization, owing either to a reduction of the religious arena or to a decrease in the intensity of religious experience. It is true that many aspects of the modern experience, such as the development of science and education and involvement in economic markets and modern political institutions such as state bureaucracies and more generally in organizations of all kinds, seem to have extended the sphere of human experience where nonreligious explanations look increasingly plausible and religious ones rather redundant, in Spain as in so many other countries. And it is also true that the expectation of liberation from certain kinds of suffering, and certainly from scarcity, and the subsequent gratification of a rather wide range of desires and needs have considerably increased as a result of technical and economic growth, the development of liberal democratic states, and more liberal and permissive social mores, all this without much religious reference. But it is no less evident that some aspects of modernity have been quite oppressive, and indeed that even at its best, modernity cannot eradicate the roots of human ignorance and suffering. In their search for knowledge and happiness people confront limits that they may expand but cannot eliminate, for the more they know, the more they become conscious of what they do not know. A similar dialectic can be applied to other dimensions of their experience. Therefore, even under the best of circumstances a place can always be reserved for demands for explanation, salvation, and community of an ultimate nature which, in principle, can take many different forms and be met by very diverse religious offers and a wide variety of institutional arrangements.

Modern conditions may enhance, for instance, the likelihood of a church based on largely autonomous local congregations, which would be compatible with an intensely personal religious feeling as well as with very different attitudes toward the temporal order. Such a church would be able to formulate its religious message in terms of the legitimation of that order or in terms of a prophetic denunciation of it; or it could even dispense with the temporal order, recognizing that whatever human value action in this world may have, it is impossible to interpret the specific *religious* content of that action, in the way that it could be defined by God himself, since the inscrutability of God means that any pretension to interpret him, including that of the church, would be in vain (although that may imply entering into Barthian reasoning, probably incompatible with the fundamentals of a church such as the Catholic church). By testing all these messages under different local conditions and before different audiences, and more particularly by testing all the possible mixes and combinations of them, that church might possibly be able to recuperate, or even extend, its influence in the world.

An example of this capacity is offered by the resurgence of Protestant fundamentalism in the United States (Roof, 1984; Hunter, 1985; Cox, 1984). Bound up within it is an intense and emotional religiosity, the prominence of local churches, styles and forms of authority which are at times democratic and at times authoritarian, and certain specific messages about the nature of temporal activities. The limited size, the activism of the shepherd, the creation of a vigilant collective opinion, and the very literalness of interpretation of the Word combine to ensure in these communities of spiritual kinship stability in the definition of the group situation and consistency of meaning of the behavior of its members (Ault, 1984; Bittner, 1963). But a Catholic fundamentalism may also be observed which paradoxically accepts the role of a lay priesthood, the importance of the local church, an emphasis on the message and the Word, and even an attitude of prophetic denunciation of power (which Paul Tillich considers the "Protestant principle" par excellence; see Tillich, 1957), or at least the power of totalitarian regimes, and which, nevertheless, makes all these innovations compatible with the pope, the sacraments, respect for fragments of a popular magical religion, and an otherwise very catholic eclecticism successfully practiced throughout the history of the church, as exemplified by the work of John Paul II. Of course, this Catholic fundamentalism coexists with the church, with liberal theology—which had its best moments during the Second Vatican Council—with the curious situation of the masses of believers who have come to the conclusion that they can be Catholics, and good Catholics, without accepting substantial proportions of church teaching as to questions of faith and social mores, whether these be of a public or a private nature. What we observe here is a far more complex and colorful Catholic pluralism than that of the schism which occurred between liberals and hard-liners in the nineteenth and early twentieth centuries, or, more recently, between progressives and conservatives.

There was a time when observers of religious phenomena thought that there was a clear process of secularization affecting the religious as much as the ecclesiastical sphere, and they forecast a reduction of the importance of religion and the churches, pushing to its limits Weber's ideas on the disenchantment of the world. They even thought that, in a situation of religious pluralism, there was a tendency for the religious offer, being flexible and sensitive to demand, to become homogeneous under the pressure of homogeneous demand, in the belief that in the convergence of the Protestant denominations, liberal Judaism, Catholicism, and secular humanism in the United States was to be seen a corroboration of this hypothesis (Berger, 1971). We now see, on the contrary, the persistence of the religious phenomenon and an increase in the differentiation of religious demand as much as of the religious offer and, as a result, a growing pluralism in the world of Christian belief, Catholic or otherwise, and in the non-Christian world as well, as is seen in the ferment in the world of Islam.

4

Region, Economy, and the Scale of Governance: Mesogovernments in Spain

Any government needs to justify itself in the eyes of the people under its domain. In order to do this it makes an appeal to various sources of legitimacy. Max Weber concentrated his attention on three of these: faith in personal or institutional charisma, adherence to tradition, and acceptance of legal forms (Weber, 1978, pp. 212ff.). But in addition to coercion and the factors mentioned by Weber, there is another reason for obedience, namely, instrumental consent to authority by reason of its success in resolving certain basic problems of society. In the long term, society will agree to the authority of politicians only if this capacity is present. In other words, modern social consent implies contract: obedience is given in exchange for successful leadership. This argument applies in particular to liberal and capitalist societies. In these societies consent to authority on the condition that it demonstrates a capacity to solve (or reduce) certain basic problems is an explicit principle regulating the relationship between civil society and the political class. Periodically society chooses from among competing segments of this class and hands power over to one or the other on the condition that it be efficient (or at least less inefficient). If this condition is not fulfilled, power is withdrawn and handed over to the opposition.

In contemporary times, however, the capacity of not just one sector or another of the political class but the political class as a whole, and by implication the political regime itself, to solve the problems of modern societies has been called into question. There has been talk of a crisis of governability or of a trend toward ungovernability in many countries. So it would seem that the liberal societies were governable during the 1950s and 1960s, but since then the situation has worsened substantially. Between the Vietnam war and the Watergate affair, the United States lived through a period of turbulence and confusion. Europe suffered intense distributive conflicts, youth rebellions, the resurgence of various peripheral nationalist movements, and spectacular explosions such as those occurring in May 1968 in France, or the Autunno Caldo in Italy in 1969, which seemed to be redolent of a crisis in society itself. This is the historical context in which the literature of governability first appeared in political science.[1]

Let us accept as a starting point that the advanced liberal capitalist societies of today face a crisis of governability, the solution to which depends on the capacity of their governments to solve certain basic problems. Among these are matters of defense and territorial integrity vis-à-vis other countries, law and order, economic growth, and social integration. In many of these countries an attempt has been made to make the agent for resolving these problems not just the government in its widest sense, including the executive and legislative branches, but also what I call intermediate governments, or mesogovernments; indeed, extensive authority has been delegated to these mesogovernments. I take this term from the Greek root *mesos* (middle) to denote institutionalized sets of positions of authority and their corresponding administrative structures in associations of domination whose authority is reinforced by that of the central state; whose activity is directed toward satisfying the interests and social identities of subnational groups which are functionally or territorially differentiated; and where these groups are of a scale or scope that lies between the large scale of macrogovernance at the state or national level and to the small scale of local or sectional microgovernance.

I shall focus my discussion on two types of mesogovernments: those which are territorially defined, and those which are functional or economic in nature.[2] According to my definition, the authority of these mesogovernments is reinforced by that of the state, and their social bases are territorially differentiated populations or functionally defined economic classes, such as employers and workers, whose interests and identities they try to defend. These mesogovernments may adopt many and varied organizational forms. Territorial mesogovernments may be grouped into federated states, as in Germany; autonomous governments, as in Spain; or regional governments, as in Italy. Various types of economic mesogovernments may be lumped together under the title of neocorporatism, a term which describes a system of intermediation of interests and of a participation in the definition and execution of the economic policy of the state (Schmitter and Lehmbruch, 1979).

THE ROLE OF THE POLITICAL CLASS

I do not believe that we can get very far in discussing the reasons for the appearance of intermediate governments by attributing them to the needs or requirements of capitalism, the modern state, or any other entity of this type. This would force us into the fallacy of abstraction by attributing purposes, aspirations, or needs to these institutional complexes or by reifying great historical tendencies such as progress, democratization, bureaucratization, organizational revolution, and so on.[3] This is not to imply that these institutions and trends are irrelevant, but they may best be taken *cum grano salis,* to identify the context or situation within which specific historical agents may be found and motivated to act. Mesogovernments must be understood as the result of the actions, many of them deliberate, of these real protagonists who naturally are neither omniscient nor omnicompetent, nor are they always able to avoid the undesirable consequences of their behavior. Such agents operate not within the framework of an ideal empty space but within a circumscribed historical context, an accumulation of trajectories, and a legacy of possibilities and constraints.

Thus, I consider these intermediate governments to be instruments designed by particular human agencies for the purpose of solving certain problems. More specifically, these mesogovernments are an institutional construction of the political class which controls the government or state with the cooperation of certain social elites and the support, to a greater or lesser extent, of the people. If the concept of the state refers to the whole collection of roles of authority and administrative functions within an association that enjoys a monopoly over the legitimate use of force, then the expression *political class* refers to the set of individuals who occupy these roles (the incumbents) plus the set of individuals who make it their business to oppose or ally themselves with these incumbents in the more or less remote expectation of being able to succeed them in their posts.[4] This political class is composed of professional politicians, usually organized into political parties; administrative bodies, including both civil servants in the widest sense, encompassing employees in the public sector or those who are dependent on public funds, and the officers of political parties and organizations; and the military or members of party militias. It is well to restrict the use of the term to the civilian political class, as I shall do throughout this discussion.

This political class may be divided for the sake of analytical convenience into two groups, *incumbents* and their allies, and their *opposition*. This division can vary as to degree, reflecting in different ways the divisions in the social strata which support one or the other segment. In liberal societies the political division is normally softened by a fundamental pact, generally implicit, whereby one of these groups governs on condition that it guarantee its adherence to certain rules of the game which could result in its eventual replacement by the other group. To this may be added other factors which contribute to bringing the political adversaries closer together. These are the result of their frequent interaction and the fact that their socialization processes are similar; this generates a certain code of conduct among politicians as well as certain ways of looking at things, their own language and style, which distinguish them from the rest of society. This unity is also a product of their common interest in demonstrating that they control the state in such a way that it will not fall into the hands of historical competitors such as the clergy, the military, the squirearchy, or extremists of one type or another. This common interest in occupying by turns the state and government of civil society is probably the decisive factor in the configuration of the democratic political class. In fact, the phrase *governing society* has a double meaning: on the one hand, it means trying to solve the problems of the country, which is one of the keys to the legitimization of the political class; on the other, it means the group that is dominating civil society, exercising, preserving, and extending its power of domination.

The arrangement which exists within the political class is not enough to make orderly government possible. The consent of society is also needed. Society is internally structured and differentiated by region and class and other criteria. The social groups may be more or less organized and ruled over, with a greater or lesser degree of firmness, by regional or socioeconomic elites. The central political class at the national or state level confronts a dilemma with regard to these elites. It may reduce, ignore, or eliminate them, or back some of them in order to reduce the power of others, running the risk that resistance might rupture the linkage of consent between society and the political class. Or it may respect them and their autonomy, running the risk that the power of these subnational elites which then limit the power of the central authorities. Therefore, the political class has to choose between two basic strategies: either to submit these social powers to its authority, or to associate these powers with its authority. Choosing the second option may involve the development of a system of mesogovernments.

The political class is more likely to opt for a strategy of constructing mesogovernments the weaker it is with regard to solving the problems of social integration and economic crisis and the more it must deal with regional or socioeconomic elites who already have de facto veto powers but who are nonetheless prepared to compromise. The strategy may also depend on the moral and technical resources available to persuade the people of the desirability and technical feasibility of intermediate governments, and the generic support, or at least the acquiescence, of a significant segment of that population for any formula that seems capable of reducing the level of conflict among the competing elites.

The weakness of a political class may be the result of its internal division into several parts, none of which would be capable of imposing itself on the others. The formula of consociational democracy applied in Holland or Switzerland, for example, came about through scenarios of this nature (Lijphart, 1975). In turn, this experience facilitated the subsequent appearance of corporatist formulas (Katzenstein, 1984). Weakness might also be due to the fact that the political class does not enjoy the loyalty of the bureaucratic system and/or of the armed forces, or that it does not have the support of grass-roots parties, as is usually the case during a transition toward democracy such as Spain has experienced in the recent past. Weakness may also be rooted in the precariousness of the political regime resulting from war, defeat, or occupation by an enemy, as happened in Germany and Austria after the Second World War. It may even stem from the fact that the party which has predominated historically does not have sufficient resources to impose its will on major social forces in civil life, as was the case with the Scandinavian social democrats for a long time, and which forced them to accept an equilibrium of sorts with business associations, trade unions, and the bourgeois parties. But whatever its causes, the point is that such weakness is relative to the intensity of the problems to be solved and to the nature of the system of alliances and conflicts among politicians, business groups, unions, and regional elites. The political class may be confronted with extraordinarily serious problems of social integration and/or economic crisis. As, during the 1930s, the corporatist arrangements which would subsequently be developed after the Second World War were sketched out, the impetus in many countries was the twofold crisis of a very high level of unemployment and of extremist threats to social stability from the fascist right and the communist left (Lehmbruch, 1979a).

Throughout the postwar period these corporatist arrangements developed, *pari passu*, with the pressure of inflation and distributive conflicts. It has been argued that the extraordinary vulnerability of some countries in the context of the world market made them more prone to this kind of arrangement, as danger from the outside calls into question the capacity of the government to control the situation and moves actors toward social dialogue. Countries such as Sweden, Norway, Holland, and Switzerland, for example, reacted to their economic dependence with semicorporatist arrangements. This made it possible for Sweden to have a policy directed toward export, whereas in Austria the same kind of arrangement was connected with a more protectionist policy (Katzenstein, 1984).

For the response to these problems to take the specific form of mesogovernments, the political class must be able to avail itself of the support of social elites with the capacity and will to share in the burden of governance. In the case of corporatist arrangements, this seems to require the presence of business and trade union organizations with a wide array of resources. It is usually argued that this in turn calls for unions with high membership figures and centralized structures (Lehmbruch, 1979a), as might have been the case with northern and central European unions. By contrast, British trade unions did not have the capacity to control local disputes. Up to the 1970s the French and Italian unions had low membership figures. However, it may be possible to make up for the absence of these enabling resources with a strategic capacity for vetoing public decisions, which can occur when the lack of union membership is balanced by a high degree of union influence at a difficult point in the process, as happened in Spain during the transition from authoritarian rule. In the case of territorial mesogovernments, the importance of the factors of timing and momentary influence is even more evident. Territorial reforms by the state are unlikely to occur in the absence of powerful peripheral nationalisms (Gourevitch, 1980). An ethic, national, or regional potential is not enough. It must be articulated through an energetic political organization.

The construction of mesogovernments also depends on whether or not certain cultural resources exist. It is difficult, not to say impossible, to construct a stable system of corporatism without a minimal ideological basis of interclass national solidarity, or without any confidence that agreements will be honored or that actors wish to cooperate (Lehmbruch, 1979a). It is difficult for functionaries who have been educated in the cult of the state and who on principle distrust social groups to agree to share public responsibility with them. Nor is it easy for a "statist" political party to agree to delegate part of its powers once it is in office. The difficulties of neocorporatism in France have been due precisely to these attitudes: the deep-rooted ideology of the class struggle among leaders and militants of certain unions, and the statism of the political class (Berger, 1985a).

But ultimately in a liberal state the agreement to construct a system of mesogovernments requires the support or the acquiescence of the people. This might come about because the people trust their social or political leaders and their organizations, owe them loyalty, and even become attached to certain charismatic personalities. Or the people may share a sense of threat or of the seriousness of a given situation and therefore adopt a feeling of solidarity. This may involve solidarity against *external competition*, which has characterized Sweden and other countries, or solidarity against *political reaction*, which has characterized several countries during their transition to democracy. These dispositions may be reinforced by the memory of a dramatic historical event which brought about values of solidarity and compromise, such as defeat in a foreign war, forced submission to a foreign invader, resistance to foreign domination, or civil war. In some cases corporatist agreements have been tried out before, in times of war or in the midst of an emotional climate of national unity or "sacred union." In many European countries the experience of the Nazi invasion favored understandings in the postwar period within the political class and among the social elites. In countries such as Spain and Austria, the memory of a civil war fostered the search for a compromise some ten or even forty years later.

PROBLEMATIC EFFECTS OF MESOGOVERNMENTS

One cannot deduce from the fact that the mesogovernments may be constructed to solve certain problems of governability that this will be their actual effect. The earliest neocorporatists took for granted that such arrangements amounted to instruments for the control of contemporary society which therefore improved its governability. Philippe Schmitter, in addition to ascribing the emergence of corporatism to the requirements of advanced capitalism (Schmitter, 1979), attempted a partial empirical test of the hypothesis concerning the greater governability of corporatist societies. He maintained, in fact, that corporatism correlated negatively with at least one of the multiple dimensions of ungovernability, which he called *unruliness*. To this end he constructed an indicator which combined figures relating to collective protest, violence or civil war, and industrial conflict (Schmitter, 1981) and found a significant relationship for the period 1960–1974. However, the question is still a long way from being resolved.

In the literature on neocorporatism several analysts have insisted on its functionality with regard to capitalism. It has frequently been associated with economic policies of a Keynesian or social democratic bent, to which part of the credit for the growth of western economies was ascribed, at least until the 1960s. For some, arguing from different political or ideological positions, this was proof of its bias in favor of the interests of the capitalist class (Panitch, 1980). Both factions supposed that neocorporatism, since it rested on a standing agreement between government, unions, and employers, would improve the efficiency of economic policy, which in turn would consolidate or save the capitalist system. The disputants all seemed to lose sight of the possibility that the policies of government, unions, and employers might be principally directed toward obtaining immediate benefits, without necessarily conveying medium- or long-term benefits to the system as a whole.

A criticism of this type has been formulated by Mancur Olson (1982), who has argued that, in general, the development of organized interest groups results in interference with the functioning of the market and of the state, to the disadvantage of both. Such operations may function within the framework of a *pluralist* system of many and varied groups, or within a *corporatist* system with a few coordinated protagonists, but in both cases the typical tendency is that of influencing policy and diverting resources in the direction of particular regional or sectoral interests. This would interfere with the objective of satisfying the public good (for example, promoting economic growth or curbing inflation). Colin Crouch (1983) has argued against this, saying that Olson accepts the possible existence of what he calls "all-encompassing organizations," which, because of their size or scope, are in a position to internalize the general consequences of their conduct. For example, they would feel the effects of inflation on the buying power of salaries, or of the fall in the investment rate on the level of unemployment. In that case, according to Crouch, Olson should accept the possibility that organizations act responsibly and, as a consequence, have favorable effects on the economy.[5] However, one might reply that these all-encompassing organizations may produce two types of policy: they could either adopt responsible policies directed toward the public good or redefine the public good in such a way that as to give priority to attaining selective benefits for themselves and for the social bases closest to them at the expense of consumers, taxpayers, the unemployed, and even future employers and workers. Perhaps in order to avoid the second possibility, Crouch (1983) suggests that the organizations be situated "in the public eye," which would make them more sensitive to the wishes of the nation and to its economic needs. But what is a suitable public forum in this sense? Is it not a space dominated by the initiative and presence of the political class and, perhaps to a lesser degree, those same organized interests? Unless we are willing to attribute to the political class the status of a "universal class" as Hegel did,[6] there is no guarantee that being in the public eye will prevent politicians, bureaucrats, and socioeconomic leaders from directing their efforts toward improving their chances in the next elections (whether general political elections or specialized associational ones) by pandering to the immediate interests of their corresponding electoral bases. This can be done at the expense of the "functionally non-privileged groups" (Schmitter, 1983), whose electoral weight and presence in that public eye is lower. To the degree to which this possibility is effectively carried out, neocorporatism tends to produce a dual society, with an extensive set of interests protected by mesogovernments and another set of interests which are not protected. Thus, there can be no opposition between corporatism and dualism, for under certain conditions, they are complementary phenomena.[7]

Regional and socioeconomic elites are also interested in reinforcing their domination over their organizations and their social bases, at the same time that the state is interested in the effectiveness of whatever agreements they might reach with those elites. This means that the leaders of organizations must be capable of persuading or compelling their own bases to comply. Such discipline is considered the sine qua non for strong corporatism. If this is the case, then the scenario of social dualism, or segmentation, may be combined with a situation in which, as a consequence of these social agreements and the setting up of their respective mesogovernments, the sphere of social action unregulated by the public authorities would diminish, and at the same time the degree of submission of individuals to the political and economic authorities would increase. The market sphere and, in general, the scope of independence for individuals (that is, the liberal component of western democracy) would thereby be reduced to a minimum. If neocorporatist agreements produce an economy which is not very efficient and a dualist and submissive civil society, then the contribution of mesogovernment to the governability of modern liberal democracy and capitalism will in the long run be negative regardless of any short- or medium-term benefits with regard to orderliness.

Analogous doubts may be cast on the effects of regional mesogovernments. Federalism (or one of its variations) might improve the efficiency and the efficacy of political and administrative agencies. Or it might reduce both, blocking the decision-making processes,[8] as was the case in West Germany, a country where it operated with initial success. It may contribute to social integration in certain regions, satisfying legitimate aspirations for a degree of self-government. Yet, regional elites may exacerbate interregional conflict all the more, as well as popular mistrust of the central government. Without prejudging the question, I just wish to alert the reader to the problematic nature of the effects of the mesogovernments, and, therefore, of the need to analyze the nature of and special circumstances surrounding such experiments with the scale of authority, interest, and identity.

Spain is especially relevant to the general discussion for three reasons. First, in recent years Spain has been a laboratory for experiments in mesogovernance, both territorial and economic. A "state of autonomies" was established during the transition between regimes, and economic and social policy has depended on a series of social contracts or pacts between the state and interest groups almost without interruption from 1977 to the mid-1980s. Second, Spain is one of the advanced capitalist societies of western Europe. It may rank fairly low, but it is definitely within this category by virtue of the nature and complexity of its economy and because of the level of education and the cultural orientation of its people. Third, the fact that the experiments with mesogovernments have taken place within the framework of a transition to democracy makes Spain a special case. Certain characteristics of the formation process and certain general problems of the effects of the mesogovernments may be observed with greater clarity and intensity. Political transitions increase the risk of ungovernability and the vulnerability of the political class. Regional elites and interest associations emerge from the long authoritarian period with very poor organizational resources, at the very moment when the fragility of the situation increases their strategic power. Under these circumstances greater-than-normal importance attaches to the sentiments of the people—sentiments which neither the national political class nor the regional elites nor the social powers understand or can determine. Therefore historical memory, especially of the civil war and of nearly forty years of an authoritarian regime which has been decisive in the formation of these sentiments, acquires particular salience.

THE FORMATION OF REGIONAL MESOGOVERNMENTS

The national integration of Spain is a problem which has not been satisfactorily solved for the last two hundred years. At the time of the Hapsburgs, Spain was a correlate of the monarchy, a collection of people and institutions set up under the authority of the king of Spain. It was not just a political union; the people felt that they were united by Catholicism and certain common economic interests, that they were involved in an ever-growing process of communication with one another, and that they were becoming increasingly different from their neighbors, France and Portugal. The process of political and administrative unification, occasionally punctuated by the force of arms, was spurred on in a rather sporadic fashion by the Hapsburg dynasty and then, more systematically, by the Bourbons. By the end of the eighteenth century these efforts appear to have been successful. During the grave political and social crisis occasioned by the peninsular wars of 1808–1814, there were no attempts to take advantage of the circumstances in Catalonia or in the Basque region. However, the dramatic period which began during the 1830s with the first Carlist war and culminated in the 1930s with the civil war bears witness to the explosive nature of a complex national problem and to the confrontation between the various nationalist movements.

This confrontation was the result of a combination of factors: a strong ethnic potential in Catalonia and the Basque region, and the incongruity in the distribution of economic and political power between these two regions and the central region. This encouraged the development of central and peripheral movements characterized by a political and exclusive nationalism, that is, one based on the definition of a nation not simply as a differentiated community, united by feelings of belonging to a group based on history, language, or race, but as a community which demands the undivided loyalty of its members, and which is considered indistinguishable from an autonomous political entity or an independent state. Such was the Spanish nationalism that aimed at the integration of Basques and Catalans, denying them their own nationalistic sentiments; and such were the Basque and Catalan nationalisms which in turn aimed at acquiring a monopoly over political authority within the territory they considered their own. In particular, this meant local control over a resident Spanish emigrant community which had grown in size and which had to be assimilated, subjugated, or expelled. The definition of all these types of nationalisms as exclusive and incompatible with one another, the idea of nations as being incomplete without their own state, and the will of the national community to assimilate the peoples living in their territory: this was the basic repertory of beliefs and attitudes underlying Spain's several nationalisms in the nineteenth century and continuing throughout the twentieth.[9]

Despite the fact that the Spanish market and the Spanish state, Spanish society and Spanish culture, in other words Spain itself, had become an ever more complex reality with a greater density of internal interaction, and that many Catalans and Basques had reconciled their sense of belonging to Catalonia or the Basque region with the idea of belonging to Spain, exclusive nationalist movements became stronger during the years of the Second Republic (1931–1963), culminating in the civil war. After the war the victors imposed their own solution of an exacerbated Spanish nationalism, denying the validity of any kind of peripheral nationalism, or at least trying to deny it.

The impact of Francoism on the problem of national integration was, as in so many other things, contradictory. On the one hand, it substantially improved the fit between the distribution of political and economic power, owing to the industrial development of the center of the country and above all of Madrid, as well as some other enclaves in the Spanish hinterland. On the other hand, in the crucial area of sentiment, the results of its actions were contrary to its intentions. In the long run Francoism reinforced Catalan and Basque nationalist sentiments while weakening Spanish nationalist sentiment.

The repression of nationalist culture and feelings, not to mention autonomous political institutions, in the 1940s in the Basque region and Catalonia left behind an aftertaste of injustice and indignation. After the 1960s, there was a reduction of repression, achieved with the encouragement of the church and intellectuals. In these regions the offer of compensation for political and cultural subordination with economic privileges was never accepted. This deal, implicitly offered by the Franco regime, was rejected by the people. They enjoyed their economic advantages but refused to trade them for any other obligations. Indeed, a typical effect of economic development, the massive influx of migrants, increased nationalistic preoccupations.

The peripheral nationalist movements saw the eclipse of Francoism as a double opportunity, first, to achieve democracy for Spain as a whole, and second (and above all), to satisfy their aspiration for self-governance and the assertion of nationalism. Both expectations mutually reinforced each other. The central (as opposed to the peripheral) political class which emerged during the transition read the situation in a different way. Their position was ambivalent and, therefore, indecisive. This Spanish political class was unable to oppose a substantial proportion of the peripheral nationalists' aspirations for a number of reasons, some of which were of a moral or emotional nature. Among them was the internalization of a sense of historical guilt over the repression of claims which they themselves considered to be legitimate. Another was the reflection of a loss of conviction in Spanish nationalism, which was one of the paradoxical consequences of the "nationalist" Franco regime.

Francoism's grandiose yet superficial interpretation of Spanish history associated the country with an empire, Catholic unity, and a unitary and authoritarian state. The importance of Spain in Europe, however, had been lost at least three hundred years earlier. The delusions of a new empire faded with the defeat of the Nazis and fascism at the end of the Second World War. Dreams of moral and cultural leadership in Latin America were just talk. Pretensions to Catholic unity ended up by being discreetly discarded by the church itself. In this way Francoism exhausted the whole gamut of standard nationalist topics and emotions. The very concept of Spain had become tainted by association with notions of grandiloquent and vacuous imperialism, enforced Catholicism, and centralized and authoritarian unitarism. The effect was to inhibit Spaniards, not only of the left but also of the center and even of the right, from asserting their nationalistic sentiments during the early years of the transition to democracy. Many felt uncomfortable with the term *Spain* and systematically went out of their way to avoid using it, replacing it with the term *Spanish state*. But the willingness of the central political class to yield to the claims of the nationalists had two key limitations: a suspicion that the ulterior motive of the nationalists was to reduce central governance to a minimum, and above all a fear of the willingness and capacity of the armed forces to intervene in the nationalist question.

The Spanish armed forces, whatever their innermost feelings might have been (two of which were loyalty to the crown and a conviction that Francoism without Franco was not viable), showed that they were prepared to accept the transition to democracy as long as certain basic conditions were met. These were the opposite of the conditions which, in their opinion, had brought about the collapse of the Second Republic, led the country to civil war, and justified the subsequent military reaction. Official declarations or silence apart, the Spanish armed forces have always believed in the legitimacy of their actions in the 1930s. They have justified them on the grounds of the need to prevent the disintegration of the country through class struggle, moral breakdown (partly as the result of religious persecution), and nationalist separatist movements. Being very much aware of these issues, as well as defending their own corporate autonomy, the armed forces observed that two of these dangers were very much muted during the transition. Economic and social conflicts, much less serious than in the 1930s, were channeled through social contracts; and church and state were able to reach an understanding, assisted by the internal transformation of the church during the 1960s. However, military attention continued to be focused on the problem of separatist movements firmly linked to the problem of terrorism, all the more since terrorists have principally attacked the police and the armed forces. Moreover, the capacity of the armed forces to intervene remained intact during these years. They very quickly imposed, discreetly but firmly, the condition on political parties that they exclude political propaganda from the barracks. They also ruled out any kind of civilian control over the recruitment and training of military personnel, demanding and obtaining considerable corporate autonomy. They remained united by eliminating factions such as the UMD (Democratic Military Union) right from the start in swift and radical fashion (Fernández, 1982), and by neutralizing attempts to create conflicts between democratic and Francoist military factions or between officers of different generations. At military headquarters there developed among officers of all ranks an acute awareness of political problems, especially regional and nationalist ones, and the army made its voice heard more or less continuously, and through more or less informal channels, throughout the nation and the political class.

Thus, the transition began in a climate of mixed feelings and expectations. A majority of Spaniards held tepid Spanish nationalist sentiments, tempered by a certain sense of guilt. There were also peripheral nationalist minorities with very strong feelings who formed a relative majority in their own territories. The armed forces, united, disciplined, and alert, followed the course of events, suppressing their deep and growing indignation at what they considered to be the lukewarm attitudes of the Spanish nationalists and the excesses of peripheral nationalists. It was in this context that the central political class began, indecisively, to take the first few steps toward forming autonomous communities.

THE THREE-STAGE FORMATION PROCESS

The process of the formation of the Spanish system of regional autonomies can be broken down into three phases. The first extends from the beginning of the Suárez government in June 1976 to the approval of the Constitution in December 1978. Adolfo Suárez began his government by giving priority treatment to the regional question. He concentrated on "Operation Tarradellas," that is, the return from exile of a historical Catalan leader, as a test case and the key to future developments. He avoided making pacts with political parties, and reached an agreement directly with Josep Tarradellas on the restoration of the Generalitat (or government) of Catalonia, making Tarradellas himself president. Suárez and Tarradellas insisted on the priority of the establishment of a political relationship of mutual trust and recognition of the identity and right to self-government of Catalonia, as well as its integration within Spain. But in Catalonia there was no terrorist movement. Suárez could not find a similar leader among the Basque nationalists. Moreover, the PNV (Basque Nationalist party) gave primary importance to the release of political prisoners, including terrorists, which Suárez had delayed on account of pressure from the armed forces, and because he believed that those released would subsequently return to terrorist activities. This delay further inflamed the conflict.

In mid-1977 Suárez initiated the "pre-autonomies" by attributing a presumed desire for self-government to all the regions of Spain. The decision was backed by the political class as a whole. The reasons were varied and complex. The central political class understood that it could easily create and manipulate regional political classes. Thus, these leaders believed that by establishing a general system, they could reduce the severity of the Basque and Catalan problems. By placing them within the framework of a whole set of regional claims, the political class sought to set against the Basque and Catalan claims not just the centralism of Madrid but also the equally legitimate claims of the other regions. The regional political classes were to be converted, apparently, into appendages of or electoral agents for the Madrid parties.

The commission for drafting the Constitution, with no representative from the Basque nationalists, inserted section 8 into the Constitution covering regional autonomies in a way which was consistent with the experience of the "pre-autonomies." It went much further than the Italian Constitution in the direction of a regional state, and sketched out a system which was de facto federal (Burgos, 1983). The projected law included a reference to the Spanish "nation" together with other "nationalities" (article 2 of the Constitution) and allowed for unlimited delegation of the powers of the central state (article 150.2). In fact, section 8 of the Constitution was a compromise which postponed the problem of the effective transfer of powers to the autonomous communities, leaving this to the outcome of later political negotiations.[10]

The Constitution was passed by the parliament and by the nation by the end of 1978. General euphoria was tempered for two reasons. First, the PNV had abstained from voting in favor. The Basque nationalists wanted a mention of certain "historical rights" existing prior to the Constitution. This would have left the door open for subsequent negotiation with a view to obtaining the so-called right of self-determination, which was in principle denied by the Constitution itself. The PNV did not accept the Constitution until later, when the provision they wanted was taken up in the Basque Statute of December 1979 (in the additional ordinances). Second, terrorism by the ETA (Euskadi Ta Askatasuna, or The Basque Region and Freedom), responsible for thirty-five deaths during the last two years of Francoism (1974 and 1975) and another twenty-seven in the first two years of the transition, intensified in 1978, when sixty-four people were killed, resulting in the growing unease of the armed forces.

The second phase lasted from the approval of the Constitution to the attempted coup d'état in 1981. During this period two parallel processes took place. There was the process of discussing and passing the Basque and Catalan Statutes in 1979. Suárez was confronted with certain projected statutes which had been drawn up by nationalists (the Statutes of Guernica and Sua) which reduced central government to an absolute minimum and even restricted freedom of action in foreign policy. Suárez did not enjoy a majority in parliament, and the Socialists were in favor of these statutes. Under the circumstances, Suárez and the nationalists reached a consensus, the main thrust of which was an extremely broad declaration of exclusive powers for the autonomous governments, with the sole cautionary introduction of an ambiguous clause: "without prejudice to the powers which, with a similar exclusiveness, the Constitution grants to the central state for the same matters." The two adversaries thus achieved a double Pyrrhic victory, leaving it for the future (and the Constitutional Court) to decide who the real victor was (García de Enterria, 1984).

In light of what was in fact a government strategy to bring about a minimum level of consensus and governability by means of ambiguities and limited concessions to the nationalists, a second process was initiated parallel to the first throughout the rest of the country, namely, the activation of regionalist sentiments in other regions. These were encouraged for two reasons. First, there was the suspicion that discriminatory treatment in favor of the Basques and Catalans would redound unfavorably on the rest. There could be many types of distributive conflicts between regions, involving taxes, investment, energy, natural resources, and so on. Mistrust was exacerbated inasmuch as many of these regions, especially in the south, felt that Catalonia and the Basque region had dominated the Spanish economy for at least a century. For many, such as the Andalusians, the economic development of Catalonia or the Basque region had come at the expense of their own underdevelopment and the exploitation of their migrants. Second, to this motive of correcting economic imbalances was added another: a claim for equality of status. It was unacceptable that some regions (the "historical nationalities" of Catalonia, the Basque region, and Galacia) should achieve the status of full autonomy while others received only partial autonomy, or that some should reach autonomy quickly while others achieved it slowly and with difficulty (as articles 143 and 151 of the Constitution suggested).

A series of incidents, blunders, and political maneuvers made the autonomy of Andalusia a test case for this double injustice with regard to both the economy and status. When the government called a referendum in Andalusia, its proposal for a lesser degree of autonomy for the region was rejected in February 1980 by the Andalusian people. The problem was aggravated by party rhetoric, a tendency of the media to dramatize conflicts, and the desire of local political figures to seize a share of the limelight. Offenses to the prestige and the status of the region were magnified in the eyes of public opinion. The formula proposed by the government seemed to imply a distinction between one rapid form of full autonomy, suitable for developed regions such as Catalonia and the Basque territory, and a formula for a limited, slow autonomy in the underdeveloped regions with less status. Presented with the problem in these terms, the Andalusians felt the urgent need to assert themselves as full equals of the Basques and Catalans. A new Andalusian national consciousness was generated.

Throughout 1980 this competition for the prestige of national status was repeated all over the country. Intense nationalist or regionalist sentiments were felt everywhere. It is difficult to say how genuine were the feelings of the masses (López Aranguren, 1983; Linz, Orizo, and Gómez Reino, 1982) or if they were projections of the regional political classes upon their environment. The degree of mobilization was not equal in every case. The voting to pass the statutes, and the national and regional elections in turn, showed the limitations of the phenomenon. Nevertheless, in 1980 the issue filled the front pages of the newspapers and caught the imagination of the politicians.

The process had disconcerting effects on the political class. The PSOE (Spanish Socialist Workers' party), which had just emerged from a serious internal crisis both ideological (the debate about Marxism) and organizational (the debate about organized factions), which had led to the resignation of Felipe González as secretary general, saw the opportunity to make its political comeback. The centrist UCD (Unión de Centro Democrático) crumbled. This was in part due to the fact that this was the moment chosen by several of the party's political families to engage in internal battles, some over programs and others over the distribution of power. The personal leadership of Suárez, harshly attacked by the PSOE, was called into question by his own party.

The political crisis was aggravated by terrorism, as 1979 and 1980, with 181 deaths, were critical years for terrorist assassinations. These were also the years during which the problem of the governability of the Basque region intensified. In fact, in some areas of the province of Guipuzcoa and in part of Vizcaya the state apparatus almost withered away: judges were intimidated, police were confined to urban ghettos, and those parties of the center and right which represented Spanish nationalism disappeared. The "revolutionary taxes" imposed by the terrorists affected both professional people and businessmen, quite a number of whom left. All these developments reinforced the effects of a serious industrial crisis which focused on a region with a predominance of basic industries incapable of resisting world competition. The unemployment rate in the Basque region was soon higher than that of Spain as a whole. A segment of the region's youth found themselves in a position midway between apathy and sympathy for terrorist subversion. Terrorist activity received the support of 15 percent of the region's voters, a figure that, when abstentions are counted, represented 10 percent of the electorate. This was the historical background against which, in mid-1980, the first indecisive attempts were made by the central political class to reform the devolution process granting autonomy in the regions (Martín Villa, 1984). More important, military restlessness increased, culminating in an attempted coup in February 1981.

The third phase began with that coup. This was an enormous trauma of which it is necessary to recall some of the more significant details. The coup began at 6:25 P.M. on February 23, 1981. Lieutenant Colonel Antonio Tejero seized the Cortes building and held the entire government and parliament hostage. The political class reacted as a whole with extreme moderation. There were no calls for a general mobilization, and there were no spontaneous uprisings. The nation gathered in front of its radios and television sets. The drama was acted out by the king and the army. Apparently the king made it quite clear that he would neither accept the situation nor abdicate. The rebels would have to shoot him. The contrary example of his grandfather Alfonso XIII and his brother-in-law Costantine of Greece probably served as decisive models, for their acceptance of military coups had led to the dissolution of the monarchy in their respective countries. The king appeared on television at 1:24 on the morning of February 24, approximately seven hours after the initiation of the coup, and made it clear that he had the army's official support. The incident ended peacefully in a matter of hours. One plausible hypothesis is that during those seven very long hours, a complicated process of discussion between the Crown and the armed forces had taken place. In the end, the armed forces put a stop to the coup, emphasizing that they were doing so out of loyalty to the Crown and in obedience to its orders. The implicit exchange was clear: the armed forces had sent an unequivocal message to the political class that they would exact a moral commitment from it to give priority to maintaining the unity and territorial integrity of Spain. In exchange for suppressing the coup, the army pressured the political class into adopting a clear, explicit, and consistent policy toward the regional problem. Also, the agreement implied the slowing down of the transfer of powers to the autonomous regions, the reduction of nationalist rhetoric with separatist overtones, and the imposition of a legislative framework which would safeguard the powers of the central government.[11]

A new climate quickly developed within the political class. The final drafting of the map of regional communities was accomplished. A new law was drawn up, based on the April 1981 agreement between the UCD and the PSOE, the so-called LOAPA (Organic Law for the Harmonization of the Autonomic Process; see García de Enterria, 1984). Although the Basques and Catalans challenged it and the Constitutional Court later declared it unconstitutional in August 1983, the law provided a model for a series of regional statutes passed over the next several years. Furthermore, a substantial part of the content declared unconstitutional by the court had been accepted by the same tribunal since 1981, since rulings about conflicts of powers have set certain important precedents in favor of the prevalence of central over regional norms. Finally, a provisional understanding on the transfer of economic resources was worked out between the central government and the regional ones.

The result of this laborious and dramatic process was a set of pacts between the central government and the difference regional political elites. On behalf of the central political class, not only did the UCD and the PSOE take part in these negotiations, but so did parties to the right and to the left of them. These pacts were invested with the moral authority of other institutions of the political system, such as the Crown and the Constitutional Court, and they have been backed by the people in successive referenda. They are enshrined in section 8 of the 1978 Constitution, in the Catalan and Basque Statutes of 1979, and in the remaining statutes of the different regions or peripheral nationalities which have been passed since then. To this set of norms of a general nature should be added those institutions which ensure an orderly framework for a process of permanent negotiation over the effective transfer of services from the central to the regional administration.

THE FUNCTIONING OF THE MESOGOVERNMENT SYSTEM

The national political class and the regional political classes jointly established, by means of these pacts of autonomy, a system of communication between central and regional governments which presupposes a compromise over certain content and certain rules for interpreting the pacts, negotiating their boundaries, and settling conflicts. How has this system worked, and what have been its principal effects during its brief existence? Let us consider just some of the immediate effects: those on national integration, on certain aspects of the relationship between the state and civil society, and on social integration within some of the communities.[12]

It seems, on balance, that the regional pacts have reinforced the degree of national integration. They have managed to incorporate into the political system almost all the regional movements and the greater part of the peripheral nationalist movements. Catalan nationalism exists inside the system, with all (or nearly all) this implies. One indication that this is the case is the active role played by Catalans in Spanish politics on the left, as well as in the center and on the right.

The Basque PNV, while still keeping to the fringes, has manifested a halfhearted willingness to cooperate with the central government, as shown by the limited legislative pact between the president of the Basque autonomous government, José Antonio Ardanza, and the Basque branch of the PSOE. The PNV's ambiguous path between "semi-loyalty" (see Linz, 1981, pp. 87–88) and full acceptance of the Constitution appears in the repeated mention by its party members and officials of the need for an eventual renegotiation of the regional statute in terms of those historical rights which were supposed to have been acquired prior to and independent of the Constitution, the abstract or formal recognition of which has been granted in the statute itself. Many Basque nationalists hope this recognition will one day open the door to the acknowledgment of a supposed right of national self-determination. Figuratively this is expressed in their reluctance to use the symbols of Spanish unity such as the flag or even the name of Spain (which does not appear at all in the Basque Statute). Even so, the presence of the PNV on the fringes, but nevertheless *within* the political system, is significant for the time being. Furthermore, once the critical device was used by PNV's leader to take responsibility for the governance of the Basque region in some alliance with the PSOE, the actual consequences of that choice in the everyday experience of regional government seem to have strengthened their commitment to the rules of the game and broadened their appeal to the Castilian-speaking population. This in turn has softened somewhat the nationalistic thrust of their linguistic and media policies (Mezo, 1990). However, at the same time, a sizable segment of the PNV split from the party to create the Eusko Alkartasuna (EA); and a significant fraction of Basque nationalists still support terrorist activities (about 10 percent of the registered voters, or about 15 percent of the vote) and remain outside the system.

In general, the political system of the regional autonomies has been able to absorb and channel a considerable (if unequal) volume of social pressure and unrest. Social mobilization has been continuous and substantial in Catalonia and the Basque region. At times, demonstrations of hundreds of thousands of people have supported specific regionalist symbols or policies. These were frequent and fervent in Andalusia on the occasion of the referendum in 1980. They have dwindled somewhat, though they remain relatively numerous in the other regions, where they have frequently been confined to declarations by intellectuals and diverse associations. Critics of the system argue that it has generated, or at least encouraged, social pressure without absorbing the consequences. But the fact remains that referenda have shown the people to be overwhelmingly in favor of these autonomies in every region. Nevertheless, the percentage of those abstaining from voting in those referenda as well as in regional elections has been very high. Once more it is necessary to distinguish between regions. In the Basque territory and in Catalonia the desire for autonomy cannot be questioned. It has been clearly expressed in regional elections throughout the period. Regionalist parties, the CIU (Convergencia i Unió, and Catalan center-right nationalist coalition) and the PNV, respectively, obtained a consistent plurality of the vote. In 1984 the CIU got 46 percent, followed by the Socialists with 30 percent, and the PNV 41 percent, followed by the Socialists with 23 percent.[13] In the other regions local feelings may have been obvious, but the will for self-government was much less so. In the "historic nationalist" regions of Galacia, abstentions ran as high as 73 percent in the referenda that passed the initial statute. In the subsequent regional elections in 1981 the entire range of Galician nationalist and seminationalist parties obtained around 12 percent of the vote. In the other regions an abstention level of 40 percent was normal when the enabling statutes were passed, and no party whose *main* identity was nationalist or regionalist obtained more than about 10 percent of the vote.

The system has been successful in absorbing intense regional feelings and the propensity toward mobilization in Catalonia but not in the Basque region. It has provided a channel for more moderate feelings and for a lesser degree of activism in other regions. This relatively positive result has been achieved by running risks and paying costs that must be taken into account, the first of which was uncertainty.

The policy of granting autonomy has constructed an unstable system with a high degree of indeterminacy. The constitutional texts and the statutes have made the distribution of power between central and regional governments an area of permanent political negotiation.

Given that any revision of the Constitution is very unlikely in the short or medium term, that its interpretation by legislative means is impossible (as illustrated by the relative failure of the LOAPA), and that any reforms of the statutes would be quite difficult to decide on since they would require qualified majorities and popular referenda, disagreements between central government and the regional governments, especially where the two are not controlled by the same party, can lead to institutional conflicts and to claims of unconstitutionality before the Constitutional Court. The rulings of this tribunal have compensated for deficiencies in the pacts themselves. And although the content of these rulings has been favorable at times to the arguments of the central government, asserting the prevalence of the state norm in matters of dispute,[14] the ruling against the central government in the case of the LOAPA has balanced and reinforced the tribunal's image of moral authority over the different sides. However, its decision to declare part of the LOAPA unconstitutional has placed upon its own shoulders the task of settling a growing number of conflicts between governing powers. For example, by late 1985 twenty-six claims by the central government against decisions of the Basque government had accumulated, countered by fifteen claims by the Basque government against the central government. A similar number of counterclaims had been filed between the Catalan Generalitat and the central government. And the number of legal claims and counterclaims between the central state and the regional governments has increased steadily over the years. Moreover, nationalist parties have intimated that if the ruling of the Constitutional Court were not in their favor, they would disregard it.[15] These constant conflicts bear the risk of lengthening the time needed for decisions to be reached, intensifying the controversy over rulings and enhancing the possibility that the rulings might not be accepted, thereby eroding confidence in the court.

If the system of autonomies is inherently unstable, what other political and social mechanisms exist to compensate for it? The intervention of national institutions over and above the party political game might reinforce the system. The Crown has been and remains a crucial factor in the process of national integration. This was strikingly evident when the king faced down the attempted coup d'état in February 1981; but it also demonstrated every day in a quieter fashion as the Crown is seen as the locus of the moral and symbolic unity of the country. However, by the very nature of the Spanish political system, the specific intervention of the Crown in such complex affairs can occur only very occasionally without running the risk of an erosion of its moral authority.

Only limited trust can be placed in the capacity of the political parties to understand and to compromise. In the past, partly owing to the fear of a military coup, they showed a growing willingness to compromise in this area. This fear and the caution it induced have now been substantially reduced. One cannot rule out a learning process whereby the parties would give primary importance to the value of national integration as a prerequisite for their own government. Although moral or philosophical considerations may by themselves seem to be of little influence in the heat of party competition, politicians may come to perceive the people's sympathy for cooperation between central and regional governments, their distance from party politics, and their desire for administrative efficacy. Only then may they recognize their own party's electoral interest in following state policy on the regional question. Evidence of such a learning process can be observed in the PSOE's actions on regional issues before and after 1981.

These political mechanisms for integration may be complemented, or compensated for, by social mechanisms. What politicians might not be able or willing to do may be accomplished by cultural associations, intellectual circles, the church, trade unions, and business associations. It is hard to say, however, who has the greatest relative influence. Politicians are fond of arguing that without them, the country would fall to pieces, torn apart by its centrifugal tendencies, and if one observes the performance of the cultural elite, it would seem they may be right. Intellectuals, mostly ideological and literary, have responded to the problem of national integration during these years in a rather disappointing way. While receiving from the politicians a set of ambiguous constitutional definitions, many have restricted themselves to the old game of radicalizing nationalistic aspirations and taking them to the extreme where they become aspirations to exclusive nationalism. Or, in some regions, they have created a new nationalism with dubious social roots. Those who feel most alienated from the political class have placed themselves above the situation and have scorned the whole debate, arguing that nationalistic sentiments of any sort are inferior or extravagant. Such contempt for the feelings of the majority of the population has led to ingenious games in questionable taste.[16] Curiously enough, intellectuals have made hardly any effort to analyze real popular feelings about the matter, particularly among those very numerous groups who feel that they are at one and the same time Basque and Spanish, or Catalan and Spanish, despite the fact that these groups pose an intellectual puzzle of great interest, for they appear to refute by their very existence the theory of incompatible nationalisms. They constitute an empirical fact that demonstrates the error of conventional nationalist thinking. As for the church, it has been like a boat trying to reach too many ports simultaneously. In general, clergymen have tended to defend their links with the community nearest to them and over which they have wished to maintain their moral influence.

The effect of businessmen and trade unions has been greater and more constructive than the rather modest influence exercised by intellectuals. The image politicians like to put forward of themselves as holding together the world which is breaking apart seems plausible when one compares them with the cultural groups, but much less so if they are compared with socioeconomic groups. The market and industrial development have been important binding forces throughout the Spanish territory for the last century and a half. Businessmen and trade unions have been powerful centripetal forces, tending toward the integration of the national community. Catalans and Basques have occupied positions of leadership in employers' and workers' organizations: Carlos Ferrer, a Catalan, and Nicolás Redondo, a Basque, were the first leaders of the CEOE (the Spanish Confederation of Employers) and the UGT (the socialist unions of the Unión General de Trabajadores), and the convergence of the CEOE and the UGT has been the cornerstone of the social contracts of the late 1970s and early 1980s. The activities of employers' representatives and unions have responded to global strategies of an integrating nature, as employers have pressed for the explicit recognition on the part of all regional leaders of the unity of the Spanish market, and the unions, as much as if not more than the employers, have wished to ensure the supremacy of central organizations within the corresponding confederations. The CEOE and the UGT have committed themselves firmly (and the CCOO less so) to a policy of concert or neocorporatism at a national level. All of them have demanded from the central government a homogeneous social and economic policy.

All the same, a note of caution should be sounded. The restructuring of the production system, both agricultural and industrial, made necessary by world competition and, more specifically, by the entry of Spain into the European Economic Community in 1986, has affected the regions of Spain in very diverse ways, creating strong tensions. The political class and social forces and their respective strategies change from one region to another and from one moment to another according to the course of events. The combination of sectoral interests with regional and local political pressures in the few instances where it has happened can be worrisome. Partisan calculations have reinforced sectoral demands to prevent, slow down, or increase the cost of industrial restructuring in the steel and shipbuilding industries. This has happened with Socialist regional authorities in Valencia, nationalist ones in the Basque region, and conservative ones in Galicia. In Andalusia the regional authorities have created a climate of optimism with expansive policies of agricultural supply (connected to modest agricultural reforms which are themselves of dubious compatibility with the Constitution), bound to clash with the ceilings set by entry into the Common Market, making national readjustment in this difficult sector even more painful.

The articulation between the state or the political class and civil society introduces yet another dimension into the problem of national integration. One general effect of the combined Statutes for Regional Autonomies has been a great expansion of activities, powers, and resources in the political system as a whole, taken from the social sphere. This process has only just begun. It was simply a matter of time before the regional parliaments started legislating within their own spheres. The fact is that all regional parliaments engaged in significant legislative activities in the 1980s, although the intensity and the range of these activities varied from region to region.[17]

Given that most regions were prepared, even eager, to legislate, it was to be expected that they would do so by interfering further in private activities, watching over and guiding them, and extracting even more resources from society. This would make deregulation and the minimization of government intervention quite difficult at a time when the rest of Europe is moving, hesitantly, in that direction, but so far there has not been much evidence of this interventionist strategy. In turn, the share of regional and local governments in public spending has increased considerably, and, as a result, public spending as a whole has increased quite significantly. The central government's share in public spending fell from 90 percent in 1980 to 84.5 percent in 1982, 73.9 percent in 1986, and 67.4 percent in 1991. The regional governments' share rose from 5.9 percent in 1982 to 13.3 percent in 1986, up to 19.2 percent in 1991. And the combined share of regional and local governments rose in 1991 to 32.6 percent of public spending, and from 5.3 to 14.5 percent of the gross domestic product (Bel i Queralt, 1991).

The sheer number of the members of the political class in positions of power has multiplied during this period. The system of autonomies has led to the creation of parliaments and seventeen governments, with ten or so councilors each, and a plethora of directors general, civil servants, and advisers. To these should be added appointments to administrative posts of a more or less interim nature, but soon to be consolidated. This is in part justifiable because new activities have to be carried out. In theory this is to be done by central civil servants transferred to the regions, but they are proving reluctant to leave Madrid. In principle, almost every Madrid-based ministry should hand over between 60 and 80 percent of its powers, along with its corresponding personnel. It is easy to guess what is in fact happening: the majority of civil servants remain in their posts, at first in a situation of underemployment and later in that state of feverish activity aimed at finding new activities to justify their existence. As a matter of fact, between 1982 and 1991 the number of civil servants increased twelve-fold (from 44,475 to 565,460) in the autonomous communities, with only a minor decrease (from 1,181,820 to 900,576, a drop of about 23 percent) in the central administration (*El País*, February 22, 1992, p. 11). In addition, one of the results of the corporatist pacts between the state, the unions, and the employers' organizations has been to encourage the access of the leaders and staff of these organizations to state and para-state structures, including the seventeen autonomous communities.

Spain is just emerging from its first decade of mesogovernance. The financial dimensions of the process were initially quite modest. In 1982, for example, the share of the regional administrations in the

GDP was no more than 2.1 percent. This expenditure was certainly far from extraordinary, particularly in comparison with the losses incurred by private banks, such as Banca Catalana, and public companies, such as Seat or Renfe, not to mention the cumulative losses of Rumasa as a result of private and public inefficiency, or with lost investment in the nuclear power plant of Lemoniz (200 billion pesetas), all of which were covered by treasury funds. Given such losses, which are indicative of the degree of inefficiency in the country as a whole, the substantial alteration of the distribution of public expenditures between the central and peripheral administrations, the relative haste of the devolution process, and the initial additional increases in public expenditures generated by the autonomies must be taken philosophically. The real problem lies in the trend toward a general expansion in public spending and in the public deficit, which has been fueled by those expenses, and by the fact that, short of being financed by the state, the regional governments would be tempted to reduce their deficits by increasing fiscal pressures (as the Socialist government of the Madrid region tried to do in 1984, although it backed off in the face of public protest), or by going heavily into debt (as the rightist government of Cantabria has done, followed also by Madrid's regional government; Bel i Queralt, 1991, pp. 34ff.).

At the same time, although the experience has been brief and recent, there is already some evidence of disturbing patterns in the selection of public officials and their expansion throughout civil society, which suggests carelessness, an eagerness to occupy posts, and intense partisan spirit. Posts in various regional administrations have been preferentially occupied by members or supporters of the parties in power. The same thing has occurred in economic institutions of a public or semipublic nature which autonomous governments are trying to convert into the instruments of their policy, through the control of their boards of directors and the placement of partisans in key positions. This double strategy of widening public space at the expense of civil society and of occupying and using it for parties' political ends can also be observed in the field of cultural and educational institutions. Systematic attempts at discrimination in the cultural and linguistic areas of Catalonia and the Basque region have been reported, and similar attempts have been noted in the appointments of teachers for higher, secondary, and primary education and in the preparation of textbooks. This attempt at partisan control over the educational system may also be repeated in the mass media. Radio licenses, for example, have been handed out and pirate radio stations tolerated according to party criteria, while all the autonomous governments have tried to get their own regional television stations, with few doubting that these were the choicest prizes savored by the ruling party leaders.

These takeover attempts have been encouraged by the fact that in almost every region power is in the hands of parties in positions of clear electoral superiority. Political opposition is weak and has little moral credibility in these areas, as the opponents can always be accused of similar practices in those regions where they are in power. It is obvious that the consolidation of these patterns would call into question the nature of communication, understanding, and confidence between civil society and the political class. It is frequently argued in favor of federalism (or an analogous system such as the Spanish one) that in such a dispersed system society controls its rulers better, takes a greater part in public debate, and applies more effective pressure in the search for solutions to its problems. The contrary outcome could lead to the alienation of civil society with regard to the political system, and the fragmentation of the country into a caste of professional politicians and organized interest groups and a mass of relatively passive citizens.

At the same time, the effects of the mesogovernment system on the social integration of certain autonomous communities have also been problematical. The main reason for attributing the label "nation" to a specific aggregation of human beings is the existence of a shared feeling that they belong to a historically differentiated group. This feeling may be based on diverse factors such as race; memories of a shared past; occupation of a common territory; linguistic, cultural, or religious community; or simply belief in a common future.[18] According to this criterion Spain is a plurinational country. Within its territory there coexist a majority Spanish nation and two or three minority nations, including the Basques and the Catalans. According to this same criterion, Catalonia and the Basque region are also plurinational countries in whose territories coexist a minority who feel that they constitute the Catalan or the Basque nation, a minority who feel they belong to the Spanish nation, as well as a minority who feel both Spanish and Catalan or Spanish and Basque at the same time, that is, who have feelings of dual nationality.[19]

To this complicated tangle of collective identities must be added the complexity of the distribution of authority and political power, since Spain as a state includes Catalonia as a Generalitat and the Basque region as a set of Basque political institutions, or Basque government in the wider sense. How anyone can live at this crossroads of national sentiments and political organizations is the great question for the coming years. The main test depends on what will happen inside the Basque region and Catalonia. Can these plurinational countries and plurinational semistates respect the complex national identities of the people within their own territory without imposing discriminatory practices on access to public posts and positions of influence and prestige that would lead either to assimilation by repressing their multiple collective identities or to the segmentation of their societies into two communities?

Despite occasional alarms and certain excesses, relatively understandable as emotional and symbolic compensation for so many excesses of an opposite kind for so many years, there does not seem to be much danger in Catalonia. However, in the Basque region the potential for the segmentation of society seems to be a much more critical problem, and one which is directly related to the role of violence in that region. A double phenomenon may be observed there. On the one hand, an enormous potential for linking up the community is being invested in the operation of regional, provincial, and local self-government, and in the dramatic self-assertion of identity and culture. This augurs well for a process of learning and moral development, but there has been an erosion of trust between communities and a breakdown in the social fabric. People have become accustomed to exasperation and violence, to the emotional evaluation of their own interests, and to the rejection of possible reasons on the part of their adversaries. All of this of course delights militant and belligerent groups, but makes it ever more difficult to sustain a policy of economic recovery, and paves the way for all kinds of demagogy. It suggests a process of increasing chaos and tension where only violence itself can be established.

The problems of achieving internal peace in the Basque region and of the continuous renegotiation of its role within Spain are difficult. But even more worrisome is the moral and emotional climate which the cleverness of politicians and the exasperation of so-called men of action have allowed to prevail in that territory. For example, a dual scale has been established for measuring insults. There are insults which are perceived as "sacrileges," for which there is no expiation and which apparently require infinite revenge; and there are insults hurled at an adversary which are invariably "acts of justice." Under these conditions the exchange of insults always results in an escalation of feelings of indignation. It is obvious that there can be no lasting compromises based on such emotions or such a lack of a sense of proportion. With all this, there is a grave risk of the establishment of a fragmented society with communities that cannot achieve any kind of moral unity, some of which are exasperated, others terrified, and still others indecisive, but all blinded by a violence which drives them inexorably forward. There have been many deaths, but the tragedy of Basque society lies in the fact that these deaths do not draw its components together but divide them even more deeply. This is a dangerous situation.

ECONOMIC MESOGOVERNMENTS
AND THE NEOCORPORATIST EXPERIENCE

At the time of the democratic transition the political class "invented" neocorporatism spontaneously, as if it were impelled by the circumstances. After some initial moments of tension and disarray, it found itself making pacts reaching consensus all around. The person who began this process was Prime Minister Adolfo Suárez. In the summer of 1976 he faced a situation which was rife with difficulties. He decided that he could solve these only by means of explicit compromises between existing regional, social, and political powers. His survival instinct made him seek the language of moderation and the practice of compromise, which very soon became general. To start with, Suárez needed these pacts in order to extend and cement the foundations of the country's new political class. His starting point was the ambiguous coexistence within the Francoist political class of the so-called intransigents and evolutionists. Once this uneasy coexistence had turned into open conflict ending in victory for the latter, the problem consisted of overcoming the historical division between the evolutionists and the anti-Franco political class, that is, overcoming forty years of war, exile, and persecution. The very existence of the memory of such a bitter historical experience constituted, paradoxically, the foundation for an understanding between adversaries of so many years' standing. The lesson that could be drawn from this memory was that democracy had been impossible in Spain during the 1930s because the political class had exacerbated the conflicts of the nation and had split into two irreconcilable groups; therefore, if a second chance to achieve democracy was not to be missed, it was necessary to reduce the existing level of conflict, starting with political conflict itself. The assimilation of this historical lesson was assisted by the presence of the armed forces, which were in a state of alert and beyond the control of the political class.

The new political class also had to achieve legitimacy in the eyes of public opinion. Civil society aspired to democracy, and one sector of the population was even pressing for it, although only within certain limits. No one was prepared to repeat the experience of the 1930s. Popular support for democracy was not unconditional. The message was that it should neither imply too many risks nor endanger the governability of the country. The political classes had to be able not only to understand one another but also to solve substantial problems, such as those of the regional autonomies and the management of the economy and social conflicts. However, it turned out that the transition to democracy was taking place at a very difficult moment in Spanish economic history.

The Spanish economy has developed over the last few decades in three discrete stages. Between 1960 and 1973, during the second phase of Francoism, the economy grew at an extraordinary rate; from 1974 to the mid-1980s, that is, during the last two years of Francoism and throughout the transition and the democratic consolidation, there was a permanent state of crisis. Certain figures serve to sum up the experience of economic development: during this phase the Spanish economy grew by 7 percent per annum and exports by 10 percent. The structure of supply also changed substantially. The country became industrialized, ranking tenth among western economies. Three million jobs were created. The labor market reached full employment. Real wages per person increased at an annual rate of 6.5 percent (higher than productivity, which grew at 5.5 percent). As a proportion of national income, wages, and salaries, income advanced (in gross terms, that is, including payments to social security) from 53 percent to 61 percent. At the end of the period income per capita reached $1,600, 20 percent lower than in Italy, but 60 percent higher than in Portugal (Pérez-Díaz and Rojo, 1983). During these years

Spain took the most important steps in its recent economic history toward creating a modern economy.

The picture changed considerably after 1974, however. The last two years of Francoism were dominated by the impact of two events, one economic, the other political: the oil crisis and its consequences, and the crisis following the assassination of Prime Minister Luis Carrero Blanco. The economy entered a phase of increasing difficulty which would in any case have required various adjustments to economic policy. These adjustments would have implied serious distributive conflicts since during the previous ten or fifteen years there had developed, together with industry, a dispersed but significant trade union movement. It existed in a climate of partial tolerance and was demonstrably capable of calling strikes, with an average annual loss of a million working days during the early 1970s (Pérez-Díaz, 1979). The Franco regime did not feel that it had the political force necessary to confront the social discontent which would have resulted from the implementation of a tougher economic policy. Franco himself was weak; he lacked a faithful and strong second-in-command; the prince was an unknown quantity; and the Francoists were divided. Therefore, the government decided to allow the rate of inflation to increase, thus maintaining levels of production and employment. It did not dare to raise energy prices, contain the growth of salaries, or limit public spending. Its objective was to survive: *après nous, le déluge.*

During the first two years of the transition, 1976 and 1977, the economic situation worsened markedly. Although the economy had grown very little during these years, the increase in nominal salaries accelerated substantially. Inflation stood at around 26 percent (it had been at 7.5 percent during the period 1969–1973). Unemployment now affected 6 percent of the working population, and the level of foreign reserves fell substantially. Although the government and other political entities were aware of the magnitude of the crisis, they decided to give priority to the achievement of political agreements at the expense of all other decisions until after the first general election in June 1977. Only then did they begin to discuss economic problems seriously.

The contrast between the economic development of the previous authoritarian regime and the crisis in which democracy was born was ominous, not least because of the fearful memories it evoked. The Second Republic had also arisen out of an economic crisis following a dictatorship which had coincided with a period of growth. The Republic did not fall as a consequence of economic difficulties per se, but its failure was partly a result of the virulent social conflicts that accompanied them. During the transition period the new political class decided not to "solve" the economic problems, but rather to "soften" them in such a way that social conflicts were reduced to manageable proportions, while at the same time each party tried to improve its own chances in the complicated contest leading up to the election of 1977, which produced only a small majority for Suárez.

Meanwhile, economic experts had been observing with growing preoccupation the phenomenon of an economy threatened by accelerating inflation, rooted in the indexing of salaries, a collapse of the external trade sector, and a high degree of unemployment. They focused on the inflation problem. Their fear was that Spain could go the way of Argentina, and that the indexing of wages, Italian-style, could be the mechanism to push Spain along that dreadful path.[20] From their point of view, there were only two possible options. Either a fairly restrictive financial and monetary policy could be imposed, which would contain inflation, balance the external sector, and confront social discontent head on; or the money supply could be gradually reduced and an attempt made to introduce a policy of explicit contracts between the different political and social forces, the nucleus of which would be commitment on the part of the workers to accept a limitation on the growth of their salaries in exchange for an expected reduction in inflation, and a set of measures of a social and distributive nature (fiscal reform, social services, and transfers, as well as declarations of principles about structural reforms). The key to the agreements would consist in persuading the workers (or better, their representatives) to agree to calculate their wage increases on the basis of future rather than past inflation. The government did not have enough political capital to enforce the first option, but it did have enough to attempt the second. This was the nucleus of the proposal of the Banco de España and of Enrique Fuentes Quintana, who was to be appointed vice president with special responsibility for economic affairs by Prime Minister Suárez.

The proposal was welcomed enthusiastically by Suárez. In general, the political parties declared themselves favorable to the contract. The parties of the center and the right had no alternative. The Communists needed a sign that they belonged to the political establishment.

They were eager to make the symbols of the new regime their own, including the national flag and the monarchy if necessary. Their leaders needed to acquire the reputation of statesmen. The Socialist party reacted ambiguously and cautiously. Their plans were uncertain, and they were only gradually moving away from radical Marxist language. They instinctively mistrusted anything that appeared to favor the government and the Communists. And yet, the Socialists were aware of the unstable political situation, the difficult economic juncture, and their own need for time to organize their resources.

Thus the Moncloa Pacts came into being. They were signed initially in October 1977 by the main political parties although not by the employers, who were still organizing themselves; the CEOE (Confederación Española de Organizaciones Empresariales) appeared only at the end of 1977. The trade unions did not sign them either. Their attitude was ambivalent but basically favorable. The UGT and the CCOO were organizations controlled by the Socialists and the Communists, respectively. Tension between these unions and their parties over the signing of the pacts was minimal at the time. The unions were aware of the need to reinforce democracy as a sine qua non of their own existence; they were also aware of their own weaknesses in terms of economic resources as well as organizational ability and membership, for which only state backing could compensate. However, by not explicitly signing the pacts, the unions acquired an additional margin for action, enhanced their credibility for being independent of the parties, and also avoided being swamped by more radical unions or assembly-type movements.

What began as an ad hoc solution to the threatening state of the Spanish economy in 1977, and to the initial discussion of the text of the Constitution throughout 1978, became, after a short parenthesis in 1979, a pattern of almost uninterrupted social agreements up to 1986. The starting point was the basic agreement between the CEOE and the UGT in July 1979, which culminated with the AMI (Interconfederal Framework Agreement) in January 1980. Parallel to this, consensus was reached between the UCD and the PSOE on the Worker's Statute, which was finally passed in March of the same year. The AMI remained in force until July 1981, when it was replaced by the ANE (National Agreement on Employment) negotiated between the government, the CEOE, the UGT, and the CCOO. In 1983 the employers' organizations and the unions (although not the Socialist government) signed the AI (Interconfederal Agreement). At the beginning of 1984 talks were held which did not result in any agreement. But in the autumn of the same year they were renewed, and the AES (Economic and Social Agreement) was signed in October 1984 by the government, the CEOE, and the UGT, effective for two years.

This policy of repeated social agreements, with the participation of the economic organizations in the definition of certain key aspects of economic policy, slowly reinforced the role of these organizations. They had come into being with hardly any association with the old state corporatism of the Franco regime. The new unions were organized in opposition to the old "social sections" of vertical trade unionism, although the CCOO had been infiltrating certain local sectors of that machinery for a number of years. There was a limited degree of continuity between the former "economic sections" of the Francoist system and the new employers' organizations.

With the initial transition to democracy no one imagined that these new organizations would manage to oblige their respective social bases to join them or, least of all, that they might aspire to govern the behavior of their members. The very principles of the new constitutional order seemed to rule out such a possibility. Nevertheless, with the passage of time one employers' organization became the undisputed representative of Spanish business, and two trade union confederations between them obtained the necessary representation to commit the majority of the working classes (with the partial exception of the Basque region) to negotiations and agreements during these years. Thus, even if the control of these economic organizations over their bases seemed weak, their degree of representation and influence was significant.

CORPORATIST PACTS

The social or corporatist pacts entered into between 1977 and 1984 formed the nucleus of a series of wider agreements which were reflected in several laws and decrees, for example, the Workers' Statute of 1979 or the government's rulings on temporary contracts of November 1984. Although not without tension, economic and social policy, first under the UCD government and then with the PSOE in power, moved within an area bounded by the relative convergence of the CEOE and the UGT and showed quite remarkable continuity.

The CEOE and the UGT, and to a lesser degree the CCOO, were involved in the most important decisions concerning these policies, especially wages and labor market policy. They were somewhat less capable of making their opinions and even their veto felt in social security policy (the reform of which they blocked) and other matters. To this should be added the direct entry of the economic organizations into the institutions of the state. After the AES, a network of committees was set up to monitor and control the agreements. In essence, a modest system of functional mesogovernments with control over specific policy matters was constructed during these years, based on agreements between government and the chief organizations of employers and labor. Moreover, these developments depended on significant support from the social bases of these organizations, in particular the workers.

The agreements were actually carried out to a considerable extent. In the first place, development of real salaries did not outstrip the limits set by the agreements (or it has done so but very minimally). In the second place, labor conflicts tended to decrease. This should not lead one to believe that the unions, strictly speaking, controlled their social bases. The unions were not, and never have been, in a situation where they could exercise such formal control. Union membership was very low. A survey carried out in 1978 among industrial workers gave a figure of 57 percent; two years later the figure was only 33 percent; and by 1984 the percentage had fallen to 24 percent. If one assumes a somewhat lower membership rate in the service sector, and an even lower one in agriculture, then the membership rate for the fully employed wage-earning population must have been somewhere between 15 and 20 percent in 1984–85. By 1987 that affiliation rate had fallen below 15 percent. It is true that the unions exerted a greater influence over the workers than these figures suggest. This is shown by the fact that union candidates were regularly elected to most factory committees (affecting around 40 percent of the wage-earning labor force), and by the fact that the unions assumed the leadership of workers in negotiations over wage agreements and in calling strikes. It is obvious that the union leaders could not push the workers in directions contrary to their preferences and aspirations.[21]

Bearing in mind the rate of unemployment, which rose from 6 percent in 1977 to 20 percent in 1984, the union strategy through the signing of social contracts mainly ensured short-term advantages for those workers who were still employed. The contracts permitted a slight growth in real wages, made dismissals extremely difficult to put into effect, and for a number of years extended social benefits (pensions, social security payments, and so on). These were of central importance to the Spanish working class, in the defense of which it seemed prepared to act with considerable militancy. This does not mean that behind their adherence to these values there lay a radical or critical opinion of the company, of capitalism, or of the state. On the contrary, to judge by both the effective conduct of the workers and their answers to questions about their opinions and attitudes, the economic system was accepted by the majority of the working class, which was prepared to reach agreements and compromises with its leaders. This being the case, one might introduce the hypothesis of the implicit social contract (Pérez-Díaz, 1980a). That is, the workers behaved as if they in fact had a social contract with both their employers and their government. Within the terms of this contract, workers would consent to the exercise of economic authority in exchange for the satisfaction of certain basic claims to be heard through representation or participation, claims not recognized during the Francoist period but secured under democracy (the recognition of free trade unions, worker or factory committees, and other institutions), and certain substantive benefits in terms of wages, job security, social security, and the like. The neocorporatist contracts between the state, the employers, and union leaders were fulfilled not because the unions controlled their workers, but because these explicit contracts were congruent with the implicit contract desired by the workers themselves.

The pacts were built around a nucleus involving a commitment to the containment of wage increases, and an implicit commitment to the reduction of conflict, in exchange for commitments to control inflation. This nucleus was surrounded by sonorous declarations and negotiations on a variety of topics. To some extent the consequences of these contracts should be measured in terms of their core issues: wages, strikes, and inflation rates. However, the rhetorical periphery and the content of the subsidiary agreements may have been much more important than they initially appeared.

In the first place, the periphery of the agreements contained significant symbolic messages and some important substantive elements. In many cases it was stated overtly that it was impossible to change the status quo, and evidence was given of the balance between opposing forces and of the blockage of the decision-making process. This happened in matters such as dismissals and temporary contracting. It also occurred in the reform of social security and in measures to promote productivity. But only the mention of these things kept them alive in public opinion and on the agenda of negotiations, perhaps in the hope of more propitious times which might permit an eventual improvement in attitudes on both sides, as well as in their capacity for reflection and argument about such complex matters. In some cases a substantial decision was built into the core agreement, as happened in the AES with certain increases in public investment and the establishment of various commissions to monitor the progress and execution of the agreements. The latter constituted an organizational innovation which contained the outlines of an authentic system for the mesogovernance of class relations and economic policy, the development of which was discontinued in the late 1980s and early 1990s.

In the second place, the pacts existed within the framework of permanent negotiations between political and economic forces, and their content should not be disassociated from these negotiations. This affected four crucial policy areas: the system of industrial relations, labor market policies, industrial restructuring, and public spending. Thus, the Workers' Statute, which was the basic piece of legislation for the new system of industrial relations, was not part of the pacts reached between the CEOE and the UGT in 1979–80, but was agreed to by the UCD and the PSOE at the same time and in the light of what had taken place in those other negotiations. The public spending policy of governments during the transition was relatively generous as to social benefits as part of a deliberate inducement to get the unions to compromise when it came to signing the pacts. The issue of the norms governing temporary and part-time contracts almost blocked the decision-making capacity of the actors until a few days after the signing of the AES (in 1984), when a government decree was published making significant alterations in the flexibility of temporary contracting, and the policy of industrial reconversion, although also outside the social contracts, was the object of almost continuous discussion between the government, employers, and unions. In these two respects (temporary contracts and industrial reconversion) the socialist union went along with the general policy of the Socialist government (which was pushing a policy already initiated by previous governments) as a way to block more drastic moves for a thorough liberalization of markets. Finally, particular attention should be given to the growth of public spending, which was one of the main policy and institutional features of the social pacts. Public spending as a percentage of GDP in Spain went from 25 percent in 1975 (well below the 38 percent in the OECD) to 42.1 percent in 1987 (compared to 38.7 percent for the OECD). This was the result of a political consensus: public spending grew from 25 to 37 percent between 1975 and 1982 under a centrist government, and from 37 to 42.1 percent between 1982 and 1987 under a Socialist government (Alcaide, 1988).

In the third place, the relative importance of these peripheral and contextual aspects of the contracts was confirmed by the very fact that the signing of the pacts was always accompanied by an air of expectation and ceremony on the part of politicians, the media, and the general public. The signings were major symbolic events, the culmination of a dramatic process with a message of compromise, moderation, discussion, and the assertion of common objectives, joint responsibility in the progress of the economy, and mutual recognition between the signatories. The spectacle of a political game, along with the ornamental rhetoric surrounding the pacts, was an important and to a limited extent educational part of the efficacy of the agreements.

Pacts in this broad sense have had contradictory effects on the Spanish economy. The main positive result has been the legitimation of a reformed modern capitalism, in which the market economy is flanked by the state, unions, and employers' organizations. The greatest negative effect has been the rigidity and the delay the pacts have caused in the adjustment to economic crisis. On the positive side, the corporatist agreements have reinforced the implicit pact between the workers and economic managers and have contributed to the acceptance by workers of the enterprise of entrepreneurial authority and of the economic system as a whole (see Chapter 5). This acceptance should not be taken for granted. On the contrary, many observers, assuming that the radicalism of Spanish workers was deep-seated, somewhat overdramatized labor developments in the first thirty years of this century. The spectacle of the industrial conflicts of 1975, 1976, and 1977 seemed to lend support to these interpretations. Conflicts were at times very bitter, and it was believed by some that a radical movement was on the increase. However, the process of negotiating and signing the pacts strengthened those unions that wished to reinforce the role of their corresponding parties and to consolidate the constitutional aspect of the transition. In exchange for their freedom and recognition, and for certain compromises in economic and social policy, these unions were prepared to ensure a relatively peaceful social climate. Moreover, they found among the working classes increasing evidence of moderation, along with a willingness to compromise. In fact, after some initial uncertainty and ambivalence, the level of conflict dropped in 1979 and 1980, and remained relatively low in the succeeding years, though much higher than in neighboring countries.[22]

The pacts seemingly reinforced those organizations that signed them. By the late 1980s the CEOE had a de facto monopoly over the representation of employers' interests despite some competing challenges, and it enjoyed a high degree of confidence among employers. The effect of the pacts on the unions has been even more spectacular. The closer a union has been to the process of negotiation, the stronger it has become. The divergent paths the CCOO and the UGT have taken would seem to corroborate this hypothesis. In 1978 the CCOO had twice as many members as the UGT among industrial workers. In the years that followed, the unions developed different attitudes toward the pact-making process. The UGT was clearly in favor. It took part in all the negotiations and initiated some of them. By contrast the CCOO was ambivalent and at times hostile, and on occasion it gave the negotiations only reluctant support. By 1980 the total membership of two unions was practically the same: in the elections for factory committees in 1980, the UGT had 29 percent of delegates, the CCOO 30 percent. By 1982 the percentages were 36 percent for the UGT and 33 percent for the CCOO; in 1986 the figures were 40 and 34 percent. These unions which excluded themselves completely from the negotiations or which were excluded owing to pressure from the UGT and the CCOO either have disappeared or are in a very precarious condition.

Such has been the effect of the pacts on the legitimization of the economic system, the relative integration of the various economic classes, and the development of their representative organizations. But the effect of the pacts (and of the whole set of agreements and negotiations between political and social forces of which the pacts are a key factor) on the actual performance of the economy still remains to be discussed.

In the mid-1970s Spain was a typical industrial nation, covering 65 percent of its energy needs by importing petroleum. The increase in the price of crude oil in 1973 caused a daunting problem, greater than any suffered by the majority of the other countries in the OECD. The balance of payments rapidly became negative. However, for political reasons it was decided not to pass on the increase as fuel costs. Nor was there any attempt to conserve energy in the years that followed. Quite the contrary, in Spain the demand for energy per product unit increased by 10 percent between 1973 and 1979, in clear contrast to the seven major industrial nations of the OECD, where demand dropped by 9 percent. The second oil crisis in 1979 brought about a swift and drastic reduction in disposable income, even though this time energy prices were adjusted.

However, the defense of the level of economic activity and employment, and therefore the demand for investment, made it necessary to go beyond the internal adjustment of energy prices. It became necessary to reduce labor costs to a minimum. For, together with the shock caused by the oil crisis, the world economy during these years had undergone a deep transformation in the structure of the relative prices of industrial products. This was the result of the introduction of new technology, the competitiveness of new industrial nations, and falling demand for certain basic industries such as steel and shipbuilding, which had acquired great importance in Spain during the industrialization process of the 1960s and early 1970s.

But things happened the other way around in Spain. This was the moment chosen for increases in labor costs (including contributions to social security) far beyond the productivity or inflation rate. Between 1970 and 1982 the real unit cost of labor increased by about 40 percent over productivity. To the impact of the increase in labor costs was added an increase in the inflexibility of the labor market. Francoism had tried to offer an arrangement to the working classes whereby they would renounce the right to trade unions and strikes in exchange for job security as well as a system of social security and other benefits. Although this deal was not accepted, the Francoist state remained deeply involved in the labor market. At the moment of transition, with the expectation of a prolonged economic crisis, there was no political force that had either the capability or the inclination to deregulate this market or make it more flexible. In fact, the degree of inflexibility of the labor market increased as the pacts made salaries more rigid, affecting both their level and their structure, as methods of contracting were kept rigid (with minor rectifications in 1984), as the cost of dismissal remained high, and as the historical tendency to reduce the length of the work day accelerated. (Working hours were reduced by 11 percent between 1973 and 1983 as a result of modifications to the legal maximum, as well as the fact that overtime had become more costly and thus more limited in use; Malo de Molina, 1984.)

Under these conditions, and with the uncertainty caused by rather sluggish internal demand, businessmen tended to reduce their investments, to invest in the replacement of work by capital, or to "invest" in compensated dismissals. The public sector reacted by opting for a spectacular increase in public spending, which rose from 25 to 38 percent of gross internal product (45 percent if public companies are included) between 1975–76 and 1983. The increase was directed not toward public investment, which dropped from 9 to 5.3 percent between 1973 and 1982, but toward the financing of unemployment subsidies, increases in pensions, growing costs of social security, subsidies to unprofitable companies (especially public companies), and other all-consuming expenses (Pérez-Díaz and Rojo, 1983).

The consequence of this combination of decisions was a drop in the rate of gross investment from 23 percent to 18 percent for the period. There was also a loss of 1.8 million jobs between 1973 and 1982. The losses occurred in all sectors, but mostly in the industrial sector, where the number of people employed in 1982 was 19 percent lower than in 1973. Not only did Spain's unemployment rate become the highest among the OECD countries (it stood at 20 percent of the working population by the mid-1980s), but the working population as a percentage of the whole was one of the lowest (about 48 percent). The loss of jobs mainly affected women and young men. Half the population under age 19 was unemployed, and the rate of unemployment among women, who make up 31 percent of the work force, was 27.5 percent. Part of the unemployed population was absorbed into the underground economy, notable for its lack of social security contributions, controls on working hours, and minimum wage limits. It may be for this reason that the mass of 2.5 million unemployed showed no outward signs of alienation or hostility to the economic and political system. In fact, there were abundant signs that the underground economy was vital and flourishing.

In light of the actual performance of the economy, how is it possible to characterize the complex of pacts and economic policies for these years as well as its effects? In discussing economic and social policy, one must differentiate among several diverse elements. Monetary policy, for example, was aimed at gradual, moderate growth in liquidity, along with the idea of containing inflation within tolerable limits (which, in the years following the Moncloa Pacts, stood at around 14 to 15 percent of annual growth) and maintaining a level of economic activity which would prevent a further sharp drop in employment. Wage policy was passably consistent with monetary policy, as carried out principally through the pacts. It aimed to make the rise in wages compatible with inflation forecasts. This system of contracted salaries introduced a certain rigidity in the way wages behaved. The wage spectrum, in fact, was compressed around the maximum, imposing an artificial homogeneous norm upon an enormous variety of positions within companies. Furthermore, wage rates did not reflect labor costs, which included contributions to social security, compensation for dismissals, and reduced workday, and other factors such as promotions, changes in professional categories, seniority, and so on. Real labor costs, therefore, grew steadily until 1982. The greatest deceleration in nominal wages took place in 1984, one of the few years in which there were no pacts (Malo de Molina, 1984).

Despite these reservations, it is evident that there was relative congruence between monetary policy and wage policy during these years. These could be described as twin factors in a policy of gradual adjustment to the economic crisis involving gradual growth in liquidity, a modest drop in inflation, and relative moderation in wage increases. But this congruence extended to other area policies only to a limited extent.

Public spending policy was directed toward reducing the immediate social costs of the economic crisis by financing unemployment subsidies, increasing pensions and other benefits, and providing subsidies to help companies in difficulty maintain jobs artificially. The policy of industrial reconversion was designed according to a similar pattern. It aimed at negotiating layoffs with collectives of workers who were particularly opposed to them for two reasons: first, because many of these workers were employed in public companies, and second, because the companies in crisis were located in areas such as the Basque region, Asturias, and Galicia, where labor's resistance could easily end in political crisis. The result was a policy of smoothing out the political consequences by maintaining jobs and providing for extremely high compensation costs, as well as a de facto neglect of retraining and of a consistent policy of finding alternatives. Labor market policy tended to minimize the cost of the crisis to the working population by guaranteeing the stability of their employment. It did this at the cost of work prospects for young people and future generations. Finally, the efforts to create infrastructure and provide personnel training, education, research, and health coverage were largely reduced to sporadic lip service in the absence of any capacity or will to carry out needed reforms.

Professional politicians and the public bureaucracy, in their attempt to give a rational and systematic appearance to what was in fact a set of ad hoc improvised policies, christened their efforts a "policy of gradual adjustment." In fact this title should be applied only to monetary and to some extent wage policy; the other policies should be called a gradual maladjustment to crisis. Thus, the social contracts, with their implications for wage policy, the labor market, and public spending, were part of a set of contradictory policies. The final consequence was a combination of relative moderation in inflation and salaries, together with a deterioration in the production system, a loss of jobs unparalleled in the western economies, and the creation of an underground economy of major proportions.

Thus, two economic spheres have been created in Spain. One is subject to a visible order in which legal norms operate by means of contracts, political discourse, and the dissemination of information in the media. The other is hidden, chaotic, and subject to its own rules; here "submerged" employers operate, as well as "invisible" workers, who may also be drawing unemployment benefits. The local authorities decline to interfere with or protect these industries, and the unions regard the situation indecisively. It is obvious that this hidden area has come into being partly as a reaction to the growing rigidity of the visible economy, with its increases in social security and wage difficulties resulting from temporary contracting and dismissals. Insofar as this rigidity is attributable in some way to the negotiation of corporatist pacts and the operation of mesogovernments, one would have to conclude that not only has Spanish neocorporatism shown itself to be compatible with the dualism of the economy and the segmentation of society into heterogeneous spaces, but in fact it has generated and even reinforced this dualism and segmentation.

COMMON CAUSES AND PARALLEL PROCESSES

The Spanish experience during these years fits well with the scheme outlined at the beginning of this chapter explaining the appearance and development of mesogovernments in liberal and capitalist societies, both territorial and functional. The political class which came into being around 1977, whether in the government or in opposition, could not sustain its projected domination by coercion or through Weberian sources of legitimacy. The traditional and formal legality of the previous forty years had broken down, and the dramatic contemporary history of Spain prevented an unequivocal and unanimous appropriation of any of several previous traditions. There were no charismatic personalities on the scene. The very nature of the transition, with its need for formulas of compromise and with protagonists who showed neither expertise nor any inclination to heroism, excluded this type of politician. To govern the country and to solve or at least reduce the severity of problems was the principal way of legitimizing a new regime and its political class. This class now found itself in an initial position of apparent weakness. Its control over the army was nil. It had no grass-roots party organization. It was divided by bitter memories, ideas, and opposing interests. However, certain crucial facts of political life obliged its members to understand one another. They had to survive, exorcising the fear of a military coup which afflicted almost all of them. They had to design rules of the game, as well as a Constitution, with its guarantees for mutual survival. The elections, when they took place, produced a balance of power which made them seek alliances among themselves.

This political class was faced with two very serious problems, one involving the regional division of authority in the country, and the other the management of the economy. Both had deep-seated historical roots, but both had been intensified by recent events. This intensity was caused by a combination of external and internal factors. Among the internal factors was a hard-line or radical nucleus of the population that hoped to convert the problems into insoluble issues.

Both were also dependent on certain external circumstances. The Spanish economic crisis was derived from the worldwide economic difficulties of the early 1970s: the oil crisis, which affected Spain more than other countries, and subsequent alterations in the structure of relative prices for industrial products. The nationalist crisis had roots which were more or less indigenous, but it must not be forgotten that the resurgence of peripheral nationalisms was a relatively generalized phenomenon in Europe during the 1960s and 1970s, and terrorism had an international dimension which was as obvious as it was significant.

External difficulties combined with internal factors to create a serious crisis of governability in Spain. In the case of the economy, adjustment was made more difficult by the apparent need to satisfy the expectations of a wage-earning population whose aspirations were encouraged by the development of the recent past and by the sudden attainment of democracy. These difficulties were increased by the presence of a radical group (a role played only in part by the CCOO) that wished to delay the moderation of expectations and frustrate the establishment of compromise. In the case of the regional problem, adjustment was made difficult by the apparent need to satisfy the wish for self-government in all regions. The difficulties were magnified by the presence of two radical protagonist groups: on the one hand, the Basque nationalists and their extreme wing, the Basque terrorists; and on the other hand, part of the armed forces and their extreme wing, the architects of military coups.

However, the central political class was able to lean on intermediate groups with the capacity and will to compromise. These played the crucial role of broker, initiating or consolidating compromise. In the case of the territorial autonomies Tarradellas played this part at the beginning, and to a lesser degree the Catalan nationalists have seemed inclined to play it since then. In the case of the economic organizations, the UGT and the CEOE played this role, especially at a critical moment in 1979–80, in contrast to the indecisive position of the CCOO.

The technical instruments were available, and some social knowledge had been accumulated by economists, jurists, and other experts for the creation of mesogovernments. The federalist and regionalist experience was a known factor, although perhaps only partially so since the design for the autonomies (section 8 of the Constitution included) suffered from considerable defects. The policies of various European social contracts of the 1950s and 1960s were known superficially. Among the Socialists there was some interest in these experiences, but at the beginning there was considerable mistrust and ignorance about what was known as social democracy. As for economic expertise, this was very unequally distributed across the political spectrum and sections of the administration. It was probably insufficient, although this insufficiency was widely shared throughout Europe as the crisis of the 1970s began. If the accumulated social and economic knowledge was modest, the normative disposition of the political class, of intermediate groups, and of the population in general was favorable to the solution of mesogovernments. Attitudes favoring bargaining, moderation, and compromise were commonplace at this time in order to ensure the peaceful transition to democracy and to organize civil coexistence. On this point the church and the majority of intellectuals as well as the mass media had an important role to play. This ensemble of forces and attitudes facilitated the negotiations, which eventually led to the establishment of mesogovernments as well as understandings with the armed forces and the church.

This finally brings us to those Spanish people not controlled by the political class and its parties, by regional elites, by class organizations, or by the church or other cultural institutions. Their support for the mesogovernments was constant, systematic, decisive, and, to a certain extent, unforeseeable. It was welcomed with a sigh of relief by the leaders, who thanked them for their common sense. One explanation for this common sense lies the collective memory of the 1930s and the civil war, with its counterexample of a failed democratic transition, of nationalist separatism, of bad management of the economy, and of exacerbated class struggles.

The Spanish experience contradicts all simplistic theories about the positive or negative effects of mesogovernments on the governability of a democracy. These effects are complex and contradictory. The positive effects of the regional and the social contracts and of the corresponding mesogovernments have been an increase in the legitimacy of the political and economic system in force, as well as in the degree of national integration. The pacts have served to convert the country into a forum for permanent negotiation among a wide variety of people seeking consensus and compromise, and who, in doing so, have learned to trust one another. This has been of crucial importance to political change in Spain. Any process of transition toward democracy requires a massive investment of confidence by the public, not only in a particular government or a new political system, but also in the national community and key institutions such as the economic establishment. If this confidence does not exist, if it does not stem from the shared sentiments of identity, unity, and integrity, then there is the risk that the transition to democracy will lead not to a simple change in the political system but to the disintegration of the community which supports that political system (Rustow, 1970). If there is insufficient confidence in economic institutions, then there is the risk that the transition to democracy will be a prelude to a social revolution and to the emergence of a different socioeconomic system.

A liberal democracy is ideally a community of free and equal men and women who justify their self-governance in terms of a social contract. The concept of the social contract contains two analytically different ideas: a pact of government between the ruling class and its subjects, and a pact of association among the members of a society by which they agree to join together (Barker, 1960). These ideas do not attempt to explain the historical genesis of a particular social formation, but they represent an effort to make explicit the logical and moral implications of a community of free and equal individuals. So the constitutional contract, the regional contracts, and the social contracts, as well as the related understandings with the army and the church, make up a set of pacts that collectively form the basic social and political contract of democratic Spain. They incorporate dimensions of both a pact of association and a pact of government. As such, the regional pacts and the social pacts, with their corresponding mesogovernments, have played their part not only in the legitimization of Spanish nationalism and Spanish capitalism but also in the legitimization of Spanish democracy.

It was no easy task to legitimize nationalism and capitalism, since both complexes of institutions and symbols have historically had great difficulty in taking root, at least in some sections of the country. Both were contaminated by their links to the previous authoritarian regime, a regime which the transition has retrospectively converted into an illegitimate experience, that is, into something which should never have occurred but which is justifiable only as a reaction to something else which also should never have occurred: the civil war. As we saw in

Chapter 1, the civil war has been the moral and emotional reference point of the contemporary Spanish transition to democracy in much the same way that the English civil war was the moral and emotional reference point for the sociopolitical promises that opened the way to modern western liberalism and contractual theories. The Spanish civil war was the national drama, ever present in the public mind, and the pacts have been part of the symbolic ceremony which has nullified that experience—an anti–civil war, pro–class reconciliation ceremony. The political class and the social leaders have been the main agents and officiators at this ceremony, with the country acting as spectator, chorus, and accompaniment. The state has acted as the locus and pay-master for the ceremony.

As Clifford Geertz pointed out in his study of the Indonesian states in the last century (Geertz, 1980), the state has a double dimension: as the agent of domination and solution to collective problems, and as the exemplary symbolic focus for society. In the latter instance the state performs a drama which is not a reflection of private tensions, but the negation and the defeat of these tensions in the creation of a peaceful and prosperous community.

Attention should be paid to this dramatic, symbolic, and affective dimension of the state if one is to understand the Spanish transition, and in particular the extraordinary role which institutions such as the pacts and the Crown have played in it, all the more so inasmuch as in Spain under the transition the ceremony of calming the community has had a continuous counterpoint in the violence that has afflicted it. This has accentuated the necessity for and the urgency of ceremonial rituals such as pacts which are part of the activity of the state aimed at exorcising the destructive (demonic) forces threatening coexistence. The dramatic function of the pacts is all the more important the more serious the tensions within the country and the more bitter the memories of past disintegration. The "pact fever" and the obsession with consensus which have been seen in Spain during these years (as well as the intensive surge of sympathy for and gratitude to the king for his conduct) can be explained only by these special circumstances.

Now, if it is true that the effects of the mesogovernments and pacts have been positive, in the sense that they have reinforced the legiti-macy of Spanish nationalism and of capitalism, thus cementing the social contract of democracy, there is nonetheless another side to the coin. Although they have been carried out in a public forum, the pacts and the mesogovernments have had a specific content which has to a large degree reflected the balance of power, the preconceived ideas and short-term interests of the politicians, bureaucrats, trade unions, employers' organizations, and regional elites. The consequence has been to a large extent a lack of coherence and rigidity in the functioning of the economy, society, and the public decision-making process.

In the case of the regional autonomies, there is a clear danger of an unstable system overloading institutions such as the Constitutional Court and blocking the decision-making process, with the consequent possibility of frustration as the number and the power of regional political classes increase with the consequent risk of clientelism and political interference in the readjustment of productive factors.

In the case of the corporatist agreements, experience shows that they have formed part of an incoherent economic and social policy of gradual adjustment or maladjustment, which has as a consequence produced the segmentation of sectors which were protected by the agreement from those which were not, inflexibility and delay in adapting to the conditions of the world market, and an increase in state intervention and the size of the public sector. This pattern has not been exceptional in western Europe, where economic and social policy in general has suffered from a similar lack of coherence in facing up to the current crisis, which in turn has led to the loss of a massive number of jobs in recent years. In this sense Spain is an extreme case within a general tendency.

If these dangers become a reality and these tendencies are sustained, then the mesogovernments and pacts will turn Spain into a society where there is a split between a controlled nucleus and a peripheral margin (underground economy, backward regions, political apathy), and where that nucleus will be more and more inflexible and indecisive. Spain will have been an extreme case of experimentation with territorial and functional mesogovernments, some of whose positive effects will have been more pronounced, and some of whose negative effects will also have been more serious.

5

The Spanish Workers: Between Radicalism and Moderation

One crucial condition for ensuring the governability of Spain during the democratic transition and the years that followed, and for the relative success of functional mesogovernments (see Chapter 4), was the industrial working class's relatively moderate demands and behavior. The workers adjusted both to the new political regime and to a severe economic crisis. Whether this was due mainly to the influence or leadership of unions and parties which were supposed to represent them or rather to the predispositions of the workers themselves is an intriguing question. In this chapter I suggest that, contrary to the expectations that followed from theories emphasizing the capacity of unions and parties to shape social demands and to mediate between social constituencies and the socioeconomic and political system, at least in this case these organizations followed rather than led, or at most accompanied, their constituencies. I also suggest that workers' accommodation both to their firms and to their unions was compatible with the fact that Spanish rank-and-file labor took a position of relative detachment from and harbored ambivalent feelings toward the enterprises and the unions they belonged to. In Chapter 6 I shall explore the interplay of the workers' ambiguous stand and the unions' strategic uncertainties in more general terms, linking that interplay to the topic of the public sphere and to the western European scenario.

At the end of the Francoist regime, the Spanish working class was a great unknown quantity. For forty years its freedom had been substantially limited, its aspirations practically silenced, and its fighting spirit subdued. What would the working class do with its new-found freedom? What would its attitude be toward its employers, toward the unions, and in short, toward society and the social order as a whole?

The eruption of the Spanish working class onto the public stage in 1976 and the years that followed was spectacular. Social conflict multiplied tremendously. Between 12 and 16 million working days were lost annually through strikes between 1976 and 1978—three times more than in France.[1] Workers joined the communist and socialist unions in droves, at least to begin with. From the very first elections they also voted in huge numbers for leftist candidates. But what did all these phenomena really mean? In no way could strikes, unionism, and the vote be interpreted as unequivocal signs of radicalism. To be precise, they were signs as spectacular as they were equivocal of a working class which was emerging from a long and complex experience of political subordination and economic growth under Francoism. Were the strikes an expression of aspirations for more substantial change, or were they rather conflicts of interest within the context of the existing order? Was support for unions and political parties based on what these organizations had to offer as the apparent alternative to the existing order, or on their ability to act as means for airing grievances and for expressing aspirations for improvement and reform? In short, to simplify the question to the maximum, was Spain faced with a radical working class responding to the political repression and economic difficulties of the past, or with a moderate class resulting from economic development and the semitolerance of Franco's final years and the peaceful transition to democracy?

These questions were the driving impulse behind the research I carried out between 1978 and 1984, which I summarize here. The purpose of that research was, first, to gather all available evidence about the behavior, attitudes, and opinions of Spanish rank-and-file workers.[2] In order to do this I conducted three surveys in 1978, 1980, and 1984 based on very large national samples (about 3,500 industrial workers in 1978, about 2,200 in 1980, and about 2,200 in 1984) classified by sectors and the size of firms, to which quotas were applied on the basis of age, region, and professional qualifications. A random process was used in the selection of firms and interviewees. The individual interviews, of approximately one hour's duration, were carried out in the workplace.[3] Although I favored the direct survey among industrial workers as an instrument for obtaining data, I did not limit myself to this method, and complemented it with interviews of union leaders and an analysis of the available documents and statistical material, newspapers, and other sources. Second, it was the purpose of this research to analyze systematically the relations of workers with the firm, with the unions, with political parties, and with the social order in general, and to consider these relations in a temporal sequence over several years (between 1978 and 1984), thus allowing me to explore some of the ongoing tendencies. Finally, I tried to obtain an answer to my original questions and explain the basic attitudes of the majority of these workers by means of what Cardinal Newman (1985) referred to as the "illative sense," by increasing the plausibility of my overall explanation as a result of the convergence (fit or consistency) of specific theories which applied to various segments of the empirical evidence.

THE IMPLICIT SOCIAL CONTRACT

My discussion of workers' opinions of, and their attitudes and behavior toward, the firm begins with a definition of the firm as an organization in which there is an exchange of contributions between management and workers. Management contributions can be grouped under five headings: wages, job security, working conditions, treatment, and opportunities for a voice (which is to say, participation in decision making in the widest sense). Workers' contributions are their labor and their consent to management authority. I shall concentrate on their consent. I assume that the degree of worker consent to, or belief in the legitimacy of, management authority depends on a relative level of general satisfaction with management contributions. If, from all the available evidence, it can be inferred that these contributions are satisfactory, then a high level of consent is to be expected. The corollary of this is a nonantagonistic view of the firm on the part of workers. That the level of management contributions was satisfactory in the case of these Spanish workers should be inferred, in my opinion, from the bulk of the evidence. Most of my data come from the 1980 survey, with occasional references to the 1978 and 1984 surveys.

First, Spanish workers achieved levels of real wages and well-being far superior to those at the beginning of the 1970s, similar to those of other European workers, and sufficient to place them, in the opinion of the workers themselves, on a par with those of the average Spaniard. Real wages increased at an annual rate of 3.6 percent between 1973 and 1979, in spite of the ongoing economic crisis (by contrast, the average annual increase for OECD countries was 1.9 percent). Income and the index of family living standards (50 percent owned their own flat, 48 percent their own car, and large percentages owned a wide range of household appliances and other goods) placed these workers close to the level of their French and Italian counterparts. Finally, 66 percent of Spanish workers in 1980 (68 percent in 1984) considered their economic situation to be at least similar to that of the majority of Spaniards; 70 percent said the same in regard to their education (80 percent in 1984), with 68 percent having completed primary or secondary school; and another substantial majority held the same opinion of their general opportunities (66 percent, and 79 percent in 1984) and circumstances (78 percent, and 86 percent in 1984).

Second, 80 percent of workers in 1980 said that they did not want to change firms (83 percent in 1984). Of course, this was influenced by the situation of the labor market, which was increasingly difficult, and by the growing importance given to job security, with the accompanying overvaluation of a job with a large firm or a state-owned enterprise.

Third, Spanish workers evaluated their working conditions in a positive way (this being compatible with support for reforms, above all in certain sectors and for certain age categories or levels of qualification). We know this to be so because it was expressly stated by workers in large numbers, in 1980 as well as in 1978 and in 1984, in answer to a wide range of specific questions. In effect, they stated that they were satisfied with the physical conditions of their job (79 percent in 1980, 77 percent in 1978, 83 percent in 1984), the tempo of work (82, 80, and 87 percent), the risk of accident or illness (62, 63, and 71 percent), the diversity of tasks (70, 67, and 76 percent), opportunities for applying their professional knowledge (69 percent in 1980 and 79 percent in 1984) and the margins for personal initiative in carrying out their work (57 percent in 1980, 59 percent in 1978, and 65 percent in 1984).

Fourth, Spanish workers, for whom humane treatment was of prime importance, according to the evidence gathered in this survey, considered that the treatment which they received from the firm was satisfactory. This can also be deduced from their satisfaction with the attention that their complaints and requests received (70 percent in 1980), to which can be added the fact that these were addressed directly to the firm (78 percent, and 86 percent in 1984) rather than being channeled through a union (16 percent, and 9 percent in 1984), even in large firms; their relative satisfaction with the information they received (50 percent, and 58 percent in 1984); and the relative minority of those who resented the policy of rewards (17 percent, and 9 percent in 1984) and punishments (22 percent, and 13 percent in 1984) of the firm.

Fifth, Spanish workers did have unsatisfied demands for a voice, but their demands were for a consultative voice or for decision-making powers on minor matters, not on major ones. Between 53 and 61 percent of Spanish workers wanted a deciding voice on hours and the tempo and conditions of work, with a limited though significant proportion of them (between 26 and 35 percent) claiming to have this. However, only a minority (between 13 and 19 percent) wanted a deciding voice on matters of sales policy and investment.

Sixth, as a consequence, and in corroboration of my argument, Spanish workers accepted the legitimacy of management authority. Some 85 percent of them (89 percent in 1984) believed that even if they were able to make some decisions about the organization of their work, the responsibility for managing the firm, deciding on investment, and so on belonged to the management; likewise, 72 percent considered that the unions should achieve the maximum possible incomes, but should endeavor at the same time to raise production without participating in management (only 2 percent advocated union participation).

From what we can see, the balance of exchanges between Spanish management and workers seems to have resulted in an attitude of moderate satisfaction on the part of labor and their acceptance of management authority. Implicit in this satisfaction was a view of the firm as an entity with two different but reconcilable sides. This corresponded to the available evidence to quite a significant degree. The behavior, attitudes, and opinions of the majority of workers were organized as if they held such a theory. The logical conclusions from the data were that workers accepted the leadership of the management; they considered the firm a moral community with common objectives and bonds of solidarity; they perceived the social climate as being moderately satisfactory; and they conceived of the institutions for collective and union action as mechanisms for pressure and reform, but not for a radical transformation of the authority structure of the firm. All these conclusions were borne out empirically to a significant degree in Spain at the time. For instance, the view of the firm as a team and not as the setting for fundamental conflict was shared by some 56 percent of Spanish workers (49 percent in 1978, 57 percent in 1984, in contrast with the view of most union leaders, as shown in Fishman, 1990, p. 40); and some 53 percent (57 percent in 1984) believed that the majority of their co-workers were content with the firm.

Collective action implies exchanges between workers and the unions or other organizations through which some of this collective action is carried out. These exchanges are regulated by an implicit contract of mandate or representation. The object of such a contract consists of an exchange of leadership and articulation of demands by the union for a variety of workers' resources: votes, membership, dues, sympathy, militant participation in union organizations, and so on. We can distinguish two dimensions in the workers' expectations of the union leadership. One has to do with the *nature* of the objectives they hope to achieve, whether they are moderate objectives or radical ones aiming at a total transformation of the institutional framework of industrial activity. The other refers to the *quantity* of resources with which workers provide the unions to achieve these objectives, the degree of confidence they have in them and to which they identify with them, a spectrum of possibilities which ranges from total identification to minimum involvement. I shall assume that the greater the workers' satisfaction with the services received from the unions in light of their own objectives (in other words, the more efficient unions are in matters which are important to workers, and the more the unions' articulation of workers' demands coincides with the real wishes of the workers themselves), the larger the quantity of resources given by workers to the unions and the greater their identification with them. I believe that the evidence gathered in these surveys indicates clearly that the attitude of Spanish workers toward the unions, as well as to different kinds of collective action, was moderate (that is, they expected the unions to help them attain moderate goals) and instrumental, with a modest degree of involvement.

First, workers valued the unions (and other organizations of collective action in general) more in terms of their capacity to obtain favorable collective agreements (62 percent, and 69 percent in 1984) and to provide professional advice or other similar services (56 percent, and 58 percent in 1984) than in terms of their capacity to put pressure on the government for a change of policy (12 percent, and 15 percent in 1984).

Second, they valued different kinds of collective action, such as strikes, in terms of their suitability for achieving results within the framework of the existing order. In keeping with this, they were in favor of the legal regulation of strikes (64 percent, and 73 percent in 1984) and prudent recourse to them within the context of collective bargaining (77 percent, and 91 percent in 1984). This fact should be considered in light of the evolution of strike activity. After many years of significant though partial repression in the 1960s and early 1970s came the explosion from 1976 to 1979: the level of conflict jumped from approximately 1.5 million days lost annually in the early seventies to a figure oscillating between 12 and 21 million. The level of conflict fell by the end of 1979, but even so, between 1980 and 1983 about 10 million workdays were lost to strikes each year. By 1980 the workers' assessment of strikes in which they had taken part over the previous twelve months was not enthusiastic; only two out of seven considered the results worthwhile (one out of five in 1984), and only 40 percent would have gone on strike had they known the consequences (30 percent in 1984). This stands in clear contrast to the attitude of most workplace union leaders (Fishman, 1990, pp. 226ff.).[4]

Third, in keeping with the foregoing observations, workers emphasized their preference for unions to be independent of political parties (55.5 percent, and 57 percent in 1984), or at most to establish occasional agreements with them on specific matters (33 percent, and the same in 1984). This could be seen as a telling comment on the strong links existing between the socialist union and the Socialist party, and between the communist union and the Communist party.

Fourth, with these considerations in mind, workers were willing to concede a wide margin of confidence to the unions as their representatives for the purpose of collective bargaining, but not to grant them a monopoly over this representation. When it came to deciding who should lead the collective bargaining, workers were divided in their preferences between the unions (25 percent), enterprise committees (17 percent), a mixed commission of the two (22 percent), or the assemblies (5 percent). It is true that when it came to choosing representatives for the enterprise committees, union candidates obtained majorities (probably in the order of 75 to 80 percent of the effective vote); but workers insisted categorically that their choice of candidate was a function of his or her personal characteristics (93 percent, and 86 percent in 1978) and not the result of union backing (5.5 percent, and 13 percent in 1984). Furthermore, they preferred candidates to run on open ballots (57 percent) and, if elected, to be able to be dismissed at any time (75 percent), all of which substantially reduced any control the unions might exercise. Likewise, workers insisted on the value of assemblies as places in which to meet and exchange information, although quite definitely not as organs for collective bargaining or, in general, for decision making.

Fifth, based on these criteria of efficiency in the negotiation of agreements and strikes, workers judged the performance of the unions and gave them only a modest rating. I have already indicated their reticence toward strikes. Their assessment of the unions active in their respective firms over the previous twelve months was somewhat critical (64 percent of workers in firms where the CCOO had been operating judged its performance as ranging from average to very poor; 65 percent of workers in firms where the UGT had been operating considered it in the same terms).

Sixth, given the importance of the results of agreements and strikes, given that in order to benefit from the activities of the unions in this field it was not necessary to belong to one, and given that assessments of union performance were not enthusiastic, the dramatic fall in union membership from 1978 to 1980 and then 1984 down to a decidedly modest level hardly seems surprising. From a membership of 57 percent of industrial workers in 1978, the figure dropped to 33 percent in 1980 and 24 percent in 1984.

Consistent with all these points is the fact that this reduction most deeply affected the smallest and most radical unions, causing them practically to disappear from the scene. Within the majority unions, it affected the CCOO far more than the UGT, for the former had insisted on a relatively more radical image and was perhaps more readily identifiable with the strategy of a relatively radical political party, the Communist party.

Workers' attitudes of moderation regarding firms and the unions may either be carried over or modified as they focus on the macro level of the political and economic order of capitalism or the market economy. We may assume that the consistency between workers' attitudes from one level to the other depends on their general interpretation of their own place in the social order. There is a wide range of possible interpretations. At one extreme workers may see themselves as belonging to a class which is segregated from, peripheral to, or negatively differentiated from the rest of society, and in antagonistic relation to what they consider a dominant class. The reasons for adopting such an attitude are various, but may include the fact that they have been socialized in a Marxist or quasi-Marxist organizational culture corresponding to a strong class consciousness. At another extreme, they may have a less structured or less simplified interpretation which is also less in conflict with the social order; they may see themselves more on a par with the rest of the country and feel more satisfied, or at least less resentful within that social order. This interpretation corresponds to a weak class consciousness. By these standards the Spanish working class had a weak class consciousness. Only 37 percent of industrial workers identified themselves as working class in 1980 (dropping spectacularly to 20 percent in 1984), while 37 percent thought of themselves as middle class (44 percent in 1984). In addition, only 47 percent of workers thought that belonging to any particular class was of great or moderate significance, while 39 percent thought it of little or no importance. Then, when comparing themselves with the majority of Spaniards, workers placed themselves on a level similar to that of the majority with regard to income, education, prestige, influence, the ability to achieve the "good things in life," and their situation as a whole.

Now, I would assume that if one finds workers' theories on microsocial organizations such as the firm and the unions to be consistent with their general outlook on the social order as a whole, in such a way that both views imply moderation and a weak class consciousness, then a similar attitude is to be expected in relation to areas such as the market economy and the political order, which are logically implied by the micro-organizations that they encompass and by that social order of which they are a crucial part.

An attitude of moderation toward the established economic order can be understood in terms of the relatively satisfactory contributions received from the ruling groups within the context of an implicit social contract. These contributions should ensure acceptable living standards and working conditions, as well as opportunities for a voice and representative institutions such as unions. This implicit social contract has regulated the exchanges between the working class and their political leaders in western countries for many years (see Chapter 2); it has contained conflicts and pressures within the existing framework; it has proved to be compatible with workers' frequent majority support for left-wing parties and for the unions. At the same time, from the workers' consent to (though not necessarily their enthusiastic embrace of) the capitalist or market economy, two consequences follow. First, even if a majority of workers supports left-wing parties, whether socialist or communist, this does not mean that they are voting in favor of an alternative kind of society and asserting the desirability of a radical social transformation. Second, even if this vote does imply support for an alternative government, if not an alternative society, this does not imply a rejection of the policies of the incumbent (perhaps center or right-wing) government. These policies may be judged in terms of their probable effect on the functioning, and eventually the gradual reform, of the existing order; and if, when considered in these terms, the policies of the opposition are perceived as being as unconvincing as, or no more convincing than, those of the government, some combination of workers' acceptance of the prevailing policies, uncertainty, and resignation may be expected. Correspondingly, workers' evaluations of the political parties and their leaders in general can be expected to show low levels of approval, although continuing to reflect dimly the distribution of the vote.

The empirical evidence corroborates these arguments and hypotheses in the case of Spanish workers. Just as they voted for left-wing unions, the majority of Spanish industrial workers also voted for left-wing parties. In the elections of 1977, according to the 1978 survey, 48 percent of workers voted for the PSOE and 20 percent for the Communists, while 20 percent voted for the centrist UCD. The distribution was not substantially different in 1979. However, this vote for socialists and communists did not mean a vote for an alternative type of society. Asked about the general features of the society in which they would like to live, Spanish workers replied that a society similar to the one in which they were living was desirable in a proportion of two to one over those who preferred a socialist society. Asked to name the foreign country in which they thought workers enjoyed the most power, the overwhelming majority selected the capitalist countries of western Europe (with West Germany, France, and England at the top of the list), and preferred capitalist countries to socialist countries in a proportion of ten to one.

It is reasonable to suppose that the majority vote for the combined opposition of socialists and communists indicated preferences for policies compatible with the existing model of society but different from those of the government. However, the empirical evidence does not show unequivocal majority support from workers for the policies of the opposition such as, for example, their economic policy. This is a question which calls for special attention since the economic policy of the government was designed to overcome the economic crisis so as to ensure the survival and consolidation of the market economy. Workers were asked to judge this policy in two ways. First, they gave an evaluation of one crucial portion of it, the Moncloa Pacts, which had been accepted with varying degrees of reservation by the left-wing parties and unions. Second, they gave an evaluation of the economic policy as a whole, which had not met with the approval of the opposition. In both cases the bulk of worker opinion was divided almost equally between acceptance of the pacts and the government's economic policy (25 percent and 22 percent), no opinion (39 percent and 32 percent), and a feeling of hostility toward this policy unaccompanied by any support for an alternative policy (22 percent and 27 percent), while only a small minority opted for such an alternative (14 percent and 19 percent).

This mixture of acceptance, uncertainty, and resignation was in keeping with the relative receptivity of workers toward the key justifications for the economic policy of the government, even when it was precisely these key arguments which were contrary to their immediate interests. Thus, 33 percent accepted the argument that the rigidity of labor markets was responsible for the crisis of many firms in the sectors in which they worked (47 percent rejected it, and 20 percent did not know), and 39.5 percent accepted the argument that blamed the rise in unemployment on wage increases (16 percent only partly accepted this, 25 percent rejected it, and 19 percent did not know). Such a model of acceptance, uncertainty, and resignation was repeated, with some variations, in workers' attitudes toward regional policies and the security policy of the government, there being only a small minority (around 11 to 14 percent) who supported an alternative policy on these matters.

In sum, Spanish workers behaved with moderation toward the firm, suggesting that they accepted the legitimacy of management authority and adopted the theory that the firm consisted of two different but reconcilable sides; they behaved with moderation toward the unions, using them as instruments, suggesting that they gave them a vote of confidence (without actually joining in vast numbers or identifying with them), on condition that the unions attempt neither to monopolize nor to politicize collective action, and that such action be oriented toward moderate and realistic objectives within the existing framework; and they also behaved with moderation toward the political class, the market economy, and the established social order, suggesting that they had established an implicit social contract according to which they gave their consent on condition that they obtain certain substantive advantages and some opportunities for a voice. In my view these three sets of evidence show that the views of the Spanish workers were moderate, and their strikes, union membership, and votes for left-wing parties were signs not of their radicalism but precisely of their moderation.

However, I wish to qualify this conclusion in four ways. First, the theory of an implicit social contract differs from a theory of neocorporatism, which expects explicit social pacts to follow from the unions' moderate strategies and from their ability to persuade and discipline their own constituencies. In my interpretation the Spanish workers' moderation was largely independent of the union leaders' (and leftist politicians') original definitions of the situation, and have remained so. Second, at the same time, there are limits to the implicit pacts and to the moderation of the Spanish workers. Not only were there minorities (of greater or lesser importance) who did not share in that moderation, but even the majority's moderation might include the desire for reforms in the direction of greater autonomy for workers within the firm, the unions, and the political system, greater equality, and probably an expansion and reinforcement of the spheres of moral community.[5] Third, the economic crisis called into question some of the terms of the implicit social contract (and explicit social pacts such as the Moncloa Pacts and others) and reinforced both the workers' ambivalence and the unions' strategic uncertainties vis-à-vis the social order (see Chapter 6). And fourth, the question still remains as to how and why the working class reached this evaluation of the situation. This leads us to a series of questions which cannot be answered here. How can workers' attitudes be explained in the light of their experience of the Francoist regime, especially since the mid-fifties, and the various dimensions of economic growth, partial tolerance, ideological quasi-pluralism, and political repression? What were the effects of the strategies of the unions and political parties from the mid-seventies onward? In what ways did the conditions of the political transition and the economic crisis influence worker attitudes and organizational strategies?[6] In the remainder of this chapter I will expand on and provide further evidence for the argument I have outlined with regard to workers' attitudes vis-à-vis the firms and the unions by concentrating on the findings of the 1980 survey.

WORKERS' ATTITUDES TOWARD THE FIRM

What experience did the Spanish workers of 1980 have of the firm? In the light of this experience, to what degree did they consent to the authority structure of the firm, or what degree of legitimacy did they attribute to management? Consequently, what was their global perception of the firm? Considering the firm as a system of exchanges between workers and management, the workers contributed their labor and their consent to management authority, to a greater or lesser extent, and in exchange they received a salary, job security, certain working conditions and treatment, and the opportunity for a voice, also to a greater or lesser extent. In this way a balance may have been established between contribution and compensation. The degree of consent to, or of legitimacy attributed to, the authority of the management on the part of the workers depended on how they perceived that balance, and, therefore, on the level of their satisfaction with the compensation received from the management. I shall examine the contributions made by the management relative to wages, job security, working conditions, treatment, and the opportunity for a voice. Given that consent was part of the system of exchanges, it could be expected that the more satisfactory the contributions received by workers, the greater would be their consent. But levels of satisfaction are very hard to establish. Sufficient remuneration, tolerable working conditions, acceptable treatment, satisfactory opportunities for a voice: all these values require definition within a frame of reference, and my discussion in this respect can only be tentative. I also relate the level of consent to the workers' perception of the firm. My conclusions can be summarized by the fact that there is proof of a relatively high level of consent and a perception of the firm approximating that of a theory of two different but reconcilable sides.

Jobs and Wages

That circumstances had been making job stability increasingly difficult was evident in Spain during the transition to democracy. Against this background, we must consider what the workers themselves said about the stability of their jobs: 80 percent of Spanish workers had no wish to change their place of work in 1980 (up from 75 percent in 1978). Neither did they express a wish to do so within the next five years, in spite of the fact that this period offered some latitude for making plans less subject to present limitations: 64 percent wished to continue in the same firm (up from 59 percent in 1978). Attachment to the firm might reflect satisfaction with it, but it also reflected perceptions of the labor market. In 1978 a sample of workers were asked if they believed that for people of their age and occupation finding work was more or less difficult than it had been two years previously; 94 percent replied that the situation was considerably more difficult (93 percent in 1978). This perception of difficulty corresponded to an obvious fact: the rate of unemployment, between 8 and 11 percent from 1978 to 1980, jumped to 20 percent in the mid-1980s, and fell to about 15 or 16 percent in the early 1990s.

The importance attributed to job security by workers was not, therefore, surprising. Asked what the principal factor was for them in choosing a job, they mentioned motives of all kinds—intrinsic (relative to the factors of interest or education) as well as extrinsic (pay, security, prestige, promotion possibilities; see Brown, 1970). But job security stood out from all of these, with 41.6 percent of the respondents emphasizing this factor. Concern with job security was corroborated by other data. Workers were asked about their preferences for large or small firms, and for firms in the public versus the private sector. There was a clear preference for large firms (51.5 percent, compared with 15 percent for medium-size firms and 11 percent for small ones), and the reason for this preference was also job security (51 percent). Likewise, job security explained workers' preference for firms in the public sector: 36 percent preferred a public company compared to 19 percent who preferred a private one, while 38 percent were indifferent (14 percent of the sample did work in the public sector, compared to 85 percent in the private sector), and again the main reason for this preference was job security (59 percent).

As for income, the average worker had a monthly income of about 42,000 pesetas (roughly $520), and the average working-class family had a monthly income of about 53,000 pesetas (roughly $662).[7] They were asked if these incomes were sufficient or satisfactory, and in relation to what. A worker's income could be sufficient (or not) in relation to either an ideal level which implied having satisfied the expectations of a real increase in income over the previous five to ten years; an ideal level which implied access to goods which were generally perceived as necessary; an ideal level which was not markedly different from that which corresponded to the pay of industrial workers in countries with which comparison was frequent; or an ideal level perceived as on a par with the situation of the majority of workers in the country.

The evidence regarding the Spanish workers was as follows. From 1973 to 1979 the real wages of Spanish workers increased appreciably; in fact, the annual increase was 3.6 percent, much higher than that of the OECD countries (1.9 percent). (These increases were concentrated particularly from 1973 to 1976.) Workers' incomes permitted appreciable levels of consumption: 50 percent of workers were homeowners (3.3 percent owned a second home and 2.8 percent owned some land), 48.4 percent had their own car, 90.8 percent had a television set, 93.6 percent a refrigerator, 64 percent an automatic washing machine, 42 percent a telephone, and 31.1 percent a phonograph. It is difficult to make precise international comparisons on standards of living; variations in the cost of living, the volume of social transfers, and cultural trends, as well as in the procedures for obtaining data and statistical definitions, must all be taken into account. Even so, an initial comparison between Spanish and French workers indicates only moderate income differences. According to the 1979 statistical yearbook of the OIT, or International Organization of Labor, the average hourly salary (in nonagricultural sectors) in 1977 was 15.5 francs in

France (approximately 248.2 pesetas at the time), and for the same period the average hourly salary in Spain was 179.8 pesetas. Other statistics on home ownership and possession of consumer goods indicate that, in 1973, 36.6 percent of French workers owned their own home; in 1976, between 67 and 75 percent (depending on categories) owned a car; and, also in 1976, 90.3 percent had a television set, 92.4 percent a refrigerator, 80.9 percent a washing machine, and 18.4 percent a telephone (INSEE, 1978).

Workers were asked how they saw themselves in relation to the majority of the country with respect to their level of income, their education, their political influence, their capacity to achieve the "good things in life," and their position in general. This was an attempt to find out in what proportion workers felt they were similar to the majority of Spaniards and in what proportion they felt themselves to be negatively differentiated or discriminated against. The 1980 results showed that around two thirds of workers considered themselves to be in a situation similar to that of the majority of Spaniards with regard to income as well as education, access to the good things in life, and their position in general; only one fifth believed that they were in a position of relative inferiority (these proportions were almost the same as those obtained two years earlier). Moreover, if the relative level of income was compared not with that of the majority of the country but with the closest professional categories of technicians and clerks, the inequalities were more marked; but even so, only one third of workers resented the inferiority of their incomes in relation to those of technicians, and scarcely one fifth felt the same way vis-à-vis clerks. In short, the evidence appeared to demonstrate that workers had experienced a real gain in their levels of income over the previous six or seven years, had reached appreciable levels of consumption roughly comparable to those of French workers, and felt relatively equal to the majority of their countrymen with regard to income and other variables.

Working Conditions

The significance of the answers to questions about job satisfaction is quite problematical, and the problems of interpretation are various. The opinion expressed may not correspond to the real opinion of the interviewee; the subject may overvalue his job as a way of avoiding pity or self-pity; or he may give in to the opposite temptation and exaggerate his grievances. A useful way of reducing the effect of these biases is to repeat the question over a period of years and compare the results. Other problems ensue from defining the concept of job, since a job is a set of task-related activities and social relations. For this reason the surveys included not just one question on job satisfaction in general but a battery of questions about various relatively specific aspects of the job. Thus, workers were asked to express their agreement or disagreement with statements such as: "Most of the time my work is too monotonous and boring"; "In my job I am allowed to put my own ideas about how things should be done into practice"; "The normal tempo of my work is tolerable"; "The physical conditions in which I do my work are satisfactory"; "The risk of illness or of a professional accident at work is minimal"; or "I am allowed to apply a substantial number of very professional skills in my job."

Although the workers' degree of satisfaction was influenced by variables such as age (it increased with age), the size of the firm (it decreased as the firm got larger), and other circumstances, the general trend was quite clearly one of moderate satisfaction. Approximately two thirds of the answers (between about 56 and 81 percent, according to the topic, in 1980) indicated satisfaction with the variety of tasks to be performed (70 percent), the opportunities for using initiative (56 percent), the tempo of work (81 percent), and physical conditions and the level of the risk of accident or illness (62 percent). In all these respects the level of satisfaction tended to increase from 1978 to 1984. Consistent with this trend were workers' answers to the question about the application of knowledge of their trade (the term *oficio* indicating the sum of professional knowledge acquired by workers, whether from direct experience or from a formal apprenticeship). In 1980, 69 percent (79 percent in 1984) reported that they applied their professional knowledge in all, almost all, or a large number of the tasks they performed. It should not be forgotten, however, that a significant minority (20 to 25 percent) expressed dissatisfaction with various aspects of their working conditions, and this fraction increased for certain intrinsic aspects of job content, such as the margins permitted for personal initiative, where the percentage of dissatisfied workers rose to 40 percent (down to 32 percent in 1984). Even so, the bulk of the evidence is clear: about two thirds of workers perceived and valued their experience at work as positive and showed no feelings of anger, grievance, or alienation with regard to their jobs.[8]

Humane Treatment

Under the umbrella term *treatment* I include the overall social behavior of the firm and/or the management toward the workers insofar as this behavior expresses their degree of concern for the general welfare of their workers both in the workplace (as shown by the readiness of the firm to attend to complaints, to distribute sanctions or rewards fairly, and to provide information) and outside the workplace (as shown by services or subsidies for the education of children, sporting and cultural activities, and so on). This behavior does not, in itself, alter the authority structure of the firm; but it does illustrate the extent to which the firm treats its workers merely as a work force as opposed to what in everyday moral discourse is referred to as human beings. I use here, as in the survey, the term *treatment*, rather than *human relations*, to refer to this behavior because it seems to me that the term *treatment* is broader, less controversial, and closer to the immediate perception of the Spanish workers, and better reflects their moral frames of reference. A term such as *human relations* has connotations of sophisticated techniques, book learning, and use by experts and bureaucrats in personnel policies, bureaucratic organizations, and large firms. The term *treatment* refers to the basic rules of coexistence in everyday social interaction between persons who respect one another, whatever their origin or educational level, and whatever the organizational framework in which they coexist. To "treat" others and to "be treated" as a person implies a sense of self-respect, rules of reciprocity, and a common basic equality. Now, I used these terms in this sense, in the face of a fairly generalized assumption according to which the question of "treatment" (or "human relations") is merely cosmetic or rhetorical. This is a prejudice that fits two different assumptions. For some employers, and some experts, the subject is irrelevant because, for the purposes of production, the important thing is to juggle wage incentives with threats of dismissal. For some union leaders or labor politicians and other experts the subject is also irrelevant because they assume that the treatment workers receive from managers is virtually by definition humiliating or manipulative, and suggesting that it might be otherwise encourages paternalistic practices. But in fact, in order to learn what a firm looks like from the workers' viewpoint, the subject is of considerable importance.

In the survey of 1980 workers were asked what they would decide to do in this dilemma: "I am going to describe two types of firm to you. If you had to choose one of them, which one would you choose? (a) A firm which pays very well but which is not interested in you and provides no assistance when you are ill or in other unfortunate circumstances; (b) a firm which is more humane although it pays somewhat lower wages." Worker response was unequivocal and overwhelming: 91.5 percent opted for the second alternative, and only 4.3 percent for the first. The proportion by which a more humane employer was preferred was twenty-two to one. Note that care was taken to include a reference to remuneration levels which were somewhat higher in the "inhumane" case than the "humane" case; thus interviewees were forced to reflect somewhat more carefully on their answer. Note, however, that Spanish workers were no exception in showing this preference. The question in this survey replicated an identical question formulated by Ronald Dore in a study comparing British and Japanese firms (for which the fieldwork was done in 1969; see Dore, 1973). The distribution of answers was practically the same for Spanish workers and Japanese workers, although it was rather different from that of British workers (59 percent to 34 percent in favor of the "humane" employer).

What interpretation should be put on these data? What questions and problems arise from this interpretation? In the first place, although the examples make explicit reference to activities outside the workplace, I suggest that the focus of the contrast was the humane treatment of the firm in general and not specific social benefits. In support of my interpretation it can be proven that worker discontent was usually more widespread in larger firms, in spite of the fact that these were generally the employers which provided more outside social benefits. In the second place, taken literally, the reply suggested not only that workers wanted humane treatment but that they were willing to pay for it (or rather to be paid less in exchange for it). Should it be inferred from this that they would be willing to enter into negotiations in which there were formal and explicit discussions of an exchange of money for better treatment? Would wage increase be renounced in favor of rules governing disciplinary procedures, provision of information, and a "social salary" in the form of housing, education, and so on? These topics remain to be researched.

Finally, how were the basic attitudes and feelings of workers toward humane treatment to be understood? They could be understood as an

expression of deference toward, and expectations of, paternalistic attitudes on the part of employers. This is not my interpretation,
although I hasten to add that it would seem logical to me that such
feelings existed among the workers, since they exist in all social categories, and in particular among those who occupy subordinate positions, and that this should be to some extent expected, for it is
expected that ambivalent feelings toward authority, experienced for
the first time within the confines of the family, should then be projected onto the organizations and communities in which adult life
unfolds (Freud, 1969). I would suggest, however, that there is
another way of interpreting workers' responses. Workers desired
humane treatment not because they missed a paternalistic attitude but
because they wished to be recognized as members of a moral community and to receive the respect which was their due as members of such
a community. This is why—and this is a crucial fact in support of my
interpretation—they wanted humane treatment together with opportunities for a voice, or participation in decision making. At the same
time, to have a voice was not to occupy the place of the management;
that is, they seemed to want neither an omnipotent father figure nor
the death of the father; neither absolute monarchy nor anarchy nor a
revolutionary government but rather, perhaps, a limited constitutional
government. The fact is that the evidence available as to how Spanish
workers judged the way their employers treated them shows that more
than two thirds believed that the management was sensitive to their
requests and complaints. They were asked: "When you file a request
or a complaint, do you have the impression that you are being listened
to and attended to properly?" The answer was affirmative in 69 percent of cases (72 percent in 1984) and negative in 19 percent. Moreover, about four fifths (77 percent in 1980, and 86 percent in 1984)
of workers used channels within the firm for their complaints and
requests, while only 16 percent (9 percent in 1984) used union channels.

Attention and the readiness to listen were indicators of good treatment, but there were others. No less important was the fairness of the
rewards that management gave for professional conduct on the part of
workers. More than half (52 percent) of the workers believed that the
management gave just recompense for good performance at work,
while 43 percent believed that management was indifferent to individual performance (that is, they had the impression that even if they

worked hard, competently, and with care, this would have no positive repercussions on their salary, on their chances for promotion, or on the treatment they would receive, nor was it recognized by management in any other way). In turn, levels of workers' satisfaction were somewhat higher when they were asked about the fairness of promotion (59 percent in 1980, and 65 percent in 1984), lower when asked about punishments or sanctions (45 percent in 1980, and 52 percent in 1984). And the level of satisfaction with regard to information received from the firm was around 50 percent in 1980 and 58 percent in 1984.

Finally, a significant number, though not a majority, of Spanish firms organized or sponsored social services and activities of various kinds. The percentage of workers whose firms offered assistance in the education of children or in solving housing problems, promoted cultural, recreational, or sporting associations, and organized celebrations or cultural activities varied (in 1980) from 20 to 30 percent. Where these associations, activities, or benefits existed, the number of workers who participated in or took advantage of them was variable: 43 percent of the workers whose firms provided assistance for the education of their children benefited from this (amounting to 13 percent of the total number of workers); 34 percent of workers in firms which offered assistance with housing problems benefited (around 5 percent of the total); 70 percent of workers in firms in which cultural activities or parties were organized attended them (12 percent of the total); and 33 percent of workers in firms in which cultural, recreational, or sporting association existed participated in them (7 percent of the total). Here the differences between large and small firms were most marked: social services were found almost exclusively in large and medium-sized firms. At the same time, although we know the degree to which workers used these services, we do not know how they perceived and evaluated them. Did they consider them part of the social wage which was owed to them? As convenient instruments with which to solve personal problems with no connection to notions of justice or of moral obligation? As an expression of such a moral or affective bond with the firm? As an occasion in which to evoke a sense of belonging, or as an expression of humane treatment from the firm? It must be noted, however, that the relation between workers' demands for humane treatment and their utilization of social services was problematical, since it was possible that these services were provided within the framework of an impersonal bureaucratic organization and were perceived by workers as merely derivative of a situation of tension and distrust. And the fact is that the social climate in large firms, where there was a higher proportion of outside activities, was no better than that of smaller firms (in firms of fewer than twenty workers, 71 percent perceived that the majority of their companions were content with the firm; this percentage decreased in inverse proportion to the size of the firm, until it reached only 47 percent in the case of firms with more than five hundred employees). Hence, a note of caution must be sounded lest we overvalue the effects of social services on the social climate of a firm.

Demanding a Voice

Demands for humane treatment were combined with demands for a voice (Freeman and Medoff, 1984). This combination is proof, in my judgment, that behind the demands for humane treatment there were no particular feelings of deference toward nor expectations of paternalistic conduct from the management. Rather, workers' demands for a voice could be understood as the starting point for those who aspired to participate in the decision-making process, to build institutions of cooperation, and to achieve some degree of constitutional government in the firm. In short, there were those who considered changes in the authority structure of the firm, or at least in the exercise of that authority, to be desirable.

The question is crucial to both the present and the future of firms in advanced capitalist societies. Two factors, politicocultural and economic, make its formulation essential. The first factor consists of the effects which the values of liberal democracy have on the functioning and the organizational structure of the market economy system in the long term. These effects imply the gradual decline of absolute or unconditional forms of authority and the consequent emergence of mechanisms for voicing legitimate opposition in all spheres of social life, including the economic sphere. The second factor consists of the effects of economic crisis, which create the opportunity for an exchange in which substantial increases in wages may be renounced (including a social wage by means of an increase in public spending), in exchange for better treatment and a more powerful voice in decision making, particularly if and when the firm's survival can be shown to depend on the loyalty and motivation of a skilled labor force.

Now, in order for this discussion not to become mired in the rhetoric and confusion of ideological and political debates, it is necessary to define the varieties of demands for a voice. In the first place, there are variations with regard to the *theme* and *content* of voice. We can distinguish two types. On the one hand, there are relatively minor themes relating to the day-to-day functioning of firms, the characteristics of the job, the way in which the work is done (hours, tempo, the physical conditions at work), and other similar themes. On the other hand, there are the major strategic themes relating to critical decisions about the direction of the firm in the medium term, for example, decisions about investment in new machinery, new production proceedings, and commercial policy.

In the second place, there are variations as to the *degree* or *intensity* of the voice being demanded. Having a voice at the deliberating or consulting stage (with the expectation that notice will be taken, advice will be followed, or reasons will be forthcoming as to why it is rejected) is not the same thing as having a deciding voice (which obliges or imposes).

In the third place, it is important to distinguish between demands for a voice on specific matters (both major and minor) and demands for a voice on generic matters, such as those regarding fundamental decisions about the firm. This distinction is necessary because making decisions about specific matters, considered separately from one another, is very different from making mutually interrelated strategic decisions related to a complex and ever-changing external environment. It could be argued that consideration of fundamental decisions in generic terms incorporates additional complexity and uncertainty (a defining characteristic of the entrepreneurial role), which distinguishes it qualitatively from consideration of those decisions in specific terms.

Finally, a distinction should be made between two types of institutional mechanisms for having a voice. On the one hand are mechanisms from which the management of the firm is excluded, such as institutions for workers' collective action (enterprise committees, assemblies, union action). On the other hand are the institutions within which there is a place for the employer, or persons designated by the employer (such as meetings of employees with their foremen or team leaders in Japanese firms, or codetermination or vigilance committees in large German firms).

Two other distinctions may also be drawn: there is the distinction between demands which emphasize the voice or power to be achieved, and demands which emphasize the content of this voice. That is, there are those individuals or groups who are out to achieve power, and those who are primarily interested in solving a problem. It is the difference between power primarily as an end in itself and power as means. Typically, people in top organizational positions aim primarily at the first, whereas the average person with no specific ambition or vocation for power aims at the second. Then there is the distinction between those "integrative" demands that foster cooperation and those "radical" demands that create the basis for further conflicts between management and labor, although it is necessary to specify whether the distinction is made by reference to the intention, spirit, or ideology of the actors, or to the effective outcomes of their actions in the short or long term.

Now, the voice which the Spanish workers interviewed in this survey wanted varied depending on the subject under discussion. In matters concerning the daily functioning of the firm, such as tempo and working hours, 53 percent and 61 percent respectively of Spanish industrial workers (55 percent and 67 percent in 1984) wished for decisions to be made on the basis of agreement between the management and the employees; around 25 percent wanted decisions to be made by management after consultations with the workers; and around 10 percent wanted them made by management alone. On strategic matters, such as investment policy and sales policy, only around 15 percent of workers wished for the decisions to be made by common consent (the figure was the same in 1984); 20 to 25 percent wished for them to be made by the management after consultation; and around 50 percent were happy to leave them to management alone. Thus, the vast majority of workers wanted some say in minor matters, and around 40 percent wanted a say in major matters, but only a relatively small minority wanted a deciding voice.

To what extent did the ideal decision-making model contrast with the real one? How much voice did workers actually have in Spanish industrial enterprises? Once again, this depended on the subject matter. In minor issues (working hours, tempo, physical conditions) 23 to 35 percent of workers declared that decisions were the result of an agreement between workers and management, and another 16 percent replied that they were consulted before a final decision was made; in all, 40 to 50 percent of workers reported that they had a say in these matters. Yet on strategic matters (new investments, sales policy) the proportion of workers who had some voice fell to between 5 and 7 percent.

If we compare the ideal decision-making model with the real one, we observe several facts. Concerning minor matters, there was a discrepancy of 25 to 30 percentage points between the ideal and reality with regard to a deciding voice and 7 to 10 points with regard to a consultative voice. This could be interpreted as an indication that between 30 and 40 percent of workers were dissatisfied with the way minor decisions were made in the firm, above all because they wanted a deciding voice. Concerning major matters, there was a discrepancy of 11 to 16 points with regard to a deciding voice and 16 to 23 points with regard to a consultative voice, and this could be taken to mean that between 30 and 40 percent of workers were dissatisfied with the way major decisions were made, above all because they wanted a greater consultative voice. As additional evidence in corroboration of worker interest in obtaining a voice in major matters, I should point out that in answering the question, "On which two main subjects do you feel that you are not consulted by the management and that you should be?" workers insisted they should be consulted about the economic situation of the firm.

Nevertheless, aspirations for a voice on the part of Spanish workers were fundamentally limited by the widely accepted image of the roles of the employer and the wage earner and of their legitimate spheres of action. Workers were asked if they agreed or disagreed with this statement: "While workers should contribute to decision making about the organization of their immediate work, beyond that it is the manager's responsibility to manage, to take the bigger decisions and to ensure that there is work to be done" (taken from Dore, 1973, p. 361). Eighty-five percent declared that they agreed with this formula, conferring the right of strategic decision making to management and giving the workers opportunities for decision making with regard to the organization of their work; and 6.5 percent disagreed because they favored an extension of worker power in the field of strategic matters, while 2.4 percent advocated a restriction of worker power. Thus, if we pass from a discussion of specific strategic matters to one of how decisions should be made on strategic matters considered in a *generic* way, the proportion of workers interested in decision-making powers drops from between 13 and 19 percent to 6.5 percent.

It is interesting to compare Spanish workers' real and ideal models of decision making on specific matters with those of British and French workers. In 1971–72 Duncan Gallie (1978) posed questions very similar to those formulated in this survey to a sample of British and French workers in the petroleum industry. Gallie included questions about how decisions were made on hours, forms of payment, and wages (tactical or minor matters), on new investments and budgets (strategic or major matters), and about how they should be made. The distribution of answers on other major and minor matters in Gallie's survey do not diverge substantially from the distribution of answers in my survey on the subject of hours and investment, as examples of minor and major matters respectively. Concerning the minor question of hours, the ideal model for the Spanish, French, and British coincided; by an overwhelming majority they all wanted a voice, and also by an overwhelming majority they wanted a deciding voice, though somewhat less overwhelming in the Spanish case (78 to 82 percent of French, 82 to 90 percent of British, and 61 percent of Spanish workers wanted the decision to be made by common agreement). On the subject of new investments, the ideal model for the Spanish workers was close to that of the British but different from that of the French: while the majority of the first two would accept the management's decision or would settle for a consultative voice, the majority of the French aspired to a deciding voice (only 12 to 15 percent of British and 19 percent of Spanish workers wanted this). Concerning the real decision-making model, the situation was reversed. With respect to strategic matters, the Spanish, French, and British found themselves in a similar situation: in the immense majority of cases (between 86 and 95 percent of respondents) decisions were made by the management. By contrast, on the question of hours, the position of the Spanish workers was closer to that of the French and different from that of the British; while the immense majority of the British had a deciding voice on the question of hours (82 to 88 percent), only about one third of the French (26 to 36 percent) and the Spanish (35 percent) had the same power. In short, and although this slightly simplifies the question, Spanish workers aspired to what British workers aspired to, but they lacked the latter's real control over minor matters; and they had what the French had but without their ideal aspirations for control over major matters. The gap between expectations and achievements was greatest in the case of the French and at a minimum for the British, with the Spanish somewhere in between.

The Theory of Two Sides of the Firm

At the beginning of this chapter I said that the focus of my discussion was on the degree of consent and legitimacy attributed to the firm and the capitalist employer on the part of workers, which depended to a great extent on their satisfaction regarding the goods and services they received: job security, wages, working conditions, humane treatment, and a voice. But in turn the workers' evaluations of such goods were tied up with their particular perception of the firm. This was, in my view, a moderate version of the theory of the two sides of the firm, as it has been proposed by Ronald Dore in the context of his comparison of Japanese and British factories (1973). Dore suggested that there has been a gradual transition of workers' perceptions of the firm, so that the theory of the firm as a center of antagonism or irreconcilable opposition between two classes had gradually been replaced by the idea of the firm as an entity with two reconcilable and cooperative sides. He believed that this transition was relatively well advanced in Japan and was already starting to take place in Britain on the part of both the management and the trade unions (see also Dore, 1987).

The theory of antagonism or conflict between the two sides of the firm emerged almost at the start of the industrial revolution as the antithesis of a traditional view of the firm as an organic whole with the same interests, or as one large family. The latter view was denounced as an illusion or a deception to smooth over what was purely and simply the exploitation and subordination of the employees. To combat this, a theory of the firm as a battlefield of opposing interests was conceived, a theory of the two sides as enemies brought face to face. By contrast with this theory of antagonism, the theory of the two sides of the firm suggests that conflicts are relatively reconcilable and pacts of cooperation are possible. The theory could be formulated this way. First, there are two sides to the firm, with different interests. To deny this differentiation and the existence of conflicts of interest between these two sides (as is demonstrated by collective bargaining on the subject of the distribution of production surpluses) can only generate ambiguities and misunderstandings and obstruct realistic discussion and the possibility of agreement. Second, these different interests coexist with common interests, which are of equal or greater importance, and do not always imply antagonism or conflict, since different interests can often be complementary. Third, there is no reason why, in the relations of both sides, the conflictual element should prevail over feelings of community or complementarity to the point of undermining the moral community which can be constructed around common interests and objectives. Thus, the duality can be contained *within* the community. This is so because nothing in the nature of the firm—that is, in its authority structure and its objectives under present conditions—necessarily requires the breakdown of the community. In fact, increases in production (to which everyone agrees) may benefit all, and there may be a diffusion of the resources of voice and power operating in the firm, which may be extended to all or many of its members.

I use this model as a reference for a discussion of the available evidence about the attitudes of Spanish workers toward the firm. First, I establish what the logical implications or derivations of the model are, and then I examine to what extent the data correspond to those implications. From the extent to which they do, I deduce the relative applicability of the model for the situation in Spain. The model implies several assumptions about the workers. First, it is assumed that they do not question the basic power structure of the firm and therefore recognize the leadership and moral authority of the management; second, that they consider the firm a moral community and therefore believe that important common objectives and bonds of solidarity exist among its members; third, that they perceive the climate of social relations within the firm to be an expression of moderate contentment or satisfaction on the part of the people who work there; and fourth, that they conceive of unions and collective action as a mechanism for putting pressure on, and eventually reforming, the firm, but not as a mechanism for its destruction, and neither, therefore, as the bearer of an alternative model radically different from what already exists.

One implication of adopting the model is the acceptance of the power structure of the firm and the resulting legitimacy of management authority. In other words, this would imply the generalization among workers of the opinion expressed by Dore:

While people are to be treated with respect and should not be asked to take orders without explanations; while they can and should contribute to decision-making about the organization of their immediate work, beyond that it is the managers' responsibility to manage, to take the bigger policy decisions and to ensure that there is work to be done. The unions are there to squeeze the maximum advantage for the workers they represent, while doing all they can co-operatively to increase production so that there is more to squeeze. But beyond that these do not want the responsibilities, or the inhibitions on the ability to squeeze, of participation in management. (1973, p. 361)

In the 1980 survey two questions were formulated about the extent of the decision-making power of the management, one vis-à-vis the decision-making powers of workers and the other vis-à-vis labor union power; both were expressed in terms very similar to those used by Dore. Workers were asked: (a) I would like you to tell me if you agree with a statement such as the following: "Workers should be able to make decisions about the organization of their work, but it is the management's responsibility to manage, to decide on investment, and to guarantee that there is enough work for everyone." Those who disagreed with this statement were asked: "Would you mind explaining briefly to me why you disagree?" and they were offered the following alternatives: "Workers have no reason to make decisions on the organization of their work," or "Workers should also have responsibility for decisions on investment." Then they were asked to agree or disagree: (b) "The unions should achieve maximum possible wages but they should do this in such a way as to produce more so that there is more to be shared out without having to share responsibility with the management." Those who disagreed with this statement were asked: "What exactly do you disagree with?" and they were offered these alternatives: "The union does not have to worry about increased production," or "It has to share responsibility with the management."

The answers produced the following results: in 1980 approximately 85 percent of workers agreed with the formulation of question (a) (89 percent in 1984, and only 6.5 percent disagreed, in the sense that worker power over decisions should be expanded), while 71 percent of workers in 1980 agreed with the formulation of question (b) (73 percent in 1984, and only 11.7 percent disagreed, in the sense that they wanted an increase in union power). According to this, about 70 to 85 percent of workers in 1980 wished the management to exercise basic authority in the firm and only about 6 to 11 percent wanted a radical change in its authority structure. But this basic proposition must be qualified by two observations. First, there were pressures and demands for either a deciding or a consulting voice on specific matters, both major and minor (radical demands for a voice were very small, but reformist demands, in the broadest sense, were widespread). And second, there were indications of worker concern about whether managers were really "authentic" managers or not, since a small but appreciable number of workers wondered whether managers were capable of adequately fulfilling their role and exercising their authority as managers, and around 23 percent believed that there was a productivity problem in the firm (and this percentage included 15 percent who laid the responsibility for this problem on the managers for not organizing the work properly, for not investing correctly, and/or for not having the right personnel policy).

Now, contrary to what is sometimes claimed, a definition of the firm as a moral community, as understood in the context of the theory of the two sides, is not the most typical definition of managers themselves, and neither does its acceptance on the part of workers reflect the supposed cultural hegemony of the managers. In reality, some managers adopt a purely instrumental attitude toward the firm, and consider their links with the personnel strictly those of an exchange of work for wages, while others adopt a paternalistic or familial version of the firm as a moral community. In turn, many workers tend to create a moral environment around their experience of life and work in the factory. This is what happens with work groups, in which it is common to find an environment of moral and emotional exchanges according to an ethic of mutual assistance, solidarity, and reciprocal recognition. The importance of this environment to Spanish workers was expressed by the fact that 70 percent of them said that they would be very or quite sorry to leave their companions if they had to transfer to another workplace or firm (the same in 1980 as in 1978). This proportion was far higher than the 27 percent observed by John Goldthorpe and his collaborators (1968a) in his study of English workers (carried out between 1962 and 1964). This tendency to create moral environments no doubt underlay worker commitment to institutions of collective action and the unions (together with the instrumental attitude to which I refer later on). But this tendency also manifests itself in the sphere of the firm. The firm was the object of Spanish workers' aspirations for the constitution of a moral environment, expressed, as we have seen, by demands for humane treatment and for a voice. But this environment was not only an ideal; it was also, to some extent, a reality. In other words, the firm was a sphere in which moral authority was already exercised by the manager, in which relationships implied respect and recognition, although they were not free from pressure and conflict, some common interests and objectives, and some feelings of belonging to a community.

That this was so may be deduced from workers' answers to the question about which of these statements was closest to the way in which they saw the firm: "My firm is like a team in which there is a major common interest in producing more and better for everyone's benefit" or "My firm is not like a team because there is fundamental opposition between the interests of employers and employees." Of course, the answer to such a question can be considered only an approximate indication of the feelings and evaluative orientations of workers. Even so, the choice was clear: the first statement expressed a concept of the firm as a community, the second a concept of the firm as a battlefield. A large majority of workers (56 percent) chose the first statement, and only 38 percent chose the second. I must point out that this distribution of answers accentuated the tendency observable two years earlier, in 1978, when 50 percent chose the first statement and 46 percent the second, and was kept in 1984, when 57 percent chose the first statement and 38 percent the second. According to these data, feeling for the firm increased throughout this period. (By contrast, Fishman's study of the attitudes of workplace union leaders of the CCOO and the UGT in 1981 shows that about 70 percent of these local leaders had a "conflict interpretation" of the firm; 1990, p. 40.) In keeping with these data was the fact that a majority of workers also considered the social climate of the firm to be positive. The level of conflict in the firm might vary, but a majority of workers perceived most of their companions to be happy with the firm: 52 percent in 1980 perceived the social climate of the firm to be positive (57 percent in 1984), while about 38 percent felt that it was negative (the same in 1984).

WORKERS' VIEWS OF
UNIONS AND COLLECTIVE ACTION

Finally, I want to discuss the support that workers gave to the unions and other institutions of collective action (enterprise committees, assemblies, strikes) and the perception they had of them. Worker support for these institutions was significant, but workers did not fully identify with them, nor did they consider them an instrument for a radical transformation of the firm or of the existing economic order. Their attitude was both instrumental and moderate in its objectives, as shown by the evidence available on union membership among Spanish workers and other indicators of union influence, as well as evidence of workers' perception of the political links and functions of the unions, their assessment of union performance and of collective action in general, their participation in the interunion debate, and their tendency toward an institutional pluralism of collective action (that is, of support for the unions while simultaneously making use of enterprise committees and assemblies). Data refer mostly to 1980, but also to the overall period between 1978 and 1984.

Union Membership and Union Influence

Four main characteristics of the union membership of Spanish industrial workers stand out. First, the level of union membership fell dramatically between 1978 and 1984: in 1978 the level of affiliation was 57.4 percent; in 1980 it was 33.8 percent; and in 1984 it went down still further to 23 percent. The 23-point drop between 1978 and 1980 represented a decline of some 40 percent from the initial figure, and the 34-point drop between 1978 and 1984 a decline of about 60 percent. Second, most of the workers (about 80 percent) who joined a union preferred one of the two majority unions, the Comisiones Obreras (CCOO) and the Union General de Trabajadores (UGT). Taking into account the global reduction in membership, the consequence was the almost total collapse in membership of the minority unions (particularly the most militant ones, except for the relatively moderate nationalist unions in the Basque region). Third, within the two majority unions there was a gradual shift away from the CCOO and toward the UGT, even though the CCOO retained a larger following among industrial workers. In 1978 the CCOO had more than twice the membership of the UGT among industrial workers (31 percent versus 13.6 percent). In 1980 they were closer to each other (16.3 percent to 10.3 percent); and by 1984 they were even closer (12.2 percent and 7.9 percent). Thus, the 31 percent of workers affiliated with the CCOO in 1978 had dropped to 12.2 percent by 1984, while the 13.6 percent share of the UGT in 1978 had fallen to 7.9 percent by 1984. Although the CCOO continued to attract more members than the UGT in the industrial sector, the percentage of the decrease in relation to the 1978 level (60 percent) was much greater than the percentage of decrease for the UGT (42 percent). Finally, taking into account the total number of affiliates (from among manufacturing, construction, services, and retirees), the CCOO and the UGT had a similar level of affiliation by the late 1980s (about 800,000 affiliates each), and the overall rate of union affiliation was about 15 percent of the working population. These figures are close to those of the United States and France, but are considerably lower than those for most other industrial countries (35 percent in Germany, 41 percent in Italy, 46 percent in the United Kingdom, 59 percent in Belgium, 85 percent in Sweden).[9]

However, it is not sufficient to know only the membership figures for the unions in order to understand the extent of their influence. The sphere of influence of an organization constitutes a series of concentric circles in which the intensity of influence is in inverse proportion to the distance from the core of that organization. In the case of the unions, within their sphere of influence one may distinguish between a nucleus of members (where the influence is greater) and a periphery of sympathizers, voters, and even admiring onlookers and occasional followers of union activity (where the influence is less). One then has to ask what the extent of these zones was in this case and how it varied over the years.

Let us look closer at the situation in 1980. We have already seen that the membership level was 33.8 percent. Within this nucleus of membership, however, we should recognize the difference between a core of active, militant members and a concentric circle of relatively passive members. We have two indicators: attendance at union meetings over a twelve-month period (25 percent attended rather frequently) and active participation in the last meeting attended (18 percent). From this we can infer the existence of a militant core of around 25 percent of union members (or 8 percent of workers) and an outer circle of passive union members of around 75 percent (or 26 percent of workers).

To this we may add another 20 percent of union sympathizers in 1980 (about the same percentage as in 1978, and up to about 34 percent in 1984). If we consider that the unions' area of influence was composed of the sum of members and sympathizers, this sphere was reduced in size, parallel to the decrease in membership, from around 77 percent of workers in 1978 to around 53 percent in 1980, but steady at 57 percent in 1984. This was accompanied by a redistribution of influence between the CCOO and the UGT. In 1978 the ratio was 2 to 1 in favor of the CCOO, down to 1.3 to 1 in 1980, and 1.2 to 1 in 1984. According to these estimates about 40 percent of industrial workers were in the sphere of influence of the CCOO in 1978 (31 percent as union members), down to 26 percent in 1984 (12 percent as union members); and about 21 percent of industrial workers were in the sphere of influence of the UGT in 1978 (13.6 percent as union members) and 22 percent in 1984 (8 percent as union members).

It is worth considering, however, another three measures of the sphere of union influence. According to a first alternative, the unions' influence reaches out to encompass those who voted for union candidates in the elections for delegates and representatives to enterprise committees. There are two ways of recording the results of those elections. One consists of calculating the percentages obtained by union or nonunion candidates based on the electoral roll (including abstentions and "not voting"), in which case we obtain a figure of voters for each union close to the figure of members and sympathizers of that union. The other way consists of calculating the percentages on the basis of the effective vote (excluding abstentions and "not voting"), in which case we obtain a distribution of the vote close to the distribution of the positions of delegates and committee representatives obtained by the unions: 40 percent for the CCOO, and about 29 percent for the UGT in the elections that took place between 1978 and 1980; and 42 percent for the CCOO and 37 percent for the UGT in the elections that took place between 1980 and 1984. But this applies only to firms where these elections took place—about half the total number in the years under consideration.

We also have data on firms in which the unions were active, although of course their presence among workers could not be equated with their having an influence over them, since it might be that the unions' activities were perceived in such a way that the result, far from being one of influence, was one of reticence or even hostility. For this we would have to know how workers evaluated these activities. Thus, another (second alternative) estimate of the unions' influence can be drawn from the number of workers in whose firms these unions were active and who judged that their performance was excellent, good, or at least average. This again yielded a percentage for 1980 of about 42 percent who mentioned the CCOO and 35 percent who mentioned the UGT as being active in their firms. Similar results are obtained through still another (third alternative) estimate of union influence by including workers in firms in which the unions had been in charge of collective bargaining; here 36.8 percent mentioned the CCOO and 37.2 percent the UGT for 1980.

We therefore have different estimates available of the total sphere of union influence. On the one hand, the estimate is based on data about members and sympathizers and is in keeping with the data on the vote for union candidates at elections for representatives calculated as a percentage of the total electoral population, and the percentage of workers who were aware of the unions' activity in their firms and had a relatively favorable opinion of this activity. On the other, the estimate is based on the results of voting as a percentage of the total effective vote and the participation of the un:_ns in collective bargaining. Both came down to a figure of about 40 to 50 percent of industrial workers under the sphere of influence of the two main unions. However, it must be remembered that the real influence of the unions on events can exceed or fall short of their theoretical influence calculated on the basis of these estimates, particularly in decisions leading to strikes or collective bargaining and in the realization or implementation of these decisions.

Moderate Instrumentalism and Its Implications

One of the most important findings of the survey was that although the drop in union membership was spectacular, to leap to the conclusion that there was a drop in worker support for the unions would be unjustified. There was evidence for the first but not for the second, since union presence in firms was considerable, and the negotiating role of the unions in collective bargaining was even more so. In reality, the decline in membership was compatible with the maintenance of a relatively high degree of support because the attitude of workers toward the unions was increasingly instrumental. It was built on the exchange of support for services (above all in the field of collective bargaining), and this support was calculated in very general terms in such a way as to obtain maximum benefit at minimum cost. If the unions were seen principally as instruments for negotiation, then their services were to be obtained at the cost of limited support. It was sufficient to vote for their candidates to serve as representatives on enterprise committees (provided they displayed the necessary characteristics of honesty, efficiency, and so on) and/or support them in their job as negotiators without taking the next step of becoming a member or having a more enduring commitment to a union (Goldthorpe et al., 1968a and b, 1969). This was an attitude in between that of a committed supporter and a true free rider. A very different attitude would be to consider the unions as, above all, the promoters of a project for transforming the social order, or as an expression of values of solidarity, and to identify with them for reasons of identifying with those projects or values.

If it was the instrumental attitude which prevailed toward the unions and not one of identification with them, as I believe was the case, this would have far-reaching consequences. If this interpretation is correct, and the extension of union influence was maintained at the cost of its intensity, this would affect the capacity for union mobilization, which, at least insofar as it referred to nonprofessional or non-labor objectives, must diminish, since the mobilization of workers from a distance was not the same as the mobilization of members identified with the final objectives of the organization.

The way in which union membership was redistributed among the unions should be taken as confirmation. The majority unions continued to be so because workers wanted efficiency, and they associated efficiency with union power. But between the majority unions there was a gradual redistribution which operated clearly in favor of the UGT and against the CCOO. This corresponded to a process of differentiation between the images and the strategies of the UGT and the CCOO in the critical years between 1978 and 1980 and beyond. The UGT cultivated an image of realistic moderation and accommodation within the existing framework, whereas the CCOO opted for an image of social mobilization, more expressive of the project of transforming the existing order, the prevailing framework of industrial relations, and the formula of government. All of this illustrates my earlier hypothesis: the more workers were confronted by demands for identification with sweeping projects of social transformation, the greater their withdrawal and the subsequent decline in membership, while the more they were approached with requests for instrumental support to achieve advantageous agreements, the more stable this membership remained. This argument applies even more so to the situation created after 1982 by the accession to power of a Socialist government, which was expected to have a special relationship with the UGT.

Thus, the unions appeared to be instruments, but instruments for obtaining relatively modest objectives. This interpretation is corroborated by empirical evidence relative to workers' views of the unions and of the firm, their appraisal of collective action, the position of workers in interunion debates, and their use of various institutional mechanisms as an alternative to the unions.

That the attitude of workers was not only instrumental but also moderate can be confirmed by analyzing worker preferences and orientations toward the unions. Of course, the workers' view of the function of unions was complex and included, for nearly 50 percent of workers, their presence in public affairs and their intervention in matters of a general nature. In spite of this, it is essential to bear in mind their preferences for one or another kind of union activity or strategy. Summing up the evidence, the emphasis was on worker preference for union activity in collective bargaining (62 percent, and 69 percent in 1984), and in the provision of professional services (56 percent, and 58 percent in 1984), rather than on exerting pressure on the government for a change in policies (12 percent, and 9 percent in 1984); on the independence of the unions with respect to political parties (55 percent for complete independence versus only 4 percent in favor of their subordination, and 57 percent and 4 percent respectively in 1984); on the moderation of union objectives for union power in firms; and on considering the strike as an instrument which should be subject to regulation (64 percent in favor in 1980, and 73 percent in

1984), and as a last resort to be subordinated to negotiations (77 percent in favor in 1980, and 91 percent in 1984). In keeping with these findings was the fact that the workers' reference model was the situation of the advanced capitalist countries (61 percent, and 66 percent in 1984) but not the socialist countries (6.3 percent, and 5 percent in 1984), as well as the vision of the firm and the attitude of limited cooperation with the management.

In effect, workers wanted unions which were oriented toward negotiating agreements and providing professional advice, but which also played a part in helping to solve the social and economic problems of the country. However, when it came to specifying which should be the primary objectives, the answers emphasized two preferences from a battery of four alternatives which were clearly in favor of collective negotiations and professional advice. At the same time, the unions' own goals of social mobilization and exerting pressure on government policies were of less interest for workers; and the strong links of unions with any political party, in the form of subordination to or coordination with its strategies, were clearly rejected. The formula "The unions should be independent from political parties" was greatly preferred in 1980 (55.5 percent), followed by the formula "They should be independent but may occasionally enter into agreements with political parties on specific subjects" (32.8 percent), while a formula stating, "The unions should subordinate their strategies to the strategy of a political party of the same ideology," was rejected (only a minority of 4.2 percent accepted it).

Thus, agreements were expected to be made and bargains to be struck between unions and management, but in what spirit, and with what procedural rules? One indication of the spirit was the formula that the majority of workers considered valid relative to the ideal objectives of the unions within the firm. They were asked if they agreed with the statement "The unions should achieve maximum possible wages, but they should do this in such a way as to produce more, so that there is more to be shared out, without having to share responsibility with the management." Seventy-two percent agreed, while those who disagreed were relatively few (3.7 percent in the sense of wanting nothing to do with production levels, and 11.7 percent in the sense of being willing to exert pressure to obtain more power). That formula reflected a spirit of limited cooperation with the firm in keeping with the views I have discussed.

A final indication of the view workers had of agreements with the firm was their attitude toward collective conflicts. Such conflicts were judged realistically in light of their effects and, to a great extent depending on this, would then be repeated in similar circumstances. However, it is also important to show how the institution of the strike itself was perceived and valued. The strike could be seen either as an instrument to be used energetically when the balance of power was favorable, and which should not be limited by prior regulations, or as a last resort when negotiations had broken down, and which should be regulated for use in an orderly fashion. The fact is that the perception and normative orientation of a majority of Spanish workers toward strikes tended to the second alternative, in keeping with their general attitude of moderation. In order to corroborate or falsify this, we offered workers a series of two alternatives. In a first pair of alternatives, a strike was associated, on the one hand, with the idea of its being used with the utmost energy and in view of the tactical opportunity it offered, and on the other, with the idea of its being a last resort to be subordinated to negotiation. In a second pair of alternatives a strike was associated, on the one hand, with the idea of being an instrument of defense which should not be regulated, and on the other, with the idea of its being an instrument to be submitted to legal regulation and orderly use. In each pair of alternatives the first implied radical associations, tending toward a show of strength, as opposed to the second set, which could be characterized as moderate orientations, tending toward compromise. The results were clear. The moderate orientation was dominant. When we combined the two answers to obtain a spread bounded by the consistent radicals, who replied affirmatively to the first options (10 percent and 19 percent respectively), and the consistent moderates, who adopted the second positions (77 percent and 64 percent respectively), the consistent moderates were ten times more numerous than the consistent radicals (the former made up 56 percent of the sample and the latter only 5.7 percent).

All these findings appear to be in keeping with workers' attitudes toward matters of a more general nature: their perception of the social order and their position in it; their model of a desirable society and acceptable forms of behavior with relation to this social order; and also with their answers to the question "Would you name two countries in which, in your opinion, workers have more power than in

Spain?" By "more power" is meant more voice, not simply greater well-being. The desideratum of worker power or a worker voice was not, for Spanish workers, to be found in the socialist countries (whose governments, however, presumably represented the "rule of the proletariat" according to the communist mythology, which was presumably known by at least the nucleus of the communist-led CCOO). Rather, it was found in the western capitalist countries, for which preference was expressed in a proportion of ten to one over preference for socialist countries (in 1980 61 percent versus 6 percent, and in 1984 66 percent versus 5 percent). Within the spectrum of western capitalist countries workers looked to Germany, followed by France and England, as models (43 percent in 1980, and 47 percent in 1984), with Italy holding no attraction whatsoever (despite the influence of the Italian type of unionism among national and local leaders of the CCOO).

In keeping with this theory of moderate instrumentalism, and consistent with it, were the workers' evaluations of the unions, strikes, and agreements; their reticence toward interunion debates; and their choice of institutional pluralism through which to channel collective action (which included unions as well as enterprise committees and assemblies). The evaluation of the unions was expressed by an assessment and rating of each union by virtue of its performance over the preceding twelve months. In 1980 two out of every six workers declared that union performance had been good, three that it had been average, and one that it had been bad. It is difficult to interpret "average," which is on the borderline between adequate (meaning not quite mediocre) and inadequate (but not intolerable). It might perhaps be concluded that slightly or moderately negative evaluations predominated over positive ones, reflecting critical, distant, or doubtful attitudes underlying the vote for union candidates, and some confidence in the unions for collective bargaining. At the same time, the evaluation of collective agreements as a whole (with or without union intervention) resulted in a similar though perhaps slightly more positive assessment. These agreements affected 75.5 percent of workers. Of those affected, 39 percent considered the results reasonable, 38 percent considered them mediocre, and 15 percent thought them unacceptable.

In the survey, workers were asked to give their opinions on three general topics relative to the framework of industrial relations. These were a legislative statute known as the Estatuto de Trabajadores (Workers' Statute); the social pact of 1979, referred to as the Acuerdo Marco Interconfederal (AMI); and the issue of union plurality versus syndical unity. These opinions were formed against a backdrop of debate between the two majority unions, so without taking this into account, it is difficult to appreciate the workers' opinions of these matters. The debate over the Workers' Statute and the AMI put the UGT at odds with the CCOO, the first in favor and the second against. But it should be remembered that both the statute and the pact were long and complicated texts relating to a number of topics. Above all, these topics were ambiguous and allowed for an evaluation from three different viewpoints: from that of their impact on the formal framework of industrial relations; from that of their impact on the solution of immediate social and economic problems (of which the economic crisis and unemployment were the most pressing); and from that of their impact on the relative strength of socialist and communist organizations in the field of union activity and in the political arena. Thus, if we take into account the complexity of the debate and the low intensity of workers' identification with those organizations, it is understandable that the workers' inclination to take a stand on these matters was weak, and that in consequence the debate did not cause polarization but only uncertainty and a certain reticence. Thus, the workers who felt themselves to be most closely involved with the respective unions held an opinion, while the less involved they were, the less likely they were to hold one. The main factor was the large proportion of workers who did not hold any opinion, whereas the rest were almost equally divided between the two (a few more in favor of the pact and against the statute). At the same time, it could not be inferred from this that workers did not therefore hold an opinion about each of the referents or components of the AMI or the statute, that is, about a desirable framework for industrial relations, about desirable solutions to the economic crisis, and about their preferences for one or the other of the unions. They might or might not hold such an opinion. What happened was that the debate confused all these elements and transformed the AMI and the statute into complex and ambiguous symbols whereby identification or virtual identification with one or other of the unions was reduced to an apparently unequivocal yes or no in a minority of cases, leaving most workers undecided.

The question of unity or plurality of the labor movement was also a complex matter. Once again, it can be understood only within the context of the interplay of strategies of the majority unions. At the time, a relative acceptance of the status quo seemed to predominate; two unions of almost equal strength shared most of the territory between them and were competing for more, ensuring, wherever possible, the growth of their quasi-monopoly at the expense of the minority unions. Thus, workers, when confronted by the question of the unity or plurality of the unions, found themselves facing three kinds of declarations and behavior from the unions. First, on the level of formulating abstract ideals or values, every union leader recognized the desirability, in an indefinite future, of the unity of the working class, recognition of which was perhaps more emphatic on the part of the CCOO. Second, on the level of union policy, every union leader defended the specificity of each union—its symbols, its history, its strategy, and its tactics, insofar as they could be differentiated from the others'—a defense which was perhaps more emphatic on the part of the UGT. Finally, on the level of the effective behavior of the local leaders of firms, there was an ambiguous and constantly changing interplay of unity of action together with an emphasis on differences and competition according to the circumstances. Under these conditions a very general question was formulated in the survey on worker preference for one of these statements: "We workers all have the same interests and problems. A single central union would represent us and defend our interests better," or "Although we workers all have the same interests, there may be different ways of understanding the defense of these interests and therefore there should be various unions which represent the different ways of thinking." With the question formulated this way, the answer was divided nearly down the middle: 52 percent in favor of the first and 43 percent in favor of the second in 1980 (and 45 percent versus 51 percent in 1984).

In general, what we observe in the field of collective action is the workers opting for institutional pluralism. They backed two majoritarian unions that challenged each other, and a variety of enterprise committees and local assemblies all of which had an autonomous basis for social power. Thus, we know that where there had been elections for enterprise committees (about 40 to 50 percent of enterprises), a large majority of workers voted, with an abstention rate of around 24 percent. This represented significant participation by workers in this institution, and it was confirmed by the fact that around 10 percent of workers had formed part of these committees, and 24 percent were ready to accept a similar responsibility. Furthermore, it was clear that votes for representatives on enterprise committees and for delegates were oriented fundamentally toward candidates identified with the unions (and, as we have already seen, that meant mainly toward the CCOO and the UGT); but at the same time, when it came to stating the reasons for their choice, workers affirmed unequivocally that their main concern was for the personal characteristics of the candidates (93 percent in 1980), as opposed to their union backing (5.5 percent in 1980), and, most particularly, for their personal integrity and honesty. In general, enterprise committees were conceived of as different from the unions rather than as being either part of or in opposition to them. These committees participated, and were in fact the main actors, in collective bargaining in about 33 percent of cases.

What the workers expected from assemblies was less clear. They placed great value on assemblies as forums for expressive behavior and information, but they had little desire to see these assemblies act as protagonists in collective bargaining, and considerable doubts about the efficacy of the processes of decision making and debate which were carried out within them. That assemblies satisfied a need for information and of "being together" as a way of expressing solidarity and community, seems corroborated by the fact that workers valued highly the assemblies as a place for meeting (94 percent in 1978, 91 percent in 1980, and 93 percent in 1984), but at the same time most of them considered that the majority of those in attendance did not know much about the issues, did not participate, and, even when they did, did not speak their minds clearly.

In sum, the picture that may be drawn from the evidence regarding the relationship between Spanish rank-and-file workers and the Spanish unions during the years under consideration cannot be captured by the concepts of representation or interest intermediation. These concepts imply making assertions about the virtual identity of workers' and unions' interests and orientations, and therefore about the unions' ability to lead the workers, shape their demands, and mobilize them, which are not supported by the data. The fact is that Spanish workers and unions stood in a complex relationship, each side holding its own views, definitions of interests, and cognitive and normative orientations, while at the same time each was willing to use the other, to accommodate the other, and to put a limited trust in the other for a variety of purposes.

Workers' attitudes were different in that they were more moderate (and this is an ambiguous label I have tried to clarify in the preceding pages) than those of the union officials, as these officials knew, to their regret, only too well, and said so explicitly when asked (Fishman, 1990, pp. 43ff.). And workers acted on this difference in their handling of the unions. They "punished" unions which seemed too radical, such as the CSUT (Confederación de Sindicatos Unitarios de Trabajadores) and SU (Sindicato Unitario), which had enjoyed a period of great activism and public exposure in the late 1970s, by voting them out in a series of elections for enterprise committees. They rewarded the UGT's moderation by putting it on a par with the CCOO, despite the UGT's rather unimpressive record during the Franco regime. Then, they sent both the UGT and the CCOO clear messages to the effect that they would prefer these unions to distance themselves from their respective political parties (as they started to do, or to look as if they were doing, in the course of the 1980s). The workers also made it quite clear that they wanted a plurality of institutional mechanisms (and not only unions) for handling their problems, and that they wanted as candidates for enterprise committees primarily people they could trust, and only secondarily people trusted by their highly placed union officials.

To the extent that the CCOO and the UGT listened and accommodated themselves to these demands, workers showed themselves willing not to become union members but to support these unions, to accept their candidates for committees, and to allow the unions to engage in collective bargaining and other activities on their behalf, despite the fact that both unions maintained positions which were less moderate than their own. In explanation of this support, two arguments, which may be complementary, suggest themselves. In keeping with the instrumentalist theory, workers may have considered unionists' relative radicalism an indication of an altruistic disposition, even a fighting disposition, which would suit their own interests well. Workers would be grateful for, and ready and willing to exploit, the unionists' dispositions with no guilty feelings, since altruistic people are supposed to love being given the opportunity to be altruistic, and besides they are never supposed to be so altruistic as not to enjoy becoming powerful, which they might be by becoming union leaders. The alternative to altruistic militants would be well-paid militants (who could easily be suspected of being self-serving, willing to cut a deal with management, or even being utterly corrupt).

But a softer version of this instrumentalist theory would allow significant room for an additional, and complementary, explanation. In this view unions could be seen as depositories or embodiments of an inherited, accumulated capital of trust. A collective memory at work would provide laborers with arguments for the defense of their interests, and for their common-sense view of the world, with an additional rhetorical strength as well as moral persuasiveness which otherwise would be missing. This may be one of the reasons why the confused yet unending, intense conversation between unions and workers would go on, and the workers' (limited, conditional, yet real) attachment to the unions would stand. This is the theme I will explore in the next and final chapter.

6

Unions' Uncertainties and Workers' Ambivalence: The Moral Dimension

The public sphere is the locus of a debate among individuals and social participants who are required to advance the pursuit of their goals within the framework of an argument about the public good. The defense of their particular interests must be embedded in general justifications of public policies and political institutions, and in a view of the kind of well-ordered society that is the goal of the people implementing those policies and supporting (or transforming) those institutions. Moreover, these arguments are expected to be acted out by those who advance them: to be embodied in actual behavior, mores, or traditions. Therefore, they are supposed to arise not out of detachment but out of commitment. They are not theoretical statements of uninterested debaters but prudent, practical judgments of committed participants. The capacity these participants have for listening to others' arguments and for fully understanding the experiences from which these arguments arise is a limited one, though the limits may change over time for better or worse. Under these circumstances, learning through debating may be expected to be a difficult and always precarious undertaking.

At least on principle, the rules of the game of the public sphere tend to exclude the attribution of a privileged voice to any specific agents or institutions. This applies, first of all, to the state itself, which, rather than being the agent in charge of providing an authoritative definition of the common good (or of giving voice to a moral-political consensus about policies and institutions), is just one of the participants in the debate. Furthermore, the state is also one of the key topics of the debate. Thus, the public sphere is the arena where the limited role of the state as a service provider and coercive agent, and as a distinguished performer in the public theater (see Chapter 2), is to be assessed and debated.

But this applies not only to the state but also to every other social agent and institution of civil society, such as the church, regional elites, business, the professions, and labor, among others.[1] Their voices may be crucial, yet they are limited in their role of giving content and shape to the public sphere. In assessing their contribution we must also consider the internal complexity of each voice. Thus, the voice of labor is rather a polyphony, with a strong component of chaos, of voices linked to different traditions and debating one another.

Chief among the internal controversies surrounding labor stands the one regarding the claim of unions and parties of the socialist tradition (understood in its broadest sense, as opposed to the anarchist tradition) to have their voice taken as representing that of the entire class of "workers" (often loosely defined, and ranging from a nucleus of manual workers in manufacturing and construction to the whole of the wage-earning population), and to speak for them. This claim is a familiar one, which parallels the claim of political representatives to the "virtual representation" of the entire population, as well as that of the church to speak for the entire body of religious believers.[2]

This claim would assume a virtual identity between the interests, as well as the normative and cognitive orientations, of union officials (as "representatives"), affiliated members of the unions (as "electors"), and the rest of the working class (as "nonelectors"). It may be conceded that general acceptance of the unions' claim to be the virtual representatives of the working class as a whole laid the groundwork for the unions' added moral weight and moral stature in the public sphere. This "moral surplus" has traditionally allowed the unions to be seen generally as more than mere interest groups, and has invested their voice with a larger significance. In fact, for a long time they were, and still are to a minor extent, the bearers of rather extraordinary moral projects which have been shared or recognized in both explicit and tacit ways by broad segments of the population. Now, the points I intend to make in this chapter concern the internal complexity and moral ambiguity of the voice of labor, not just in Spain but in advanced capitalist societies in general under present circumstances, and to the fact that this theory of virtual representation or tacit delegation no longer applies, with the result that labor is faced with a series of crises of representation.

This final chapter addresses some general questions concerning the voice and the consciousness of trade unions and workers in the context of a changing political economy, which is in fact a crucial piece in the larger puzzle of a changing world. I stress that there is an important moral dimension to union officials' and workers' behavior and attitudes, and that the current crisis has precipitated and brought to the forefront a series of moral dilemmas that underlie their strategic uncertainties. The crisis of capitalism has revealed, paradoxically, an even more profound crisis among its critics. At a time when capitalism is most vulnerable, its critics have shown a lack of the ability and the will even to attempt to bring it down and replace it with at least a variant of capitalism that would entail qualitative change in the system or steer it in the direction of a form of socialism. This had always seemed to be the intention of the European unions and socialist parties, whether Marxist or revisionist, at least according to their declarations of principle. Their ideals took the form of a project for society which was an alternative to the existing society. Despite all the compromises imposed over the years by what we may call the reality principle, these organizations could hardly renounce this ideal, since it had become a crucial symbol of their identity. Amid the continual changes in historical context, generations, political tactics, organizational structure, alliances, and political agenda, a fixed and immutable point of reference was needed in order to preserve the sense that this identity was being maintained. This point of reference was a collective memory of fights, victories, defeats, truces, and compromises, organized around a continuity in the fundamental ideals and principles of the organizations. Without it there seemed to be some danger that moral confusion and a loss of direction would spread through working-class organizations, a development seemingly incompatible with the mobilization of the moral energies necessary for success in the struggle for power, for benefits, and for social victories. Such a loss would seem to endanger the trust that the masses were asked to place in their leaders and the self-confidence of the latter.

For this reason, a considerable part of the culture surrounding an alternative project for society survived a hundred years of historical change and compromise. It survived in the rhetorical *ritornelli* of speeches, songs, flags, raised fists, statements made at conferences, texts for training courses for militants, and propaganda leaflets, sometimes in the form of nostalgic evocations of the past, sometimes in the form of hopeful appeals to a utopian future. In other words, it survived in numerous aspects of exhortative moral discourse of the organizations in question.

For reasons whose explanation is not relevant here, this culture of an alternative project for society or a left-wing culture was more vital in western Europe than in the United States or Japan. Curiously enough, it was also in Europe where the objective vulnerability of the existing model of society seemed greater during the last quarter of the twentieth century. This means that, when compared with other parts of the liberal capitalist world, Europe has constituted an area of higher risk, where the subjective will and the objective opportunity for a radical transformation were greater. Europe was, therefore, an extreme case, in which we can examine the relative importance of cultural factors in terms of explaining the strategies of social and political agents, as well as the resulting processes of conservation or change in the current socioeconomic structure.

Now, when we examine this cultural factor regarding the attitudes and behavior of unions and workers vis-à-vis the economic system, it is essential to distinguish between the cognitions and moral values of these two groups, so as to avoid the fallacy that may be implicit in terms such as *labor, the workers' movement,* or *the working class* (in the Marxist or Lukácsian sense of a class in itself, which incorporates labor organizations into the definition of the class; Lukács, 1960). These expressions may serve to confuse two quite different (though, depending on the circumstances, often interrelated) groups: on the one hand, the organizations themselves, in this case especially the trade unions, or rather the more specific groups of leaders, officers, and active militants of such organizations; and, on the other, the rank-and-file workers who supposedly constitute the social base of these organizations, be it current (the affiliated members) or potential (those susceptible to following these organizations or assumed to be represented by them).

In my comments I take western Europe as my context. After a brief review of the circumstances leading up to the current crisis, I analyze both dimensions of this concept of subjective will: the strategic uncertainties of union leaders and officials (as well as a considerable number of activists), and the ambivalent attitudes of the workers themselves (which are finally resolved in an attitude of moderation). Finally, I suggest the moral dilemmas implicit in this uncertainty and ambivalence.

The objective vulnerability of Europe can be measured in terms of the economic crisis and its associated political and social problems (see Chapter 2). European countries as a whole have suffered a prolonged economic crisis from the mid-1970s up to the present, which has brought sizable rates of inflation and unemployment. The range of factors giving rise to this crisis was quite complex. Among them were the drop in demand for certain products, the rise in interest rates (linked, to an extent, to American trade deficits), and the rise in the costs of fuel and especially labor. The crisis affected gross capital formation and thus called into question the system's capacity for sustained growth and absorption of the increasing mass of unemployed workers. This has occurred in Europe at a time of intense competition in international markets among the United States, Japan, and some of the new industrialized countries, and a subsequent increase in the rate of technological innovation. The sources of the decline in profitable productive capacity were thought to lie in a series of factors discouraging investment, three of which stood out from the rest: the excessive rise in real wages, the considerable lack of flexibility of external and internal labor markets, and the disproportionate weight of the public sector. According to this diagnosis, in order to surmount the crisis, governments should try to contain the growth of wages while refraining from fiscal and monetary policies that might stimulate inflation and create balance-of-payments problems; they should introduce a greater degree of flexibility into internal and external labor markets; and they should reduce the weight of the public sector.

Now, these conclusions, if accepted, call into question the basis of the social compromise that had been the foundation of reformed capitalism and the welfare state in postwar Europe. Under the terms of this compromise, the unions and the social democratic parties had been able to achieve increases in workers' purchasing power, the dense network of regulations limiting managerial authority, and raises in social or indirect wages based on increases in social security and other expenditures either as social victories or as part of a social compromise, the other side of the story being their acquiescence to the foundations of the capitalist system. This compromise was the implicit regulating principle for electoral contests between the major political parties and for many aspects of the stability and actual functioning of European economy and society. It placed a limit on conflicts of interests among organized groups and allowed continuity through changes of government; and it also appeared in various countries at different times in the form of explicit contracts or agreements, such as experiments in consociational democracy, grand coalitions, or neocorporatist institutions. The economic crisis therefore affected not only the economy but also understandings that had been crucial for preserving the fabric of society, for its integration and cohesion throughout the entire period.

Moreover, as this crisis unfolded between the mid-1970s and the mid-1980s, it seemed to be taking place at a time of considerable vulnerability for the political institutions themselves. This vulnerability came about through the confluence of several factors, some of which proved to be, in time, of a rather transitional character. First was Europe's increasing vulnerability as a broader region, which was in turn the effect of East-West tensions in the late 1970s and early 1980s over the defensive rearmament (within the European nuclear scenario) of NATO and the consequences of the continuing crisis in Poland, soon to be overcome by the collapse of communism in the late 1980s. Second was the increasing difficulty in building a united Europe as a result of internal problems, especially of an agricultural and financial nature, and the problem of enlarging the EEC with the inclusion of Greece, Portugal, and Spain, which gave way to a climate of Euro-optimism in the second half of the 1980s. Third were problems of governability, which seemed to be on the rise in many countries since the 1970s as a consequence of the increase in distributive conflicts, the upsurge of various new social movements, and regionalist or nationalist tensions, all of which led to the formation of new collective identities of a territorial or social nature which posed a threat to the internal cohesion of European political systems. To all of this can be added, in certain southern European countries, the problematic experiences of "difficult democracy" (Italy) or democracy in transition (Spain, Portugal, and Greece).

The result was an emotional and intellectual climate in which the whole of the established order lost its "naturalness," or at least the kind of naturalness it had attained during the period following the Second World War, as the result of a lengthy experience of liberal democracy, the growth of the welfare state, and the experience of prosperous capitalism (see Chapter 2). It ceased to be considered a given order, one that could be taken for granted. Its foundation, in a consensus involving a large part of society, was laid bare; the implicit had to be made explicit. (Perhaps this was one of the main reasons for the rise of corporatist agreements, or attempts at the same, during this period, for even if they did not solve many economic problems, they were perceived as being able to reinforce social cohesion; see Chapter 4.)

Under normal circumstances the cultural foundations of economic, social, and political structures are taken for granted. This creates the impression that events in the economy, society, and politics are more or less structurally determined and autonomous from the cognitive and evaluative point of view of society. But in times of crisis one can observe the opposite. Whether existing structures are maintained or modified depends, at such points, on how the actors define the situation, how they explain and evaluate it, what alternatives they can see, what consequences they foresee for different courses of action, what decisions they make, and what moral resources they can muster in support of one decision or another. These actors are, in the last analysis, individuals, since organizations in such situations are obliged to take into account the commitments that these individuals decide to make to them, for not even the continued existence, identity, or strategy of these organizations can be taken for granted any longer. It is true that even under such circumstances not everything is possible, whether for individuals or for organizations; but it is clear that in a situation of disorder and turbulence the range of possibilities is much greater than one might previously have supposed.

In western Europe this range of possibilities, as far as the socioeconomic system was concerned, included several options: holding to the course of reformed capitalism, the welfare state, and what some have called the social democratic model;[3] drastically pushing this model beyond its present limit toward the primacy of the public sector, and establishing a new balance of socioeconomic forces in favor of the trade unions by increasing union power either in companies or in the economic life of the country (as was suggested by Swedish and Italian unionists in the late 1970s);[4] reversing the historical tendency and heading toward neoliberalism, reducing state regulation and the weight of the public sector; or choosing between hybrid forms of social democracy and neoliberalism adapted ad hoc to the situation and the moment in each country (see Chapters 2 and 4).

STRATEGIC AND MORAL UNCERTAINTIES OF THE TRADE UNIONS

Faced with the current challenge and with this broadening in the range of options, the leaders, officers, and activists of the trade unions showed signs of profound uncertainty. Yet we must remember that, despite the overall growth in trade union membership in the 1970s (Visser, 1984, 1990), the relative intensification of industrial disputes in that decade, the legislative improvements obtained by trade unions, substantial increases in the public sector, and some advancement in the development of neocorporatist institutions (Therborn, 1984), nonetheless, in the latter half of the 1970s and especially the first half of the 1980s the situation became more complicated and considerably more gloomy for union action (Baglioni and Santi, 1985).

In the first place, it became much more difficult to aggregate the basic interests of various types and categories of wage earners. With the high levels of mass unemployment in recent years, a substantial part of the labor force either remained outside the formal economy (being unemployed or forming part of the underground economy), or remained within the formal economy but in a very precarious position. This happened throughout almost all of Europe, thus creating a breach between the interests of those employed in relatively stable jobs and the interests of the rest of the work force. But even the difficulty of unifying interests among the population employed in the formal economy grew considerably. There was an increase in the internal differentiation and heterogeneity of the economy. In fact, the crisis affected the different sectors, subsectors, and types of companies in different ways. The difficulties encountered in part of the public sector and in the traditional industrial sectors contrasted with the opportunities for growth facing many firms in other areas as a result of different rates of technological innovation, ability to attract foreign capital, and penetration into overseas markets. This created differences within the labor force between those working in expanding firms and those working in companies experiencing difficulties. Moreover, differences of interest sharpened among various categories of workers according to their field of work and their professional qualifications, for example, between technicians and highly skilled workers in research and development, design, entertainment, or sales on the one hand and semiskilled workers in production and administration on the other.

In the 1970s there had been a trend toward centralized agreements which standardized the treatment of different sectors, companies, and professional categories, aiming at a compression of salary ranges. Thereafter this trend clashed with the interests of wage earners who were in an especially powerful position to demand higher pay, and whose interests coincided with those of employers seeking to establish specific agreements with their personnel or company unions. This coincidence of interests was facilitated by the growth strength of workers' representative bodies within many companies (Streeck, 1984). Furthermore, not only was the growing differentiation of workers' interests by sector, type of business, and professional category related to salaries; it also affected the operation of the internal labor market, job organization, working conditions, and the length of the workday. All these depended more and more on the particular conditions in each company, and these were items that employers were interested in discussing on a case-by-case basis.

Under these circumstances the trade unions experienced increasing difficulties in aggregating the interests of the workers as well as in diagnosing the situation and formulating a moral argument to strengthen their appeal for mass mobilization. The defense of the interests of nearly all wage earners required something more than simple aggregation of their interests as formulated at the grass-roots level; it required minimizing the differences between groups of wage earners so as to render them compatible with a medium-term plan for social and economic policy. It was here that one could see a serious moral and intellectual crisis developing in the unions, which was only partly a reflection and result of a parallel crisis in the corresponding political parties.

Many trade unionists hardly dared to believe anymore in the possibility of carrying out the projects of the previous era. During the period following the Second World War, trade unions and socialist parties reached a compromise with capitalism. They still recognized, rhetorically, the ideal of overthrowing capitalism, but in practice they managed to reach a compromise with capitalism based on the latter's ability to fulfill union objectives such as incorporating reforms, improving workers' purchasing power, guaranteeing jobs, reducing inequalities, and giving the workers more say in industrial matters. This compromise was therefore compatible with a project to improve the terms of capitalism. It could be said to generate a series of social victories for the masses, as well as to enlarge the spheres of power for union and party leaders. Such a project based on the improvement of capitalism and a gradual widening of social victories seemed feasible at a time of economic growth and full employment; under circumstances of economic crisis, however, it no longer looked that way.

It was nonetheless true that many trade unions continued to encourage such projects during the second half of the 1970s. For a while they gained modest victories over reluctant social democratic parties (such as the Labour party in Britain or the German Social Democrats) or over liberal-conservative parties (the Swedish bourgeois government of 1976–1982, the Italian Christian Democrats, the UCD in Spain). But the result was the opposite of what they had sought: those governments that made concessions saw their economic policies fail and themselves fall from power; and in the end, stricter monetary and financial policies were adopted along with austerity measures. In central and northern Europe this meant defeat for the social democrats, or, in the case of the Swedes, an opportunity to be more cautious in implementing their economic policy. In southern Europe the mirage of Eurosocialism listing to the left gave way to the reality of socialist governments following orthodox economic policies (after François Mitterrand's brief semiradical experiment of 1981–82) as the only way of ensuring reelection; they have even gone as far as to ignore, if necessary, neocorporatist institutions (Berger, 1985a).

In addition to watching their repertoire of policies and their diagnosis of the situation fail them, unions were also losing their moral momentum. At the critical moment of struggle to defend the social gains of thirty or forty years, they appeared to lack moral force, and their reserves of moral indignation seemed to be depleted, except perhaps in relatively isolated or marginal sectors and communities (as in the case of the 1984–85 miners' strike in the United Kingdom). Yet this element had been crucial to trade unions, and to socialist parties in general, since their foundation, and it had been a decisive factor in their ability to mobilize. The unions typically compensated for weaknesses in organization, financial resources, and technical know-how with numbers and enthusiasm. Without this enthusiasm there were no militants or, at critical moments, masses to be present in the right place at the right time, nor were there leaders who inspired confidence, nor a base membership who would hold out in times of hardship. This show of enthusiasm was essential, moreover, to move those among the general public who were sympathetic, and to inhibit opposition. All this depended on the unions' ability to dramatize a situation and stir up feelings of loyalty toward one group and indignation toward the other.

Trade unionism began, in fact, with two highly dramatic elements in its makeup. One was the conflict with capital, which was seen as evil, an almost diabolical force. In the beginning part of trade unionism's appeal lay in its ability to evoke quasi-religious sentiments among its members and the masses: feelings of hostility toward the god Baal, the golden calf, or the merchants turned out of the temple; feelings of indignation (or resentment) toward those who accumulated wealth, who had been traditionally viewed, in both urban and peasant Christian societies, as being excluded from or on the margin of the moral community. The secular morality implicit in theories of the class struggle incorporated many of these feelings and endured time and time again by evoking the moral drama of the confrontation between good and evil. The religious aim of salvation or liberation from the domain of sin or evil was transmuted into an attempt to seek salvation or liberation from economic exploitation, political oppression, and the affront to individual dignity. "Good" became socialism (or, in a variation, anarchy), seen as the way to achieve a morally integrated or virtuous community from which capital (and, for the anarchists, the state) would be excluded. But at the same time, the labor movements did not adopt a gnostic view of the world; therefore, neither did they believe in the permanent struggle between good and evil. Good had to prevail. And so a second dramatic element rested on the hope offered for a final triumph of virtue, already anticipated through contemporary struggles which gave the labor movement meaning.

Now, more than a hundred years of protracted historical experience brought about a second-order secularization, a disenchantment, to use Weber's term, and finally a moral de-dramatization of the conflict. Moral ambiguity and ambivalent feelings with regard to capitalism set in. This process had been going on for many decades and could be perceived in Germany as early as the period prior to the First World War (Moore, 1978). But the process was particularly evident in the period since the Second World War as a result of status leveling, economic prosperity, political stability, and a strengthening of national feelings.

The weakening of sharp status divisions within society intensified conflicts of interest (Goldthorpe, 1978), but it also reduced much of the basis for the development of feelings of moral indignation, of having been humiliated and offended, of having had one's dignity abused. No matter how intense and frequent these conflicts about status were in some countries (more so in the English-speaking and Latin countries than in central Europe or Scandinavia), they were not zero-sum conflicts; instead they brought about a considerable improvement in the position of both sides. Therefore, in the long run there was an institutionalization of industrial relations of either a pluralist or a corporatist kind, reciprocal acceptance of the legitimacy of the other side, and to some extent the formation of a quasi-community between adversaries. Similar developments occurred in the area of political institutions and national sentiment. Initially the workers' movement took the state to be a tool of the enemy and felt a keen ambivalence with respect to the national community. But in time, unions and socialist parties came to grant a considerable degree of legitimacy to the state in liberal democratic regimes, which implied the devaluation of the view of the state as an instrument of the capitalist class. This was greatly facilitated by the alternative experience of totalitarian states, be they fascist or communist, and, last but not least, by the fact that since the Second World War the liberal state had frequently been in the hands of social democratic parties. All this in turn was reflected in the development of feelings of national solidarity across classes. The state was one of the key factors in the development of these feelings, along with experiences of national solidarity in time of war (as occurred during the Second World War), social agreements struck in order to overcome internal conflicts of a religious, ethnic, or linguistic nature (as occurred in small European countries; see Lijphart, 1977), and situations of international economic competition which have brought both sides closer together in internal economic disputes (Katzenstein, 1984).

Certain elements of the present economic crisis also made it more difficult for the leaders, officials, and active members of trade unions to achieve a convincing dramatic tone and effective manipulation of the masses' feelings of moral indignation. First, the crisis placed more emphasis, among the trade unionists themselves, on collective or national goods such as fighting inflation or improving the domestic economy's competitiveness abroad. Second, the crisis divided the working class by provoking an intensified strategy of dual closure (Parkin, 1979) among its organizations. This strategy attempted to narrow the wage, status, and employment gap with respect to those at the top (employers and professional people) but at the same time also to widen the gap between unionized or "core" workers and those below (such as immigrants, ethnic minorities, women, young people looking for their first job, people near retirement age, or socially stigmatized minorities). To a greater or lesser extent this duality had always been part of the workers' experiences, but whereas in times of economic growth they had been relatively open and generous with those below, in hard times their organizations closed ranks and established a clear hierarchy of priorities at the expense of those at the bottom. Even corporatist institutions that employed rhetorical claims of solidarity tacitly accepted this veiled dualism.

As a result, union leaders, officials, and activists found themselves heading for what could be called realism, pragmatism, or opportunism, but which really entailed an adjustment of moral and intellectual discourse. Motivated by concern for the survival of the organization and for their own leadership position vis-à-vis the working classes, these trade unionists defended tooth and nail the wages and jobs of the core of workers in the formal economy, who formed the nucleus of the unions' membership. They were thus obliged to take another step (in addition to those taken in times of prosperity) in the direction of accepting the logic of capitalism. This acceptance in turn meant that they must also give priority to the accumulation of capital, which ensured the long-term future of the system, over the redistribution of wealth. Eventually this logic also implied that unionists had to defend the interests even of the core workers in a very qualified way, by going on the defensive and accepting concessions with respect to wage levels, flexibility of external labor markets, and social benefits. All this was very difficult and embarrassing to do, and even more so to explain, because it implied an acceptance of capitalism that Marxist or revisionist trade unionists, who attempted to preserve their union's class identity, could never state explicitly.

The union leaders' position was all the more painful by contrast with their ambitions of the 1970s, when they had dreamed of occupying a central position in the public arena. They had believed that they could bring governments to their knees (as happened in Britain under the Heath and Callaghan governments), impose their will on the political parties (as seemed for a time to be the case in Italy), or develop economic policy on equal terms with employers and the state even to the point of implementing a new model of economic development (according to the Italian EUR line; see Martin and Ross, 1980). They thought they could go beyond the basics of bread-and-butter issues toward more ambitious, qualitative, and power-oriented issues, and they were brought down to earth with a shock.

It is only in this context that one can understand the current transition from a language of moral objectivism to one of moral subjectivism on the part of many union leaders, officials, and activists. Previously it had seemed as if the future of mankind was at stake when it came to adopting certain union and political stands. People had committed themselves to an objective undertaking, which they called a historical task. There were many moments of intense commitment and even heroism. Now it was a question either of trying to regain the feelings of the past, which were linked to the belief in the historical task—a belief that no longer existed—or of renouncing those feelings. The drama now consisted of adapting to a situation from which it was no longer necessary to save oneself, or in which salvation was no longer salvation from the moral evil of capitalism or the state but rather from the daily routine of committees, negotiations, bureaucratic hierarchies, the fluctuations of the market, or the life of party politics. Although this may have been important to some groups of intellectuals and militants, for the masses it was no more than a minor matter. So the trade union and political drama of the past increasingly became a private drama; and what was once an epic struggle became a lyrical one, a rear-guard action on the part of some trade union leaders and activists who tried to regain an identity through a search for a time gone by.

THE CRISIS OF IMPLICIT DELEGATION

During this difficult period governments and employers, especially in Europe, needed a great deal of cooperation from the trade unions and the work force. Europe is a region of many historical fissures and all sorts of tensions (nationalist, ethnic and linguistic, religious and ideological, economic, political, social), where, precisely for this reason, and in order to counteract these tensions, a delicate balance of power was set up over the postwar years. This took the form of a network of institutions and a pattern of mutual tolerance which could not be ignored or called into question with impunity, since to do so would stir up relatively recent, dramatic historical memories. The power of the unions within this web of institutions was still quite considerable. For this reason, an economic policy that would systematically exclude unions from the public decision-making process would, in the long term, be too costly and too risky.[5] Yet if European governments still needed to support their economic policies through understandings reached with the unions, or directly with the workers, something similar was also occurring among European employers, who required a loyal, motivated, and responsible work force in order to be able to introduce a greater degree of flexibility into their organization, human relations and training policies, and production processes, which was essential to survival in the current competitive climate. Therefore, the unions' problems resulting from their moral and intellectual crisis were compounded by the fact that the unions were being asked at the same time to cooperate with governments and employers who needed their assistance in the task of redefining and curtailing the historical compromise of the postwar era. The unions, however, were not only puzzled and reluctant to cooperate with such a task but were also less able than they had been in the past to deliver the acquiescence of the workers.

In the past, the trade unions and, to a certain extent, the socialist parties had been the guarantors, and in part the creators, of working-class acquiescence, but now this was proving much more difficult to achieve. First, as we have seen, the unions were deeply uncertain about which strategy to adopt in order to aggregate interests and formulate viable alternatives, and they were experiencing a prolonged internal crisis. Second, the unions had hardly any control over their members, which was partly the result of the uncertainty of the unions themselves but was also principally due to a cultural change within the work force. This change reflected the development of feelings of moral autonomy and a newly rational (or experimental) attitude toward the union on the part of the workers. As a result, the relationship of implicit delegation which had once linked the two groups was substantially eroded.

The theory of implicit delegation as a link between the working class and workers' organizations was developed primarily within the socialist tradition as a seemingly realistic counterpoint to the more romantic anarchist line which held that a workers' organization should be, in the strictest sense, organized by the workers themselves. This was based on a literal interpretation of the principles of the Internationale. Since its beginnings, however, the socialist tradition had given a different interpretation to the creed of workers' self-organization. The socialist interpretation was based on the supposedly hard facts of a class made up of workers who were ignorant; who had neither the time to reflect upon their situation nor the cultural capacity for interpreting it; who could not express their ideas in public or in writing; who were influenced by governments, companies, the media, schools, and churches; and who could see no further than the immediate needs of their families, neighborhoods, or companies. Under these circumstances, working-class organization and working-class action meant that workers should place their confidence in, and follow the initiative of, a group of intermediaries or professional organizers, some from other social groups, some from the working class, but all still separated from the working class by a specific process of socialization that supposedly gave them the cultural resources that workers lacked to be morally and intellectually independent of the ruling classes.[6] Under ordinary circumstances the working class would implicitly delegate problems of ideology, strategy, and organization to this group, and this act of delegation would be corroborated periodically by rank-and-file support for strikes or demonstrations called by these professional organizers, as well as by rank-and-file votes in political, local, or union elections. This theory of implicit delegation was a key part of the Marxist interpretation of the relationship between the working class, on the one hand, and the workers' organizations or workers' movements, on the other.[7] But it can also be found in the work of authors such as Pierre Bourdieu, who seems to suggest that the implicit delegation by the lower classes to these intermediary or professional politicians would be the only alternative such classes have to dependence on, or deference to, the ruling classes (Bourdieu, 1981).

In fact, however, the relationship between the rank-and-file workers and the leaders and cadres of the workers' organizations can take different forms. To begin with, we can observe a range of basic attitudes toward the trade unions on the part of the workers that varies according to the nature and quantity of resources that workers contribute to these organizations. These resources include a capacity for moral autonomy and critical judgment, as well as various other factors such as time, money, enthusiasm, votes, information, social relationships, and technical know-how. If we focus on moral and intellectual resources, we may distinguish three basic types of attitudes that constitute three modes whereby the working class can be related to the organizations that represent them. I call them *heteronomous-traditional, heteronomous-charismatic,* and *autonomous* attitudes. The main distinction is between an attitude of moral heteronomy and one of moral autonomy.

In a case in which the workers adopt an attitude of moral heteronomy, they convince themselves (or allow themselves to be convinced) that their liberation or their well-being, however defined, depends on their placing full trust in the organization. Only in this way can the workers counteract their cultural deficiencies, their isolation, their feelings of impotence and frustration, and their apparent defenselessness in the face of real oppression and symbolic manipulation by a powerful, determined enemy or of arbitrary fluctuations of the economy. Those who adopt this attitude identify with the organization, develop a high degree of loyalty toward it, and constantly enact their implicit faith in, and delegation to, the organization—to its core of officials and activists—which thinks, evaluates, and decides for them. In turn, this heteronomous attitude may assume two ideal-typical forms, or in Weberian terms the *traditional* form and the *charismatic* form. In the *heteronomous-traditional* form the workers acquire a class ethos or habit one of whose features is precisely this faith in, and implicit delegation to, the union or the party. In this case these organizations form part of the workers' everyday experience, of their own identity, and even of that of the local community. The organization's values and its definitions of the workers' identity are accepted as self-evident. The workers live for, or loyally follow, the party or the union, with a minimum of critical reflection on the means and tactics used and on the details of the organization's program. Loyalty toward the organization stems from the workers' faith in the organization's ability to maintain a sense of identity and coherence in their everyday lives and in the routines of their community.

In the *heteronomous-charismatic* form the workers are guided not so much by the past as by the future. Their loyalty toward and identification with the organization stem from its seemingly extraordinary ability to fight for and create a new world or a different future, to attain historical protagonism. Faith in this future, in the organization, and in its leadership go hand in hand, since the leadership and the organization are seen as the key to this new future. Neither form of identification with the organization excludes criticism of its means, calculations of personal, family, or local benefits likely to be gained from organizational action, or proposals for readjustment in light of the consequences of the organization's action, but typically these instrumental or experimental considerations are played down. Despite some criticism and even the possible frustration of workers' expectations for personal gain or collective success, the union (and the party) can count on seemingly limitless reserves of identification, loyalty, and confidence on the part of the workers.

These reserves of identification, loyalty, and confidence are not present to the same degree when the relationship between workers and their organizations follows the mode of *moral autonomy*. For the workers to adopt an attitude of moral autonomy, and therefore of independent judgment, means that they decide to make their own decisions, to make their own judgment of the organization's decisions, and therefore to maintain a sort of irreducible distance between their individual judgment and the organization's. There is neither implicit delegation nor implicit faith: at critical moments one must decide on the basis of one's individual values and judgment of the situation.

This represents a rational, instrumental, or experimental attitude toward the unions or parties which is very different from the attitude of implicit delegation; and if it is embedded in a tradition, it is in the critical rationalism tradition of Popper (1972, pp. 120ff.). The union is seen as an artifact created by a group with the aim of attaining certain values, gains, or benefits, and it is judged rationally, or instrumentally, in terms of both the desirability of those aims (substantive rationality) and its ability to achieve such aims (instrumental or formal rationality). The workers' relationship with the organization is one in which support is exchanged for benefits. However, these need not be material benefits such as defense of wage levels, jobs, working conditions, or social security. Values or gains may be defined quite broadly to include public goods (for example, keeping the economy in good working order or reforming socioeconomic institutions) as well as intangible moral benefits, such as the sense of belonging to a moral community or of having prestige, power, or influence within the community. The defining feature of this attitude is not which kind of objectives are valued but the fact that once these objectives have been agreed upon, the organization is judged according to its ability to achieve them. Even if workers hold the values of group solidarity and collective action in high esteem for their own sake, it still remains to be seen whether these specific organizations (that is, unions and parties) embody such values better than other institutional alternatives such as families, neighborhoods, ethnic or national communities, and churches. Therefore, the degree of loyalty or credit given to the organization for achieving even these objectives is relatively modest, and the workers' relationship with the organization is periodically adjusted in light of its performance. If the results are disappointing, the relationship becomes weaker or ceases to exist.

I believe that there has been a trend over the last several decades toward precisely this sort of autonomous, rational, instrumental, or experimental attitude at the expense of one of implicit delegation. In the 1960s Goldthorpe found a growing incidence of instrumentalism (although he did not link it with these elements of moral autonomy, formal rationality, and experimentalism) among workers in England (Goldthorpe et al., 1969). Today there are numerous indications that this instrumentalism has become a dominant feature of industrial relations, and there are more and more instances of workers who remain outside the unions while still benefiting from its action ("free-riders"; see Olson, 1971), or who support the union conditionally without joining, or who join without becoming active, or who join and commit their loyalty to the union but still keep a critical eye on it and decide whether to renew their commitment on the basis of the union's performance. This has occurred as a consequence of a series of deep-rooted processes, of which I shall mention but a few.

Structural changes in the economy and the great migratory movements of recent decades in most parts of Europe eroded workers' traditional communities, limiting them to areas and industries in decline, like the remains of a past era. The growth of generalized social benefits provided by the state, the transformation of large sectors of the traditional middle class into wage-earning employees, and improvements in the conditions of industrial wage earners reduced the differences between the standards of living of the two groups. This, along with the spread of mass consumer life-styles, undermined the socioeconomic and cultural bases for feelings of self-identification as members of a strictly defined working class, one of whose features ought to be unconditional loyalty to a class-based union or party. The practices of reformist unionism and social democracy, based on a compromise with capitalism, also unintentionally strengthened the instrumental attitude. Of their two typical messages, radicalism and practical reformism, it was the latter that prevailed, and people became accustomed to focusing their attention on concrete problems and to judging such organizations according to the visible results in the short or middle term. This was true to such an extent that even radical proposals for nationalization of companies during the late 1970s and early 1980s (in France), a shorter working day (in Germany), or wage investment funds (in Sweden; see Korpi, 1978), which might otherwise have had ideological connotations or evoked feelings of hostility toward capital, were presented with a heavy emphasis on their practical features and experimental character. It was a matter of persuading public opinion that the results of these experiments would be beneficial, or at least not harmful, to the economy, and that they would work. This practice also tended to immunize working-class organizations and their social bases against new strains of revolutionary prophecy. It did not prevent the periodic resurgence of grievances and resentments fueled by the everyday frustrations of industrial life, nor did it exclude the occasional appearance of millenarian movements of an agrarian, religious, or generally precapitalist nature, either within or outside the working class. However, the new collective actors created under the protection of such movements were either gradually routinized and aggregated into a plurality of interest groups or incorporated into existing organizations, forming the unions' or parties' so-called critical tendencies, youth branches, or nonconformist redoubts.

There was also a variety of other factors that enhanced the value attached to individual moral autonomy and rationalism. They were just as important as the structural factors and political practices, and they displayed increasing weight in the life of western societies. These included the internal complexity and multiplicity of individuals' roles in contemporary societies, which were marked especially by a substantial reduction in the importance attached to people's roles as workers; the softening of authoritarian or hierarchical structures in the spheres of family and civil associations; the spread of education and the development of the influence of science over society; the evolution of the churches and a shift in the content of their messages toward an emphasis on the importance of personal conviction and religious feeling; the consolidation of liberal democracy, pluralism, and a regime of political liberty; and the development of the market and its penetration into widely differing fields. All these developments tended to pressure individuals to make their own decisions and to develop an ethic or self-fulfillment and social commitment that associated self-respect and dignity with successful personal decision making (for example, in politics, personal relationships, and religious life), and militated against any expansion of the sphere of implicit or explicit delegation of one's personal responsibilities to others.

WORKERS' AMBIVALENCE TOWARD BUSINESS AND THE CAPITALIST ECONOMY

If workers saw the trade unions more and more from a rational, experimental, autonomous point of view and therefore more as an instrument, one can ask, an instrument for what? To what end? And, more specifically, to what end in relation to the capitalist firms and the capitalist economic order? Some of these objectives seemed obvious: workers expected unions to defend wages, job security, working conditions, and social security provisions, and to come into conflict with employers over the distribution of surplus production and the ways and means of power. But beyond these basic issues unions and workers might differ considerably in their assessment of the situation and of what objectives were to be achieved.

It appears that capitalist firms, at least in western Europe, did not command any deep traditional loyalty from the work force, even if the game of patronizing and deferential relationships between bosses and workers had long been played in certain industrialized areas. Neither, given its formal rational characteristics, did capitalist businesses generate any charismatic support on the part of their employees, except in sectors linked to highly advanced technology or among highly qualified personnel. However, business did receive a type of instrumental support that included a considerable degree of respect and sympathy; and, as in the case of the unions, this covered objectives that might go well beyond the achievement of tangible individual benefits, extending to collective benefits such as the smooth running of the company or, more particularly, to intangible benefits such as the feeling of belonging to a moral community.

In this light we can see that all potential understandings, pacts, or agreements between unions and management stood on shaky foundations, for, underlying all their economic agreements and their economic disputes, there was a more fundamental struggle to secure the moral leadership of the workers, to impose on them competing definitions of the prevalent moral community, and to determine the appropriate hierarchy of loyalties between union and management. The battlefield was the system of moral attitudes and cognitive tendencies of the workers themselves.

If we look first at workers' attitudes, judgments, and feelings toward business firms, as evidenced in several reports from a variety of countries in the late 1960s and throughout the 1970s,[8] these seem to have been characterized by a basic ambivalence. Various conflicts of interest were obvious, and perhaps even intense and frequent. But they existed alongside positive attitudes that implied the acceptance of the authority of the employer as legitimate. Most workers showed little desire to diminish this authority in a fundamental way. They seemed to think that it was the task of the employer to manage and be responsible for the company. Workers' demands for more information, better treatment, and more participation in decision making indicated in many cases that they did not see the company as an adversary; rather, it was as if the whole enterprise were made up of two contrary yet complementary halves which formed a whole, a team, with common fundamental objectives. Their demands sometimes implied recognition of the company as their own moral community, in a form that was perhaps not the case at the time but could become fully realized without any radical alteration in the authority structure of the firm (see Chapter 5).

At the same time, these attitudes were marked by an ambivalence that was cyclical; phases of trust alternated with mistrust. But signs of a confidence in everyday company life, beyond the mere routine of work and acceptance of orders, were evident and constant. Broad groups of workers exchanged acceptance of the employers' authority for wages, working conditions, and opportunities to have a say, all of which they considered acceptable, tolerable, and even satisfactory. What this implied was that for many workers, support for the trade unions, in defense of their basic interest vis-à-vis the company, was limited by an implicit social contract between the workers and the company, a tacit agreement not to attack the company to the point of placing it in jeopardy or reducing its competitiveness in the market, and not to make radical alterations in its authority structure. True, current economic conditions were endangering this relationship, since the companies' ability to improve wages, guarantee jobs, and sustain the existing (and often-negotiated) working routines had been reduced. At the same time, however, the crisis itself, by accentuating the differences between companies and creating a growing sense of their vulnerability in the face of new challenges from technological innovation, the internationalization of capital, foreign competition, and experimentation with new ways of organizing production, might enhance the positive side of the workers' ambivalent relationship with the company. It might develop a company spirit and favor microcorporatist agreements.

A similar ambivalence existed in the relationship between the workers and the capitalist order as a whole. A diffuse anticapitalist feeling persists within the European working class, the result of a collective memory imbued with a record of moral protest, repeated over nearly two centuries by cultural and intellectual leaders belonging to both the culture of the left and the culture of the right, by secular as well as religious leaders. This moral tradition underlay contemporary unionism. The initial moral impetus for unionism came from nostalgia for a community, which was apparently being destroyed in an implacable way by the commercialism and mechanization of capitalist civilization. *Commercialism* referred to the rift between people who exchange goods and services without any affective and moral ties, *mechanization* to the rift between people brought together within a production process and, likewise, to the distance between these workers and their means of work, their products, and their natural environment. These ruptures left people isolated and defenseless. The workers' movement, before becoming an instrument for defending certain economic and political interests, was a response to the need for a moral community. In the final analysis it offered a community patterned according to the ideal of a large family of proletarian brothers, apparently without protective or domineering parents.

To the extent that present-day workers clung to this ideal vision of a harmonious and reconciled society, it was obvious that they could not consider capitalism "just" (in the sense of perfect), given its implications of tension, competition, and conflict. The situation was different when their judgments simply indicated a preference from among available alternatives (for "preference" values versus "commitment" values, see Klein, 1981). In this case the value of capitalism, its desirability, might be enhanced if it was seen as a means of access to other values such as individual freedom, material prosperity, and social protection, and/or because of its compatibility with other moral communities such as the union and even the company itself. In such circumstances capitalism might appear to be just, not because it was perfect or ideal, but because it could be reasonably justified. In that case capitalism would not be the object of an intensely positive valoration, but it would be accepted and defended as morally tolerable and sufficiently just, all the more so if it was open to reforms or improvements in the direction of the ideal. And that positive evaluation could be either explicitly verbalized or, more likely, embedded in actual behavior.

In general, those workers who had the most difficulty in expressing a positive valuation of capitalism seemed to be those within the workers' movement who had been most deeply socialized in the Christian or the Marxist culture. Normally such people could get no closer to the acceptance of capitalism than the moderate admission that it was a minor evil, a demon of modest size, with which one could uncomfortably coexist, waiting for better times. In this way it was possible to maintain an ideal and doctrinal purity as well as symbols of identity for the party, union, or church, as the ideal became converted into a dream which could not be given up. But when the masses of rank-and-file workers came around to the view that capitalism was morally tolerable, and even the ideological elites shifted their ideal of an alternative society into the realm of nostalgia and dreams, then a situation was created whereby capitalism acquired plausibility as a moral structure, while at the same time a "crisis of plausibility" (Berger, 1971) threatened its socialist alternative.

This crisis of plausibility was precipitated by events in the late sixties, and developed throughout the seventies and eighties. From a historical point of view, the most important events of 1968 took place not in Paris but in Prague: the apparent refutation of the hypothesis of the compatibility of full-fledged socialism with respect for individual and associative freedoms and democratic procedure in public decision making. From then on, the left in Europe had to reactivate memories of Berlin in 1953 and Hungary in 1956, reconsider what was happening in Vietnam and Cambodia, and reflect on signs of dissidence in the Soviet Union, Poland, and Afghanistan. The commitment that could be attached to this alternative to capitalism suffered a severe blow. Meanwhile, the preference for capitalism felt by the masses became stronger and finally ended up being adopted by a large part of the political and social leadership of the left itself and by its militants. As a consequence, the workers' potential support for the attempts of the unions and socialist parties to reform capitalism was limited by their moral acceptance of capitalism, a tolerance based on the ambiguity of their value judgments and by the moral hesitancy of the unions and parties themselves.

CRISES OF UNION REPRESENTATION

Under these conditions we were seeing not just *one* crisis of representation in the trade unions (as suggested by Regini, 1984) and the corresponding parties, but rather the combination of several different crises of representation. For some time the unions experienced a crisis of representation vis-à-vis their militant and relatively radical members, who had high hopes and expectations regarding the transformation of the economic order: a crisis of representation on the left. The unions' defensive battles to ensure that the economic system functioned well, thereby reducing the rate of unemployment in the core of the formal economy and the rate of deceleration in the growth of social public expenditure, produced feelings of discontent and frustration among those activists and union members who remembered the period of expansion in the cycle of struggles at the end of the sixties and throughout the seventies (Pizzorno et al., 1978). But during the second half of the 1970s and the first half of the 1980s these signs of discontent were counteracted by signs of another crisis of union representation vis-à-vis moderate workers (Pérez-Díaz, 1980b; Urbani and Weber 1984; Accornero et al., 1985), that is to say, a crisis of representation on the right. In other words, there was a potential crisis of representation in the trade unions with respect to radical members if the unions were not aggressive enough; but there was now a more serious crisis with respect to larger numbers of moderate workers if the unions tried systematically to violate the rules of the companies and the economic system. The crisis of representation on the radical side manifested itself in loud and visible signs, in the voice of those concerned, while the crisis for the moderates most often manifested itself in silent, less visible signs—in their exit from the union, in their abstention and passivity. Only rarely did the moderates resort to mass demonstrations, for instance, in the crucial response to the unions' appeal to strike at the Fiat factory in Turin in 1981 (Accornero et al., 1985). Local leaders and militants were aware of this situation,[9] and their confusion reflected a sharp conflict between their own evaluative outlook and those they saw as being prevalent among their social base (Fishman, 1990).

Therefore, the main problem for national trade union leaders consisted not so much in controlling the crisis of representation among the radicals as in avoiding a possible crisis of representation among the moderates, should the unions prove incapable of carrying out an effective moderate strategy. Hence, a trade union strategy aimed at saving the economy did not entail a cost in terms of moderate representation, as Regini has suggested (1984); rather, it promised a benefit, since many workers saw this objective as a public good. With respect to this majority of workers, union leaders did not need to use alternative means to control the crisis of representation, for these workers accepted, though with varying degrees of reluctance, the objectives of saving the capitalist economy and, if necessary, of wage moderation. Giving up frequent and intensive use of the strike was not a grave sacrifice for these moderate workers. In fact, the majority of them may have considered current levels of conflict excessive, accepting these conflicts only as defensive measures, reluctantly consenting to their necessity, and even demanding that such matters be decided through secret ballots by all the workers. Indeed, many workers resented the attempts of the radical militants to force strike decisions through control of the union apparatus and the manipulation of public meetings (see Chapter 5). This was one reason why the 1985 miners' strike in the United Kingdom did not enjoy the unanimous backing of the working communities or subsequent support from other national unions. The radicals were cognitively and evaluatively oriented toward conflict with management, whereas the moderates were predisposed to agreement; for them, agreement was the rule and conflict the exception.

Now, while these crises of representation were based on a cultural difference between the unions and the workers, there was a further crisis based on structural tensions of a socioeconomic nature within this collectivity. In fact, despite the differences in their explicit declarations, both radicals and moderates accepted a strategy that gave priority to protecting the core of workers in the formal economy; they therefore accepted a strategy of veiled dualism which maintained the inferior position of unemployed immigrants, young people, women, and the elderly. This strategy was apparently compatible with declarations of principle of a universalist nature, and implied a high degree of de facto tolerance toward the underground economy, at least in its initial phases and with the reservation, perhaps, that such activity should eventually be legalized. In this case universalist declarations of principle served to control a potential crisis of representation among the unemployed and those in precarious work situations, minimizing the possibility that they might express their interests in the terms proposed by antisystem parties (fascist or extreme left wing), or at least in terms contrary to the interests of the core of employed workers.

The unions were therefore faced with a third crisis of representation with respect to a heterogeneous group of people who were fully or partly excluded from the work force of the formal economy: marginal workers, the unemployed, members of the underground economy. Although this constituted an important problem for the unemployed or underemployed, it seemed only a minor problem to the unions, at least in the short run. It was obvious that the link between these groups and the unions was weakening; but the costs and risks of a de facto union strategy of benign neglect with respect to these groups appeared relatively low, so long as it remained difficult for them to build rival organizations or to articulate their interests in terms that contradicted the interests of workers employed in the formal economy.

For these reasons, the crisis of representation for the left-wing parties was probably even more serious than that of the trade unions. There were relationships of closeness, familiarity, and frequent contact between workers and unions. The unions were part of the workers' everyday lives. The parties were much further removed from daily experience, and, although party traditions varied from country to country, there was a general trend toward a weakening of the connections between party and social class. Hopes for a distant, extraordinary future, one of the fundamental impulses that led activist minorities to join political parties, faded and became even more tenuous in this time of crisis. As for the hopes and expectations of the majority of workers with respect to the performance of the political class, everything seemed to point to a moderate shift toward the center of the ideological spectrum. This implied a lowering of hopes and expectations with regard to the left-wing parties' potential to transform society. In this case, opting for the left ceased to be a natural choice and became a renewable option, according to the personality and programs offered by the candidates of the moment.

Here again the distinction between radical and moderate workers came into play; and the evidence pointed to the growing volatility of the moderate workers' vote. The defeat of many of the social democratic incumbents in northern and central Europe in the 1970s and early 1980s depended in a crucial way on the move among moderate workers to vote in favor of conservative opponents (for example, Margaret Thatcher in the United Kingdom, and the Christian Democratic Union in Germany). Even the 1982 Swedish election could not be construed as a mandate for radicalism on the part of the workers, despite signs to the contrary, in view of the poor performance of the bourgeois governments of the time and the more effective government of the social democrats. Something similar might be claimed in southern Europe. The social democratic element of Italian communism became more and more marked with the passage of time, and the moderate social democratic nature of the policies of Spain's Socialist government was obvious. Nor could Mitterrand's victory be interpreted as a public demand for a radical program, and the realignment of his policies after one year and a few months in office was partly an attempt to move closer to prevailing currents of public opinion. In general, signs of the working people's skepticism with regard to radical measures such as nationalization multiplied in those years.

One consequence was that social democratic parties had to rewrite their messages in order to bring them into line with the inclinations of the electorate and the majority of workers. The message concerning their own identity always included two contradictory elements: on the one hand, of being national, popular interclass parties with a sense of state, and on the other hand, of being class-based parties; and current circumstances obliged them to emphasize their interclass aspect. In the same way, their programmatic message always included two further contradictory elements: their goal was to administer the system well, introducing modest, viable reforms with the object of making the system work, or work better; but also they were bearing a message of radical transformation and change. Current circumstances obliged them to restrain the rhetoric of change, or to use it simply as rhetoric, and to tend to the business of good administration and of adjusting the system to the crisis.

Left-wing parties might try to dramatize their differences with liberal or conservative parties by means of a rhetoric that made the latter out to be the champions of a policy aimed at excluding the workers' movement and dismantling the welfare state. However, the rhetoric turned out to be at best only partly convincing because, among other things, these liberal or conservative parties were often careful to incorporate a large measure of compromise, realism, and pragmatism in their strategies. Consequently, conservative politicians realized that they could not systematically exclude workers' organizations or dismantle the welfare state; nor did they appear determined to do so. In reality, there was in Europe a great deal of constitutional and legal protection for workers' and unions' rights, and the indications were that this would remain the case. At the same time, although the courses of action pursued by center or right-wing parties and governments were quite far removed from a neoliberal utopia, the position of left-wing governments and parties also shifted toward the center; they adopted in great measure the objectives of containing wage increases and public spending, and of making the labor market more flexible. Thus, the variants of this program belonged to a common stock of measures and experiments practiced by all European governments and parties—policies such as heeding external imbalances, modestly reducing the length of the working day, and privatizing some public companies or submitting these companies to market conditions.

In short, the workers' hopes and expectations with respect to all political sectors, right, center, and left, did not lend themselves to intense polarization. And although prevailing patterns whereby many workers vote for the left might be maintained, ever larger sectors of the working class appeared to exercise a volatile vote, that is to say, a rational, instrumental vote which changed from one election to the next, in view of the government's achievements.

The economic crisis beginning in the mid-1970s called into question the compromise that had been a foundation of the European social fabric over the preceding forty years. This coincided with a moment of vulnerability for political institutions, and required unionists (and party politicians) to face some critical choices, and to make an appeal to the workers to support these choices. At that critical juncture it was demonstrated that culture mattered in explaining both the organizations' strategic uncertainties and the workers' attitudes and actual behavior. There were no structural adjustments between conflicting interests. Previously interests had had to be recognized as such, and this could happen only in the light of values and cognitions which were usually embedded in already existing or emerging institutions. Only then could unionists articulate strategies and look for ways to mobilize emotional resources in support of them through the application of practical reasoning, including moral suasion.

But the crisis coincided with a time of great uncertainty among the trade unions. Their perplexity stemmed from the objective difficulties of aggregating workers' interests and from the inadequacies of the unions' long-standing intellectual and moral resources for comprehending and reacting to the situation. On the one hand, the unions had to deal with three different crises of representation, as they faced three different kinds of constituencies: unions had to deal with militants and radical workers unhappy with what they saw as a policy of concessions to capitalism; with a not-so-silent majority of moderate workers willing to reach an accommodation with business and governments, with or without unions; and with those workers excluded from, or relegated to the margins of, employment in the formal economy.

On the other hand, the unions', and to an extent the parties', moral uncertainties stemmed from a painful coming to terms with their sense of the loss of plausibility of a real transformative socialist alternative to the existing order, either in times of prosperity or in times of crisis. They might aspire only to become managers (as parties within government) or junior partners (as unions in corporatist or tripartite arrangements) of the established order. They could also aspire to bring to these endeavors a program of social and economic reforms, a discourse on the historical protagonism of the working class and of power sharing with that class (or the people), as well as an appeal to universalistic principles. But most of these unionists and party leaders understood that their reforms (in fields such as income policies, industrial policies, industrial relations, and industrial democracy) must either be compatible with the smooth functioning of capitalism or would have to be revised in a matter of years, if not in a matter of months. Moreover, many saw that there was not much point in stressing their working-class credentials, since not only were the industrial workers a permanent minority within the labor force, but also many of them denied their class identity. They equally realized that if and when they were to hold a substantial measure of power, they would face a crucial test of their leadership capacities. Therefore, they felt it was, or would be, their responsibility *not* to share power, other than rhetorically, with an ill-defined working class, internally heterogeneous, and lacking a clear sense of direction. They also understood that even their universalistic claims could not easily be reconciled with the imperative they felt to defend the short-term and medium-term interests of the national working class, especially since these interests often conflicted with those of other sectors of the population, including marginal segments of the working class itself, and those of the working classes of other nations.

These sobering thoughts, and the perplexities that follow from them, were reinforced by the moral and cognitive development of the workers themselves. Their increasing moral autonomy, and increasingly rational or experimental attitude, rendered these workers critical followers of their organizational leaders, if not free riders or volatile voters. The moderate stand of most workers vis-à-vis capitalism made them a skeptical audience for a discourse of grand projects for an alternative society or for radical breaks with the past. These workers shaped their hopes and expectations so as to focus on the ability of unions, parties, and the state to solve most of their problems within the limits of the established institutional framework. They were therefore unlikely to be attracted by planning programs and promises to control fate. This was accompanied by a decline in political polarization, since their outlook shifted gradually toward the center, and they become more attracted to moderate or even conservative programs. In turn, all of these trends constituted an incentive for socialist parties to moderate their socioeconomic proposals. Unions and political parties could not but follow a strategy of de facto accommodation with capitalism. And so they came out of this period appearing mildly aggressive while in opposition or excluded from power, while looking cautious, responsible, and statesmanlike when in government or associated with it, and in any case somehow more pragmatic, opportunistic, and willing to learn, readier than in the past to try new experiments—ranging from neo-Keynesianism and macrocorporatism to microcorporatism, deregulation, and privatization—within the limits posed by the rules of their political games and their ideological proclivities.

Notes

1. The Emergence of Democratic Spain

1. For the literature on "the problem of Spain," see Laín (1956). Earlier versions of portions of this chapter were presented at a meeting of the Société Tocqueville (sponsored by Young and Rubicam) in Paris in 1989, at Nuffield College, Oxford, and the London School of Economics in 1990, and at the Department of Political Science, University of California at San Diego, in 1992. Joaquín P. López Novo (as well as Pedro L. Iriso, Ana M. Guillén, and Susana Aguilar) provided me with up-to-date information for the last section.

2. On the relation between *transition* and *consolidation*, see also Linz (1990, pp. 143–162).

3. Traditions can be constructed on purpose, as a result of deliberate human design (or "invented" proper), or they may arise from the actions of many people who did not know, or half knew, what they were doing. In the first instance we usually speak of the *invention* of a tradition, in the second of the *emergence* of a tradition. In real life most traditions arise both ways. See also Hayek, (1978, p. 58).

4. As Weber would maintain regarding traditional behavior (Weber, 1978, 1:25). Yet Hayek points out that his "distinction between . . . purposive and rule-governed aspects of action is probably the same as Max Weber's distinction between what he calls *Zweckrational* and *Wertrational*" (Hayek, 1978, p. 85).

5. Numancia (Numantia), a town located near modern Soria in Spain, was the center of Celtiberian resistance to Rome. Scipio Aemilianus blockaded it

(133 B.C.). After an eight-month siege the population was reduced by hunger, and the survivors preferred to die before surrendering the city, which was finally destroyed by fire. This is similar to the case of Masada, a fortified city in southeast Israel, renowned for its resistance to the Roman siege of A.D. 72–73. After the fall of Jerusalem and the destruction of the Temple (A.D. 70), the Masada garrison was besieged by the Romans, who found that the defenders, having preferred death to enslavement, had taken their own lives.

6. See data on changes in religious attitudes in Orizo (1983). See also Toharia (1989).

7. The archetypal examples of this evolution were, among the Falangists, that of Dionisio Ridruejo (1964, 1977), and, among the communists, that of Jorge Semprún (1977).

8. The terms *consolidation* and *transition* are used in this section as interchangeable to the extent that the former may be considered the final test of the success of the latter.

9. Social movements are only one among many manifestations of civil society. O'Donnell and Schmitter seem to equate social movements with civil society, and this may be the reason why they speak of a "resurrection" of civil society in connection with strikes and social movements (O'Donnell and Schmitter, 1986, pp. 26, 48) at some stage in their description of the transition process. Thus, from the fact that these phenomena are relatively rare under authoritarian regimes, they conclude that societies under those regimes are passive and atomized (pp. 48ff.). This underestimates the ability of large segments of the population in those societies to resist political coercion, economic exploitation, and cultural indoctrination exercised by the state in collusion with different social elites. They do resist with a measure of success by using a variety of means, and especially through market mechanisms of various kinds. Owing to such resistance, some of the meta-rules of the political game are already in place before the actual game begins.

10. See López Pina and López Aranguren (1976). See also López Pintor and Wert Ortega (1982); Gunther (1988).

11. Or to adjust itself to a new political regime. This point would be tested (and proved) by the readiness of the Francoist political class to submit to Adolfo Suárez's pressures and arguments in the fall of 1977.

12. This is why Fernando Claudín and Jorge Semprún had lost their posts in the central committee of the Communist party by 1964.

13. This was something the PSOE (Partido Socialista Obrero Español) had never done in nearly one hundred years of its agitated history, and a choice it would soon repent. By 1979 the same party leaders who had introduced Marxism as a symbol of identity for the party at the Twenty-seventh Party Congress in Madrid in December 1976 had downgraded it to just one among the many ideological influences to which party members should be sensitive. They also

commended Marxism to socialist militants as the most appropriate method of scientific analysis.

14. See in particular Suárez's television speech of September 10, 1976, transcript in *ABC* (Madrid), September 11, 1976, pp. 6–8.

15. Another was the economic crisis; see Chapter 5.

16. On industrial restructuring, see Navarro (1990). On the financial system, see the papers gathered in *Papeles de Economía Española,* nos. 43, 44 (1990). On the creation of new enterprises, see *Anuario El País* (1990, p. 405).

17. See Pérez-Díaz (1987, chap. 4); Martínez (1984); and González Olivares (1985); as well as other papers gathered in *Papeles de Economía Española,* no. 22 (1985, pp. 38–201).

18. Ministry of the Interior, Register of Associations (Law 161/1964). On the matter of social activism in the areas of health and education, see Pérez-Díaz (1987, pp. 261–351).

19. Thus, the Spanish Socialist party had about 215,000 members in 1988 (Share, 1989, p. 28); the Italian party had about 510,000 in 1980 (Di Scala, 1988, p. 317); the Austrian about 713,000 in 1981 (Sully, 1986, p. 165); the German about 954,000 in 1981 (Braunthal, 1983, p. 79); and the Greek about 200,000 in 1987 (Gillespie and Gallagher, 1988, p. 181).

20. "For a change" was in fact the slogan of PSOE in the electoral campaign of 1982 which led the party to power.

21. This appeal was included in the socialist platform for the first regional elections in the Basque region in 1980, and has been haunting the socialists ever since (*El País,* December 11, 1990, p. 22).

22. On the sociology of political scandals, see Markovits and Silverstein (1988); and Philp and Pinto-Duschinsky (1989). In general, the literature of moral denunciation in Spain has included clichés about the salvation of souls, or the salvation of the country (as in the past, during the Francoist regime); or (more recently) moral clichés about modernization, progress, solidarity, or justice.

23. Of course, these shady aspects of the funding of political parties is hardly an exclusive characteristic of Spanish politics, as indicated by recent scandals in France (see the debates surrounding the passing of the amnesty law of December 7, 1989, in the National Assembly) as well as in Greece (the "Koskotas affair"), Japan, and other countries. With regard to Spain, see, for instance, the debates concerning the affair of Juan Guerra (the brother of then Vice Prime Minister Alfonso Guerra), January–February 1990; the Tribunal de Cuentas's hesitancy to exercise control over the accounting of the political parties (see *El País,* February 13, 1990, and the following days); and the press coverage of the Filesa and Malesa affairs of April 1991 and of the Ibercorp affairs in February and March 1992 (see, for instance, *Economist,* February 29, 1992, pp. 90, 95; *Financial Times,* February 20, 1992, p. 15).

24. By 1992 the official unemployment rate in Spain was 16 percent; but according to the OECD (Organization for Economic Cooperation and Development) report on the Spanish economy, the real rate, once employment in the underground economy is taken into account, was about 10 to 12 percent (OECD, 1992, p. 20).

25. Therefore ensuring the control of the party by the tandem of González and Guerra as long as they worked together, since southern delegates made up about 40 percent of the total vote in the party congress.

26. This may or may not be done with the tacit complicity of local authorities, political parties, churches, and unions. Sometimes this tacit alliance may break down. See, for instance, the case of the two union leaders who denounced a fraud of 1.6 billion pesetas by the city governments of several towns of the province of Seville, during the first two quarters of 1991 (*El País*, October 29, 1991, p. 42).

27. For example, a call for a social pact between the political class and the productive classes in defense of "democracy" or the "national economy" may be no more than a justification for arrangements of this type.

28. Sometimes, too, these local arrangements may be viewed with ambivalence by condescending foreigners, who would not accept them in their own open, universalistic societies, but who, in a show of superficial sympathy and some complacency, are quite prepared to respect them, if not to admire them, in societies in which they have no intention of settling, as an indication of an "art of living" which their compatriots (though not necessarily themselves) would appear to have lost (Enzensberger, 1989).

2. *The Return of Civil Society*

1. For a history of the distinction between civil society and the state in the period 1759–1850, see Keane (1988b). See also Pérez-Díaz (1978), and Poggi (1978, pp. 77ff.). A nearly final version of this chapter was presented at the Minda de Gunzburg Center for European Studies at Harvard University in the winter of 1991–92.

2. On spontaneous extended orders, see Polanyi (1951); Hayek (1960, p. 160; 1978, pp. 72, 90); Gray (1986, pp. 34ff.).

3. See, for instance, Bailyn (1967) for an assessment of the different intellectual traditions that converged on the American Revolution: a classical tradition, the rationalism of the Enlightenment, the tradition of common law, the covenant theology of Puritanism, and the radical thought of the Commonwealth period (see also Ball and Pocock, 1988; and White, 1978). More generally, such different traditions, which are compatible with the institutions of civil society, have contended with and influenced one another for several centuries in countries on both sides of the Atlantic. While their content has changed

over time, the labels put on them continue to be a matter for unending schol-
arly and ideological argument. These debates are part of the problem as well
as of the potential for developing the public sphere in societies of this sort.

4. This is the same use I made of the term in Chapter 1.

5. See Sartori (1987, 2:265ff.). Still, it does not follow, as Giovanni Sartori suggests, that the meaning of words may be stabilized by an endless trial and error
process. Indeed, if the process is endless, there is no reason to expect that
meaning would ever become stabilized. On the contrary, the debate about the
terms is to be expected as part of an endless debate about the nature of the
institutions to which these words refer (*pace* Popper). As Hayek has shown,
serious problems may be obscured by our use of words which imply explanations of political and moral institutions, and which correspond to earlier modes
of thinking and earlier historical experiences (Hayek, 1978, p. 72).

6. This has been largely the result of journalists', social elites', social observers',
and, to some extent, politicians' taking on the term, which had been advanced by academics in previous discussions.

7. At the same time, from the assertion that we must take into consideration the
several linguistic uses of the concept in different historical contexts it does not
follow that the concept is "historically bounded" in the sense that it would fit
(or would allow itself to be applied to) only a unique historical development,
for instance, European history of the last few centuries, as Habermas (1992)
suggests, or a particular stage of that development. Rather, I use the concept
as an analytical tool that may help us map out critical problems, assemble the
evidence in an orderly manner, formulate relevant questions, and eventually
answer them with regard to a variety of historical settings. Nonetheless, "civil
society" also has a normative dimension, one I do not attempt to address in
an explicit and systematic manner in this book. (See, however, my discussion
in Chapter 1.)

8. See Zbigniew Pelczynski's interpretation of the recent Polish experience, in
the light of Jeffrey Weintraub's reading of Tocqueville (Pelczynski, 1988,
pp. 361–380, esp. 368, 379).

9. Antony Black's otherwise quite instructive inquiry is based on this market-
centered, or, in John Keane's words, property-centered, interpretation of civil
society (Black 1984; Keane, 1988b, p. 64).

10. See, for instance, Andrew Arato's understanding of civil society as organized
around independent associations or social movements against the background
of the Polish experience of 1980–1982 (1981, pp. 23–47; 1981–82,
pp. 19–48). See also Tismaneanu (1990).

11. And opposed to the "life-world" (Habermas, 1992). Habermas goes on to
illustrate what he means by voluntary associations, and in so doing he produces
statements that are self-contradictory. He speaks of voluntary associations
outside the realm of the state and the economy, ranging from churches and

cultural associations to occupational associations, political parties, and labor unions. But occupational associations, parties, and unions are core participants, and thus belong in the realm of the state and the economy.

12. Or rather the market as a scenario for a class struggle. See Gouldner (1980, p. 357) and Pérez-Díaz (1978).

13. This is the distinction proposed by Hayek (1960, pp. 222, 258). Other distinctions which are related to Hayek's although different from it are those of Michael Mann between "despotic" and "infrastructural powers" (1986a, pp. 144–175; 1986b, 109–136), and Giovanni Sartori between the "vertical dimension" and the "horizontal dimension" of politics (1987, p. 131). From a different perspective, see also Oakeshott (1990, pp. 185–326).

14. Although Weber refers to legitimacy in general, he addresses only the issue of formal legitimacy (1978, p. 36).

15. A point most forcefully made (and, in my opinion, overemphasized) by Theda Skocpol (1985a, pp. 3–37).

16. On sociopolitical coalitions, policy networks, and patterns of intermediation and interaction between interest groups and public bureaucracies (and parties), see Gourevitch (1986), Katzenstein (1978), and Lehmbruch (1991).

17. See Hegel (1956, p. 90). See also Hegel (1967, para. 247, p. 151), where the sea is related to civil society and the land to the family.

18. Needless to say, therefore, that while the substance of the metaphor may be Hegelian, its spirit and meaning are not. Hegel's state is supposed to incorporate and overcome civil society, not to play a game of alternating protagonisms with it. The fundamental Hegelian metaphor for social order is that of "the edifice of human society" (1956, p. 27).

19. Thucydides (1972, pp. 34–46, 143–151). See also Hayek's comments (1960, pp. 64, 459; 1978, p. 122; 1988, pp. 43ff.).

20. Or "extraction-coercion cycle" (Finer, 1975, p. 97).

21. See Skocpol (1979) and Mann (1986a) following Hintze (1975).

22. And prior to that in the Netherlands in the 1570s.

23. Absolute politics would attempt to recast the entire society in an operation of utopian engineering. See Popper (1966) and Pizzorno (1987).

24. As well as the process of diffusion of that institution everywhere in the world (see Thomas and Meyer 1984).

25. This dramatic script was most notably developed from the beginning of the nineteenth century on by the new politics of nationalism through the use of national myths and symbols and the use of a liturgy (Mosse, 1975, p. 2).

26. As Nietzsche suggested, "as soon as any war breaks out, there also breaks out . . . a pleasure that . . . is kept secret: rapturously, they throw themselves into the new danger of death because the sacrifice for the fatherland seems to them to offer the long desired permission to dodge their goal; war offers them a detour to suicide" (1974, p. 270).

27. Or, in other words, one path led to a situation in which civil society would challenge the state's rulers and the other to a situation where civil society would be exclusively an object of rule (Poggi, 1978, pp. 77ff.).

28. Hegel's ambiguous use of the term *civil society* parallels his equally ambiguous use of the term *state*. See Pérez-Díaz (1978, p. 7) and Pelczynski (1984, p. 1). Hegel tries to reduce the impact of his ambiguity by referring to the "strictly political state" (1967, para. 163, 267, 273, 276). Yet Hegel's thinking regarding this "correspondence" between the "speculative development" and historical developments is, once again, deliberately unclear. See, for instance, Hegel (1967, para. 32 and its addition) and Pérez-Díaz (1978, p. 7). All these ambiguities justify Popper's exasperation with Hegel's way of expressing himself (1972).

29. See Hegel's insistence on the public authority's surveillance of the corporations (1967, para. 252, and his addition to para. 255); and on the joint appointment of the corporations' officials by the government and local election (1967, para. 288). For a reassessment of Hegel's views of the corporations, see Black (1984, pp. 202ff.).

30. See Hegel (1956, paras. 189, 289, 244, 245, 255, 301).

31. In Hegel's terms, universality would be the basic principle of civil society, even if it were still only an inward principle (see 1967, paras. 181, 157, 182–188, 249–255).

32. See Hegel (1956, pp. 12, 18–19).

33. On the bureaucratic ethos, see Hegel (1967, p. 133); and on the bureaucracy as a "universal class," see p. 205. Yet, as Lehmbruch (1991, p. 149) has suggested, Hegel was the main exponent of the notion of bureaucratic autonomy as it developed in the Prussian administrative tradition.

34. For a rather more positive assessment of Hegel's contribution to a theory of civil society, see the essays gathered in Pelczynski (1984) and Riedel (1962).

35. Beginning with Eduard Gans, one of Marx's teachers. See Cornu (1955, p. 85).

36. The thesis of the separation between the state and civil society runs through Marx's thinking from his analysis of the early 1840s of the American and Prussian political regimes to his discussion of the French Second Republic and Bonapartism and his analysis of the Paris Commune. See Pérez-Díaz (1978, pp. 55ff.).

37. At least in the terminology Marx used in the 1840s (see 1967, pp. 249–264).

38. See a summary of the discussion in Laskey, Stolp, and Weiner (1984); also Niskanen (1971) and Borcherding (1977). See also the critical assessment of the literature in the late 1970s, on the basis of a comparative analysis of the size of the public sector in eighteen relatively developed countries between 1960 and 1975, in Cameron (1978).

39. This seems consistent with A. T. Peacock and J. A. Wiseman's theory (1961) about the impact of extraordinary events changing the public's degree of

tolerance of fiscal pressure, on the basis of their analysis of the growth of public expenditures in Great Britain between 1890 and 1955.

40. See Habermas (1962, 1975). See also O'Connor (1973) and Offe (1984).

41. Such as teachers or university professors and hospital doctors, as well as artists or intellectuals commissioned by the state.

42. See Aron (1968); and for a more sympathetic witness to the events, see Epistémon (1968).

43. The Grenelle accords, soon to be followed by a successful adjustment of the French economy and the French political system. See Salvati (1981).

44. In countries such as Spain, trying to persuade labor to accept limits on wage increases was the main reason for creating these institutions.

45. As against John Goldthorpe's assumption (1984b) of the incompatibility between dualistic and corporatist strategies.

46. See Streeck (1989), Dore (1987), and Piore and Sabel (1984). Streeck, for instance, assumes the existence of "production patterns" which are coherent, mutually supportive configurations of demand, marketing strategies, modes of capital formation, product ranges, production technology, work organization, utilization of work skills, labor market structures, and relative and absolute wage levels (1989, p. 26).

47. On the labels (neo)conservative and (neo)liberal, see Hayek (1978, pp. 397ff.).

48. This is the assumption in Schmitter (1979), as a result of which he conflates his concept of neocorporatism by including two components: a concerted policy (as a result of that pattern of consultation), and a monopoly on representation on the part of unions.

49. In turn, the Conservative party put stringent limits on some traditional practices of the unions through legislation that by the early 1990s the Labour party was no longer committed to reverse.

50. By contrast, it did not start, as a rule, from the assumption that the public arena was a mere political marketplace for individuals seeking their narrow interests, as has been argued by Paul Starr (1987, p. 127).

51. See, however, Starr's comments on the proven capacity of private firms (for instance, in the defense equipment and health services sectors in the United States) to manipulate state regulations aimed at increasing competition to their own advantage and at the expense of the competition (1987, pp. 128ff.).

52. See Friedman and Friedman (1980), Jencks (1972), Cazes (1981), and Glazer (1981). See also, for the joint support of British unions and employers to proposals of the use of vouchers for professional training, Rose and Wignanek (1990, p. 112).

53. For an application of this argument to the case of Spanish universities and Spanish hospitals in the 1970s and 1980s, see Pérez-Díaz (1987, chaps. 10, 11, 12).

54. For the pressures generated by the implications of economic openness on French policies, see Peter Hall (1990b). This seems to contradict the generalization (Cameron, 1978) according to which internationalization of the economy strengthens the welfare state, which is needed as a buffer against international shocks.

55. Even if there were no moral link to be established between market outcomes and merit, as Hayek emphasizes (1978, pp. 85ff.). Goldthorpe takes this as a starting point for asserting the moral erosion of capitalism (1987, pp. 363ff.).

56. For current discussions of the relevance of the term *totalitarianism,* see Rupnik (1988, pp. 264–289), and Z (1990, pp. 298ff.).

57. See, for instance, John Hall (1986b): "The Soviet Union pioneered a form of industrialization based on central planning by a monopolist elite armed with a salvationist ideology. The efficacy of this model has been clearly recognized by many regimes the world over" (p. 170).

58. Incidentally, it also demonstrated that Carl Schmitt's characterization of liberal democracy as the stage for an endless debate with no final decision in view was wrong and missed the point, since totalitarian states could obviously be more rhetorical and inefficient than parliamentary democracies (see Schmitt, 1985).

59. This includes the Russian tradition of liberal reforms, referred to by Frederick Starr (1989) and by Solzhenitsyn (1991, pp. 107ff.).

60. As later on, during the 1980s, the West would also provide examples of experiments with socioeconomic policies, ranging from Swedish-style social democratic policies to policies of liberalization and privatization, and with democratic transitions (hence the interest of many in the example of the Spanish transition) see Geremeck (1990), Michnik, 1990).

61. According to Pelczynski (1982), by 1955 Polish intellectuals were already loudly questioning the practical and theoretical value of Marxism-Leninism; he mentions a survey of Warsaw student opinion conducted in 1958 in which 60 percent of the students described themselves as religious believers.

3. The Church and Religion in Contemporary Spain

1. As Suzanne Berger has argued in reference to similar developments in France (1985b). Patricia Newey translated the original Spanish version of this chapter, which I then used as the basis for the final version.

2. Geertz (1973), Bellah (1970), and Bell (1980) consider religion the combination of an explanation of the world, which manages to give an answer to the ultimate questions of existence, and of a coherent social ethos or morality. Geertz and Bellah also stress the integrative function of religion. I see religion as comprising views of the world and of morals constructed by reference to supernatural forces (in the western tradition, gods and other divine or de-

monic agents) and focusing on the interaction between humans and those supernatural forces. I do not think that the integrative role that religion may play in some societies for some periods of time allows us to take it as a defining characteristic of religion as such; see my discussion of the limited fit between religion and society later in this chapter.

3. Manuel Azaña's statements (in his speech to the Cortes, October 13, 1931) were in fact a combination of a descriptive statement and a normative one and were related to a deliberate anticlerical strategy. See, for instance, Azaña's discussion of his own crucial moves regarding the ban on liberal teaching by the religious orders and the dissolution of the Jesuits (1968, p. 178).

4. As Cardinal Gomá described the work of the "diabolical enemy": "Jews and Masons poisoned the national spirit with evil tales [which were] converted into social and political systems in the nations of darkness manipulated by Semitic internationalism." From this followed the prelate's moral advice to the leaders of the military uprising when they took power: "Do not make a pact with the devil, even in the face of demands for social freedoms; conceding rights to the citizens . . . is to bring about the ruin, in the longer term, of the nation which you govern" (Laboa, 1985, pp. 142–143).

5. Thus, for example, in an interview granted by Cardenal Tarancón to the magazine *Cambio 16,* December 10, 1984, the cardinal was asked: "During the civil war, the Spanish church and the Vatican openly supported the Nationalists; however, at the end of the dictatorship, relations between the church and the state were not always cordial. What happened?" He replied: "For a large part of the period in which the civil war was taking place, the Vatican did not pronounce in favor of either side until, at a given moment (and they should know why), the Vatican sent a nuncio to visit the National zone, something which everyone understood as official backing of the Movement's cause. However, the Vatican always had its differences with the Franco regime. On the one hand, Francoism looked for support from the church, but on the other, the church did not always approve of all that Francoism did. For example, no sooner had the war ended than a pastoral by Cardinal Gomá was published in which he said that we were to search for reconciliation and forget any kind of revenge, something which the Francoist authorities did not like at all, to the extent that the pastoral was prohibited."

6. Although, as Alfonso Alvarez Bolado points out, this was used earlier as a term of praise by the defenders of the Francoist regime (1981, p. 231).

7. See the reference to the position of Cardinal Ottaviani in González de Cardedal (1985).

8. Such was the general history of the Spanish church during this period, but this does not include the Basque church. To the main tendency of the alliance with the state and the secondary one of dissidence in connection with the handling

of the intellectual, social, and moral problems I discuss in this chapter, a third trend of dissent by the Basque church (and in a much more mitigated way by the Catalan church) should be added, which was the result of a marked historical singularity of the church and Catholicism in that region. This singularity can be deduced not only from what happened in 1830, the civil war, and the first stage of Francoism, but also from what occurred in the second stage, as the moderation of the state in the rest of Spain from the 1960s on was in sharp contrast to the increasing repression in the Basque territories. The political and moral evolution of the Vascongadas provinces also diverged from that of the rest of Spain during the transition to and the consolidation of democracy. Throughout the rest of Spain this evolution led to a moral pacification of the country, whereas in the Basque region it led to the routinization of violence. The political and moral problems related to the tolerance of violent terrorism and the so-called right to self-determination of nations are problems which have been posed in different ways and with differing intensity in the Basque church and the rest of the Spanish church. But it is too large an issue to be discussed in the short space of this note.

9. For the distinction between moral experience and moral theory, see Aranguren (1958).

10. In Mary Douglas's words: "To the consumers themselves consumption is less like pleasure for its own sake and more like a pleasurable fulfillment of social duties . . . to one's wife to buy a labor-saving piece of domestic capital equipment" (Douglas, 1988, p. 479).

11. Although, in general terms, the inclination to vote Socialist decreases in relation to the intensity of religious practice, the French example shows the complexity of the vote of practicing Catholics. In a 1982 survey in the region of Grenoble, this vote was broken down into support for Socialist leaders which did not correspond with left-wing sympathies (9 percent); a vote for leaders of the center compatible with left-wing sympathies (10 percent); and a vote for leaders of the center entirely apart from left-wing sympathies (45 percent); (Brechon and Denni, 1983).

4. Region, Economy, and the Scale of Governance

1. On the subject of ungovernability, see Birch (1984); Crozier, Huntington, and Watanuki (1975); Rose (1980); Barry (1982); Bell (1979); Brittan (1975); Offe (1975); and Habermas (1975). A version of this chapter was presented and discussed in the Committee on Western Europe of the Social Science Research Council, "Experimenting with Scale," 1983–1985.

2. There are also non–economic-functional mesogovernments, for example, churches whose educational or moral authority is backed by the state, and which may be treated as social or cultural mesogovernments; see Chapter 3.

3. As, for instance, the macrohypothesis of Philippe Schmitter (1979) concerning the emergence of neocorporatist arrangements would suggest.

4. By "political class" I mean a segment of the population which is more restricted than that referred to by Gaetano Mosca (1939), who identifies it with "ruling class," but wider than that which is deduced from Schumpeter's definition as that group of people which competes for the votes of the people in order to gain power (1943). See also Aron (1960).

5. This would be a way of saying that if we looked at one of these organizations, the unions for example, we should be able to distinguish between unions with a narrow, sectoral, short-term outlook (in Spain and other Latin countries these are usually referred to as corporative unions, the term *corporative* or *corporativism* having a different meaning from that which the terms *corporatist* and *corporatism* have here), which would produce negative results, and unions with wider horizons, which are responsible, and would consider the interests not only of their own class but of society at large.

6. Including their relationship with the leaders of corporations (see Chapter 2). See also Pérez-Díaz (1978), Black (1984), Lehmbruch (1991).

7. For a different view, see Goldthorpe (1984b).

8. On this possibility, see Scharpf (1988).

9. This is the type of nationalism Ernest Gellner refers to when he states: "Nationalism is primarily a political principle, which holds that the political and the national unit should be congruent" (1983, p. 1); see also Hobsbawm (1990, p. 9). The trouble is that "congruence" allows for quite different interpretations. Political nationalism, strictly speaking, tends to interpret "congruence" as requiring the establishment of an independent state. By the same token political nationalism tends to be nationalism of an exclusive kind and cannot easily accept the possibility that fellow nationals may hold *plural* national identities.

10. Within the framework of this chapter it is unnecessary to go into the full complexity of the constitutional norm. It is sufficient to say that under the Constitution one can find different types of autonomies depending on whether they have used article 151 (Catalonia, the Basque region, Galicia, and Andalusia) or article 143 (with or without article 150.2, which makes Valencia and the Canary Islands a different case), all of this without mentioning the peculiarity of Navarre and the specific nature of the economic pacts between the central state, this region, and the Basque territory.

11. This essential nucleus, wrapped in the language of royal proclamations, appeared in the declaration read by the king to the party leaders when they were released (*El País*, February 26, 1981).

12. I shall not discuss the effects on the degree of administrative efficiency, or the management of economic problems, in the hope that the passage of time will make it possible to replicate studies such as those which Robert Putnam et al. (1985) have made of the Italian experience.

13. Moderate nationalists in both regions (the Basque PNV and EA and the Catalan CIU) obtained a similar share of votes in the second half of the 1980s. The power of the nationalists was much less at the start of the process. In the 1977 elections the PNV had fewer votes than the PSOE in the Basque region, and Convergencia i Unió had fewer votes than the PSOE and the UCD in Catalonia; the abstention rates in the referenda for passing the autonomy statutes in both regions was around 40 percent.

14. For example, in the critical issue of public debt by autonomous governments, which would require the approval of the central government (ruling of February 2, 1984), or in consideration of the orders of the Banco de España as the basic norms for fixing the cash ratios of banks and savings institutions throughout the country.

15. This has already happened with the ruling of the Constitutional Court of April 7, 1983, which confirmed the constitutionality of the designation of secretaries of municipalities in the Basque region by the central government, the PNV mayors having refused to hand over the posts to these secretaries. Similarly, Xavier Arzalluz, the leader of the PNV, suggested that state laws that were contrary to the regional statute should be "obeyed, but not implemented" (*El País,* May 31, 1990, p. 27). At the same time, the jurisdictional conflicts have become so numerous that the minister for territorial administration of the central government was making an offer to the regions to take out of the Constitutional Court one hundred such conflicts (out of four hundred which had accumulated since 1984; *El País,* December 30, 1989, p. 16).

16. See, for example, the telling debates at the meetings of intellectuals in Gerona in February 1984 (*El País,* February 21 and 29, 1984, and *Cambio 16,* no. 641 [1984]).

17. By comparing legislative activities of regional parliaments during the first four years of their existence, we may observe that Navarre made full use of its legislative capacities (103 laws passed), followed by Catalonia (58 laws), and then by Asturias (47), the Basque region and Valencia (44 each), Madrid (42), and Galicia (40). At the other extreme, Rioja (12), Extremadura (17), Castilla-León (22), and Castilla–La Mancha (25) made little use of that capacity (*El País,* November 11, 1991, pp. 18–19).

18. See note 9. By the same token, the theory of Ortega y Gasset (1959) that the nation implies "a common project" cannot be accepted since, by implication, this combines the concepts of nation and political power for the carrying out of this project. But, as Weber has pointed out (1978), the relationship between nation and political power is a contingent one. Throughout history there have been numerous plurinational states. What is more, the plurinational state has been the norm to such an extent that the national state must be considered the exception that proves the rule. Furthermore, national self-determination may be the aspiration of the nation at a particular moment in

its history, but it is not a natural right or a normative requirement which can be derived from the essence or concept of nation. On this point, see also Popper (1972).

19. On this dual national identity in connection with this experience of Spain's autonomous communities, see also Smith (1986, p. 259).

20. See, in particular, Banco de España (1978), Rojo (1978), and Fuentes Quintana (1982).

21. See Chapter 5 and also Pérez-Díaz (1979, 1980a).

22. The official statistics issued by the Ministry of Labor on labor conflicts are of very poor quality. The ministry has no strict control over the compilation of information. Normally it does not count strikes lasting for less than a day, and since 1980 it has included only sporadic information about conflicts in Catalonia and the Basque region. The statistics which the CEOE has been publishing since 1980 are more complete. Various estimates of the number of strikes between 1976 and 1979 vary considerably from year to year. However, they do coincide on a degree of magnitude of between 11 and 21 million working days lost every year during this period. After 1980 both the ministry and CEOE figures agree on a substantial reduction in conflict. The CEOE statistics show that conflict for the period 1980–1983 involved 13 million days lost in 1980, 9 million in 1981, 7 million in 1982, and 9 million in 1983. The ministry statistics reflect the same trend at a much lower level. In 1984 there was a considerable increase in conflict, which might have been caused by the restlessness over industrial restructuring and the absence of social pacts.

5. The Spanish Workers

1. Between 1980 and 1983 Spain (with 7.8 million wage earners) lost about 10 million workdays a year; France (with about 17 million wage earners) lost about 1.7 million; and Italy (with about 14 million wage earners) lost about 14.5 million (see *Papeles de Economía Española* 22 [1985], 242–243). Patricia Newey translated the essays on which this chapter is based, which I then combined and used as a first draft. Modesto Escobar provided assistance and up-to-date information for the final version of this chapter.

2. For a view from the perspective of local union leaders, see Fishman (1991).

3. Surveys were conducted in 1978 and 1980 under the sponsorship of the INI Foundation and in 1984 with the help of the FIES Foundation. Results from the 1978 survey are gathered in Pérez-Díaz (1979 and 1980a). Most of the data in this chapter came from the 1980 survey. The survey of wage earners in the industrial sector in 1980 was planned as an interview of a sample of 2,400 wage earners in industry, representative of the wage-earning population of each of the industrial sectors and subsectors in the regions selected, and including white-collar technicians and employees as well as industrial workers.

The sectors were mining; food, drink, and tobacco; textiles, clothing, foot-wear, and leather goods; chemicals, rubber, and oil and coal derivatives; metals (basic metals, machinery, electrical equipment, and transport equipment); and construction. The regions in which the interviews were carried out were Asturias, Catalonia, the Basque region, the Levant, Andalusia, and Central Spain.

The sample represented 64.45 percent of the total wage-earning population in industry; the total number of wage earners in industry was 4.49 million, and the total number of wage earners in the six sectors selected was 2,893,855 (Encuesta de la Población Activa, EPA, fourth quarter, 1978, INE). The reliability index for the sample as a whole was 95.5 percent, with a margin of error in the worst possible case of ±2 percent. By sectors and regions the margin for error in the worst possible case was between ±5 percent and ±5.8 percent.

In order to establish the sectoral structure by regions and provinces, the data were taken from the Frequency Tables of Industrial Establishments (*Tablas de Frecuencia de Establecimientos Industriales*, TFEI) of 1978 for the food, textile, chemical, and metal sectors; from the survey of the working population (EPA, fourth quarter, 1978) for the construction sector, and from the survey of 1978 for mining. The last had been obtained from a correction made in the industrial statistics of the INE in 1976. Four hundred twenty-five interviews were allocated to each sector, with the exception of mining and textiles, which were allocated 350 interviews, since, because the concentration of these two categories was greatest, fewer interviews were necessary to obtain the same level of reliability.

The distribution of the interviews by zones within each sector corresponded to the real weight of each one in each sector, but not for the distribution of interviews by sectors within each zone. This was done in order to increase the number of interviews which corresponded theoretically to zone 1 (Asturias) and reduce the excess number of interviews which corresponded to zones 2 (Catalonia) and 3 (the Basque region), maintaining the required levels of reliability in all of them. Finally, once the distribution of the sample had been decided by the two representative variables, quotas were fixed for another set of variables so that their representation in the sample was the closest possible to that of their real weight. These quotas were fixed by taking into account the distribution of wage earners in industry as per the EPA for the fourth quarter of 1978. In the same way a quota of interviews was fixed to be carried out outside the capital of each of the provinces selected, according to the data of the municipal census of 1975. The final choice of firms was left to the team leaders in light of the location criteria and the quotas. Once the fieldwork had been carried out, the real sample was established as 2,418 valid interviews: 29 percent of the interviews were done in firms of less than 20 workers; 29.6 percent in firms of between 20 and 100 workers; 20.5 percent in firms of between 100 and 500, and 20.8 percent in firms of over 500 workers.

The information was collected between June 25 and July 30, 1980, except for forty interviews in Valladolid and another thirty in the textile sector in Barcelona which were carried out in the first week of August. Because of the complexity of the study, a complete plan of personal briefings was implemented for all the interviewers, coordinators, and zone leaders. Furthermore, all the interviewers carried out two test interviews, which were subsequently checked, before beginning their work. The majority of the interviews (around 93 percent) were carried out in the workplace during working hours once authorization had been obtained from the firm. Interviewees were selected at random and as a function of the quotas established by the field headquarters for each region, which set a certain number of interviews depending on the size of the firm. The selection of interviewees was carried out by applying a table of random numbers to the lists which the firms used for their social security statement. The interviews always took place in private, individually, and with no one present who was not participating in the survey. Furthermore, the quality of the fieldwork was carefully controlled. A coordinator or zone leader did an initial review of the questionnaires. Then there was supervision by telephone of 962 questionnaires (39.4 percent of the sample) from the office in Barcelona for Catalonia and from the office in Madrid for all other regions. This supervision also served to clarify ambiguous data from some of the questionnaires. Finally, the questionnaires were checked in terms of the correct utilization of filters, the coherence of specific answers, the complete and codifiable nature of the information, and the coherence of the data from various interviews at the same firm. Those questionnaires which did not fulfill the necessary requirements were returned to the field department. The questionnaires were distributed in seven sets for the work of codification, and this work underwent several quality controls. Twenty percent of the work done by each codifier was subsequently reviewed.

4. The downward trend in industrial conflict has continued, with the exception of 1988 general strike. On this strike, see Gillespie (1990) and Aguilar and Roca (1989).

5. On this point, see Pérez-Díaz (1980a, chap. 1).

6. See Pérez-Díaz (1979, chap. 1), and Fishman (1990).

7. These industrial workers declared the following monthly incomes: 7.2 percent, less than 25,000 pesetas; 24.3 percent, between 25,000 and 35,000; 43.3 percent, between 35,000 and 50,000; 20.3 percent, between 50,000 and 70,000, and 1.8 percent, more than 75,000. These figures were a reasonable approximation of the official statistics (Banco de España, 1979). If to this income we add that of the other working members of the family, the distribution was the

following: 0.7 percent, less than 25,000 pesetas a month; 11.9 percent, between 25,000 and 35,000; 35.7 percent, between 35,000 and 50,000; 31.2 percent, between 50,000 and 75,000; and 12.4 percent, more than 75,000.

8. I believe that in any discussion of the qualities of a job there is a place, and an important one, for the systematic observation of working conditions by an outside observer. Nevertheless, that is no reason for accepting the conclusions of the criticism of opinion surveys of jobs that it is necessary to choose between opinion surveys and outside observation of the (supposedly) objective conditions of the job, and settle for the latter (Roustang, 1977, p. 314). To accept this conclusion is to deny the value of judgments by workers on one of the topics which is closest and most immediate to them. To deny them on this point may be only a preamble to denying them on everything else; and it is obvious that such a procedure implies throwing overboard the very intentions of sociology as a science of significant human conduct.

9. According to Visser's estimates of union density rates, employed only in 1988–89 (1990).

6. *Unions' Uncertainties and Workers' Ambivalence*

1. See Chapter 3 for a discussion of the voice of the Spanish church. See also Pérez-Díaz (1987, pp. 125–175) for a discussion of the voice of Spanish business and of that of some segments of the Spanish medical and educational professions (pp. 261–353); and see Pérez-Díaz (1992a) for a discussion of that of the Castilian peasants.

2. For an illustration of a debate about virtual representation in the political arena, see Bailyn (1967, p. 167).

3. As it had been basically accepted by most conservative or Christian-democratic parties, in line with British "butskellism" (Douglas, 1983).

4. For instance, in the EUR line, according to Martin and Ross (1980).

5. In the United Kingdom, where something akin to such a policy has been carried out, Prime Minister Thatcher managed it only by attempting to justify her policy as the one most appropriate to the reality of the situation of acute crisis (hence her "contract with realism" as contrasted with a possible "social contract"). That crisis was presented in turn as a result of the previous policy of granting concessions to the trade unions, and therefore Mrs. Thatcher could claim to be rectifying a prior excess and a tendency toward excessive broadening of the power of the trade unions and the public sector. In addition, she put a great deal of effort into mobilizing the support of public opinion, including a very sizable vote from the workers themselves; see Williams (1983), Hague (1983), and Crewe (1983).

6. This is the common assumption that Lenin's and Michel's analysis shared with regard to the predicament of the workers at the beginning of the century.

7. Or between the "class in itself" and the "class for itself," in the Hegelian-Marxist formula of Lukács (1960).
8. See Dore (1973); Gallie (1978); Pérez-Díaz (1979, 1980a, 1980b, and 1981); Urbani and Weber (1984); Accornero, Carmignani, and Magna (1985).
9. See, for instance, the attitude of Spanish local unionists in Fishman (1990).

Bibliography

Accornero, A., F. Carmignani, and N. Magna. 1985. "I tre 'tipi' di operai della FIAT." *Studi e Ricerche,* 5. Fondazione Cespe.

Adam, G., and J. L. Reynaud. 1978. *Conflits du travail et changement social.* Paris: Presses Universitaires de France.

Aguilar, S., and J. Roca. 1989. "14-D: Economía política de una huelga." Fundació Jaume Bofill. *Butlletí Informatiu,* February.

Alcaide, J. 1988. "El gasto público en la democracia española: los hechos." *Papeles de Economía Española,* 37.

Allison, G. 1971. *Essence of Decision.* Boston: Little, Brown.

Alvarez Bolado, A. 1981. "Tentación nacional católica en la Iglesia de hoy." *Iglesia Hoy,* 94.

Anderson, C. 1970. *The Political Economy of Modern Spain.* Madison: University of Wisconsin Press.

Aranguren, J. L. 1958. *Etica.* Madrid: Revista de Occidente.

Arato, A. 1981. "Civil Society against the State: Poland 1980–81." *Telos,* 47.

——— 1981–82. "Empire vs. Civil Society: Poland 1981–82." *Telos,* 50.

Aron, R. 1960. "Classe sociale, classe politique, classe dirigeante." *Archives Europeennes de Sociologie,* 1.

——— 1968. *La revolution introuvable: reflexions sur la revolution de mai.* Paris: Fayard.

Artola, M. 1959. *Los orígenes de la España contemporánea.* Madrid: Instituto de Estudios Políticos.

Ault, J. 1984. "The Shawmut Valley Baptist Church: Restructuring a Traditional Order of Family Life in a Fundamentalist Community." In R. Samuel, ed., *Religion and Society.* London: Routledge and Kegan Paul.

Azaña, M. 1968. *Memorias políticas y guerra, 1931–1939.* In *Obras completas,* vol. 4. México: Ediciones Oasis, S.A.

Baglioni, G., and E. Santi, eds. 1985. *I sindicati europei fra il 1983 e il 1984.* Bologna: Il Mulino.

Bailyn, B. 1967. *The Ideological Origins of the American Revolution.* Cambridge, Mass.: Harvard University Press.

Ball, T., and J. G. A. Pocock, eds. 1988. *Conceptual Change and the Constitution.* Lawrence: University Press of Kansas.

Banco de España. 1979. *Informe Anual 1978.* Madrid.

Barker, E. 1960. *Social Contract.* London: Oxford University Press.

Barry, B. 1982. "Is Democracy Special?" In B. Barry and R. Hardin, eds. *Rational Man and Irrational Society: An Introduction and Sourcebook.* Beverly Hills: Sage Publications.

Bel i Queralt, G. 1991. "La financiación de las comunidades autónomas." FEDEA, *Cuadernos de Economía y Finanzas,* 4.

Bell, D. 1979. *The Cultural Contradictions of Capitalism.* Oxford: Heinemann Educational Books.

——— 1980. *The Winding Passage.* New York: Harper.

Bellah, R. 1970. *Beyond Belief: Essays on Religion in a Post-Traditional World.* New York: Harper and Row.

Bellah, R., R. Madsen, W. Sullivan, A. Swidler, and S. Tipton. 1991. *The Good Society.* New York: Knopf.

Benton, L. 1990. *Invisible Factories.* Albany: State University of New York Press.

Berger, P. 1971. *The Social Reality of Religion.* Harmondsworth: Penguin Books.

Berger, P., and T. Luckmann. 1967. *The Social Construction of Reality: A Treatise on the Sociology of Knowledge.* New York: Anchor Books.

Berger, S., ed. 1981. *Organizing Interests in Western Europe.* Cambridge: Cambridge University Press.

——— 1985a. "Protest under the French Socialists." Unpublished manuscript. Massachusetts Institute of Technology. In Spanish: "El conflicto social en la Francia socialista," *Papeles de Economía Española,* 22.

——— 1985b. "Religious Transformation and the Future of Politics." *European Sociological Review,* 1.

Birch, A. 1984. "Overload, Ungovernability, and Delegitimation." *British Journal of Political Science,* 14, no. 2.

Bittner, E. 1963. "Radicalism and the Organization of Radical Movements." *American Sociological Review,* 28, no. 6.

Black, A. 1984. *Guilds and Civil Society.* Ithaca: Cornell University Press.

Bobbio, N. 1988. "Gramsci and the Concept of Civil Society." In Keane (1988a).

Borcherding, T., ed. 1977. *Budgets and Bureaucrats: The Sources of Government Growth.* Durham: Duke University Press.

Bourdieu, P. 1971a. "Une interpretation de la théorie de la religion selon Max Weber." *Archives Européennes de Sociologie,* 12.

—— 1971b. "Genèse et structure du champ religieux." *Revue Française de Sociologie,* 12.

—— 1972. *Esquisse d'une theorie de la pratique.* Geneva: Droz.

—— 1981. "La representation politique." *Actes de la Recherche en Sciences Sociales,* 36/37.

Bourdieu, P., and M. Saint-Martin. 1982. "La sainte familie: l'episcopat français dans le champs du pouvoir." *Actes de la Recherche en Sciences Sociales,* 44/45.

—— 1984. "Espace social et genese de classes." *Actes de la Recherche en Sciences Sociales,* 52/53.

Braunthal, G. 1983. *The West German Social Democrats, 1969–1982.* Boulder: Westview Press.

Brechon, P., and B. Denni. 1983. "L'univers politique des catholiques practiquants." *Revue Française de Sociologie,* 24, no. 3.

Brittan, S. 1975. "The Economic Contradictions of Democracy." *British Journal of Political Science,* 5, no. 2.

Brown, J. A. C. 1970. *Psicología social en la industria.* Mexico City: Fondo de Cultura Económica.

Burgos, J. de [pseud.]. 1983. *España: por un estado federal.* Barcelona: Argos Vergara.

Cameron, D. R. 1978. "The Expansion of the Public Economy: A Comparative Analysis." *American Political Science Review,* 72, no. 4.

Carsten, F. L. 1954. *The Origins of Prussia.* Oxford: Clarendon Press.

Casals, M., and J. M. Vidal Villa. 1985. "La industria sumergida: el caso de Sabadell." *Papeles de Economía Española,* 22.

Castillo, J. J. 1979. *La subordinación política del pequeño campesino.* Madrid: Ministerio de Agricultura.

Cazes, B. 1981. "The Welfare State: A Double Bind." In OECD (1981).

CIS. 1984. "Iglesia, religión y política." *Revista Española de Investigaciones Sociológicas,* 27.

Cornu, A. 1955. *Karl Marx et Friedrich Engels: leur vie et leur oeuvre,* vol. 1. Paris: Presses Universitaires de France.

Cox, H. 1984. *Religion in the Secular City.* New York: Simon and Schuster.

Crewe, I. 1983. "The Electorate: Partisan Dealignment Ten Years On." *West European Politics,* 6, no. 4.

Crouch, C. 1983. "Olson, Dahl, and Shonfield: New Thinking on Organized Pluralism." EUI Working Paper, no. 153. Florence: European University Institute.

Crozier, M., S. Huntington, and S. Watanuki. 1975. *The Crisis of Democracy.* New York: New York University Press.

Dangerfield, G. 1961. *The Strange Death of Liberal England 1910–1914* (1935). New York: Capricorn Books.

Di Scala, S. M. 1988. *Renewing Italian Socialism.* Oxford: Clarendon Press.

Domínguez Ortiz, A. 1973. *Las clases privilegiadas en la España del antiguo régimen.* Madrid: Istmo.

Dore, R. 1973. *British Factory–Japanese Factory.* Los Angeles: University of California Press.

———— 1987. *Taking Japan Seriously.* London: The Athlone Press.

Dostoyevski, F. M. 1964. *Los hermanos Karamazov. Obras completas,* vol. 3. Trans. Cansinos Assens. Madrid: Aguilar.

Douglas, J. 1983. "The Conservative Party: From Pragmatism to Ideology and Back." *West European Politics,* 6, no. 4.

Douglas, M. 1988. "The Effects of Modernization on Religious Change." *Daedalus,* Summer.

Eisenstadt, S. N., and L. Roniger, eds. 1984. *Patrons, Clients, and Friends.* Cambridge: Cambridge University Press.

El País. 1990. *Anuario El País 1990.* Madrid.

Enzensberger, H. M. 1989. *Europa, Europa.* Barcelona: Anagrama.

Epistémon. 1968. *Ces idées qui ont ébranlé la France.* Paris: Fayard.

Esping-Andersen, G., L. Rainwater, and M. Rein. 1985. *Stagnation and Renewal in Social Policy.* Armonk, N.Y.: Sharpe.

Evans, P., D. Rueschemeyer, and T. Skocpol, eds. 1985. *Bringing the State Back In.* Cambridge: Cambridge University Press.

Feldstein, M. 1985. "The Social Security Explosion." *Public Interest,* 81.

Ferguson, A. 1980. *An Essay on the History of Civil Society* (1767). Ed. L. Schneider. New Brunswick, N.J.: Transaction Books.

Fernández, C. 1982. *Los militares en la transición española.* Barcelona: Argos Vergara.

Finer, S. 1975. "State- and Nation-Building in Europe: The Role of the Military." In Tilly (1975).

Fishman, R. 1990. *Working-Class Organization and the Return to Democracy in Spain.* Ithaca: Cornell University Press.

Flora, P., and A. Heidenheimer, eds. 1981. *The Development of Welfare States in Europe and America.* New Brunswick, N.J.: Transaction Books.

Foster, G. 1967. "Peasant Society and the Image of Limited Good." In J. Potter, M. Díaz, and G. Foster, eds. *Peasant Society.* Boston: Little, Brown.

Fox, A. 1974. *Beyond Contract: Work, Power, and Trust Relations.* London: Faber.

Freeman, R., and J. Medoff. 1984. *What Do Unions Do?* New York: Basic Books.

Freud, S. 1962. *The Future of an Illusion.* Ed. J. Strachey. London: Hogarth Press and The Institute of Psychoanalysis.

———— 1969. *Psicología de las masas.* Trans. L. López-Ballesteros. Madrid: Alianza Editoriál.

Friedman, M., and R. Friedman. 1980. *Free to Choose.* London: Secker and Warburg.

Fuentes Quintana, E. 1982. "Economía y política en la transición democrática española." *Pensamiento Iberoamericano*, 1.

Fundación Foessa. 1981. *Informe sociológico sobre el cambio político en España, 1975–1981*, vol. 1. Madrid: Euramérica.

Fussel, P. 1981. *The Great War and the Modern Memory*. Oxford: Oxford University Press.

Gallie, D. 1978. *In Search of the Working Class*. Cambridge: Cambridge University Press.

García de Enterria, E. 1984. "El futuro de las autonomías territoriales." In E. García de Enterría and J. Linz, eds. *España: un presente para un futuro*, vol. 2, *Las instituciones*. Madrid: Instituto de Estudios Económicos.

García Sanz, B. 1989. *Los campesinos en la sociedad rural tradicional*. Valladolid: Diputación Provincial de Valladolid.

Geertz, C. 1973. *Islam Observed*. Chicago: University of Chicago Press.

——— 1980. *Negara: The Theater State in Nineteenth-Century Bali*. Princeton: Princeton University Press.

——— 1983. *Local Knowledge*. New York: Basic Books.

Gellner, E. 1983. *Nations and Nationalism*. Ithaca: Cornell University Press.

Geremeck, B. 1990. "Postcommunism and Democracy in Poland." *Washington Quarterly*, Summer.

Gillespie, R. 1988. *The Spanish Socialist Party: A History of Factionalism*. Oxford: Clarendon Press.

——— 1990. "The Break-Up of the Socialist Family: Party-Union Relations in Spain, 1982–1989." *West European Politics*, 13, no. 1.

Gillespie, R., and T. Gallagher. 1988. "Democracy and Authority in the Socialist Parties of Southern Europe." In T. Gallagher and A. Williams, eds. *Southern European Socialism*. Manchester: Manchester University Press.

Glazer, N. 1981. "Roles and Responsibilities in Social Policy." In OECD (1981).

Glock, C. 1971. "Sobre las dimensiones de la seglaridad." In J. Matthes, ed. *Introducción a la sociología de la religión*. Madrid: Alianza Editorial.

Goldthorpe, J. H. 1978. "The Current Inflation: Towards a Sociological Analysis." In F. Hirsch and J. H. Goldthorpe, eds. *The Political Economy of Inflation*. London: Martin Robertson.

———, ed. 1984a. *Order and Conflict in Contemporary Capitalism*. Oxford: Oxford University Press.

——— 1984b. "The End of Convergence: Corporatist and Dualist Tendencies in Modern Western Societies." In Goldthorpe (1984a).

——— 1987. "Problems of Political Economy after the Postwar Period." In Maier (1987).

Goldthorpe, J. H., D. Lockwood, F. Bechhofer, and J. Platt. 1968a. *The Affluent Worker: Industrial Attitudes and Behaviour*. Cambridge: Cambridge University Press.

——— 1968b. *The Affluent Worker: Political Attitudes and Behaviour.* Cambridge: Cambridge University Press.

——— 1969. *The Affluent Worker in the Class Structure.* Cambridge: Cambridge University Press.

González de Cardedal, O. 1985. *España por pensar.* Salamanca: Ediciones Universidad Pontificia de Salamanca.

González Olivares, L. 1985. "Crisis en la mediana empresa industrial." *Papeles de Economía Española,* 22.

Gouldner, A. 1980. *The Two Marxisms.* London: Macmillan.

Gourevitch, P. 1980. *Paris and the Provinces.* Berkeley: University of California Press.

——— 1986. *Politics in Hard Times.* Ithaca: Cornell University Press.

Gray, J. 1986. *Hayek on Liberty.* Oxford: Basil Blackwell.

Groethuysen, B. 1927. *Origins de l'éspirit bourgeois en France.* Paris: Gallimard.

Gunther, R. 1988. *Politics and Culture in Spain.* Ann Arbor: Center for Political Studies, Institute for Social Research, University of Michigan.

Gunther, R., and R. Blough. 1981. "Religious Conflict and Consensus in Spain: A Tale of Two Constitutions." *World Affairs,* no. 143.

Gunther, R., G. Sani, and G. Shabad. 1988. *Spain after Franco: The Making of a Competitive Party System.* Berkeley: University of California Press.

Habermas, J. 1962. *Strukturwandel der Offentlichkeit.* Nerwied: Luchterhand.

——— 1975. *Legitimation Crisis.* Boston: Beacon Press.

——— 1992. "Further Reflections on the Public Sphere." In C. Calhoun, ed. *Habermas and the Public Sphere.* Cambridge, Mass.: MIT Press.

Hague, R. 1983. "Confrontation, Incorporation, and Exclusion: British Trade Unions in Collectivistic and Postcollectivistic Politics." *West European Politics,* 6, no. 4.

Hall, J. ed. 1986a. *States in History.* Oxford: Basil Blackwell.

——— 1986b. "States and Economic Development." In Hall (1986a).

Hall, P., ed. 1989. *The Political Power of Economic Ideas: Keynesianism across Nations.* Princeton: Princeton University Press.

——— 1990a. "Governing the Economy in Britain and France." Seminar, Universidad Menéndez y Pelayo, Santander.

——— 1990b. "The State and the Market." Unpublished manuscript. Harvard University.

Hankiss, E. 1990. "In Search of a Paradigm." *Daedalus,* Winter.

Havel, V. 1988. "Anti-Political Politics." In Keane (1988a).

Hayek, F. 1960. *The Constitution of Liberty.* Chicago: University of Chicago Press.

——— 1978. *New Studies in Philosophy, Politics, Economics, and the History of Ideas.* London: Routledge and Kegan Paul.

——— 1988. *The Fatal Conceit: The Errors of Socialism.* Chicago: University of Chicago Press.

Hegel, G. W. F. 1956. *The Philosophy of History*. Trans. J. Sibree. New York: Dover.

——— 1967. *Hegel's Philosophy of Right*. Trans. T. M. Knox. London: Oxford University Press.

Held, D. 1989. *Political Theory and the Modern State*. Stanford: Stanford University Press.

Hermet, G. 1985. *Los católicos en la España franquista*, vol. 1. Madrid: Centro de Investigaciones Sociológicas.

Herz, J., ed. 1982. *From Dictatorship to Democracy*. Westport, Conn.: Greenwood Press.

Hintze, O. 1975. *The Historical Essays of Otto Hintz*. Ed. F. Guilbert. New York: Oxford University Press.

Hirschman, A. 1970. *Exit, Voice, and Loyalty*. Cambridge, Mass.: Harvard University Press.

Hobsbawm, E. 1990. *Nations and Nationalism since 1780: Programme, Myth, and Reality*. Cambridge: Cambridge University Press.

Hobsbawm, E., and T. Ranger, eds. 1983. *The Invention of Tradition*. Cambridge: Cambridge University Press.

Hunter, J. D. 1985. "Conservative Protestantism in the American Scene." *Social Compass*, 32.

Immergut, E. 1990. "Health Care: The Politics of Collective Choice." CEACS (Juan March Institute). *Estudios/Working Papers*, 1990, vol. 5.

INE. 1978. *Encuesta de poblacion activa*. Madrid.

INSEE. 1978. *Données sociales*. Paris.

Jencks, C., et al. 1972. *Inequality: A Reassessment of the Effect of Family and Schooling in America*. New York: Basic Books.

Jung, C. 1967. *Symbols of Transformation*. Princeton: Princeton University Press.

Karl, T. 1990. "Dilemmas of Democratization in Latin-America." *Comparative Politics*, 23.

Katzenstein, P., ed. 1978. *Between Power and Plenty: Foreign Economic Policies of Advanced Industrial States*. Madison: University of Wisconsin Press.

——— 1984. *Corporatism and Change. Austria, Switzerland, and the Politics of Industry*. Ithaca: Cornell University Press.

Keane, J., ed. 1988a. *Civil Society and the State: New European Perspectives*. New York: Verso.

——— 1988b. "Despotism and Democracy." In Keane (1988a).

Klein, R. 1981. "Values, Power, and Policies." In OECD (1981).

Koenigsberger, H. G. 1955. "The Organization of Revolutionary Parties in France and the Netherlands during the Sixteenth Century." *Journal of Modern History*, 26, no. 4.

Korpi, W. 1978. *The Working Class in Welfare Capitalism*. London: Routledge and Kegan Paul.

Laboa, J. M. 1985. *El integrismo: un talante limitado y excluyente*. Madrid: Narcea.

―――― 1986. "La religiosidad de los españoles." In J. M. Laboa et al., eds. *Diez años en la vida de los españoles*. Barcelona: Plaza-Janés.

Laín Entralgo, P. 1956. *España como problema*. Madrid: Aguilar.

Laitin, D. 1988. "Political Culture and Political Preferences." *American Political Science Review*, 82.

La Palombara, J. G. 1987. *Democracy, Italian Style*. New Haven: Yale University Press.

Laskey, P., C. Stolp, and M. Weiner. 1984. "Why Does Government Grow?" In T. Miller, ed. *The Public Sector Performance*. Baltimore: Johns Hopkins University Press.

Lehmbruch, G. 1979a. "Consociational Democracy, Class Conflict, and the New Corporatism." In Schmitter and Lehmbruch (1979).

―――― 1979b. "Liberal Corporatism and Party Government." In Schmitter and Lehmbruch (1979).

―――― 1982. "Introduction: Neocorporatism in Comparative Perspective." In G. Lehmbruch and P. Schmitter, eds. *Patterns of Corporatist Policy Making*. Beverly Hills: Sage Publications.

―――― 1991. "The Organization of Society, Administrative Strategies, and Policy Networks." In R. Czada and A. Windhoff-Heritier, eds. *Political Choice: Institutions, Rules, and the Limits of Rationality*. Frankfurt: Campus Verlag.

Lerner, D. 1958. *The Passing of Traditional Society*. Glencoe: Free Press.

Lijphart, A. 1975. *The Politics of Accommodation: Pluralism and Democracy in the Netherlands*. Berkeley: University of California Press.

―――― 1977. *Democracy in Plural Societies*. New Haven: Yale University Press.

Lindberg, L. N., R. Alford, C. Crouch, and C. Offe, eds. 1975. *Stress and Contradiction in Modern Capitalism: Public Policy and the Theory of the State*. Lexington, Mass.: Lexington Books.

Linz, J. 1978. *Crisis, Breakdown, and Reequilibration*. Baltimore: Johns Hopkins University Press.

―――― 1981. "A Century of Politics and Interests in Spain." In Berger (1981).

―――― 1987. "Innovative Leadership in the Transition to Democracy and a New Democracy: The Case of Spain." Conference, "Innovative Leadership and International Politics," Leonard Davis Institute for International Relations, Hebrew University, Jerusalem, June.

―――― 1990. "Transitions to Democracy." *Washington Quarterly*, Summer.

Linz, J., and E. García de Enterría, eds. 1984. *España: un presente para el futuro*, vol. 1, *La sociedad*. Madrid: Instituto de Estudios Económicos.

Linz, J., F. Orizo, and M. Gómez Reino. 1982. *Informe sobre el cambio político en España*. Madrid: Fundación FOESSA.

Lipset, S. M. 1959. "Some Social Requisites of Democracy: Economic Development and Political Legitimacy." In *American Political Science Review*, 53.

Lipset, S. M., K. R. Seong, and J. C. Torres. 1991. "A Comparative Analysis of the Social Requisites of Democracy." Mimeographed. Hoover Institution and Stanford University.

Locke, J. 1970. *The Two Treatises of Civil Government* (1690) London: Dent.

López-Aranguren, E. 1983. *La conciencia regional en el proceso autonómico español*. Madrid: Centro de Investigaciones Sociológicas.

López Pina, A., and E. López-Aranguren. 1976. *La cultura política de la España de Franco*. Madrid: Taurus.

López Pintor, R. 1982. *La opinión pública española: del franquismo a la democracia*. Madrid: Centro de Investigaciones Sociológicas.

López Pintor, R., and J. I. Wert Ortega. 1982. "La otra España." *Revista Española de Investigaciones Sociológicas*, 19.

Luckmann, T. 1969. "The Decline of Church-Oriented Religion." In R. Robertson, ed. *Sociology of Religion*. Harmondsworth: Penguin Books.

Lukacs, G. 1960. *Histoire et conscience de classe*. Trans. K. Axelas. Paris: Editions du Minuit.

Maier, C. ed. 1987. *Changing Boundaries of the Political: Essays on the Evolving Balance between the State and Society, Public and Private in Europe*. Cambridge: Cambridge University Press.

Malo de Molina, J. L. 1984. "Distorsión y ajuste del mercado de trabajo español." *Papeles de Economía Española*, 21.

Mann, M. 1986a. *The Sources of Social Power*, vol. 1. Cambridge: Cambridge University Press.

———— 1986b. "The Autonomous Power of the State: Its Origins, Mechanisms, and Results." In Hall (1986a).

Maravall, J. M., and J. Santamaría. 1986. "Political Change and the Prospects for Democracy." In G. O'Donnell, P. Schmitter, and L. Whitehead. *Transitions from Authoritarian Rule: Southern Europe*. Baltimore: Johns Hopkins University Press.

Markovits, A., and M. Silverstein, eds. 1988. *The Politics of Scandal: Power and Process in Liberal Democracies*. New York: Holmes and Meier.

Martin, A., and G. Ross. 1980. "European Trade Unions and the Economic Crisis: Perceptions and Strategies." *West European Politics*, 3, no. 1.

Martínez, R. 1984. "Business Elites in Democratic Spain." Ph.D. dissertation, Yale University.

Martínez Estévez, A., and L. García Menéndez. 1985. "La economía sumergida en la Comunidad Valenciana." *Papeles de Economía Española*, 22.

Martín Patino, J. M. 1984. "La iglesia en la sociedad española." In Linz and García de Enterría (1984).

Martín Villa, R. 1984. *Al servicio del estado*. Barcelona: Planeta.

Marx, K. 1967. *Introduction to the Critique of Hegel's Philosophy of Right*. In L. Easton and K. Guddat, eds. *Writings of the Young Marx on Philosophy and Society*. New York: Doubleday.

Maura, M. 1966. *Así cayó Alfonso XIII*. Barcelona: Ariel.

Mezo, J. 1990. "Organizations versus Decision-Makers: The Case of the Basque Television." CEACS, *Estudios/Working Papers*, 1990, vol. 7.

Michnik, A. 1990. "The Two Faces of Europe." *New York Review of Books*, July 19.

Mommsen, W. J. 1981. *The Emergence of the Welfare State in Britain and Germany, 1850–1950*. London: Croom Helm.

Montero, J. R. 1986. "Iglesia, secularización y comportamiento político en España." *Revista Española de Investigaciones Sociológicas*, 34.

Moore, B., Jr. 1978. *Injustice. The Social Bases of Obedience and Revolt*. London: Macmillan.

Mosca, G. 1939. *The Ruling Class*. New York: McGraw-Hill.

Mosse, G. L. 1975. *The Nationalization of the Masses*. New York: Howard Fertig.

Navarro, M. 1990. *Política de reconversión: balance crítico*. Madrid: Eudema.

Newman, J. H. 1985. *An Essay in Aid of a Grammar of Assent*. Oxford: Clarendon Press.

Nie, N. H., S. Verba, and J. Petrocik. 1979. *The Changing American Voter*. Cambridge, Mass.: Harvard University Press.

Nietzsche, F. 1974. *The Gay Science*. Trans. W. A. Kaufmann. New York: Vintage Books.

Niskanen, W. 1971. *Bureaucracy and Representative Government*. Chicago: Aldine, Atherton.

Oakeshott, M. 1990. *On Human Conduct*. Oxford: Clarendon Press.

O'Connor, J. 1973. *The Fiscal Crisis of the State*. New York: St. Martin's Press.

O'Donnell, G., and P. Schmitter. 1986. *Transitions from Authoritarian Rule: Tentative Conclusions about Uncertain Democracies*. Baltimore: Johns Hopkins University Press.

OECD. 1981. *The Welfare State in Crisis: An Account of the Conference on Social Policies in the 1980s*. Paris.

——— 1992. *OECD Economic Surveys: Spain*. Paris.

Offe, C. 1975. "The Theory of the Capitalist State and the Problem of Policy Formation." In Lindberg et al. (1975).

——— 1984. *Contradictions of the Welfare State*. London: Hutchinson.

Okun, A. 1979. *Our Blend of Democracy and Capitalism: It Works But Is in Danger*. Washington, D.C.: The Brookings Institution.

Olson, M. 1971. *The Logic of Collective Action*. Cambridge, Mass.: Harvard University Press.

——— 1982. *The Rise and Decline of Nations*. New Haven: Yale University Press.

Orizo, F. A. 1983. *España entre la apatía y el cambio social*. Madrid: Mapfre.

Ortega y Gasset, J. 1959. *La España invertebrada*. Madrid: Revista de Occidente.

———— 1963. *Obras completas,* vol. 1. Madrid: Revista de Occidente.

Panitch, L. 1980. "Recent Theorizations of Corporatism: Reflections on a Growth Industry." *British Journal of Sociology,* 31, no. 2.

Papeles de economía española, nos. 22 (1985), 43/44 (1990).

Parkin, F. 1979. *Marxism and Class Theory: A Bourgeois Critique.* London: Tavistock.

Payne, S. 1967. *Politics and the Military in Modern Spain.* Stanford: Stanford University Press.

———— 1984. *Spanish Catholicism: A Historical Overview.* Madison: University of Wisconsin Press.

Peacock, A. T., and J. A. Wiseman. 1961. *The Growth of Public Expenditure in the United Kingdom.* Princeton: Princeton University Press.

Pelczynski, Z. A. 1982. *Poland: The Road from Communism.* Oxford: Pembroke College.

————, ed. 1984. *The State and Civil Society: Studies in Hegel's Political Philosophy.* Cambridge: Cambridge University Press.

———— 1988. "Solidarity and 'The Rebirth' of Civil Society." In Keane (1988a).

Pérez-Díaz, V. 1973. "Processus de changement des communautés rurales de Castille." *Etudes Rurales* (Ecole Pratique des Hautes Etudes, Paris), 51.

———— 1978. *State, Bureaucracy, and Civil Society.* London: Macmillan.

———— 1979. *Clase obrera, partidos y sindicatos.* Madrid: Instituto Nacional de Industria.

———— 1980a. *Clase obrera, orden social y conciencia de clase.* Madrid: Instituto Nacional de Industria.

———— 1980b. "Los obreros españoles ante el sindicato y la acción colectiva." *Papeles de Economía Española,* no. 6.

———— 1981. "Los obreros españoles ante la empresa en 1980." *Papeles de Economía Española,* no. 7.

———— 1984. "El proyecto moral de Marx cien años después." In L. A. Rojo and V. Pérez-Díaz. *Marx, economía y moral.* Madrid: Alianza Editorial.

———— 1987. *El retorno de la sociedad civil.* Madrid: Instituto de Estudios Económicos.

———— 1992a. *Structure and Change of Castilian Peasant Communities: A Sociological Inquiry into Rural Castile, 1550–1990.* New York: Garland.

———— 1992b. "Real Politics and Symbolic Politics: The Political Symbolisms of Liberal Democracies." Manuscript. Complutense, University of Madrid.

Pérez-Díaz, V., and L. A. Rojo. 1983. "Economic Responses to Political Transitions." Conference of Europeanists, Washington, D.C.

Philp, M., and M. Pinto-Duschinsky. 1989. *Political Corruption and Scandals: Case Studies from East and West.* Vienna: VWGÖ Publishers.

Piore, M., and C. Sabel. 1984. *The Second Industrial Divide.* New York: Basic Books.

Pizzorno, A. 1987. "Politics Unbound." In Maier (1987).

Pizzorno, A., E. Reyneri, M. Regini, and I. Regalia. 1978. *Lotte operaie e sindicato: il ciclo, 1968–1972 in Italia.* Bologna: Il Mulino.

Poggi, G. 1978. *The Development of the Modern State: A Sociological Introduction.* London: Hutchinson.

Polanyi, M. 1951. *The Logic of Liberty: Reflections and Rejoinders.* London: Routledge and Kegan Paul.

———— 1967. *The Tacit Dimension.* London: Routledge and Kegan Paul.

Popper, K. 1966. *The Open Society and Its Enemies.* London: Routledge and Kegan Paul.

———— 1972. *Conjectures and Refutations.* London: Routledge and Kegan Paul.

Portier, P. 1986. "La philosophie politique de l'église catholique: changement ou permanence?" *Revue Française de Science Politique,* 36, no. 3.

Preston, P. 1986. *The Triumph of Democracy in Spain.* London: Methuen.

Putnam, R., R. Leonardi, R. Nanetti, and F. Pavoncello. 1985. "Il rendimiento delle istituzione: il caso dei governi regionale italiani." In G. Pasquino, ed. *Il sistema politico italiano.* Bari: Laterza.

Quine, W. V. 1953. *From a Logical Point of View.* Cambridge, Mass.: Harvard University Press.

Ramírez, M. 1969. *Los grupos de presión en la Segunda República española.* Madrid: Tecnos.

Regini, M. 1984. "The Conditions for Political Exchange: How Concertation Emerged and Collapsed in Italy and Great Britain." In Goldthorpe (1984a).

Ridruejo, D. 1964. *Escrito en España.* Buenos Aires: Losada.

———— 1977. *Casi unas memorias.* Barcelona: Planeta.

Riedel, M. 1962. "Hegels bürgerliche Gesellschaft' und das Problem ihres geschichtlichen Ursprungs." *Archive für Rechts- und Sozialphilosophie,* 48, no. 4.

Rodríguez Buznego, O. 1986. "El grupo Tácito y la transición a la democracia en España." Undergraduate thesis. Facultad de Ciencias Políticas y Sociología, Universidad Complutense de Madrid.

Rojo, L. A. 1978. "La economía española ante la liquidación del franquismo." *Foro Internacional,* 19.

Rona-Tás, A. 1990. "The Second Economy in Hungary." Ph.D. dissertation, University of Michigan.

Roof, W. C. 1984. "American Religion in Transition: A Review and Interpretation of Recent Trends." *Social Compass,* 31.

Rose, R., ed. 1980. *Challenge to Governance: Studies in Overloaded Polities.* Beverly Hills: Sage Publications.

Rose, R., and G. Wignanek. 1990. *Training without Trainers?* London: Anglo-German Foundation for the Study of Industrial Society.

Roustang, G. 1977. "Encuestas sobre satisfacción en el trabajo o añalisis directo de las condiciones de trabajo." *Revista internacional del trabajo,* 95.

Ruiz Rico, J. 1977. *El papel político de la iglesia católica en la España de Franco (1936–1971)*. Madrid: Tecnos.

Rupnik, J. 1988. "Totalitarianism Revisited." In Keane (1988a).

——— 1990. "Central Europe or Mitteleuropa," *Daedalus,* Winter.

Rustow, D. 1970. "Transitions to Democracy: Towards a Dynamic Model." *Comparative Politics,* 2, vol. 3.

Salvati, M. 1981. "May 1968 and the Hot Autumn of 1969: The Responses of Two Ruling Classes." In Berger (1981).

Sartori, G. 1987. *The Theory of Democracy Revisited,* 2 vols. Chatham: Chatham House Publishers.

Scharpf, F. 1984. "Economic and Institutional Constraints of Full-Employment Strategies: Sweden, Austria, and West Germany, 1973–1982." In Goldthorpe (1984a).

——— 1988. "The Joint-Decision Trap: Lessons from German Federalism and European Integration." *Public Administration,* 66, no. 3.

Schmidt, M. 1983. "The Welfare State and the Economy in Periods of Economic Crisis." *European Journal of Political Research,* no. 11.

Schmitt, C. 1985. *The Crisis of Parliamentary Democracy*. Trans. E. Kennedy. Cambridge, Mass.: MIT Press.

Schmitter, P. 1979. "Still the Century of Corporatism?" In Schmitter and Lehmbruch (1979).

——— 1981. "Interest Intermediation and Regime Governability in Contemporary Western Europe and North America." In Berger (1981).

——— 1983. "Democratic Theory and Neocorporatist Practice." EUI Working Paper. Florence: European University Institute.

Schmitter, P., and G. Lehmbruch, eds. 1979. *Trends toward Corporatist Intermediation*. Beverly Hills: Sage Publications.

Schumpeter, J. 1943. *Capitalism, Socialism, and Democracy*. London: Allen and Unwin.

Semprún, J. 1977. *Autobiografía de Federico Sánchez*. Barcelona: Planeta.

Share, D. 1989. *Dilemmas of Social Democracy: The Spanish Socialist Workers Party in the 1980s*. London: Greenwood Press.

Shils, E. 1975. *Center and Periphery: Essays in Macrosociology*. Chicago: University of Chicago Press.

Skinner, Q. 1978. *The Foundations of Modern Political Thought,* vol. 2. Cambridge: Cambridge University Press.

Skocpol, T. 1979. *States and Social Revolutions*. Cambridge: Cambridge University Press.

——— 1985a. "Introduction." In Evans, Rueschemeyer, and Skocpol (1985).

——— 1985b. "America's Incomplete Welfare State." In Esping-Andersen, Rainwater, and Rein (1985).

Smith, A. 1986. "State-Making and Nation-Building." In Hall (1986a).

Smith, P. 1967. *Disraelian Conservatism and Social Reform*. London: Routledge and Kegan Paul.

Solzhenitsyn, A. 1991. *Cómo reorganizar Rusia*. Barcelona: Tusquets.

Sopeña, E. 1970. *En defensa de una generación*. Madrid: Taurus.

Spotts, F., and T. Wieser. 1986. *Italy, a Difficult Democracy*. Cambridge: Cambridge University Press.

Stark, D. 1990. *Privatization in Hungary: From Plan to Market or from Plan to Clan?* Center for International Studies, Cornell University.

Starr, P. 1987. "The Limits of Privatization." In S. Hanke, ed. *Prospects for Privatization: Proceedings of the Academy of Political Science*, 36, no. 3.

—— 1990. "The New Life of the Liberal State: Privatization and the Structuring of State-Society Relations." In E. Suleiman and J. Waterburg, eds. *The Political Economy of Public Sector Reform and Privatization*. Boulder, Colo.: Westview Press.

Starr, S. F. 1988. "Soviet Union: A Civil Society." *Foreign Policy*, Spring.

—— 1989. "A Usable Past." *New Republic*, May 15.

—— 1990. "New Communications Technologies and Civil Society." In L. Graham, ed. *Science and the Soviet Social Order*. Cambridge, Mass.: Harvard University Press.

Stoetzel, J. 1982. *Qué pensamos los europeos?* Madrid: Mapfre.

Streeck, W. 1984. "Neocorporatist Industrial Relations and the Economic Crisis in West Germany." In Goldthorpe (1984a).

—— 1985. *Private Interest Government: Beyond Market and State*. Beverly Hills: Sage Publications.

—— 1986. "Management de la incertidumbre e incertidumbre del management (los empresarios, las relaciones laborales y el ajuste industrial durante la crisis)." *Papeles de Economía Española*, 27.

—— 1989. "The Social Dimension of the European Economy." Meeting of the Andrew Shonfield Association, Florence, September.

Sully, M. 1986. "Austrian Social Democracy." In W. Paterson and A. Thomas. *The Future of Social Democracy*. Oxford: Clarendon Press.

Swidler, A. 1986. "Culture in Action: Symbols and Strategies." *American Sociological Review*, 51, no. 2.

Taylor, A. J. P. 1955. *Bismarck: The Man and the Statesman*. New York: Knopf.

Therborn, G. 1984. "The Prospects of Labor and the Transformation of Advanced Capitalism." *New Left Review*, 145.

Thomas, G., and J. Meyer. 1984. "The Expansion of the State," *Annual Review of Sociology*, 10.

Thompson, M., R. Ellis, and A. Wildavsky. 1990. *Cultural Theory*. Boulder, Colo.: Westview Press.

Thucydides. 1972. *History of the Peloponnesian War*. Trans. R. Warner. Harmondsworth: Penguin Books.

Tillich, P. 1957. *The Protestant Era*. Chicago: University of Chicago Press.

Tilly, C. 1975. "Reflections on the History of European State Making." In C. Tilly, ed. *The Formation of National States in Western Europe*. Princeton: Princeton University Press.

Tismaneanu, V., ed. 1990. *In Search of Civil Society*. New York: Routledge.

Toharia, J. J. 1985. "Los jóvenes y la religión." In *Informe sobre la Juventud Española, 1984*. Madrid: Fundación Santa María.

——— 1989. *Cambios recientes en la sociedad española*. Madrid: Instituto de Estudios Económicos.

Ullmann, J. C. 1968. *The Tragic Week: A Study of Anticlericalism in Spain, 1875–1912*. Cambridge, Mass.: Harvard University Press.

Urbani, G., and M. Weber. 1984. *Cosa pensano gli operai*. Milan: Franco Angeli Editori.

Visser, J. 1984. "Dimensions of Union Growth in Postwar Western Europe." EUI Working Paper, no. 89. Florence: European University Institute.

——— 1990. "The Strength of Union Movements in Advanced Capitalist Democracies." Mimeographed. Sociology of Organizations Research Unit, University of Amsterdam.

Waisman, C. 1987. *Reversal of Development in Argentina*. Princeton: Princeton University Press.

Walzer, M. 1970. *The Revolution of the Saints: A Study on the Origins of Radical Politics*. New York: Atheneum.

Weber, M. 1958. *The Protestant Ethic and the Spirit of Capitalism*. Trans. T. Parsons. New York: Charles Scribner's Sons.

——— 1978. *Economy and Society*, 2 vols. Berkeley: University of California Press.

White, M. 1978. *The Philosophy of the American Revolution*. Oxford: Oxford University Press.

——— 1981. *What Is and What Ought to Be Done*. Oxford: Oxford University Press.

Wilensky, A. 1981. "Democratic Corporatism, Consensus, and Social Policy." In OECD (1981).

Williams, P. 1983. "The Labour Party: The Rise of the Left." *West European Politics*, 6, no. 4.

Z [Martin Malia]. 1990. "To the Stalin Mausoleum." *Daedalus*, Winter, 1.

Index

126; united, 127; political unrest, 185; economic crisis, 284–285, 286. *See also* Socioeconomic system; Welfare states, European
European Community, 45
Eurosocialism, 290

Fabius, Laurent, 91
Falangist party, 17, 18–19, 134; Catholic church and, 132, 133–134, 138, 142
Fascism, 161, 170, 189
Fascist party, 9, 11, 132; Italian, 9, 24, 77; German, 24, 161
Federalism, 193, 213
Ferguson, Adam, 55, 70
Ferrer, Carlos, 209
Fiat factory strike, 306
Fiscal and monetary policy, 85, 218, 228, 229, 285, 290
Flexible specialization, 87
FLP (Frente de Liberación Popular), 157, 170
Fraga, Manuel, 155–156
France, 1, 17, 65, 126, 127, 175; unionism, 81, 90–91, 189, 268, 275; student movements, 82, 83, 185; economy, 93, 154; church/state relations, 126, 128; neocorporatism in, 190; wage levels, 250–251; work force, 261
Franco, Francisco, 9, 21, 36–38, 197; death of, 17, 29, 31, 33; political strategy, 142
Francoist state, 2, 5, 10–11, 35–36, 68–69, 77; political culture, 4, 30; Catholic church and, 9, 10, 18, 35, 37, 108, 129, 130–140, 143, 144, 167–169; student opposition to, 17; economic policy, 30, 37, 154, 216–220; reform policies, 33, 153, 154–155, 169; liberal democracy and, 141–142; inner conflict, 153; national integration and, 196
French Revolution, 125
Frente de Juventudes, 132
Fuentes Quintana, Enrique, 218

Gallie, Duncan, 261
GDP, Spanish, 211, 212, 224
Geertz, Clifford, 234

Germany, 1, 76, 79, 186, 193, 292; Nazi, 9, 37, 77, 126, 127, 134, 190; Fascist, 24, 161; unionism, 81, 87, 90, 268, 275; socialist, 90; Catholic church in, 161; postwar politics, 188; work force, 258
Gibson, Edward, 70
Goldthorpe, John, 265
Gomá, Cardinal, 132, 322nn4,5
González, Felipe, 90, 202
González Ruiz, José Maria, 157
Gorbachev, Mikhail, 102–103
Governability, 184–185, 201, 202, 216, 236; mesogovernments and, 191, 194; crisis of, 231, 232, 286
Government. *See* Mesogovernments; State
Greece, 62–63, 119, 286

Habermas, Jürgen, 58
Hapsburg dynasty, 194, 195
Hegel, Georg, 62, 70–74, 147, 192
Hermandades Sacerdotales, 164
HOAC (Hermandades Obreras de Acción Católica), 149, 157
Hogares del Empleado y del Obrero, 157
Holland, 79, 188, 189
Hume, David, 70
Hungary, 104, 105, 106–107
Husák, Gustav, 107

Industrialization/industry, 4, 11–12, 74, 216, 217, 226; restructuring of, 210, 223
Industrial relations, 4, 13–14, 18, 85, 223, 275–276, 292, 299. *See also* Collective bargaining
Inflation, 41, 84, 85, 189, 226; during transition, 217, 218, 222
Insider trading, 46–47, 52, 53
Institución Libre de Enseñanza, 136
Institutions/institutionalization (general discussion), 2–3, 4, 6–7, 22, 54; based on European models, 1–3, 5, 8, 9, 13; economy and, 13–14, 92; social, 14–15, 40, 103–104; uncertainty of, 40–49; cultural, 50, 78–79; rules of, 50–51; of civil society, 55–57; institutional experiments, 88–94, 100–101; neoliberal, 93–94; design of, 94, 100–101; neocorporatist, 94, 100;